Contents

Trademarks

Preface

For most of the past four decades computer programs have been written rather than designed. It is only during the last ten years or so that the high cost of computer software became attributable to the lack of a formal approach to software development. Although many programs were constructed by mathematicians to model mathematical problem, it was rare for these scientists to apply their skills to anything other than the physical model they were portraying in their programs.

Using mathematical concepts to formally specify and sometimes verify programs is a recent innovation, but, happily, use of these techniques is rapidly gaining acceptance by software developers throughout the world. The use of formal methods is also being supported by methodologies that enable a systematic approach to be made across the complete software development cycle, which includes project planning, design, testing etc. The student computer scientist can today look forward to education and training which will equip the individual with the skills and knowledge needed to carry out the profession of a software engineer.

Abstraction is the most powerful software concept ever to be introduced into software engineering. For too long, many programs simply described the functionality of the problems they were intended to solve. Design became a fashionable pastime which achieved some discipline in its approach to program development, but very little benefit was obtained in providing methodologies that could be applied in a variety of problem areas.

Abstraction on the other hand encourages the software engineer to become aware of the importance of data, and re-focuses attention on what data the program operates, and not just the operations themselves.

The combination of abstraction and modularisation allows the software engineer to achieve the structured programs that were the goal of past years. Abstraction dominates this book and is introduced at an early stage as the principal design methodology. The term object oriented program development is sometimes used to describe this process as the ideas of abstraction are based on establishing the object data values, from which we specify our abstract data types.

The philosophy behind this book is that abstraction and specification should be used from the start of the software engineering process. Modula-2 was chosen as the implementation language as its syntax is similar to many other languages, such as Pascal, and it is therefore suitable as a beginner's language. More importantly, it fully supports the concepts of modularisation and data abstraction. The book is intended as a text for students of any discipline, and not exclusively for computer scientists.

We justify the claim that it is necessary to study program development via the route of abstraction because the correct habits of program specification design are learnt without recourse to primarily looking at the functionality of the problem. However, we recognise that many teachers of computer science do not hold this opinion, therefore we have structured the book so that it can be used as a beginner's book on program development, or as a book on abstraction and specification for students who have learnt programming without the benefit of the abstraction philosophy.

The majority of programs in this book were implemented in Metrowerks Modula-2 Professional Standalone Edition (PSE) on an Apple Macintosh LC and an Apple Macintosh SE/30. This book was created with Microsoft Word on an Apple Macintosh, and printed on an Apple LaserWriter.

Acknowledgements

Thanks are due to the following people for their help:

Dr. Graham Willis (C.W.'s brother), who read and commented on earlier drafts of the book, and gave helpful advice on presentation and layout.

Margaret Paddon (D.P.'s wife), for help with some of the typing, and for her support and encouragement during the writing of this book.

Dr. John Maher, from the School of Chemistry at Bristol University, for his generous contribution of Chapter 9, and his constructive comments on the rest of the text. (Further information on programs in this chapter can be obtained from Dr John Maher, School of Chemistry, University of Bristol, Bristol BS81TS, UK. e-mail: john.maher@uk.ac.bristol.)

Rob Thomas, for reading much of the book and offering many invaluable comments. Also for having a sense of humour, especially when sharing an office with someone (C.W.) in the throes of book authorship!

Our Head of Department, Professor Mike Rogers, for his support and encouragement during the writing of this book.

The students on the First Year Computer Science course here at Bristol, who road-tested much of the material in this book, although they didn't know it, and the students who read and commented on earlier drafts of some chapters.

Our Modula-2 supplier, Steve Collins of Real Time Associates, Croydon, Surrey.

The creators of the Apple Macintosh and Microsoft Word, without whose creations this book would have taken even longer to write!

Finally, many thanks to our publisher, John Cushion of Pitman Publishing for waiting so long, and for having almost infinite patience.

Claire Willis & Derek Paddon, February, 1992.

1 Building software

1.1 Software development

In the early days of computing, programs were normally written to satisfy a single and often simple objective. The need to plan for change in the requirements of the program seemed unnecessary and was rarely considered. It was believed that the writing of programs was an art for which good programmers had a natural talent. This state of affairs was a recipe for disaster, with programmers competing to write the most compact and clever code, often with little thought about structure, usability and documentation. Programs were often unintelligible to anyone other than the program author, with even the author sometimes failing to understand how the program had been originally implemented.

By the mid 1960s, it was recognized that programming practice had led to poor programmer productivity; programs were badly documented, often without a single comment line; programs were difficult to maintain or modify in line with the change of user requirements. Even worse, in many ways, was the failure of programmers to keep to agreed schedules. Estimates of completion dates were based on simple comparison with previous projects, with little regard to the complexity of the work involved. In short, we are describing an industry which was yet to achieve a high degree of professionalism and was often staffed by untrained personnel who proudly maintained individualistic attitudes.

From this chaos grew the discipline of software engineering. In the early days, software engineering was simply an effort to develop a structured method of programming, but today it gives the infrastructure which is needed for the production of software products to a professional standard.

1.1.1 From software craft to software engineering

Software engineering is the application of science and mathematics to the process of building a software solution to some problem. Software is not simply the program, but is the entire project solution which will include the full range of documents that describe the requirements analysis, specification, design, programs, operating procedures, test data and user and maintenance guides. The task of a software engineer is not simply to produce programs, but to introduce scientific method to all stages of the software development process. This scientific method should include the use of mathematical specification and analysis whenever possible or appropriate. At the heart of this approach is the need to be systematic in developing software, and only ideas and techniques that can be systematically applied should be used by the software engineer. A systematic approach provides a framework and a set of concepts that can be learned and used to solve many different problems. It provides a method for organising the thought processes needed for solving a problem rather than relying on the use of some arbitrary method.

In the early days of software development, the resulting product was usually a set of programs with the barest of documentation. The programs were rarely systematically designed or properly specified. The approach was that of a program craftsman akin to a cabinet maker who created a one-off masterpiece in wood by working from the most rudimentary sketch that was supplied by the customer. In the case of the cabinet maker, the object created would probably stand the test of time and eventually become an antique. But, the nature of software is not like a wooden object, instead it is a working tool that must daily give service in many applications. When out of date, the fate of software is to be discarded, but in the meanwhile, it should be efficient and maintenance free. In reality, the programs produced by software craftsmen were rarely robust and usually required a large effort to maintain, and the documentation was mostly inadequate. But worse, the software did not always match the requirements of the customer. Sometimes because of poor design and specification, and sometimes because the programmer did not fully understand the customer's requirements.

Some of the reasons for the need to change from the craftsman to the engineer are clear. The software must be correct, reliable and re-useable in a variety of related applications. Another motivation is the high cost of craftsman-built programs. We can again make the comparison between the cabinet maker and the modern approach. Today, furniture is mass produced by techniques that can be systematically applied. The methods depend on: good specification and design; modularisation so the design of components can be re-used; modularisation so that manufacturing techniques can be re-used; and most important of all is knowing the customer's requirements. Today, systematic techniques must be applied to reduce costs and increase reliability of software. For similar reasons to those described for managing the mass production of furniture, modular design and the use of modules in the production of software is considered to be essential.

1.1.2 The software life cycle

Many of us have written small programs without much attempt at design, other than to ensure that the program satisfies the problem definition. But would we apply the same unthoughtful approach to larger and more complex programs? Unfortunately, and despite what has been experienced in the past by way of the software crisis, the answer is often yes!

Let us compare programming with some other task. Suppose you are a construction engineer by profession and that you intend using a few of your skills to lay out a short garden path. You expect to buy the materials this weekend and complete the whole job by Sunday evening. Did you design the path? Did you plan the construction? Probably only in the simplest of ways by drawing on some previous experience. On Monday, in your professional job, you are responsible for the construction of a multi-lane highway, connecting major cities and passing through several towns, bridging rivers and tunnelling through hills. How do you approach this venture? By calling on some similar experience and getting on with the job? Of course, this approach would be absurd. The project needs careful planning, design, costing, manpower planning, maintenance planning, planning for modifications, environmental planning, natural disaster planning, accident planning etc. In short, at every level of the project the design and planning requirements must be of the highest professional quality. A software project has the same requirements except perhaps in the scale of the enterprise and must, therefore be approached with the same degree of professionalism.

The informal techniques that have been used for producing software in the past have been recently giving way to more formal methods where systematic design principles are used and mathematical specification is introduced wherever possible or desirable. Of course, informal methods are easier to understand, need little study and less training. And so a resistance to changing to the use of formal methods will be with us for some time to come. In time, computer aided software development tools will aid the software engineer in much the same way as automatic tools have revolutionised the specification and design of hardware. These tools for hardware design depend on modularisation, which have been made possible only because of the abstract concepts that have been introduced into the hardware design process. A similar use of modularisation and abstraction is a necessary step in the process of simplifying the production of software.

The various planning and design stages of a software project are collectively known as the *software life cycle*. An informal description of the main parts of the cycle is as follows:

- Requirements analysis: establish what the user of the software wants.

- Specification: the project requirements need to be expressed in a formal and unambiguous way.

- Project planning: estimate what the project will cost, what personnel are needed, the management structure and how long it will take.
- System design: here we transform the problem specification into a solution by describing the major hardware and software components.
- Program design: modules that were identified in the system design must now be designed as program specifications. The input, output and processing to be performed by the module must be fully specified.
- Program production: the program specification is implemented as code, usually conforming to a given format and style.
- Testing: the individual modules and the integrated system are fully tested.
- System integration: this can be a long and difficult process. The sequence of module completion and testing should be phased so that the partially completed system has some of the desired functionality even at an early stage of integration.
- Documentation: a project document, based on the specification, is the first to be produced. The detailed design documents are produced for each module. On completion of the software development, full manuals, user guides and maintenance documents are produced.
- System delivery: this stage will include full testing of the installed system and training of users.
- Maintenance: a maintenance plan must be established and implemented to deal with error reports and also to enable future improvements to the system to be introduced with the minimum of disruption to the existing system.

Maintenance costs are often high, and particularly so when the early stages of the life cycle have been badly applied. A typical breakdown of maintenance costs is as follows:

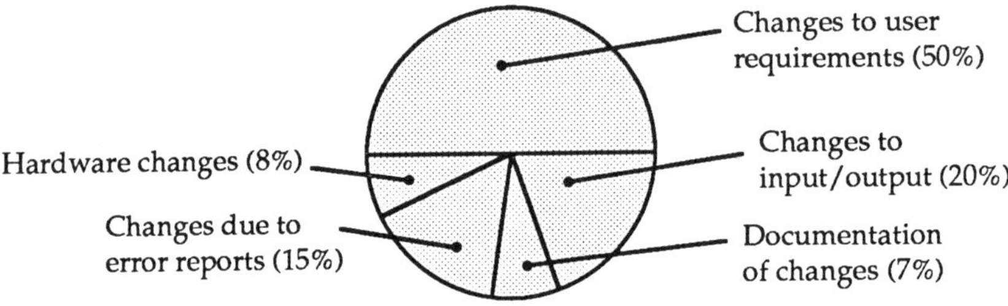

The number of software engineers involved on a project can vary from a single individual to a very large team that could be split across a number of company sites or even across different companies. Large projects, involving many individuals, require a management structure to integrate the activities of the team. The role of each team member should be clearly defined. Some members of the team have their primary interaction only with those functions which are directly related to their own responsibility, while others need to have extended liaison with many parts of the project. The customer is always involved at the requirements analysis stage, but other involvement depends on the project or even the policy of the customer.

1.1.3 Software quality

Programs should work correctly and efficiently, but is this criteria sufficient to describe the software as being a good quality product? Unfortunately, the answer is no, because a correct and efficient program may suffer from being:

- unreliable
- difficult to understand
- difficult to use
- difficult to use with other programs or application packages
- poorly documented
- tied to a particular computer implementation
- difficult to maintain and modify
- very expensive compared to similar products.

A program that suffers from these faults could not pass the quality test. Quality metrics are not easy to define, but we could use a subjective definition and say that a good quality program would avoid the list of faults we have given. The quality control engineer would avoid these faults by ensuring that the software meets a high quality standard, by first testing and checking for correctness:

- verifying that the specification of the program meets the requirements analysis
- validating that the design satisfies the program specifications
- proving the program correct by performing adequate tests to find the extent to which a program produces the required outputs for specified inputs.

And second, to ensure that the program has the extra attributes of quality which may be summarised as:

- robustness to ensure that the program can handle unacceptable input values
- reliability so that failure rates are below a previously prescribed level

- performance so that storage requirements and speed are at near optimum values
- utility, with the program meeting user requirements at a reasonable cost
- portability so that the program can run on many different systems
- easy to use
- good documentation
- easily extendible to new and varied uses
- easily maintained and upgraded.

To obtain these attributes, a consciously followed policy of specifying, designing and testing for quality must be built into the software development process. Major quality failures are usually the result of errors at the specification and design stages of development. Stringent checks should be carried out at these stages to ensure that errors are not built on. If errors that are introduced at an early stage of a project are not found then the cost of later removal grows almost exponentially with time. Therefore, the lower cost for finding errors early should be sufficient incentive to encourage the establishment of quality control checks at every stage of the product and not simply to leave all checks to the final testing stage.

1.1.4 Software failure

It is quite common for members of the general public to blame computers for errors that appear in various household accounts. Even when a request for information on the cause of these errors is referred to the offending company, the excuse usually given is that it is a computer error. Yet, true computer errors, that is hardware failure in some form, are extremely rare. Of course, the error is entirely attributable to a human and was introduced either through the software or the data on which the software operated. So, we have an example of the well known phrase – *garbage in and garbage out.*

Software faults are caused by errors introduced at all stages of the requirements analysis, specification, design and coding of the program. Errors even occur in the documentation of otherwise faultless software, rendering it useless because the software is then misapplied. This latter fault is easy and cheap to fix, as it is at the end of the development process. Unfortunately, most errors are at the beginning of the process, with more than 60% of errors occurring in the requirements analysis, specification and design stage, and most of the remaining 40%, or so, occur during the coding stage. We must ask the question: Why do these errors occur?

Let us start by examining the requirements analysis stage. This is an important stage which starts with the customer's requirements statement. But this is where the trouble immediately begins. Customers are invariably vague about their needs, often asking for conflicting or even incompatible uses of the software.

At this stage of the software process, an informal method may lead to ambiguity with the resulting implementation not conforming to the intended requirements. The need for a more formal specification that is unambiguous is clear. A danger of this method is that formal specification methods require more training and ability to understand and although the formal specification is unambiguous, it can lead to errors through the incorrect understanding of its content.

A good design method should lead to correctly implemented code. But, unfortunately, software is still produced by flawed design techniques, particularly those that consider detail first. The more detail that is considered at the early stages of a design, then the more likely it is that the design will lead to software faults.

At the coding stage, the main cause of faults is the introduction of logical errors which violate the specification. Alternatively, the errors may be related to the way that data is input and used in the program. Variables may not have been properly initialised, or the data is assigned to the wrong variable. Simple syntax errors should be detected by the language compiler, but they can be subtle. There is a famous example of a program that was used in a space mission project that had two syntax errors in consecutive statements. Unfortunately, these incorrect statements combined to form a single legal but faulty statement, which remained undetected and caused the failure of the mission. Other errors at this stage are caused by insufficient arithmetic accuracy. The accuracy of numbers depends on the number of binary digits (the word length) used in the computer's internal representation of numbers. Typically, this representation can consist of 32, 64 or 128 binary digits. An inappropriate choice of the data word length could cause unacceptable errors in a significant range of applications.

Not all faults appear early in the life of a software system. For example, most compilers are thoroughly tested, but, even after years of use, they may still throw up errors that have been previously undetected.

1.2 Requirements specification

Errors in software can be expensive to fix, particularly if the error was caused by incorrect requirements. It may appear to students who are new to computer science that it is absurd for a project to be underway without a clear definition of the project goals. But this has often been so in the past, with the consequent high cost of changes to software that were inevitable as the project developed. In some cases, it is not difficult to agree that the nature of the project is such that a clear requirement at the outset is impossible. In this case prototyping techniques are appropriate to determine the requirements of the project, rather than soldiering on with the full project and constantly being forced to change the requirements as the project develops.

Requirements analysis is often dominated by the inability of members of the customer organisation to describe the problem to be solved, and the system they require in a clear unambiguous way. Conflicting requirements can arise from different divisions of the customer organisation, and often the detrimental effect to the project of certain requirements are not fully understood by the customers.

Requirements analysis is recognised as an essential part of the software life cycle. The analysis should be systematic, because even though we know that customers may be expert at their business, they nevertheless often experience difficulty in describing their activities to outsiders. It is essential that all information gathered from a customer is recorded. Consistency must be checked as each piece of information is entered in the record in order to detect conflicting statements by the customer.

We can summarise major components of a requirements analysis as shown in Figure 1.1.

Figure 1.1 Input parameters for requirements analysis

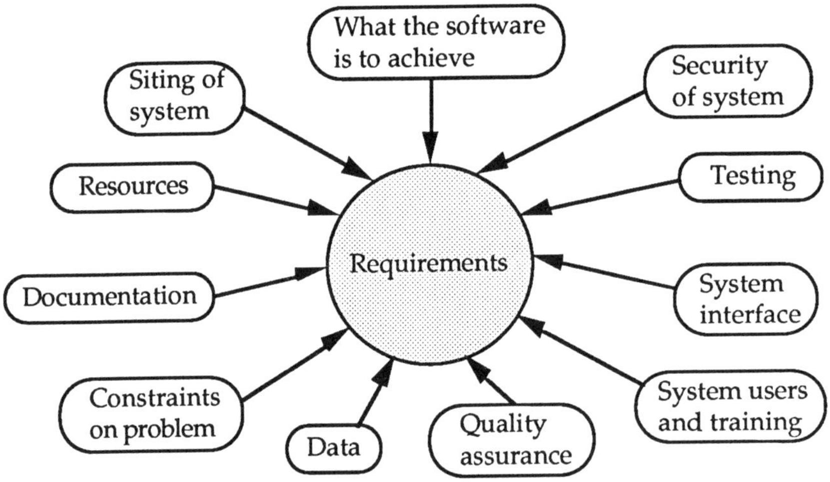

The main input parameters are as follows :

- What the software is to achieve (project goals): The problem needs to be recognised and evaluated. How will the system model the problem? Can the system be extended or changed and still satisfy the original problem?

- Constraints: There are usually constraints on the system, including speed, data preparation, response time, cost, size, manpower available, etc.

- System interface: A stand alone system is the easiest to produce. Distributed systems need to be interfaced by specific protocols.

- Siting of system: Are the systems distributed or at one location? Are the systems to be embedded in application hardware such as aircraft or military devices? Are there environmental constraints due to temperature, humidity, vibration or electromagnetic interference?

- Data: How is data input and what is the format? What precision is required?

- Testing: What level of performance is required? How are the tests needed to prove this level of performance to be evaluated?

- Security: How should access to the system be controlled? What degree of security is required on user programs and data? What system back up is required? How often should file dumps be carried out? Are off-site storage facilities needed for back-up files and data?

- Documentation: Who will use the documentation? How much documentation is needed?

- Quality assurance: What requirements are to be prescribed for reliability?

- System users and training: Who will use the system? How much training is required?

- Resources: What parameters define the system cost, environment, etc? Does the customer have the skills for maintenance? What manpower is needed to develop the system?

By necessity the requirements contain a large amount of detail, but the main characteristics of the requirements analysis can be summarised as :

1. The requirements must give a complete statement of what the customer wants.

2. What the system is intended to do should be clear.

3. The quality assurance and testing needed for the required level of assurance should be readily determined from the requirements.

1.2.1 Finding the requirements

The process starts with an initial problem statement usually written by the customer. This statement usually needs to be supplemented by information that the requirements analyst has gathered from the customer. This supplementary information must be entered in the official record of the requirements and agreed by the customer. From these combined project statements, the analyst has to build a model of the project.

Unfortunately, there are no set procedures for building the model but an agreed procedure should be established by the analyst, so that the same systematic approach is applied to each new project. One approach is as described in Figure 1.2:

Figure 1.2 Finding the requirements

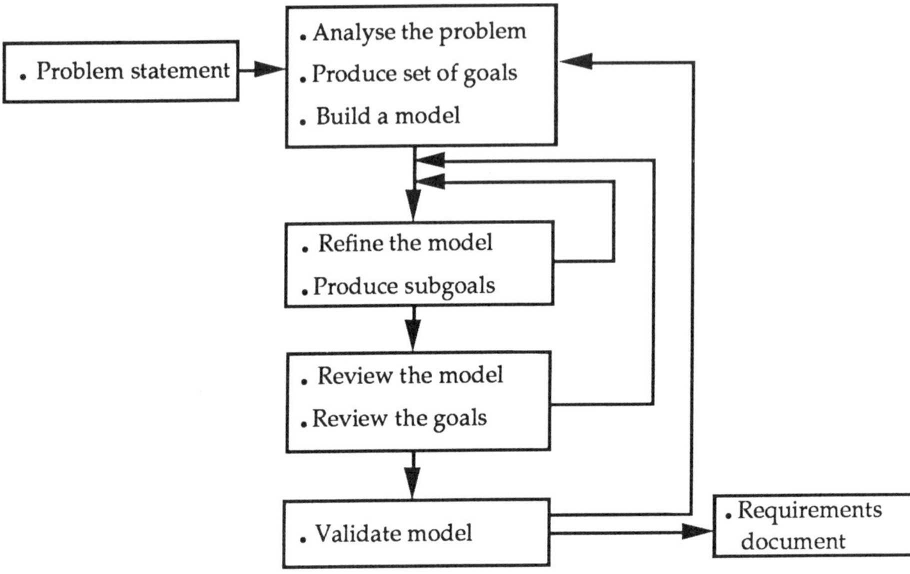

The model usually needs to pass through a number of refinement stages to fully express the required goals in terms of the model. At the end of this stage, a complete requirements statement should be available, then a reassessment of the project goals should be undertaken with additional, deleted or modified goals being proposed to the customer.

The objective of the requirements analysis is to find out *what should be done.* The detailed design stage where it is established *how it is done* is carried out after the requirements document has been completed.

Major constraints on the requirements must now be established and evaluated. The three most common constraints are :

- Resource constraints which will determine the viability of the final project. Budget, schedule, manpower and skill levels are the four most important points. Even having a good budget is not sufficient if manpower levels are too low to meet the schedule.

- Performance constraints can be associated with the raw power the system is expected to deliver, or the response time of a system, this latter point is often related to the number of users accessing a system simultaneously. Reliability is an aspect of performance that should also be considered.

- Implementation constraints will usually relate to the actual hardware, the programming language and operating systems. Normally, these are specified by the customer and will often relate to existing implementations that are being used by the customer.

The overall cost of a project must be established and modified according to the budget constraint that has been specified by the customer. Changes may have to be made to the hardware specification and the top level goals may have to be modified.

Before proceeding to the next stage of the life cycle the requirements have to be validated.

1.2.2 Validating the requirements

The requirements statement is of use only if it meets the needs of the users and is implemented within the identified constraints. Because the requirements document is the result of an informal process, there is no proof system that can be used to guarantee the correctness of the document. The customer is the final judge of the correctness or otherwise of this document. Again, a systematic approach is needed to allow a good judgment to be made on the validity of the requirements, rather than simply expressing an opinion. A good validation procedure would test the following attributes:

- Correctness – are the requirements correct? This question does not seek to establish the quality of the requirements but restricts its brief to the accuracy of the requirements.

- Completeness – are all the requirements present?

- Consistency – are there any conflicts between requirements? Is any requirement ambiguous?

- Achievability – are the requirements achievable? It is easy for a customer to specify unachievable results, especially in terms of performance and budget.

- Redundancy – are all the requirements necessary? Customers can easily ask for requirements that are unnecessary or overlap with others. Some requirements may need to be merged.

- Testability – can the requirements be tested to confirm that they satisfy the required aims? If not, changes in the requirements are needed to enable these tests to be made.

In large projects, the final document is sometimes reviewed by independent experts from consultancy companies. This is particularly useful when the consultants are expert in the problem domain. For example, you would expect control engineering consultants to examine the requirements document for the software systems of a power plant, and perhaps distributed data base consultants would be used for examining the requirements document of an airline reservation system.

1.2.3 Specification of requirements

The specification describes the set of inputs, the operations to be performed and the desired outputs. Thus, the intent of a specification is to define a set of events from input to output. There are many methods currently used to specify requirements, the simplest being natural language. A more formal approach uses programming language constructs, with the most formal using mathematical structures.

Natural language is the original specification language and is still widely applied for software requirements. For the specification to be usable, it is essential that there are no ambiguities. Every term must have a single meaning and every concept should be defined by a single term.

Pseudocode methods were particularly favoured at one time, when specifications were expressed in a semi-formal version of a programming language. This may seem an attractive method, but remember, our objective will be to design programs that are based on the principles of data abstraction, where the emphasis at this stage is on the objectives of the requirements and not how these objectives are achieved. Specifying by pseudocode or programming language may destroy the abstraction process by focusing on the functionality of the requirements. This pre-emption of the design process can only have detrimental effects on the software.

The obvious way that precision can be introduced into the specification is to use formal methods that are based on mathematics. Using these methods requires a heavy investment in training. However, companies that have done this have derived great benefit and have found that all levels of personnel are able to contribute to the requirements analysis and specification. A number of formal languages are available, the more prominent being VDM, Z and OBJ. Both VDM and Z use mathematical abstractions such as sets and mappings to describe systems. OBJ is a language for writing and testing algebraic specifications.

One of the advantages of using a formal specification language is to refine the requirements to produce a functional specification. The formal specification languages are mathematically based and can be used to verify the correctness of the functional refinement in terms of the original requirements specification. This approach, however is not so appropriate for our object based abstraction. The design process we use will produce software components that are seen as objects rather than functions. At the program design stage the emphasis will be on establishing the objects and the associated operations that will be required to act on the objects. Therefore, producing a functional specification at the requirements stage will pre-empt the design stage and may reduce the ability to use object oriented methods to produce abstract data types.

The requirements stage concentrates on *what is to be done* and does not address the detail of *how it is to be done.* Thus, the use of a traditional formal specification method such as VDM or Z should be restricted to a specification of the requirements statements and should not be further used to derive a functional specification of these requirements. In this text, we shall use natural language to specify the requirements and only use more formal methods for specifying the abstract data types from which we will build our programs.

1.3 Abstraction and modularisation

What is software abstraction and how does it affect program development? Let us start with some definitions from the Concise Oxford Dictionary.

> Abstract – the ideal or theoretical way of regarding things.
>
> Abstraction – process of stripping an idea of its concrete accompaniments (verb); the idea so stripped, something visionary (noun).

From these definitions we see that abstraction is a method of reducing the complexity of an idea. Building software is a very complex operation, therefore using abstract representations should help us to minimise the complexity of the problem.

In computer science a *data abstraction* is a set of data objects and a set of operations that can be performed on these objects. A data abstraction does not contain detail about how we store or represent the objects or how the operations are implemented. In other words the objects have been stripped of all concrete accompaniments.

Now let us explore the various abstractions with which we have some familiarity, and discover if they already exist within the computer system and in particular if they are in-built in Modula-2.

We will find that most of the common mathematical abstractions, such as numbers, are available. These simple abstractions are usually referred to as data types, and we reserve the words data abstraction or abstract data type for those types that are provided by the programmer.

Some familiar abstractions will not be found as built-in data types. From mathematics we will not find types for algebra or geometry, from physics there is no data type for power, energy, temperature or any form of electricity. There is no understanding of shape or colour, politics or business in any form. Even though these are unknown as built in data types, these abstractions can be made possible by expressing the objects in these abstractions as data and identifying the operations on the data.

1.3.1 Abstraction

Number and character abstractions

The most common abstractions in mathematics are the number systems. Much of the development of computers has been driven by the need to solve problems that arose in science and engineering, and so it not surprising that numbers should also play a major role in the Modula-2 abstractions that are provided by the language. The following types of number are inbuilt in Modula-2:

integer numbers –	INTEGER
the counting numbers –	CARDINAL
real numbers –	REAL

These numbers can be constants or variables. The variable numbers can be represented in the program in a similar way to what mathematics allows:

```
Area := pi * r * r;
```

where *pi* would be a constant number, but *r* represents a variable number. The symbol * is used to denote the multiplication operator and the symbol := replaces the equals and is read as *becomes*. This use of variable numbers is still a number abstraction and is not algebraic. Algebra is a very powerful and advanced abstraction but this is not known to most computer languages. If algebraic abstractions are used in the programs then they must be interpreted by software engineers within the abstractions that are known, such as numbers, or a new data abstraction must be defined which describes the algebraic abstraction.

The character abstraction is one of the simplest representations of data in any computer. It is designated by the reserved word CHAR and holds an 8-bit binary representation of the character (see Chapter 9). Characters can be compared to other characters, removed and inserted from a list, but not much else can be done with them. The abstractions of language and mathematics have nothing to do with the character abstraction. In other words, the character simply defines some symbol which we as humans associate with some higher abstraction.

The Boolean and set abstractions

Boolean variables are available – BOOLEAN which admit the usual operations such as AND, OR, etc. The variables can take the values TRUE or FALSE. This simple abstraction allows us to build powerful conditional structures in our software.

The set abstraction is the familiar one from elementary mathematics which allows us to define collections of objects. Boolean, arithmetic and relational operations can be applied to appropriate sets as well as the traditional set operations union and intersection.

1.3.2 Some standard data abstractions

The built in data types gives us the basic building blocks to enable us to construct all the data abstractions that are needed for the applications we will meet in our career. From time to time, we will need to exercise a great deal of ingenuity to conceive and implement original data abstractions to model our problem, and in using these new abstractions to obtain a solution to the problem. But this is not the situation at all times. Certain abstractions, such as lists and queues, occur sufficiently often in computer applications to justify them being studied to enable very efficient implementations to be achieved. Efficient implementations of these abstractions can then be made available as library modules and can be used in a wide variety of applications.

The list abstraction

A list is a sequence of data items together with the operations to be performed on the data items. Each data item is assigned some unique position in the list. The list may have some form of order or it may be unordered. The properties of a list enables us to carry out certain operations on the list such as create a list, insert an item, find an item, remove an item, size of list, etc.

Lists may have their items linked in some way. One efficient method of indicating relationships between items in a list is to link the items with a useful data type called the pointer. This is a similar idea to identifying which items in a shopping list, of arbitrary order, will be purchased at the first store to be visited, the second store, etc. In this way many different sub-lists can be defined within a list, and items with some commonality or ordering can be identified.

The queue abstraction

When we form a line to buy a hamburger, we expect the people in the queue to be served in the same order that they join the queue. This first in first out property is an essential feature of a queue abstraction.

The queue is a useful abstraction which has many applications. In later chapters, we will see it is an essential part of many implementations of program modules. Common applications of queues include controlling access to a printer in a network of computers or the sequencing of coroutines on a processor (see Chapter 8). Some queues have a variation on the first in first out principle by allowing certain queued items to have priority over other items.

The stack abstraction

The stack is a data abstraction that allows its elements to be inserted or deleted only in a last in first out order. In other words, if an item is removed from the stack then the item taken is always the most recent addition to the stack.

Most computers use stacks to support a variety of software activities, such as ordering the operations in evaluating an arithmetic expression, and controlling the order of execution of recursive calls to a procedure (see Chapter 3).

The tree abstraction

The last of the common abstractions is the tree. This is very similar to the list abstraction with the exception that each item in the list points to a number of sub-items. If the number of sub-items is two, the tree abstraction is called a binary tree. Trees are used as an efficient means of storing and retrieving information. Later, you will see that searching a tree for some item is an important topic which has wide applications.

1.3.3 Modularisation

In Chapter 2 we will examine the way in which we identify data abstractions and modules, but first let us consider some of the desirable properties of modules.

Decomposition of Modules

The way in which we decompose a problem into modules is dictated by the design method we employ

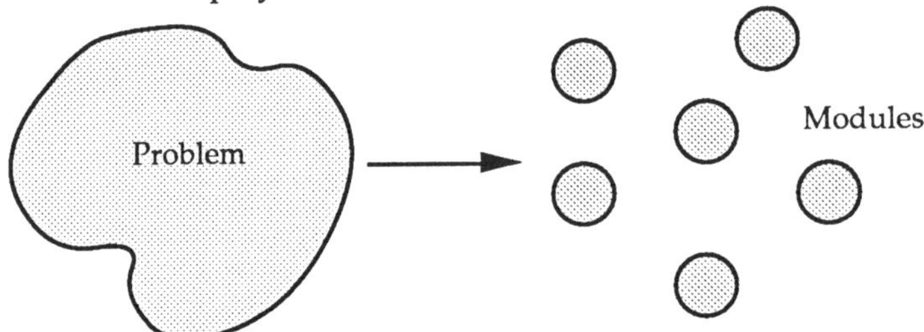

Dividing up a task into sub-tasks is not simply cutting the problem into pieces, as shown above, but is more likely to result in modules which interact with others in some way.

Let us list some of the reasons for modularisation :

- To aid the understanding of a problem by representing it as a group of coherent parts.
- To allow different individuals to work on the separated parts of the problem to increase the production rate of software.

- To group together related topics and items and separate these from unrelated topics and items.
- To minimise the effect needed for correction of errors by localising mistakes to a module.
- To reduce the cost of maintenance by restricting changes made to software as locally as possible.
- To foster the design of simple interfaces between software products.
- To enable the module to be re-used in other programs, even when the functionality of the other software is unrelated to the initial design that gave rise to the particular modules.

All of these desires are achievable if the modules are completely independent of each other, but few are achievable if there is a heavy dependence on module interaction.

Re-useability and information hiding

If a module is to be re-used, then an essential property is that its dependence on external information should be at a minimum. By extension to this argument, we can also say that if two modules do need to communicate with each other, then the information they exchange should be kept to a minimum.

If the module is to be independent of non local requirements, then an important principle that should be used when specifying a module can be formulated:

- All information about a module should be private to the module unless it is specifically declared public.

This principle is known as information hiding and is one of the most important software ideas. If we are going to hide the implementation of a module in this way, it is essential that the module's public information is clearly defined. Therefore, when two modules need to communicate, the public information should make this fact clear in both the modules.

By defining a complex problem in its most abstract form and by employing design methods that identify the data objects and operations on the data, we will demonstrate in the following chapters that it is possible to design modules that can be built as a library of reusable components. These software components can then be incorporated into new applications with little or no modification to the implemented module.

1.4 Programming languages and algorithms

Most of the problems solved in the early days of computing originated from science and engineering. The descriptions of these problems usually stressed the functionality of the requirements in terms of the physical quantities being described. There was no obvious reason for the scientist to present the problem in an abstract form, indeed abstraction that appeared in the original problem theory would have been removed long before the problem was thought to be ready for the computer. Therefore, the early computer programming languages were designed to implement this functional description of the problem in the most direct way.

1.4.1 Programming languages

A piece of software is simply a set of instructions that can be used to direct the internal operations of a computer. At the lowest level, the computer recognises machine language, which is simply a set of binary number codes which can directly control the hardware of the computer. Programming at this low level is difficult and time consuming, therefore higher level and more abstract computer languages have been developed.

The earliest high level language was FORTRAN. The language name is an acronym for FORmula TRANslation and it was intended as a language for solving problems of a mathematical style. The FORTRAN language is able to take the mathematical problem in the traditional style that scientists and engineers would express the application and formulate a line by line translation of the problem and map this to a computer program. This method maps the functionality of the application directly to the computer program and is quite effective for problems of a mathematical nature. The main criticism levelled at languages of the FORTRAN style, over the years, is that a poorly formulated solution is as easily mapped to the language as a well formulated solution. In other words, the language does not contain the inherent structures that would encourage a programmer to develop a structured and systematic approach to designing the program. This lack of structure in the language allows the programmer to develop an undisciplined approach to building software. These criticisms have led to changes being introduced over a period of more than thirty years that have slowly improved the language. Today FORTRAN still has many of its original defects, but it retains its position as the premier language for scientific use. However, by using some of the approaches described in this book the programmer can design well structured FORTRAN programs.

Attempts to improve the nature of programming languages led to the development of Algol and then Pascal among many others. Algol and Pascal each offered programming structures which encouraged the programmer to write programs in a more natural and readable form. The motivation was to allow clearer and more maintainable programs to be constructed. However, these languages still embraced the same old basic principles of program construction, that is to translate the functionality of the application directly into a program, albeit a well constructed program. During the 1970s, Wirth, the originator of Pascal, made the next step needed in program language construction and designed a language, Modula-2, which is based on the principle of data abstraction and modularisation. This means that

Modula-2 has broken with the previous principle which required a program to be designed exclusively from the functionality of an application.

The syntax of Modula-2 appears to be similar to Pascal. This is no small wonder as they grew from the mind of the same computer scientist. This fact makes it easy for a programmer who is familiar with Pascal to learn the syntax of Modula-2 programs. And so Modula-2 programs can be designed and expressed in a Pascal style. But then the comparison has been taken too far. Modula-2 is not intended to be used in this purely functional form. Indeed, if we are to take advantage of the concepts embedded in this language, we must embrace the ideas of data abstraction and model our application by first building abstract data types to represent the data objects of the original problem. The functionality of the original problem is then implemented as operations on these data abstractions.

The C programming language has become recognised as a versatile language for systems and applications, especially for low level programming. In the hands of a skilled and well trained programmer, the C language can be used to build data abstractions in a similar style to the one described in this book. Unfortunately, the language itself is not designed to encourage the use of abstraction and modularisation. In many ways, C is the latest language that encourages the purely functional decomposition of applications. In general, C is not recommended as a *good* programming language unless the disciplines of software engineering are strictly observed by the programmer.

C++ is a similar advance on C to the previously described differences between Pascal and Modula-2. C++ is an object-oriented language that fully supports the principles of data abstraction and modularisation.

1.4.2 Algorithms and programming language structures

The computer programs and modules that we will design will be coded from algorithms. This implies that the algorithm is the penultimate stage of our design process. Therefore, from the algorithms, we should be able to write a computer program in virtually any language, without having to customise the algorithm for the language itself. This means that an algorithm is a form of program, except of course, its instructions would not be directly understood by any computer system. Thus, an algorithm is a set of instructions that control some process. The process itself is carried out by some machine or device such as a computer. Let us examine a few examples of everyday sets of instructions.

A recipe for a meal is a set of instructions. The recipe specifies some food ingredients and the actions to be taken. The device in this case is the cook. A recipe, in most cases, is a very loose set of instructions, with the order of some of the instructions not always clear, and the actions leaving a degree of latitude. At best, a recipe would be classified as a very imprecise algorithm, but is better described simply as a set of instructions.

On the other hand, a plan and list of instructions to build a self-assembly kitchen unit, that has been bought as a flat pack, is very precise. Every action needed by the assembler is listed in order, with tools, screws and other needs clearly indicated for each stage of the assembly. No degree of latitude is given to the assembler, and therefore this set of instructions is an algorithm.

Similarly, the pre take-off checks that are made on the flight deck of an air liner are precisely laid out for the pilot and engineer to follow. No discretion is allowed and all procedures must be followed to the letter. This form of instruction is also an algorithm.

We can now define an algorithm more formally. An algorithm consists of :

1. a precise characterisation of a legal and possibly infinite collection of actual or potential input sets, and

2. a precise specification of the required output sets as a function of the input sets.

To achieve the required output sets, it is critical that the order of instructions in the algorithm is strictly maintained. Therefore, we need mechanisms in our language to control the sequence of events described by the algorithm. These mechanisms are sometimes referred to as *control flow instructions* and can be characterised by the set:

- direct sequencing instructions
- conditional branching instructions
- bounded iteration instructions
- conditional iteration instructions

This set of control flow instructions is sufficient to ensure the correct sequencing of program operations. They can be implemented in a number of ways, but here we will restrict attention to the form and functionality of these control flow instructions.

Direct sequencing

Direct sequencing instructions have the form:

First Do x and Next Do y

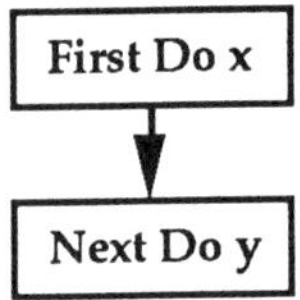

Conditional branching

Conditional branching instructions are of the form:

If Q True Then Do x Else Do y

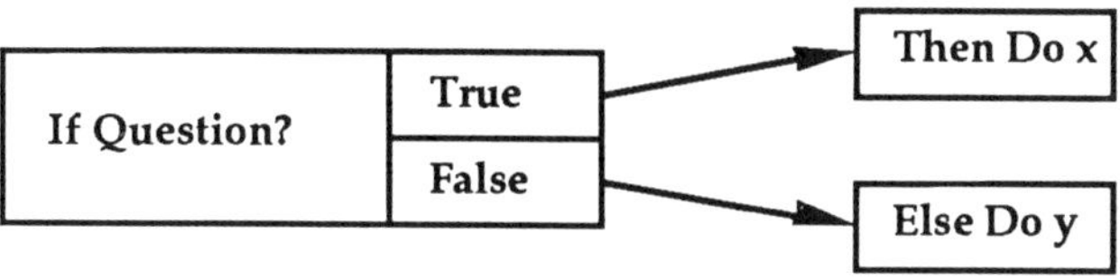

These control flow instructions are sufficient to describe simple algorithms that are fixed in length. However, many algorithms have input sets that can vary the length of the actions in the algorithm. Algorithms of this type are easily described by using control flow instructions generally named iteration constructors (or loop constructors).

Bounded iteration

Bounded iteration is of the form:

Do x N Times

This iteration construct causes the instruction to be carried out precisely N times:

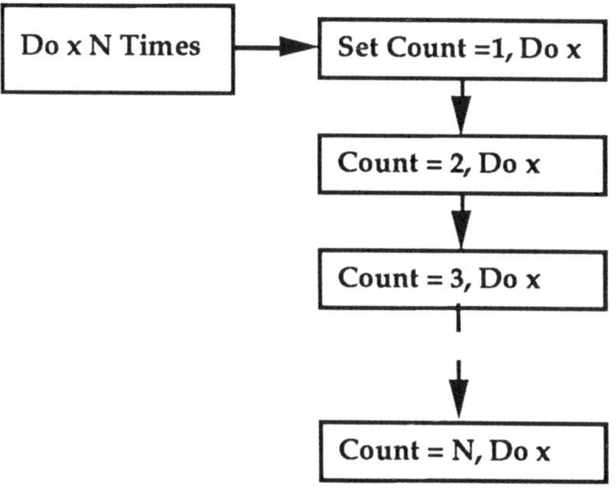

Conditional iteration

Conditional iteration (or unbounded iteration) is of the form:

While Q is True Do x

This iteration construct causes the instruction to be carried out indefinitely or until the TRUE condition is violated:

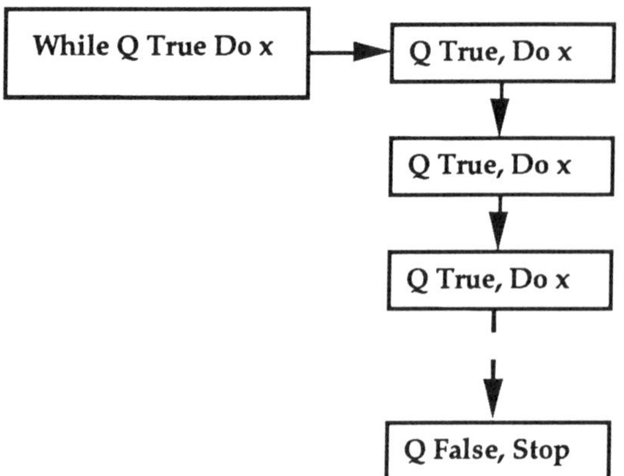

These four fundamental control flow structures are implemented in most programming languages. In Modula-2 the control flow instructions are fully implemented and are described in detail in Appendix A.

1.5 Structure of the book

This chapter has outlined the basic steps needed for building software, that is the requirements analysis, specification and design of a modular solution to a problem. The aim of the remainder of the book is to impart to the reader the skills needed to discover and specify an abstraction (or set of abstractions) for a particular problem, and further, implement and test a good solution to that abstraction. Chapters are arranged so that they collect together topics that are closely related. The only exception to this principle is Appendix A. This appendix is a tutorial on using the basic syntax of Modula-2. Many books spend a substantial part of their text reviewing simple language syntax. It is the experience of the authors that this is unnecessary. Most students confuse issues related to syntax and program development, and often mistakenly attribute the difficulties they experience with program development to simple unfamiliarity with the syntax of a language. For these reasons the description of Modula-2 syntax has been placed in the appendix where it can be easily and quickly referred to when required. Beginners should read this appendix after Chapter 2.

The first group of chapter that describe related topics are chapters 2 to 6. Chapter 2 introduces the basic steps needed to identify and specify data abstractions and build a modular solution to a problem. This is followed by Chapter 3 on procedural abstraction. Procedural abstraction is shown to be the essential ingredient in the abstraction process that is needed to describe the operations on a data abstraction. Chapter 4 brings together the ideas in the previous chapters and shows how modules can be specified and implemented. The use and need for re-usable library modules is given and illustrated with case studies. Chapters 5 and 6 are the last in this group.

Together they describe the static and dynamic implementation of the standard data abstractions: the list, stack, queue and binary tree.

The next three chapters form a natural section on low level data abstractions. Chapter 7 describes input/output and stream abstractions. together with files and random access abstractions. Chapter 8 introduces the reader to concurrency, and coroutine and process abstractions. In Chapter 9, the previous two chapters are developed further to enable hardware abstractions to be defined and modules implemented to interface real world problems to the computer. Controlling a stepper motor by a computer is given as a case study.

Chapter 10 introduces the essential task of testing software. The contents of Chapter 10 should be referred to throughout the use of the book; the need to test software at all stages of its development cannot be over emphasised. The design of test plans, unit testing, system testing, and black and white box testing are described in detail.

The final chapter concentrates on the complexity of algorithms from the point of view of making good choices of implementation. Again, this is a chapter that the reader should refer to at all stages of software development. A basic data abstraction can lead to a variety of implementations depending on the experience and good judgement of the software engineer. This chapter contrasts the good and poor choices that can be made by the software engineer by implementing and analysing some of the standard algorithms for sorting and searching lists of items.

The eleven chapters in this book, read in conjunction with a software engineering book that expands some aspects of the software life cycle, will impart to the reader the fundamental knowledge needed to develop quality software to an advanced standard.

Selected reading

Harel, D.
Algorithmics – The Spirit of Computing,
Addison-Wesley, 1987.
The delights of this book are endless. You can browse on topics as diverse as *Computer History* and *Undecidability* or concentrate on topics like *Algorithms and Data* and *Programming Languages*.

Lamb, D.A.
Software Engineering, Planning for Change,
Prentice-Hall International, 1988.
Lamb covers all the fundamentals of software engineering. The chapters on *The Lifecycle of a Software System* and *Requirements Analysis and Specification* are particularly useful at this stage.

Horowitz, E. (editor)
Programming languages: a grand tour
For those readers that wish to study the principles underlying the design and implementation of programming languages this extensive collection of papers is recommended.

Meyer, B.
Object-oriented software construction
Prentice Hall, 1988.
Part 1 of this book is recommended for its introduction to the philosophy of object-oriented design, modularisation and software re-use.

2 Modularisation and data abstraction

2.1 Why modularise?

We use modules to divide up a problem solution into smaller, logical units. The need for such subdivision does not seem apparent when we consider only simple problems with relatively short solutions, say of a hundred lines or so of source code. However, as we consider larger and more complex problems a single solution may become difficult to understand. At this stage we need to decompose the problem into smaller, independent subproblems or modules, which when solved can be used together to provide a solution to the original problem.

Modules provide several useful attributes for our problem solutions:

- They group together related items in the problem solution.
- They allow different people to work on different parts of a problem solution with little interaction between them.
- Modification of the problem solution can usually be accomplished locally in one or two modules, rather than globally across the complete solution.
- Maintenance can similarly be localised.
- They encourage the development of simple, well-defined interfaces between logical units in the problem solution.

For example, inside a personal computer the layout of the various parts is usually very modular, with separate boards for each logical unit:

- Graphics card.
- Hard disk controller.
- Floppy disk controller.
- Serial interface card.
- Parallel interface card.
- Motherboard (the main board, into which all the other boards are plugged, containing the processor and memory).

Sometimes two units will be put onto one board, for example, both the floppy disk and hard disk controllers may go onto one board, but the overall design is still very modular. By placing logically separate units onto separate boards, initial construction and repairs becomes simplified. Different boards can be built by different people, and finally assembled to produce the complete computer. If a part of the computer fails there is a good chance that only one of the boards will need replacing. If the computer had all its various units on one large board, the complete board might need replacing even if only one unit failed. Clearly this would be expensive and wasteful, so the modularisation inside a computer can be important in reducing repair costs.

This modular approach is obviously applicable to the solution of any complex problem. It is particularly useful in constructing efficient, cost effective software, as we will demonstrate in the remainder of this chapter.

2.2 How do we modularise?

We need to decompose the problem into subproblems or modules, but this decomposition must be carefully considered. Poor problem decomposition will lead to a solution which is overly complex and hard to modify or maintain, and in some cases modules will not solve the original problem when they are integrated. Learning the correct way to decompose a problem into logically separate modules takes practise. However, there are guidelines which can be followed to make the process simpler.

Firstly, the modules we decompose the problem into should all be at a similar level of detail, and each must be solvable independently from the other modules. We must avoid the situation where modules are strongly dependent on each other, as this is an indication of poor modularisation.

One of the key concepts in modularisation is abstraction (which we have already met). To recap, abstraction is used to ignore levels of detail which are unimportant, and consider only the essential concepts of an idea. In problem-solving this approach can be used to simplify the problem to be solved.

We have already mentioned two types of abstraction: data abstraction and procedural abstractions. A data abstraction is simply a set of *objects* and a set of *operations* which characterise the behaviour of these objects. For example, we can define a data abstraction to represent a set of chess pieces – the chess pieces are the objects and the operations define the ways in which each chess piece is allowed to move on a chessboard. So a pawn will have three operations, one to jump it forward by two squares (first move of the pawn only), one to jump it forward by one square, and one to jump it diagonally to take another chess piece.

A procedural abstraction is an algorithm or *operation* which embodies a single task. For example, an operation to print out a document from a computer. The important point to remember is that the operation must be abstract enough to be usable in more than one circumstance – it is not really a procedural abstraction if it can only print one particular document.

Since a data abstraction consists of a set of objects and a set of *operations*, we use procedural abstractions all the time when defining the operations of a data abstraction.

In modularisation we are particularly concerned with finding the data abstractions needed to solve a problem. Each data abstraction is then a module in the problem solution. A data abstraction corresponds directly to an object in the problem solution, so modularisation starts by trying to find the objects in the problem description, and their associated operations.

Here are some points which we can use to aid in the task of modularisation:

1. Try to find the *objects* which are used in the problem description. A noun usually indicates an object.

2. Try to find the various operations performed on these objects. A verb usually indicates an operation.

3. Each object, and the operations on it, is a probable data abstraction in the problem solution. These are the *top-level abstractions* in the problem solution, and will be the highest level modules in our implementation.

4. For each data abstraction, try to find other abstractions which will be needed to implement it. These are the *auxiliary abstractions* in the problem solution, and will be the lower level modules in our implementation.

5. At each stage in the modularisation we need to check that the data abstractions are suitable. This can be done by writing a simple algorithm to solve the problem, and seeing if the top-level abstractions provide the appropriate objects and operations for the algorithm, and if the auxiliary abstractions provide sufficient operations to implement the top-level abstractions.

Obviously, the key to modularisation is finding the data abstractions needed to solve the problem. At first you will find this very hard, and sometimes a long-winded approach to solving a small problem, but the technique becomes invaluable as the problems you need to solve become large. To illustrate the task of data abstraction let's look at a problem, and try to find the objects in it, and therefore the data abstractions needed to solve it.

The British Driver and Vehicle Licensing Centre (BDVLC) requires a new database system for holding information about all driving licence holders in the UK. In this database they need to record driver information, and provide a mechanism for indicating a driver's convictions (if any). For each driver the following information must be stored:

- name
- driver number (which is unique)
- date of birth
- address
- date licence issued
- date licence expires
- date licence ceased to be used and reason (if this is the case)
- list of current convictions for driving offences (if any)
- current penalty points accrued from driving offences.

For each conviction, the following information must be stored:

- start date
- end date
- description
- number of penalty points given.

The user of the database must be able to add, update and retrieve driver records, and their associated convictions.

Where do we find the objects (and thus the data abstractions) in this problem? You will often find that the nouns in the problem description suggest the objects you will need, whilst the verbs tend to give the operations on those objects. However, not all of the nouns will provide useful objects, so think carefully about which ones are necessary and which ones aren't. Here is a first attempt at finding the objects used in this problem, and some of the operations needed:

- Collection of driver records. Add a new driver record, find a record, update a record.
- An individual driver record. Change any of the fields in the record, get the conviction list from the record.
- A list of convictions. Add a new conviction record, find a conviction record, update a conviction record.
- Conviction record. Change any of the fields in the record.

Note that some of the operations are not explicit in the problem description, for example, changing any of the fields in a driver record. Once we have found the main objects we have also found the top-level data abstractions for the problem solution:

- Driver record.
- Driver record list.
- Conviction record.
- Conviction record list.

If we wanted to continue towards the actual implementation of the BDVLC database, we would have to start by specify these abstractions in more detail, so that they could be used to build the final problem solution. The specification of data abstractions is dealt with in detail in the next section.

2.3 Specifying a data abstraction

The technique of finding and applying data abstractions is at the heart of modularisation. We can describe a data abstraction in English, if we want to convey its meaning to others, but English is an imprecise language and is very dependent on individual interpretation. Try explaining how to stack blocks of snow in the shape of an igloo to someone. Thus, English descriptions of data abstractions run the risk of being interpreted differently by different people.

It would be much better if we could be sure of describing our abstractions more formally, so that misinterpretation is less likely to occur. The most obvious method is to use mathematics to describe an abstraction. We will find that very simple algebraic theory is all that is needed – most people have enough mathematics to be able to understand and manipulate simple axioms. An axiom is basically a rule. Our axioms are rules (which we have to write) describing how the operations of a data abstraction work. If we want to find out what a particular operation will do with a particular piece of data we look at the appropriate axiom, which describes the behaviour of the operation.

We will show how to specify data abstractions by looking at an example – the *set* data abstraction. Sets are mathematical objects, but also occur frequently in everyday life. For example, the set of primary colours {red, blue, yellow}, or the set of vowels {a, e, i, o, u}. Where we use curly braces to denote a set. We can define a set as an unordered collection of items, called the *elements* of the set. Since a set is unordered the set {u, a, i, o, e} is identical to the set {a, e, i, o, u}. A set may contain no elements at all – such a set is called the *empty set*, and this is represented by two curly braces {}, with no elements between them.

2.3.1 Data abstractions and data types

There is often confusion about the difference between data types and data abstractions. A *data abstraction* or *abstract data type* is a data type for which we know only the values and operations of the type, not how it is implemented. We have already described a data type as consisting of two parts:

- A set of values that an instance of the type can take.
- The operations that can be performed upon those values.

For example, the data type for all integer numbers allows whole number values from -infinity to +infinity, whilst the operations we can perform include addition, subtraction and multiplication. So, effectively all the data types we have talked about so far can be thought of as abstract data types.

All programming languages provide a small set of data types which can be used in programs. These data types are often called the *base types* or *built-in types* of a programming language. For the built-in types to be usable in a program, they must already be implemented in some way as part of the language. Even though we don't usually need to know how such types are implemented, it is common to avoid calling built-in types, abstract data types. We reserve the name *abstract* for those data types provided by the programmer (rather than the programming language), which consist of a set of values and a set of operations, and which can also be used without the user knowing anything about their implementations.

For example, imagine we have a data type called LibraryCatalogue, which stores the title and author of each book in a library. This data type might provide operations for marking a particular book as out on loan, searching for a book by author or by title, and adding new books or removing very old books. We could use such a data type without needing to know how each book is stored, what order the books are stored in, or how the search operation works. They might be in alphabetical order by author, or by title, or in no order at all, the search operation might check each book from the beginning of the catalogue, or it might be able to start at some point inside the catalogue. This is all hidden from the user, so LibraryCatalogue is an abstract data type, because we have no knowledge of how the books are stored or how any of its operations are stored.

2.3.2 The Set data abstraction

When we write a specification of a data abstraction we have to give that abstraction, and the data type the abstraction describes, a name. We choose a name that indicates what the abstraction is. So we might call the set data abstraction just Set.

We can define the Set data abstraction with the following operations: insert an item into a set (unless the item is already in the set), remove an item from a set, find the union of two sets, find the intersection of two sets, and check if a set is empty. We also need to include an operation to create a new, empty set. (The union of two sets is the set containing all items that occur in either set or in both sets. Thus, the union of {1, 2, 4} and {3, 1} is the set {1, 2, 3, 4}. The intersection of two sets is the set containing any items that occurred in both sets. Thus, the intersection of the set {3, 2, 1, 4} and {5, 3, 1} is the set {3, 1}.)

How do we decide what operations we need for a particular data abstraction? This is a very important problem. If our abstraction has too few operations it will not correctly model the class of data it is supposed to. If it has too many operations it may become too large and clumsy to implement and use. The operations needed for a data abstraction can be divided into three categories, constructors, modifiers and observers, which can be described as follows:

- Constructors

  Those operations which are used to create and build *instances* of the data abstraction. An instance of a data abstraction is simply an item or object which belongs to the abstraction. For example, if we are talking about the Integer data abstraction then 23 is an instance of this abstraction, so are 42, 0 and -98, but 45.76 is not an instance of the Integer abstraction (because it is a real number, not an integer).

  If we want to use a data abstraction we must be able to build all possible instances of the data which the abstraction is modelling by the use of the constructor operations. For most data abstractions there will be at least two constructors, one of which will create a new, but empty instance of the data type, and one which adds some information to an existing instance of the data type.

  For the Set data abstraction these operations are New, which creates a new, empty set, and Insert which adds integers into an existing set. All possible instances of our set type (remember it is a set of integers) can be made by performing a New operation followed by a series of Insert operations. For example, to build the set {2, -9, 72} we need the following series of operations:

New, giving an empty set {}.

Insert({}, 2), giving the set {2}.

Insert({2}, -9) giving {2,-9}.

Insert({2, -9}, 72) giving {2, -9, 72}.

- Modifiers

  Those operations which change instances of the abstraction in some way, that is they *modify* the abstraction. Modifiers are sometimes called *operators*. A modifier can change one instance of an abstraction into another instance. Delete is a modifier of the set data abstraction because, given a set and an integer, it returns the set formed by removing the integer from the original set. For example,

  Delete({2,5,3}, 3) gives the set {2, 5}

  Delete({9, 5, 1, 4, 2}, 5) gives the set {9, 1, 4, 2}

- Observers

  The observers of a data abstraction are those operations which tell us something about a particular instance of the abstraction. For the set abstraction the observers are IsIn and IsEmpty. IsIn tells us whether or not a particular element is in a given set, and IsEmpty tells us whether or not a set is empty. For example,

  IsEmpty({}) gives the answer True

  IsEmpty({3,8}) gives the answer False

Every data abstraction you design will need to have constructors (although not necessarily the same as those for the set abstraction), and you will find that a data abstraction without any observers is not very useful, as there is then no way of finding out anything about a particular instance of the abstraction once it has been created and set up. Some data abstractions do not have modifiers defined in their operations.

The first step in specifying an abstraction (in this example we are referring specifically to data abstractions, we will show where their specification differs from procedural abstractions later) is to state the syntax of the operations for the abstraction. Remember that syntax is the rules of structure that we impose on text; in particular the syntax of a programming language tells us how to build programs in the language. In this case we need a syntax to allow us to describe an operation in a data abstraction, so that we can describe all operations in a consistent manner. The syntax for an operation must state:

- The name of the operation, so we can refer to it. For example we could call the operation to add an element to a set *Insert*.
- The sort of input values needed for the operation to be performed. To make this formal we need to state the types to which the input values belong. For example, Insert would need to have two input values, one would be a set (the set in which we want to insert a new element), and therefore be of type Set, and the other would be the element that we want inserted into the set. Some of the types we need will be standard ones, such as Integer, Cardinal, Real, and Character, but others may refer specifically to the abstraction we are specifying or to other abstractions.
- The sort of output values the operation must provide – this means the types to which the output values belong. You will see that we have kept our operations to providing only one output value each, and that no input values are defined as variable, so the operation cannot change them. This means that all operations are specified as functions (although they can be implemented as procedures, if required). Chapter 3 shows how to implement functions (and procedures) in Modula-2.

Here is the syntax for the Insert operation, which adds an item into a set:

Insert: Set, Integer → Set

The first word gives the operation name Insert; we have separated this by a colon from the list of input value types, and used an arrow to indicate the output value, which follows the input values. The two input values for Insert are Set and Integer. We have given the name Set to the type which refers to our sets, and the name Integer to the type which refers to the set elements (the items we insert into the set). So Insert needs to be given a value of type Set, and a value of type Integer, and will return a value of type Set, which will be the original set with the given integer added to it.

We can specify the syntax of the remaining operations (which we will call Delete, IsIn, IsEmpty and New) in a similar manner:

Delete: Set, Integer → Set
IsIn: Set, Integer → Boolean
IsEmpty: Set → Boolean
New: → Set

Delete, given a set and an integer, will return the initial set minus the given integer. Thus Delete({5, 3, 8}, 3) will return the set {5, 8}. IsIn and IsEmpty are Boolean operations and return the values True or False. So IsIn({1, 42, 19}, 10) will return the value False, because 10 is not in the given set, and IsIn({9, 10, 11}, 9) will return the value True. New is different to all the other operations and has no input values, it has to return a new set with no items in it. In other words it creates a new set.

Although we have specified the syntax of the operations on sets this is not enough for someone trying to use the operations, since it does not give any indication of what the operations actually do. We must now find a way of describing how these operations work. To formally describe how Insert works it is not sufficient to give an example, such as Insert({a, b, c}, d) gives {a, b, c, d}. This one example doesn't tell us how Insert will work in all situations, just how it will work in these particular circumstances. We need to give axioms which specify how the operations work.

Luckily you don't have to pick axioms out of thin air, there is a method you can follow to get the structure of the axioms. First, remember that we have three types of operations: constructors, modifiers and observers. Modifiers and observers work on instances of the data type, which are themselves built by the constructors. To show how the various operations relate to each other we need to show how the modifiers and observers work on the data type instances built by the constructors. We don't want to have to write an axiom for every possible instance of the data type and every possible operation (imagine how many different integer sets you could think of!), instead we need to find some general description of an instance of the type, and use this description in the axioms.

If we look at our Set data abstraction we observe that there are two main instances of a set, first the empty set, and second an existing set to which we add a new element. This gives us two descriptions of sets, which cover all possible sets:

1. New – which returns a new, empty set. All instances of the Set abstraction must initially be created by a call to New.

2. Insert(s, i) – which inserts into the set s, a new element, i. This is a general description of any set, s.

Any set can be described by these operations, so the set {2, -9} is described by Insert({2}, -9), and the set {2} is itself described by Insert(New, 2). We can therefore give a single expression which represents the set {2, -9}:

```
Insert(Insert(New, 2), -9)
```

All sets in the Set abstraction can be described as the result of adding an item to an existing set. So the set {1, 2} is described by Insert({1}, 2), that is insert 2 into the set containing 1. More generally, any set, s, is the result of adding some item, i, into an existing set, s'. So s is represented by the expression Insert(s', i). Note that s' must be one item smaller than s, and that if we remove i from s we get s' back. Thus, Delete(s, i) = s'.

Now we have general descriptions of sets belonging to the Set data abstraction, we can build the left hand sides of the axioms showing how the modifiers and observers work. We need one axiom for each expression, that is one for the empty set produced by New and one for the non-empty set produced by Insert(s, i).

The syntax of each operation tells us what items each operation needs to be given to perform its task. Thus, the Delete operation needs a set and an integer to insert into the set. We have two general sets to use, so, if we call the integer, j, we can write two applications of the Delete operation:

```
Delete(New, j)
Delete(Insert(s, i), j)
```

The first is an attempt to delete some integer, j, from the empty set, the second is an attempt to delete some integer, j, from our general description of the non-empty set. These two applications cover all possible uses of Delete; we are deleting either from a set which is empty or a set which is not empty.

We can do exactly the same with the remaining operations of the Set abstraction, remembering to apply each operation to both the empty set and the non-empty set. In the following expressions s is of type Set, i and j are of type Integer:

```
IsIn(New, j)
IsIn(Insert(s, i), j)
IsEmpty(New)
IsEmpty(Insert(s, i))
```

It is up to us to fill in the right hand sides of these expressions correctly. First look at Delete(New, i), do we expect to be able to delete element i from an empty set? Probably yes; if we try to delete from the empty set we can simply return the empty set as the result. The empty set is described by the New operation, so we obtain the following axiom:

```
Delete(New, i) = New
```

The expression Delete(Insert(s, i), j) is more complicated to equate. Obviously we can only delete j from the set if it is already in it. From this axiom we only know one of the elements in the set, i, because it has just been added to the set by the Insert operation. If i and j are the same element then the deletion is easy, that is

```
Delete(Insert(s, i), j) = If i = j then s
```

That is, if i and j are the same element then the effect of deletion is the set we started with, s. However, what happens if i and j are not the same? In this case we need to check through the rest of the elements in the set to see if j matches any of them, this is represented by the following axiom:

```
Delete(Insert(s, i), j) = If i = j then s
                          otherwise Insert( Delete(s, j), i)
```

The *otherwise* part of this axiom probably looks very confusing. You might expect the axiom to look like this:

```
Delete(Insert(s, i), j) = If i = j then s
                                   otherwise Delete(s, j)
```

But wait, if i and j are not equal and we have to use the *otherwise* part of the axiom, what happens to item i? Even though it wasn't the one we wanted to delete we end up losing it. If we do the deletion this way we will throw away each element we reach until we come to j, which also gets thrown away. Here's an example, let's delete the number 3 from the set {1, 3, 4}. This set is built as follows:

```
Insert(Insert(Insert(New, 1), 3), 4)
```

The Delete operation is only bothered with the last Insert operation, which inserts 4 into the set {1, 3}, giving:

```
Delete(Insert({1, 3}, 4), 3)
```

Since 3 and 4 are not equal the ELSE part of the axiom is followed and the deletion now becomes:

```
Delete(Insert({1}, 3), 3)
```

Now we have the item we want to delete so the first part of the axiom is used this time, and we return the set {1} as the answer.

Can you see what has gone wrong? When 4 was found not to be the wanted item, we simply went back to the previous version of the set before 4 was inserted, to look for 3 in that version. As a result the item 4 has been discarded from the set, as well as the item 3.

Every time we find an item which is not the one we are trying to delete we have to ensure that it is inserted back into the set after the Delete operation has finished searching through the set.

We can do this with the extra Insert operation in the *otherwise* clause, which puts back the items which aren't to be deleted:

```
Delete(Insert(s, i), j) = If i = j then s
                          otherwise Insert(Delete(s, j), i)
```

Our example will now work as follows:

```
Delete(Insert({1, 3}, 4), 3)
```

will cause the ELSE clause to be used, giving

```
Insert(Delete({1, 3}, 3), 4)
```

The Delete will then go on to remove 3 from the set {1, 3}, then the Insert will put 4 back, giving us the final set {1, 4}. This is the correct result; the set {1, 3, 4} with 3 deleted is the set {1, 4}.

IsIn and IsEmpty are much easier to equate than Delete. Here are their completed axioms:

```
IsIn(New, j) = False
IsIn(Insert(s, i), j) = If i = j then True
                        otherwise IsIn(s, j)

IsEmpty(New) = True
IsEmpty(Insert(s, i)) = False
```

You can see that IsIn is very similar in definition to Delete. IsIn must search through the set, one item at a time. If the item last inserted, i, is the one we are looking for then IsIn can return true, otherwise, we must try to find IsIn in the rest of the set.

The IsEmpty operation simply returns True if it is given an empty set, and False if the set has one or more items in it. Remember that both IsIn and IsEmpty are observers of the Set abstraction and tell us something about a particular instance of a set. They do not alter the set in any way.

Specification 2.1 gives the complete specification for the Set abstraction. All the specifications we meet in the text will be described in a similar manner, by stating the name of the abstraction we are specifying (Set in this case), the types of the data items the abstraction provides (the Set type), any other abstractions needed to specify this abstraction (we need type Integer to build sets of integers), the syntax of each operation and the axioms for these operations. We also need to state the types of the variables used in these axioms. This is given at the end of the specification.

Specification 2.1 The Set Data Abstraction

Types provided: Set

Other abstractions used: Integer, Boolean

Operations:

```
New: → Set
Insert: Set, Integer → Set
Delete: Set, Integer → Set
IsIn: Set, Integer → Boolean
IsEmpty: Set → Boolean
```

Axioms:
```
   Delete(New, i) = New
   Delete(Insert(s, i), j) = If i = j then s
      otherwise Insert(Delete(s, j), i)
   IsIn(New, j) = False
   IsIn(Insert(s, i), j) = If i = j then True otherwise IsIn(s, j)
   IsEmpty(New) = True
   IsEmpty(Insert(s, i)) = False
```
Where:
```
   i, j are of type Integer,
   s is of type Set.
```

2.3.3 The Queue data abstraction

The basic operations of the Queue abstraction must include constructors to build a queue, observers to tell us what is going on in the queue, and modifiers to alter the queue.

- NewQ – creates a new empty queue.
- AddQ – adds an item to the rear of a queue.
- RearQ – gives the queue minus the front item.
- FrontQ – gives the item at the front of the queue.
- IsInQ – is a given item in the queue?
- IsEmptyQ – is the queue empty?

These operations split into the following groups: NewQ and AddQ are the constructors, RearQ is a modifier, and FrontQ, IsInQ and IsEmptyQ are observers. Specification 2.2 gives the complete specification of the Queue abstraction.

Specification 2.2 The Queue Data Abstraction

Types provided: Queue

Other abstractions used: Item, Integer, Boolean.

Operations:
```
   NewQ: → Queue
   AddQ: Queue, Item → Queue
   RearQ: Queue → Queue
   FrontQ: Queue → Item
```

```
SizeQ: Queue → Integer
   IsInQ: Queue, Item → Boolean
   IsEmpyQ: Queue → Boolean

Axioms:
   RearQ(NewQ) = NewQ
   RearQ(AddQ(q, i)) = If IsEmptyQ(q) then NewQ
      otherwise AddQ(RearQ(q), i)
   FrontQ(NewQ) = Error
   FrontQ(AddQ(q, i)) = If IsEmptyQ(q) then i otherwise FrontQ(q)
   SizeQ(NewQ) = 0
   SizeQ(Add(q, i)) = 1 + SizeQ(q)
   IsInQ(NewQ, j) = False
   IsInQ(AddQ(q, i), j) = If i = j then True otherwise IsIn(q, j)
   IsEmptyQ(NewQ) = True
   IsEmpty(AddQ(q, i)) = False

Where:
   i, j are of type Item,
   q is of type Queue.
```

These axioms are again of a very similar style to the Set axioms. However, one of them has been equated to Error. What we mean by this is that the situation represented by this particular axiom is erroneous in some way. FrontQ is syntactically defined as always returning an item; an empty queue does not have any items, so FrontQ cannot return the first item in such a queue. So we state in our specification that this is an error, and our implementation must find some way of dealing with such an error when it occurs. One possibility might be to print out an error message to warn the user of the abstraction, that an illegal operation was attempted.

In our specification we have assumed that the Error operation is available from another abstraction, but when we come to implement this abstraction we may well include Error as part of Queue itself.

Note that an operation such as RearQ can be said to have a valid result from trying to find the rear of an empty queue, because we can simply return an empty queue again. However, you may choose to make RearQ on an empty queue return an error, on the grounds that this is what the user might expect.

Let's take a more detailed look at the axioms for the FrontQ and RearQ operations when they are used on a non-empty queue, described by

```
AddQ(q, i)
```

FrontQ must return the item at the front of the queue, but unfortunately the only thing we know about our general, non-empty queue is that the item i is at the *rear* of it. We can get one item nearer to the front of the queue by ignoring the item just added to the rear of the queue. This means we are now looking at the queue described by

```
q
```

We can now try FrontQ again on this queue. Remember that each queue is really a series of AddQ operations, ending in a NewQ operation (similar to how sets were constructed). So q is equivalent to some queue q', with some item j added to it, that is AddQ(q', j) = q.

2.3.4 Removing items from a data abstraction

Algebraic specification, such as we have used for specifying the Set and Queue data abstractions, has some drawbacks. Quite often, when we are trying to define the operations for a data abstraction, we find that an operation cannot be easily specified in our algebraic form. Such an operation can often be broken down into two or more simpler operations, which we can specify algebraically.

Consider the problem of removing an item from the front of a queue. If we remove an item from the front of a queue we would intuitively expect the operation to have two consequences – the queue to have one item less, and ourselves to be left holding the item which was on the top of the queue. For example, consider the following queue of numbers:

```
Front 2  3  4  5  Rear
```

If we remove the number at the front of the queue, 2, we are left with the queue minus 2, and number 2 now separate from the queue:

```
Front 3  4  5  Rear        2
```

Now, one of the consequences of the form of algebraic specification we use is that each and every instance of a data type is built up by a create operation followed by a series of insert operations. In fact, each instance of the data type exists only as a series of such operations. For example, the previous queue of numbers would be represented in our algebraic form as the expression:

```
AddQ(AddQ(AddQ(AddQ(NewQ, 4), 3), 1), 2)
```

To remove the front item from a queue represented in this way, so that we can use the item (rather than just throwing it away), we need to find out the item's value and copy it away into a storage location or variable. This gives us one of the required effects of our remove operation.

We also need our remove operation to leave us with the queue minus the top item. This means *unwinding* the expression describing the queue, by taking off the outermost AddQ operation:

```
AddQ(AddQ(AddQ(NewQ, 4), 3), 2)
```

This then gives us the remaining required effect of the remove operation.

However, if we try to specify this algebraically as a single operation we run into problems. Each of our operations can only give a single value as a result, yet we would like our remove operation to give two results; the item that was at the top of the queue, and the queue minus its top item. Since we cannot do this in one operation we must specify two operations. FrontQ gives the value of the item at the top of the queue as its single result, and therefore leaves the queue unaltered. RearQ gives the queue with the first item removed.

Why doesn't the Set abstraction require two operations to remove an item from a set? A set is a collection of data items in no particular order; thus the set {1, 2, 3} is exactly the same as the set {3, 1, 2}. A queue on the other hand has a distinct ordering imposed on its items (for example, the ordering of a queue of people at a bus stop). It is completely valid to ask for the item at the front of a queue, or for the second, third or fourth items, because the items are ordered. However, it isn't valid to ask for the first, second, or third item of a set, because the items in a set do not have any such ordering.

To remove an item from a set we have to know which item we want removed. If we already know what the item is there is no need for an operation to find its value, and such an operation would have no meaning in the Set abstraction. So we only need an operation to return the set with the chosen item removed from it. This is the Delete operation.

2.4 Case study – a car wash simulation

The best way to see how to modularise and find abstractions for solving a problem is to go through an example of solving a problem by this approach.

2.4.1 Problem description

Simulate a car wash, which has three available car washers, and a choice of two types of wash: a simple wash or a wash and wax. There is a single queue of cars waiting to be washed. New cars arriving at the car wash join the end of the queue. Cars are removed from the front of the queue to be washed as a car washer becomes available.

2.4.2 Objects in the problem description

Remember that the nouns in a problem description often provide the objects which must be used in solving the problem, and the verbs often describe the actions on those objects. A number of objects can be found in the above problem description:

- The queue of cars waiting for the car wash.
- The car washers available.

The operations on these objects are not quite so obvious, but for the queue we need to be able to add a car to the end of the queue and remove a car from the front of the queue. For the car washers, the only action they need to perform is to wash a car, with the appropriate type of wash.

The objects in the problem give us abstractions which are central to the problem solution. We now need to define these abstractions to see if they will be suitable for implementing the problem solution, and if any other abstractions will be necessary.

2.4.3 Specifying the main data abstractions

WaitingCars

This is the queue of cars waiting for the car wash. Cars arrived and join the end of the queue, and as a washer becomes available each car is removed from the front of the queue to be washed. We should avoid trying to remove a car from an empty car queue.

The constructors needed are:

- InitialiseCarQueue – set up a new empty car queue.
- AddCarToQueue – add a newly arrived car to the end of the car queue.

One modifier, for removing a car from the front of the queue:

- RemoveCarFromQueue – remove a waiting car from the front of the car queue.

Two observers, one to tell us whether or not there are cars waiting, and one to tell us the car at the front of the queue.

- IsCarQueueEmpty – true if the car queue is empty, false if it isn't.
- FirstCar – give the car at the front of the queue.

Remember the problem with removing an item from a Queue – this is a similar abstraction, so we need two operations to give the overall effect of removing a car from the car queue and passing it on to a car washer. Specification 2.3 gives the full specification of the WaitingCars abstraction.

Specification 2.3 The WaitingCars Data Abstraction

```
Types provided: CarQueue

Other abstractions used: Car, Boolean, Error

Operations:
   InitialiseCarQueue: → CarQueue
   AddCarToQueue: CarQueue, Car → CarQueue
   RemoveCarFromQueue: CarQueue → CarQueue
   FirstCar: CarQueue → Car
   IsCarQueueEmpty: CarQueue → Boolean

Axioms:
   RemoveCarFromQueue(InitialiseCarQueue) = Error
   RemoveCarFromQueue(AddCarToQueue(cq, car)) =
      If IsCarQueueEmpty(cq) then InitialiseCarQueue
      otherwise
      AddCarToQueue(RemoveCarFromQueue(cq), car)
   FirstCar(InitialiseCarQueue) = Error
   FirstCar(AddCarToQueue(cq, car)) =
      If IsCarQueueEmpty(cq) then car otherwise FirstCar(cq)
   IsCarQueueEmpty(InitialiseCarQueue) = True
   IsCarQueueEmpty(AddCarToQueue(cq, car)) = False

Where:
   cq is of type CarQueue, car is of type Car
```

Washer

This abstraction represents a single car washer. A car washer has only two possible states: either it is washing a car, or it isn't washing a car. In other words, we can say that a car washer may be either active or inactive. A car washer becomes active when it is given a car to wash, and inactive when it has finished washing the car. Obviously, we can only give a car to an inactive car washer. Here are some possible operations for the Washer abstraction:

- MakeActive – make an inactive washer active.
- MakeInactive – make an active washer inactive.
- IsInactive – true if the washer is inactive, false if it is active.

We can now write the full specification for Washer, which is shown in Specification 2.4.

Specification 2.4 The Washer Data Abstraction

Types provided: Washer

Other abstractions used: Boolean

Operations:
  MakeActive: Washer → Washer
  MakeInactive: Washer → Washer
  IsInactive: Washer → Boolean

Axioms:
  IsInactive(MakeActive(w)) = False
  IsInactive(MakeInactive(w)) = True

Where:
  w is of type Washer

CarWashers

Now we need a data abstraction to describe a group of car washers. Remember that we have three car washers, each of which can be either inactive or active at any time. We need some way of representing a group of car washers. First, our data abstraction must have constructors, one to give us an empty group and one to put a car washer into the group.

- NewWasherGroup – create an empty washer group.
- AddWasher – add a washer to the washer group.

If we want a washer in the group to wash a car we must find an inactive one. We therefore need an observer, to tell us if there are any inactive washers in the group, and another observer to give us the name of an inactive washer:

- AvailableWasher – true if the group contains at least one inactive washer, false if it doesn't.
- GetWasher – get the name of an inactive washer in the group.

Specification 2.5 The CarWashers Data Abstraction

```
Types provided: CarWashers

Other abstractions used: Washer, Boolean

Operations:
   NewWasherGroup: → CarWashers
   AddWasher: CarWashers, Washer → CarWashers
   AvailableWasher: CarWashers → Boolean
   GetAvailableWasher: CarWashers → Washer

Axioms:
   AvailableWasher(NewWasherGroup) = False
   AvailableWasher(AddWasher(c, w1)) = True
   GetAvailableWasher(c) = If Inactive(w1) then w1
                      otherwise if Inactive(w2) then w2
                      otherwise if Inactive(w3) then w3
                      otherwise Error

Where:
   c is of type CarWashers,
   w1, w2, w3 are of type Washer
```

Specification 2.5 give the full specification for the CarWashers abstraction.

Notice that we have used the Inactive operation from the Washer abstraction to implement GetAvailableWasher.

Washes

There is one more abstraction required, which was not found in the initial search for objects. This abstraction simply provides the two types of car wash available. It is not central to the problem solution, and can be considered an auxiliary abstraction to the CarWashers abstraction.

- Wash – a simple car wash.
- WashAndWax – car wash followed by waxing.

We will not define this abstraction formally, as it is really too small, and not a true data abstraction – rather, it is two procedural abstractions, which could be implemented as part of the CarWashers data abstraction. However, we can easily give the syntax for these two operations:

Wash: Car, Washer → Car
WashAndWax: Car, Washer → Car

2.4.4 Finding auxiliary abstractions

We now have our main top-level abstractions in the problem solution. Now we have to consider what abstractions will be needed to allow us to implement these top-level abstractions. We must find abstractions we can use to implement our top-level abstractions in order to make the implementations easier.

First, consider WaitingCars. The operations and axioms of WaitingCars are very similar (except in name) to those of the Queue abstraction. This is not surprising, because we said that it was a queue of cars when we specified it! We can show how the operations of WaitingCars correspond to the operations of Queue as follows (the symbol ⇒ can be read as *corresponds to*):

InitialiseCarQueue ⇒ NewQ
AddCarToQueue ⇒ AddQ
RemoveCarFromQueue ⇒ RearQ
FirstCar ⇒ FrontQ
IsCarQueueEmpty ⇒ IsEmptyQ

where the types correspond as follows:

CarQueue ⇒ Queue
Car ⇒ Item

CarWashers does not have any obvious auxiliary abstractions. However, consider what we have defined CarWashers to be – a set of car washers, each of which may be either available or unavailable to wash a car from the queue. Can you see that we might be able to implement CarWashers using the Set abstraction?

In fact, we will only be able to get a *partial* implementation of CarWashers from the Set abstraction. The operations NewWasherSet and AddToWasherSet correspond directly to the Set operations New and Insert. However, there are no operations in the Set abstraction to implement AvailableWasher and GetAvailableWasher. We will have to implement these operations from scratch (luckily, they are likely to be quite easy to implement). The operations which do correspond are:

NewWasherSet ⇒ New
AddToWasherSet ⇒ Insert

where the types correspond as follows:

CarWasher $\Rightarrow$ **Set**
Washer $\Rightarrow$ **Item**

In more complicated problems there is unlikely to be a straight one to one map between the operations of the main abstractions and the auxiliary abstractions. In such cases it is best to try designing a rough algorithm for each operation in a main abstraction, showing how the auxiliary abstractions are used within its implementation. This will make it less likely that the auxiliary abstractions prove to be incorrect or totally inadequate when they are used in the full implementation.

It is worthwhile drawing a diagram to show all the abstractions we have identified so far in our problem solution, with arrows indicating where an abstraction uses all or part of another abstraction in its implementation.

Figure 2.1 shows the relationships between all the abstractions in the car wash simulation. You will notice that we have added an abstraction for a car, called Car. We have not bothered to define Car. It simply represents a car, and is used in the car wash queue; we might decide to represent a car as a number for example, and therefore have a queue of numbers for WaitingCars. Each data abstraction in this Figure will provide a module in our problem solution.

Figure 2.1 Data Abstractions for the Car Wash Simulation

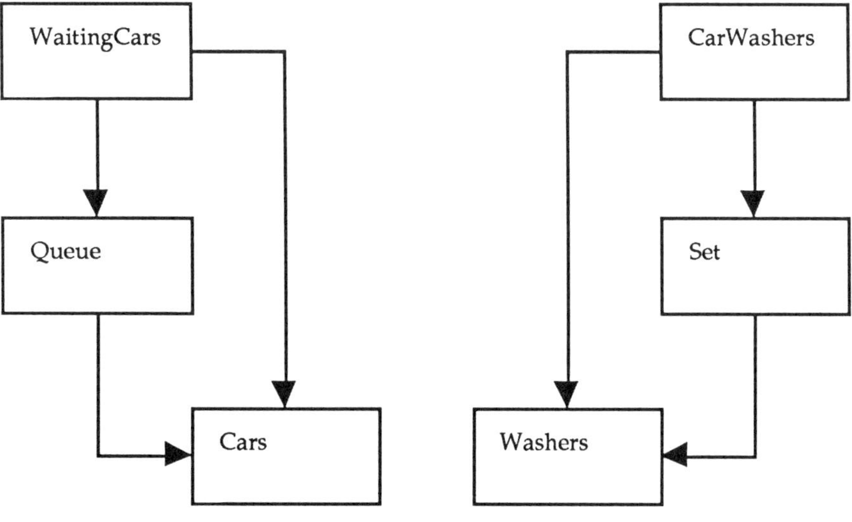

2.4.5 Informal solution using the abstractions

At this stage we can give an informal algorithm for solving the problem:

```
Loop forever
    If there is a car waiting in the queue
    and a car washer available then
        Give the car to the car washer which then washes
        the car appropriately.
    EndIf
EndLoop
```

This initial algorithm can now be refined and rewritten in terms of the abstractions we have just specified. This can be very useful in indicating whether or not we have chosen the right abstractions and the right operations within these abstractions for solving the original problem!

Here is the original algorithm rewritten:

```
Loop forever
    If IsCarQueueEmpty(carqueue) = False and
    AvailableWasher(washers) = True then do the following
        car := Wash(MakeActive(GetAvailableWasher(washers),
                               FirstCar(carqueue))
        carqueue := RemoveCarFromQueue(carqueue)
    Endif
Endloop
(where carqueue is of type CarQueue, washers is of type
CarWashers and car is of type Car)
```

There are some interesting points to note about this version of the algorithm. First the WashCar operation has a great deal going on! Wash needs an active car washer and a car, so we use MakeActive to activate a washer obtained from the GetAvailableWasher operation, then we use FirstCar to give us the car at the front of the car queue. Once Wash has finished its task the car that has just been washed (and is still at the front of the queue) can be removed from the queue by RemoveCarFromQueue.

The fact that we can use the operations specified by the various abstractions to implement the initial algorithm gives us some confidence to go on and implement the abstractions fully in the solution of the original problem. If it had been difficult or impossible to refine the initial algorithm in this way we would have had to return to the drawing board and reconsider the abstractions and our modularisation of the problem.

2.5 Case study - a company car pool reservation system

This is a larger problem than the car wash simulation, although we will find that the number of abstractions required is not very different. We will also see an example of a functional abstraction which uses several data abstractions, but does not supply any data types of its own.

2.5.1 Problem description

The requirements are for a reservation system for a company car pool. The reservation system must be capable of reserving and unreserving cars in the car pool, and giving information on the current availability of cars. Additionally, there should be a means of setting up and updating the car pool, that is putting car information into the reservation system. Each car in the car pool should have a unique record in the reservation system, which can be used to identify it, indicate its reservation status, and, if reserved, who has reserved it. Possible requests to the system are:

- Set up the car pool.
- Reserve a particular car for an employee.
- Unreserve a particular car.
- Print details for a particular car.
- List all reserved cars.
- List all unreserved cars.

2.5.2 Objects in the problem description

We can immediately see several objects in this problem description (remember that the nouns tend to indicate data abstractions), and some associated operations:

- The various requests to the car pool reservation system. Setup, reserve, unreserve, print, list reserved, list unreserved.
- An individual car record, belonging to the car pool. Change the reservation status of a car record.
- The collection of car records which forms the car pool. Add a new car record, remove a car record.

These objects now give us the top-level abstractions as a good starting point for our problem solution. Now we have to define each abstraction more formally, and find any auxiliary abstractions which may also be needed.

2.5.3 Specifying the main abstractions

Requests

There are five different types of request (see the problem description and the informal design), each of which must perform a different operation on the car pool.

Requests is not a data abstraction, it doesn't provide any data types but uses data types provided by other data abstractions. We can call Requests a functional abstraction, because it provides a higher-level of operations for several data abstractions. For this reason we don't give axioms for any of Requests' operations (it would be very difficult to do this anyway). Specification 2.6 gives the syntax of each operation in Requests.

Specification 2.6 The Requests functional abstraction

```
Data abstractions used: CarPool, Car

Operations:
    Setup: CarPool → CarPool
    Reserve: CarPool, Registration → CarPool
    Unreserve: CarPool, Registration → CarPool
    Display: CarPool, Registration → to output
    ListReserved: CarPool → to output
    ListUnreserved: CarPool → to output
```

Instead of giving axioms for the operations of Requests let's consider a simple algorithm for each operation.

We start with the setup operation which is supposed to allow the user to add and remove car records from the car pool. In this simple algorithm we haven't worried about the details of how the information is obtained from the user or how the car record is set up.

```
    Setup
        Do the following until we've finished all updates
            If we want to add a new car record then
                Get all the car information from the user
                Setup the new car record
                Add the car to the car pool
```

```
otherwise if we want to remove an existing car then
            Get the registration number of the car to be removed
            Find the car and remove it from the car pool
        Endif
    Enddo
```

The Reserve and Unreserve operations are very similar. Again we have left out details of finding the right car record and updating it in the car pool. The operations provided by the data abstractions for the car pool and a car need to be sufficient to implement Reserve and Unreserve.

```
Reserve
    Find the car we want to reserve
    Update its reservation status to reserved, and put in the
    employee number of the reserving employee

Unreserve
    Find the car we want to unreserve
    Update its reservation status to unreserved
```

The remaining three operations are all concerned with displaying information about the car pool or individual cars within the car pool:

```
Display
    Find the car we want to display
    Print out registration, status, employee number (if applicable)

ListReserved
    Do the following for each car in the car pool
        Find the status of the car
        If the status is reserved then
            Display the car
        Endif
    Enddo

ListUnreserved
    Do the following for each car in the car pool
        Find the status of the car
        If the status is unreserved then
            Display the car
        Endif
    Enddo
```

When we have specified the other abstractions required for the problem solution we will come back to Requests and try to give more detailed algorithms for each operation, using the operations provided by the other abstractions. If the operations provided by the other abstractions appear to be sufficient to implement both Requests and the main algorithm then we have probably modularised the problem correctly, and chosen the right operations for our abstractions.

CarPool

The CarPool abstraction must provide a means of storing all the information required about each car in the company car pool. It must also allow access to information about individual cars, so that a car may have its reservation status checked or altered (from unreserved to reserved or vice versa). How can we group the cars together so that each one can be accessed individually?

We looked at some data structures for grouping data together in Chapter 1, and we have already defined and used the Queue data abstraction in this chapter. However, a queue is not going to be a particularly appropriate representation for the car pool.

One structure we looked at informally in Chapter 1 was the list, which provides a list of items (such as a list of words, or a list of numbers). We could store our car pool as a list of cars.

We will need two constructors to allow us to build a car pool containing a number of cars:

- NewCarPool – Create a new, empty car pool.
- AddCar – Put a car into the car pool.

We will probably need a modifier to allow us to remove a car from the car pool (perhaps temporarily for servicing, or permanently).

- RemoveCar – Remove a particular car from the car pool.

Several observers will be necessary:

- LastAdded – Gives the car most recently added to the car pool.
- IsCarPoolEmpty – True if the car pool has no cars in it, false otherwise.
- FindCar – Find a particular car in the car pool.

Specification 2.7 gives the formal specification of CarPool.

Specification 2.7 The CarPool Data Abstraction

```
Types provided: CarPool

Other abstractions used: Car, Error, Boolean

Operations:
   NewCarPool: → CarPool
   AddCar: CarPool, Car → CarPool
   RemoveCar: CarPool, Registration → CarPool
   LastAdded: CarPool → Car
   FindCar: CarPool, Registration → Car
   IsCarPoolEmpty: CarPool → Boolean
Axioms:
   RemoveCar(NewCarPool, r) = Error
   RemoveCar(AddCar(p, c), r) = If GetRegistration(c) = r then p
      otherwise AddCar(RemoveCar(p, r), c)
   LastAdded(NewCarPool) = Error
   LastAdded(AddCar(p, c)) = c
   FindCar(NewCarPool, r) = Error
   FindCar(AddCar(p, c), r) = If GetRegistration(c) = r then c
      otherwise FindCar(p, r)
   IsCarPoolEmpty(NewCarPool) = True
   IsCarPoolEmpty(AddCar(p, c)) = False
Where:
   c is of type Car
   p is of type CarPool
   r is of type Registration
```

The syntax and axioms for CarPool need a little explanation. Note that AddCar is given something of type Car (that is, a complete car record) to add to the car pool, but RemoveCar and FindCar are given something of type Registration (That is, a registration number of a car, which will be only part of a complete car record).Both RemoveCar and FindCar need to identify a particular car in the car pool to carry out their respective tasks. Each car will have a unique registration number, so this is a good way of indicating a particular car.

The axioms for RemoveCar and FindCar use an extra operation, GetRegistration, which we assume returns the registration number from a given car record. The

GetRegistration operation will be an observer of the car record data abstraction, Car.

Car

We need to be able to store all the information for a particular car, but what information do we need? The problem requires that we can reserve or unreserve an individual car, so we need to store not only the reservation status of the car (reserved or unreserved), but also some means of uniquely identifying an individual car in the car pool. Cars usually have unique registration numbers, so we can store this information to identify a particular car. Additionally, we need to store some information indicating which employee has reserved the car, if it is reserved (see the problem description).

Our Car data abstraction must provide us with the means to store, access and alter each piece of information we need to keep about a car. A *record* allows us to store several different but related pieces of information together in a similar form to the method used on a paper record card. The record must have a name and a set of attributes. For example, the record employee could contain the information: name of employee; age; salary; starting date; position; etc. What we are talking about for representing a single car is really a record containing several pieces of information.

For a constructor we probably want something slightly different from the constructors we have needed for the earlier data abstractions. There is no need to be able to represent an empty car record – a car record must contain all the appropriate information for it to be valid. So we can have one constructor, which, given the registration number, reservation status and an employee number, builds a car record:

- BuildCarRecord – build a car record from the registration number, reservation status and employee number.

Now we need modifiers to allow us to change individual parts of a record, because we might want to alter the reservation status (from unreserved to reserved, for example). If we have separate operations for reserving and unreserving a car we can make the reserving operation alter the employee number to that of the reserving employee. However, it is unlikely that we should need to alter the registration number, so we don't need a modifier to do this.

- MakeReserved – make the reservation status *reserved*, and alter the employee number to that of the reserving employee.

- MakeUnreserved– make the reservation status of the car *unreserved*.

Finally, we will need observers to tell us about the various parts of the car record:

- GetRegistration – give the registration number of the car.

- GetStatus – give the reservation status of the car.

- GetEmployee – give the employee number of the employee who has reserved the car.

Putting all this together we have Specification 2.8, giving the full specification of Car.

Specification 2.8 The Car Data Abstraction

```
Types provided: Car, Registration, Status, Employee

Other abstractions used: none

Operations:
   BuildCarRecord: Registration, Status, Employee → Car
   MakeReserved: Car, Employee → Car
   MakeUnreserved: Car → Car
   GetRegistration: Car → Registration
   GetStatus: Car → Status
   GetEmployee: Car → Employee

Axioms:
   MakeReserved(BuildCarRecord(r, s, e)) =
         If s = reserved then BuildCarRecord(r, s, e)
         otherwise BuildCarRecord(r, reserved, e)
   MakeUnreserved(BuildCarRecord(r, s, e)) =
         If s = unreserved then BuildCarRecord(r, s, e)
         otherwise BuildCarRecord(r, unreserved, e)
   GetRegistration(BuildCarRecord(r, s, e)) = r
   GetStatus(BuildCarRecord(r, s, e)) = s
   GetEmployee(BuildCarRecord(r, s, e)) = e

Where:
   r is of type Registration,
   s is of type Status,
   e is of type Employee.
```

2.5.4 Finding the auxiliary abstractions

Now we have to find if there are any auxiliary abstractions that will be helpful in implementing the main abstractions.

The Requests abstraction is a functional abstraction which uses operations from the existing main abstractions Car and CarPool. There are no auxiliary abstractions needed to implement this functional abstraction.

However, consider the CarPool abstraction. A car pool is effectively a list of cars which constitutes the car pool. There is another data abstraction, called the List, which provides very similar operations to CarPool.

Lists are very widely used when designing software solutions to problems, but we will leave their specification until Chapter 5, where we can implement them at the same time.

Figure 2.2 Data Abstractions for a Car Pool Reservation System

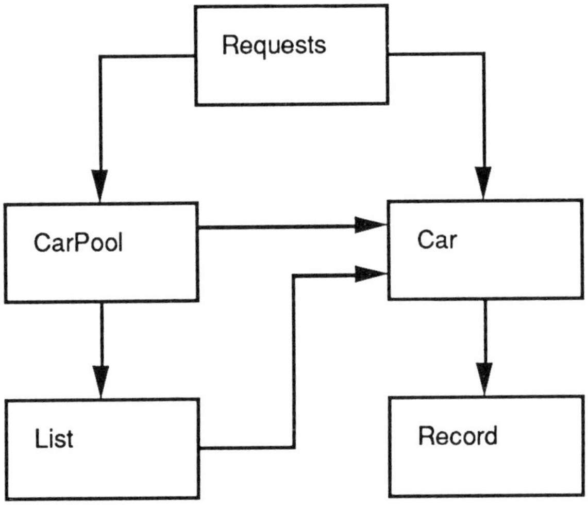

Requests

CarPool

Car

List

Record

Next, the Car data abstraction. Car, as we have said, is a record containing several pieces of information. The Record data abstraction is also one of the basic data abstractions of computer science. So basic, in fact, that most programming languages provide a method of defining and using records. We therefore don't have to implement the Record ourselves.

Now we can draw a diagram (Figure 2.2) of the various data abstractions (and therefore modules) in our problem solution, with the arrows showing which abstraction uses another for implementation.

2.5.5 Informal solution using the abstractions

Here is one possible informal algorithm for the main part of the reservation system:

```
Get a request from the user
Process the request as follows:
    If a setup request then setup car pool
    If a reserve request then reserve a car in the car pool
    If an unreserve request then unreserve the given car in the car
    pool
    If a display request then display all information about the given
    car
    If a list reserved request then list all reserved cars in the car
    pool
    If a list unreserved request then list all unreserved cars in the car
    pool
```

Remember that we have already defined the operations of the Requests abstraction as simple algorithms. We can now check if we have the right functionality by rewriting these algorithms using the appropriate operations from the data abstractions.

First consider the initial algorithm for the reservation system. There is, in fact, very little to change in this algorithm, most of the work of using the data abstractions is done in Requests:

```
Get a request from the user
If setup request then
    pool := Setup(pool)
otherwise if reserve request then
    ListUnreserved(pool)
    Get registration number of car to reserve from user
    pool := Reserve(pool, registration)
otherwise if unreserve request then
    ListReserved(pool)
    Get registration number of car to unreserve from user
    pool := Unreserve(pool, registration)
otherwise if list-reserved request then
    ListReserved(pool)
otherwise if list-unreserved request then
    ListUnreserved(pool)
Endif
```

Now the algorithms for each operation in Requests must be refined in a similar way to use the appropriate operations from Car and CarPool.

```
Setup(pool)

    If IsEmptyCarPool = True then
        pool := NewCarPool
    Endif

    Do the following
        Decide whether adding or removing a car record
        If adding a car then
            Get car information from user
            car := BuildCar(registration, status, employee)
            pool := AddCar(pool, car)
        otherwise if removing a car then
            Get registration number of car to remove from user
            pool := RemoveCar(pool, registration)
        Endif
    Until we've finished all the updates
```

Note how Setup uses four operations from CarPool and one operation from Car to perform its task.

The Reserve and Unreserve operations are not quite so straight forward. The original algorithm for Reserve was:

```
Reserve

    Find the car we want to reserve
    Update its reservation status to reserved, and put in the
    employee number of the reserving employee
```

This simple algorithm hides an important problem, how do we update a car record in the car pool? By update we mean that we want to take an existing record in the car pool and change its contents. The nature of our data abstractions means that this is not possible, but we can have the equivalent effect by taking a copy of the record we want to alter, removing the original from the car pool, altering the copy and adding the copy back into the car pool. This is exactly what we have done in the algorithms for Reserve and Unreserve. Note that we don't remove the car record until we have checked that it isn't reserved.

```
Reserve(pool, registration, employee)
   If IsCarPoolEmpty = False then
      car := FindCar(pool, registration)
      If GetStatus(car) = unreserved then
         pool := RemoveCar(pool, registration)
         car := MakeReserved(car, registration, employee)
         pool := AddCar(car)
      otherwise
         Report to user that car is already reserved
      EndIf
   otherwise
      Report to user that car pool is empty
   EndIf

Unreserve(pool, registration, employee)
   If IsCarPoolEmpty = False then
      car := FindCar(pool, registration)
      If GetStatus(car) = reserved then
         pool := RemoveCar(pool, registration)
         car := MakeUnreserved(car, registration, employee)
         pool := AddCar(car)
      otherwise
         Report to user that car is already unreserved
      EndIf
   otherwise
      Report to user that car pool is empty
   EndIf
```

The remaining three operations of Requests are the output operations Display, ListReserved and ListUnreserved:

```
Display(pool, registration)
   If IsEmptyCarPool = False then
      car := FindCar(pool, registration)
      status := GetStatus(car)
      employee := GetEmployee(car)
      Print out registration, status, employee (if applicable)
   EndIf
```

```
ListReserved(pool)
   While IsEmptyCarPool = False do the following
      car := LastAdded(pool)
      If GetStatus(car) = reserved then
         Display(car)
      EndIf
      pool := Remove(pool, GetRegistration(car))
   EndWhile

ListUnreserved(pool)
   While IsEmptyCarPool = False do the following
      car := LastAdded(pool)
      If GetStatus(car) = unreserved then
         Display(car)
      EndIf
      pool := Remove(pool, GetRegistration(car))
   EndWhile
```

ListReserved and ListUnreserved may at first glance appear to be deleting all the car records from the car pool, but input values to operations in our abstractions cannot be altered, and there are no output values to pass back any changes.

Since we have managed to give detailed algorithms for each operation in Requests and the initial main algorithm our modularisation has been quite successful, and we can continue implementing the full problem solution.

Those of you who have not used a programming language before or who have little or no experience of Modula-2 should now turn to Appendix A, which contains a simple introduction to the Modula-2 programming language. Chapter 3 introduces procedural abstractions and their implementation in Modula-2, and Chapter 4 shows how Modula-2 library modules provide the right facilities for implementing complete data abstractions.

Summary

Modules can be used to divide a problem solution into smaller, simpler, logical units, which are easier to solve than the original problem solution.

Modules also allow parts of a problem to be solved independently, and can localise modifications to a solution.

One method of modularising a problem solution is to find the data abstractions the solution requires. Each abstraction provides a module in the solution.

A data abstraction (or abstract data type) is described only by its range of possible values and the operations which can be performed on these values. It is abstract because there is no need for any information on how the operations are implemented or how the values are represented.

There are three classes of operations to fully specify a data abstraction: constructors build instances of the abstraction; modifiers transform one instance into another instance; observers tell us something about particular instance.

To specify a data abstraction we must state both the syntax of each operation (including the type of input and output values), and how the operations affect general instances of the abstraction.

In the representation of data abstractions shown here each instance of a data abstraction is represented only by a combination of constructor operations. So the set {3, 2} is represented by the expression Insert(Insert(New, 3), 2).

Selected reading

Berzins, V and Luqi
Software engineering with abstractions
Addison-Wesley, 1990
This book puts abstractions exactly where they belong – right at the centre of good software engineering practice. It shows how a problem may be analysed to find the abstractions it contains, how the abstractions are specified, and how we move from specification to implementation.

Harrison, R
Abstract data types in Modula-2
J. Wiley and Sons, 1989
This book is invaluable for its equational specifications which should be easily understood by any reader that has studied this chapter. The book uses Modula-2 to implement these abstractions.

Liskov, B and Guttag, J
Abstraction and specification in program development
MIT Press/McGraw-Hill, 1986
This is one of the best books on abstraction and specification. It is designed as a second course book, and assumes some knowledge of programming. There is an excellent section on the equational method of data abstraction specification, and a number of useful examples of such specifications. The book also shows how the specification of an abstraction can be taken through to an implementation.

3 Procedural abstraction

3.1 Introduction

So far we have only used ready-made procedures and functions, imported from library modules (for example,WriteLn and WriteString from InOut) or built in as part of the Modula-2 language (for example, INC and ORD, see Appendices A and C). Our data abstractions of Chapter 2 are each specified to have a number of operations; in an implementation of a data abstraction each operation will be a *procedural abstraction*. Even problems which do not involve data abstractions in their solution often naturally subdivide into procedures or functions.

First we will look at procedural abstractions. Just as a data abstraction specifies the values and operations of a data type without any implementation details, so a procedural abstraction specifies the task performed by a procedure or function without indicating how it performs that task.

3.2 Procedural abstractions

Procedural abstractions (or procedures) provide a method of packaging an algorithm which performs a well-defined task, in such a way that the task need only be described once, in a *definition*, and then may be performed repeatedly, simply by referring to it by name. Thus, in Modula-2, the WriteString procedure is defined only once, in the InOut library, but can be used in a program by naming it and providing the correct sort of input value, as many times as it is required. For example:

```
WriteString("Hello..");
WriteString("    world");
```

The advantages of using such abstractions are:

- A task which is well-defined, such as summing a list of numbers, converting a text file to upper case, reading in a valid filename from the user etc, is often best designed as a procedural or functional abstraction, to expose the logical structure of the overall task. That is, if something appears to stand out as a recognisable task, then it should be defined as such. We would therefore use such abstractions when one algorithm naturally subdivides into further algorithms.

- If a design of a problem solution contains a certain task or tasks which are performed repeatedly, then an abstraction can be used so that the task need only be written out once. For example, if a program is expected to read in several filenames typed by the user, it is more useful to make the reading of a filename a procedural abstraction, so that we don't have to keep repeating the same algorithm again and again.

3.2.1 Designing procedural abstractions

How do we determine the best procedural abstractions to use in a problem solution? As an example, let's see how procedural abstractions may be used to solve the following problem:

> Imagine a large computer with an attachment (such as a modem) which allows a user to dial up the computer through the phone network, and run a session from a remote site (such as the user's home). Provide a simple call logger for the computer, which automatically bills a remote user for their use of computer time. Assume that only one remote call can be dealt with at a time.

In finding procedural abstractions for this we need to consider the breakdown of the problem into separate, simple tasks. Here is one possible breakdown:

```
Loop forever
    Log call
    Calculate charge
    Bill for call
Endloop
```

Apart from the loop which makes the logger log calls continuously, each line is a simple task, and together the tasks solve the entire problem. Each task is a procedural abstraction, which can be further sub-divided:

```
Log call
    Record start time and instigator in call log.
    Wait for call to finish.
    Record finish time in call log.
```

Calculate charge
  Find charge rate per minute based on start time.
  Find length of call in minutes.
  Calculate charge for call = charge rate * length of call

Bill for call
  Send bill, showing call log and charge to instigator's electronic mailbox.

Notice that each procedural abstraction in the above example has a simple, well defined task, even though each task may further subdivide to include other procedural abstractions.

One of the properties we need in our procedural abstractions is shown in this example:

- A procedural abstraction should have a simple, well-defined purpose.

You should be able to write a short description of what the procedure does. If you can't, then your procedure is probably too complicated, and you need to try re-defining your procedural abstractions. An excellent test for simplicity is thinking of a name for the procedure. If you find it hard to think of a name which adequately describes the procedure's purpose your procedure is not simple enough.

It is possible to go too far, and define too many procedural abstractions. This can make your final problem solution unreadable. For example, CalculateCharge could be implemented with each subtask within it being another procedural abstraction, but this is almost certainly unnecessary, as each subtask is very small.

We can always define a procedural abstraction for a specific task. For example, we can define one to find the maximum of an array of ten integers. If we then wanted to find the maximum of an array of twenty integers we could write another procedural abstraction to do this task. However, it would be much better if we started by defining a procedural abstraction that was sufficiently general to find the maximum of any array of integers, regardless of length. This brings us to another property which we should try to build into our procedural abstractions:

- A procedural abstraction should, if possible, display generality (that is, usefulness in more than one situation).

There are several ways in which we can ensure generality, and most programming languages (including Modula-2) provide some means of doing this.

If we want a procedural abstraction to convert a single character from lower to upper case, we might generalise it to convert an array of characters (which will include the conversion of a single character – an array of length 1). Depending on the context in which we are using our case converter, it may well be worthwhile to go to a little extra effort and provide a case converter for a string of characters, rather than for a single character.

However, we need to avoid going too far, and over-generalising. With the procedural abstraction for finding the maximum of any size array of integers, we could decide to generalise even more, and find the maximum of any size array of integers, or reals or cardinals. In many programming languages this would be a non-trivial problem, and in some it would be unimplementable. This is one example where it is probably not worth the trouble of a completely general array maximum procedure. One for each type of array would be easier and quicker to implement.

3.2.2 Specifying procedural abstractions

A specification is a formal, and precise description of the characteristics of something, which provides anyone who wishes to build this something with sufficient detail to do so. In a specification we state only the characteristics that the final product should display, and say nothing about how to build it. The description should be precise enough to allow two different people to read the specification and both come up with exactly the same final product. For example, the specification of a teacup might state the size, shape, colour and material it is to be constructed out of, but no mention will be made of the process of making the teacup. Different people should be able to follow this specification and make teacups which all look exactly the same, even though each person may work in a different way.

- Although a specification must be precise, to avoid different interpretations, it must also be abstract, so that it does not contain any details of implementation.

To specify a procedural abstraction we need to be able to state precisely what the abstraction does. We are not only interested in avoiding giving any implementation details, but we need to ensure that any user of the procedure has sufficient detail to use it correctly.

What information do we need to specify a procedural abstraction, such that it can be used without the user needing to see the statements which actually implement the abstraction?

- The name of the procedure, so that we can refer to it. For example, LogCall and CalculateCharge.

- The sort of input values needed for the procedure to perform its task. For example, CalculateCharge needs to be given the call log as its input value. This information is given by stating the type of each input value.

- The sort of output values the procedure provides as part of its task. Some procedures don't provide any output values, and others provide more than one. In this book many of the procedural abstractions provide only single output values.

Here's an example of such a specification of the procedural abstractions from the call logger given above:

LogCall: Cardinal → CallLog
CalculateCharge: CallLog → Charge
BillForCall: Charge, CallLog → Bill

The abstraction LogCall has one input value, a cardinal number (which will be the code number for the call instigator) and one output value of type CallLog (which will be the log of the call just finished). CalculateCharge needs one input value, of type CallLog, which it uses to calculate the charge for the call, returned as an output value of type Charge. BillForCall needs to be given a Charge and the CallLog for the call, and it produces a Bill as its output value.

You have probably noticed that this is exactly the same as the syntactic specification we used in Chapter 2 to specify the operations of a data abstraction. This is not surprising because each operation was a procedural abstraction performing a single task (for example, New created an empty set, Insert added an item into a set).

However, we cannot complete the specification of the procedural abstractions given above by stating axioms. The operations of a data abstraction all act in a well-defined manner on a particular data structure, which is itself defined by the constructor operations. We can therefore write axioms showing how an example of the data structure (described in terms of the constructors) is affected by each operation. Here we are dealing with a much more general use of procedural abstractions; not to define data abstractions, but to provide some higher level of functionality for an existing data abstraction (for example, Requests in the car pool example of Chapter 2), or just to provide a useful operation. It is often very difficult, or impossible to describe the actions of such procedural abstractions using simple axioms.

We still need some way of knowing what a procedural abstraction does. The syntactic specification given above is not sufficient. So instead of axioms, we supply the information about what a procedural abstraction does with its input values by stating the pre-condition and post-condition for the abstraction.

3.2.3 Pre-conditions and post-conditions

We must not only state the input and output values for a procedural abstraction, but we must also specify the context in which each procedural abstraction will perform its task, and what that task actually is. In Chapter 2 we did this by using axioms, but here we will show a less formal, but often easier method of specifying an abstraction. The pre- and post-condition specification of a procedural abstraction must state two things:

- The pre-condition – the set of possible states before the procedural abstraction executes.

- The post-condition – the set of possible states after the procedural abstraction has been executed.

For the user of a procedure, the pre- and post-conditions indicate the circumstances under which the procedure can be expected to work, and the effects the procedure has.

- The pre-condition must be true for the procedure to work correctly. If any part of a pre-condition is false, then the procedure is not guaranteed to work correctly.

- The post-condition can be assumed to hold after the procedure has been executed.

Together, the pre- and post-condition for a procedure is sometimes called the *requirements specification* of the procedure. We can now put in the requirements specification for the procedural abstractions from the call logger, and get the complete specification, which is shown in Specification 3.1.

Specification 3.1 Procedural Abstractions for the Call Logger

LogCall: Cardinal → CallLog
  Pre-condition: A call must be starting.
  Post-condition: Returns a log of the call, giving the start and finish times and the instigator of the call.

CalculateCharge: CallLog → Charge
  Pre-condition: call must contain a valid call logged by LogCall.
  Post-condition: Returns the charge for a single call, by finding the length of the call in minutes, and then multiplying by the appropriate charge rate for the time of day the call started. The rates are: started before 8.00am 10p per minute, started from 8.00am to 6.00pm, 25p per minute.

BillForCall: Charge, CallLog → Electronic mail sent to instigator
  Pre-condition: call must contain a valid call.
  Post-condition: Send electronic mail to the instigator of the given call, indicating how much the call has cost (in charge).

It is up to the author of a procedural abstraction to ensure that its implementation matches the descriptions in the pre- and post-conditions. If pre- and post-conditions are given, the user can only assume that they are adhered to in the implementation.

3.3 Using procedural abstractions

We have seen procedural abstractions which have zero or more input values, and one (or occasionally zero) output values. In fact we have been looking at a certain type of procedural abstraction, usually called a function, which returns a single output value and does not change its input values.
The specific items given to a procedural abstraction (as input values) are usually called the parameters of the abstraction. The input values of a function are value parameters because they just supply values for the function to use in performing its task. A value parameter may be modified inside the body of the function, but any changes here won't affect the value of the parameter outside the function.

A function is a procedural abstraction which returns a result through a single output value, but this is not the only way in which a procedural abstraction may supply results. The more general form of procedural abstraction, called the procedure, does not provide an output value, but supplies results by altering one or more of its parameters. This means that several results may be supplied by a procedural abstraction.

A parameter which may be modified to supply a result from a procedure is called a variable parameter, simply because any changes made to the parameter inside the procedure will affect the value of the parameter outside the procedure.

When we use a procedure in an algorithm we say we are calling the procedure. When we call a procedure we have to give it the parameters it requires to perform its task. Remember that the types of these parameters are given in the specification of the procedure. For example, here is an earlier algorithm containing a number of procedure calls:

```
If IsEmptyCarPool = False then
        car = FindCar(pool, registration)
        registration = GetRegistration(car)
        status = GetStatus(car)
        employee = GetEmployee(car)
        Print out registration, status, employee (if applicable)
    EndIf
```

(in fact they are specifically function calls, but that doesn't matter for our purposes here). The call to FindCar provides two parameters, one called pool, which must be of type CarPool, and one called registration which must be of type Registration. GetRegistration, GetStatus and GetEmployee are each given the same parameter, car, which must be of type Car.

In the above example we are using functions. Each function must be used as part of an expression (remember that a function returns a value, which we have to do something with!), so we assign the result returned by each function to a variable, for example:

```
car := FindCar(pool, registration)
```

where the result returned by FindCar will be assigned to the variable called car. Variable car must be of the same type as the output value in the specification of FindCar.

3.3.1 Getting results from functions

So far we have defined most of our procedural abstractions as functions, which return single results via an output value, and which do not alter their parameters.

A function is used to calculate a result which can be used as part of an expression. They are very like mathematical functions such as sin, cos etc. For example, consider the following expression:

```
sin(45°) + cos(180°)
```

If we want to calculate the value of this expression we calculate sin(45°) and then cos(180°) and add the results. Sin and cos are both trigonometric functions in mathematics, but they are used in the above expression in exactly the same way we would use a procedural abstraction function. Thus, we calculate sin(45°)=0.707 and replace sin(45°) by this result in the expression:

```
0.707 + cos(180°)
```

then we calculate cos(180°)=-1.0, and replace cos(180°) by this result:

```
0.707 + (-1.0)
```

Then we just add these two values together to get the value of the expression,

```
0.707 - 1.0 = -0.293
```

The usage of a function can be summarised as follows:

- A function delivers a single result to an expression. A function may be used anywhere such a result is required. For example, if we have a function which returns a character read in from the keyboard we can use the function anywhere a character is required.

- Since a function represents a value it must be used as part of an expression. A single value on its own is useless unless you do something with it, and a function just represents a single value. Remember that you always have to do something with the value returned by a function!

- When a function is used in an expression you can assume that the function computes its result, and the result is then substituted for the function in the expression.

3.3.2 Getting results from procedures

There are some types of procedural abstraction which are not easily or naturally defined as returning a single result:

- A procedural abstraction that may need to return more than one result. For example, a procedural abstraction which finds the roots of a quadratic equation will have to return two results, because quadratic equations have two roots (although these may be equal).

- A procedural abstraction that may be best defined as altering one or more of its parameters. For example, a procedural abstraction which sorts an integer array given as a parameter into ascending order, could sort the given parameter rather than return a sorted duplicate of the parameter as a result.

Once a procedural abstraction starts altering its parameters it cannot be compared in any way to a mathematical function, so reasoning about its effects is much harder, as we cannot reason mathematically. However, there are certainly times when such abstractions are useful, for example, consider the various read operations from the Modula-2 InOut library, such as ReadCard, ReadInt etc. These operations all modify their parameters to the value read in. In fact the parameters are not used to supply any values for the read operations, they are just used to return a value from each operation.

We can specify a procedural abstraction which alters its parameters in a similar way to those which return a single output value, except that there will be no output value to specify. Here is the specification for the integer array sorting abstraction:

Sort: *IntArray
Pre-condition: none.
Post-condition: the input parameter array is sorted into ascending order, so that a[i] < a[i + 1], where a is of type IntArray and i is the array index.

In order to differentiate more easily between value parameters which can't be modified and variable parameters which can be modified, we'll precede a variable parameter by an asterisk, as in the above example for IntArray:

Sort: *IntArray

This is necessary when a procedural abstraction has some variable parameters and some value parameters.

Remember that procedural abstractions that use variable parameters to return results, are called *procedures*. Confusion can arise because *procedure* is also the generic term given to all procedural abstractions, but the two uses are generally interchangeable.

3.3.3 Formal and actual parameters

Procedure and function parameters are probably one of the most confusing parts of writing programs, so don't worry if you have trouble understanding this at the first reading, try again, it will come to you!

Formal parameters are the parameters defined in a procedure (or function) header when the procedure is declared. For example, here is a simple function header written in Modula-2:

```
PROCEDURE CountVowels(word : CharArray): CARDINAL;
```

The function is called CountVowels and the formal parameter (between the round brackets) is called word, and is of type CharArray. Since CountVowels is a function it has an output value which is given after the parameters, and is of type CARDINAL.

The formal specification of a procedural abstraction gives only the types of the formal parameters, not the names. For example, here is the formal, syntactic specification of CountVowels:

```
CountVowels: CharArray → CARDINAL
```

Actual parameters are the parameters used in any call of a procedure. For example, here are two calls of the procedure CountVowels.

```
count1 := CountVowels(firstWord);
count2 := CountVowels(lastWord);
```

In the first call to CountVowels the actual parameter is firstWord. In the second call the actual parameter is lastWord. When we call a procedure we do not have to make the names of the actual parameters (those used in the call) the same as the formal parameters, but you can give them the same names if you want to, although this is not usually good style as it can lead to confusing programs.

You can remember the difference between formal and actual parameters quite easily:

> Formal parameters are formally defined, actual parameters are actually used!

Although the parameter names do not have to be the same, the actual and formal parameters for a procedure must match in number, type and the order in which they are given.

Number

We must have the same number of actual parameters as formal parameters. So, for example, a procedure expecting three parameters cannot be given any more or less than three parameters.

Type

The type of each actual parameter must be the same as the type of the corresponding formal parameter. So, a procedure expecting an INTEGER and a REAL cannot be given a CARDINAL and a CHAR.

Order

The order in which the formal parameters appear in the procedure's header is the order in which the actual parameters must be given in the procedure call. So, if a procedure is declared as having parameters of types INTEGER, REAL, BOOLEAN in that order, it is not acceptable for the call to use actual parameters in the order REAL, BOOLEAN, INTEGER.

The reason for this last point may not immediately seem obvious – perhaps a procedure should be able to sort out a BOOLEAN parameter from a REAL parameter? There are several reasons why this can't be done – firstly that the internal representations of different types of parameter are likely to be indistinguishable (everything eventually comes down to a string of binary 0s and 1s!) and secondly, what happens if you are passing more than one parameter of the same type, but intending them for different purposes? How can the procedure know which is which?

3.3.4 Value and variable parameters

Now let's return to the way in which procedures supply results through altering their parameters, and take a more detailed look at the differences between value parameters which can't change their value and variable parameters which can.

Parameters come in two varieties: value and variable. This is nothing to do with the types to which the parameters belong, rather it indicates the way in which the parameters may be used. This is often called the *mode* of a parameter.

Value parameters provide a way to pass a procedure or function the values needed for performing its task. Any changes made to the contents of a value parameter inside the procedure will be lost when the procedure finishes, and will have no effect on the corresponding actual parameter.

Variable parameters can also pass values to a procedure, but any changes made to a variable parameter inside a procedure are also made to the corresponding actual parameter.

Consider the following header:

```
PROCEDURE GetRectangle(VAR side1, side2 : CARDINAL;
                       VAR colour : Colours; primary : BOOLEAN);
```

The formal parameters for GetRectangle are side1, side2, colour and primary. The parameters side1, side2 and colour are variable parameters, indicated by the Modula-2 reserved word VAR. Parameter primary is a value parameter.

You should see at once that this header is not a function header, but a procedure header, because it has no declaration of any return type at the end of the header, and can only supply results by altering its three variable parameters side1 and side2.

First, let's see how value parameters work. Remember that we have been using value parameters to provide the values needed by a function to calculate its result.

Value parameters can be imagined to work as follows:

- When the procedure call is made the contents of the actual parameter is copied into a new memory location, which is given the name of the corresponding formal parameter in the procedure declaration.
- The actual parameter takes no further part in the procedure.
- If any changes are made to the formal parameter it has no effect on the original actual parameter as they are stored in different memory locations.
- When the procedure is finished the formal parameter is thrown away, so any changes made to it inside the procedure are lost. The actual parameter is unchanged because it has had no part in the procedure, only being used once to make a copy of its contents into a new memory location.

We call this sort of parameter a value parameter because it can only be used to supply a useful value to the function or procedure it is passed to. Any changes made to a value parameter have no effect on its corresponding actual parameter. For example, suppose we want to write a simple procedure to swap over the contents of two CARDINAL variables, a and b. Here is the first attempt at writing such a procedure, using value parameters to supply the two values. We want parameter x to take the value of parameter y, and parameter y to take the value of parameter x:

```
PROCEDURE Swap(x, y : CARDINAL);
VAR
   temp : CARDINAL;
BEGIN
   temp := x;
   x := y;
   y := temp;
END Swap;
```

Firstly, and not on the subject of parameters, why have we used temp? If we assign the contents of y to x we overwrite the original contents of x. Unless we have saved it somewhere (in temp) we can't then assign it to y.

Now, we need to try out Swap and see what happens! Let's assume that before we call Swap the value of a is 0 and the value of b is 42. The call to Swap is then:

```
Swap(a, b);
```

The actual parameters a and b are the variables whose values we want to swap over, and they correspond to the formal parameters x and y in Swap itself.

When the call is made:

- A new memory location is given the name x and the contents of a are copied into it. So x contains 0.

- A new memory location is given the name y and the contents of b are copied into it. So y contains 42.

The identifiers x and y now refer to memory locations which currently contain copies of the contents of a and b. The variables a and b have no further part to play in the work of the procedure. Variables x and y only exist inside the procedure (we say that they are *local* to the procedure).

When the procedure is executed, x is assigned the value 42, and y is assigned the value 0. When the procedure finishes, all local variables get thrown away. This includes x and y, as well as temp. In the calling program a and b remain unchanged, with a=0 and b=42; all that Swap did was to swap the values of local copies of a and b, not a and b themselves.

Variable parameters can be imagined to work as follows:

- When the procedure call is made the memory location where the actual parameter is stored becomes temporarily renamed to the formal parameter it corresponds to in the procedure header.

- Any changes made to this formal parameter inside the procedure are therefore made directly to the actual parameter where it is stored in memory.

- When the procedure is finished the name of the memory location is changed back to the name of the actual parameter. If the contents of the memory location have been altered during the procedure then the new value will still be in the memory location on return from the procedure, thus changing the value of the actual parameter passed to the procedure.

We call this sort of formal parameter a variable parameter because any changes in its value will affect the value of the corresponding actual parameter.

Now let's repeat the earlier example using variable parameters, which should enable us to swap the contents of the actual parameters:

```
PROCEDURE Swap(VAR x, y : CARDINAL);
VAR
   temp : CARDINAL;
BEGIN
   temp := x;
   x := y;
   y := temp;
END Swap;
```

When the call is made:

- The memory location referred to by variable a is temporarily renamed x. So x (really a) contains 0.

- The memory location referred to by variable b is temporarily renamed y. So y (really b) contains 42.

At this point x=0 and y=42. When the procedure is executed the contents of x and y are swapped over, so that x=42 and y=0. But because x and y are the same memory locations as a and b respectively, we have actually swapped the contents of a and b. In the calling program after the procedure call has been done, a=42 and b=0. The identifier names x and y disappear when Swap finishes.

If we had declared only one parameter, x say, to be a variable parameter then on return to the calling program we would find that only a's value had changed (to 42) and b would still be set to its original value (also 42).

Now, consider the following call to Swap. The actual parameters are constant values.

```
Swap(10, 300);
```

What happens if we use the first version of Swap, with value parameters? This call is valid Modula-2, we are passing two constants to a procedure whose formal parameters are value parameters. Swap swaps only copies of these constants, and doesn't touch the originals at all, so it will be quite happy to swap copies of 10 and 300, and simply throw away the local copies when the procedure finishes. The net result of this will be no changes at all!

Now consider what happens with the same call, when the formal parameters are variable parameters, as in the second version of Swap. In this case, the actual parameters are still constants, but Swap expects its formal parameters to be variable parameters. The values 10 and 300 are constants, and cannot be changed by the procedure. This violates the declaration of Swap, as actual parameters which are constants can never change, so Swap would be unable to carry out its task. In this case the compiler should indicate that there is a mismatch in mode between the actual parameters in the procedure call and the formal parameters in the procedure declaration.

3.4 Implementing procedural abstractions

Much of the following discussion on implementing procedural abstractions is applicable to all procedural languages, although specific syntax will be different. Of course, all our examples are shown in Modula-2!

In Modula-2, procedures and functions are called *proper procedures* and *procedure functions*, respectively, but we will use the more common descriptions. Remember too that we also use the word procedure as a shorthand for procedural abstraction, and most of the time the two are interchangeable, but we will qualify the word when necessary to avoid misinterpretation.

Our specifications of procedural abstractions have each stated

- The name of the abstraction.
- The type of the input values required for the abstraction to perform its task (and, implicitly, the order in which they must be given).
- The type of the output value which is the result or return value of the abstraction (if it's a function).

For example, here is the specification of the AddQ operation from the Queue data abstraction:

AddQ: Queue, Item → Queue

A programming language implementation of a procedural abstraction must convey similar information. In fact, a programming language requires more information, in that we must also give unique names to the input parameters so that they can be referred to in the algorithm which implements the abstraction.

The Modula-2 equivalent of our syntactic specification of procedural abstractions is the procedure header. Here is our specification of CalculateCharge, from the call logger, which is independent of any programming language:

CalculateCharge: CallLog → Charge

with one input parameter of type CallLog and one output parameter of type Charge. Here is the Modula-2 equivalent:

```
PROCEDURE CalculateCharge(call : CallLog): Charge;
```

The reserved word PROCEDURE is used to indicate that this is a procedural abstraction in Modula-2, and is used for both procedures and functions. The name is followed by the input parameters enclosed in round brackets (only one in this case).

We have given the parameter a name, call, by which it can be referred to within the function. At the end of the header we state only the type of the return value, Charge. Since a function provides a single value as a result it is up to the user of the function to do something with the value it returns, either using it directly in an expression or assigning it to a variable.

Our specification of CalculateCharge also originally included a description of the pre- and post-conditions for the abstraction. Only a few experimental programming languages define pre- and post-conditions as part of the language, so instead we usually have to be satisfied with just stating the pre- and post-conditions in a comment under the procedure header. For example,

```
PROCEDURE CalculateCharge(call : CallLog): Charge;
(* Pre-condition: call must contain a valid call logged by LogCall.
Post-condition: Returns the charge for a single call, by finding the
length of the call in minutes, and then multiplying by the appropriate
charge rate for the time of day the call started.  The rates are: started
before 8.00am 10p per minute, started from 8.00am to 6.00pm, 25p
per minute. *)
```

Here are similar Modula-2 procedure headers for LogCall and BillForCall:

```
PROCEDURE LogCall( ): CallLog;
(* Pre-condition: A call must be starting.
Post-condition: Returns a log of the call, giving the start and
finish times and the instigator of the call.

PROCEDURE BillForCall(amount : Charge; call : CallLog);
(* Pre-condition: call must contain a valid call.
Post-condition: Send electronic mail to the instigator of the given
call, indicating how much the call has cost (in charge). *)
```

Note that BillForCall has no return value at the end of the header. Our specification of BillForCall indicated that its result was to send mail to the caller, and there is no value to return. BillForCall is an example of the second type of procedural abstraction, a procedure.

The header of a procedure (or function) is only a specification of the procedure. The procedure body, which implements the procedure, must also be written. The procedure body is very similar to the body of a program module.

In Chapter 4 we will see how Modula-2 library modules provide us with a more satisfactory way of specifying procedural abstractions, allowing the user of an abstraction to see just the headers (and any associated comments and declarations) without having to see the procedure bodies which actually implement the abstractions.

3.4.1 Functions

A function is a procedural abstraction whose only effect is to return a single value as its result. Our specifications of procedural abstractions have almost invariably described functions with zero or more input parameters and one output parameter.

We will now look in more detail at the properties of Modula-2 functions as a means of implementing procedural abstractions. Here is the specification of a procedural abstraction which finds the maximum value in an array of integers:

```
ArrayMax: IntArray, Cardinal → Integer
    Pre-condition: None.
    Post-condition: The value returned is the largest integer in
    the array.
```

Here is the Modula-2 function header, with the pre- and post-conditions added as a comment:

```
PROCEDURE ArrayMax(a : IntArray): INTEGER;
(* Pre-condition: None.
Post-condition: The value returned is the largest integer in the
array. *)
```

Remember that even though ArrayMax is defined with the keyword PROCEDURE, it is in fact a function, because it returns a single value as its result. Having a different reserved word for functions and procedures is not strictly necessary, because (in Modula-2 at least) we can always tell whether something is a procedure or function by looking at the header – in a procedure the final colon and type designator are missing.

Returning to the header for function ArrayMax, we have stated that there is one input parameter, called a, which is of type IntArray. IntArray is not a built-in type of Modula-2, and must be declared somewhere. One possible declaration for it might be:

```
CONST
    MaxSize = 20;
TYPE
    IntArray = ARRAY [1..MaxSize] OF INTEGER;
```

The value calculated by ArrayMax is not given a name in the header, instead we just need to state its type, INTEGER in this case, which is the last part of the header. This is very similar to our procedural abstraction specifications, where we also stated the type of the result returned by the abstraction. The result produced by a function is often called its *return value.*

A function may have to calculate a series of results before it reaches the final result which it has to return, so there has to be some method of indicating which of the results calculated inside a function is the intended result of the function.

The method of returning the result of a function varies between programming languages; in Modula-2 we use a special statement, the RETURN statement. Here are some examples:

```
RETURN 42;
RETURN TRUE;
RETURN count;
```

The reserved word RETURN is followed by a value, an expression, or the name of the variable whose value is to be returned. The type of the returned value must be the type indicated at the end of the function header after the colon. It is an error if these types are not exactly the same, and compilation will fail if this is the case. The RETURN statement actually performs two tasks:

- It indicates the value to be returned as the result of the function.
- When it is executed, the function terminates immediately, without any more statements being executed.

The effect of this is that when the RETURN statement is executed the value indicated is immediately passed back to the place where the function was called, terminating the execution of the function itself. Remember,

- A function must contain at least one RETURN statement.

Now all we have to do is design and implement ArrayMax. To find the maximum value in an array we must keep the current maximum somewhere and compare it with each element in the array in turn:

```
Set maximum to first element in the array
For each subsequent element in the array do the following
   If element is greater than maximum then
      Set maximum to element
   Endif
Endfor
Return maximum
```

We can now put together the complete declaration of function ArrayMax:

```
PROCEDURE ArrayMax(array : IntArray; size : CARDINAL): INTEGER;
(* Pre-condition: none.
Post-condition: returned value is the largest integer in the array. *)

VAR
   i : CARDINAL; (* Array index. *)
   max : INTEGER (* Maximum value in array. *)
```

```
BEGIN
   (* Set max to first value in array. *) ;
   max := array[1];
   (* Step through array looking for maximum. *)
   FOR i := 2 TO MaxSize DO
      IF array[i] > max THEN
         max := array[i];
      END;
   END;
   RETURN max;
 END ArrayMax;
```

Variable max therefore contains the current maximum value in the array at the start of each iteration round the loop. It must be declared as an integer variable. The variable i is used as the loop control variable and the array index, and must be declared in the function's declaration section. We start the loop from the second item in the array because the first item is already the current maximum, so there is no point checking it against itself. Note that the loop runs up to size-1, because the array is indexed from zero. Size gives the number of items in the array, so if size equals 4, the array is indexed from 0 to 3.

The last thing which happens in this procedure is that the value max is returned to the calling program, by the statement

```
RETURN max;
```

The RETURN statement doesn't have to come at the end of a function – it can come anywhere in the function's body. Also, there can be as many RETURN statements as you like in the function. The important point to remember is that the first RETURN statement reached terminates the function as soon as it is executed.

The compiler will report a syntax error if you try to compile a function without a RETURN statement somewhere inside it, or a RETURN with no value to return, or a RETURN where the type to be returned doesn't match the type declared in the function header. Remember:

- A function always returns one value.

There are no exceptions to this rule.

Another important rule to remember is that Wirth's original definition of Modula-2 only allows functions to return unstructured types. In other words, return types of INTEGER, CHAR, CARDINAL, REAL and POINTER are acceptable, but functions cannot return structured types such as array, records and sets. In our examples above, the restriction to unstructured types means that procedure LogCall would have to be changed to pass back the call log in a variable parameter, because it is a RECORD type which is structured:

```
PROCEDURE LogCall(VAR call : CallLog);
(* Pre-condition: A call must be starting.
Post-condition: Variable call contains a log of the call, giving the
start and finish times and the instigator of the call. *)
```

3.4.2 Procedures

Now we have looked at functions in detail, as the most obvious means of implementing our specifications in Modula-2, we will look at Modula-2 procedures in more detail. Modula-2 procedures provide another means of implementing procedural abstractions. To define a procedure in Modula-2 is very similar to defining a function. The main differences are:

- The header of a procedure does not have the final colon and type name; because a procedure doesn't return a value we don't have to state a type for that value!

- A procedure does not contain a statement of the form:
  RETURN variable name;
  because it is not returning a value. However it may contain a RETURN statement without a variable name. Remember a RETURN statement is not compulsory in a procedure, whereas it is in a function.

Here's ArrayMax written as a procedure (last time we saw it as a function):

```
PROCEDURE ArrayMax(array : IntArray; VAR max : INTEGER);
(* Pre-condition: none.
Post-condition: max contains the largest integer in the array. *)

VAR
   i : CARDINAL; (* Array index. *)
(* Note that there is no declaration of max - already declared in
header as a parameter. *)

BEGIN
   max := array[1];
   (* Set max to first value in array. *) ;
   FOR i := 2 TO MaxSize DO
      IF array[i] > max THEN
         max := array[i];
      END;
   END;
   (* No RETURN statement needed - the VAR parameter does
   the job. *)
END ArrayMax;
```

If you compare this declaration of ArrayMax with the earlier function declaration you will see two major differences; first, there is no return type indicated at the end of the procedure header, and second, there is an extra input parameter called maximum, declared in the procedure header. Moreover, maximum is a variable parameter. Thus, the actual parameter in the procedure call, corresponding to formal parameter maximum, will have its value altered to the maximum value in the array.

Here is one way we might make a call to procedure ArrayMax:

```
max := 0;
noOfElements := 10;
ArrayMax(myArray, noOfElements, max);
```

After this call max should contain the maximum value in myArray, not the value it was given before the call, 0. Since maximum is declared as a variable parameter, and since it is assigned the maximum integer in the array during ArrayMax, the value max will be changed.

There is nothing to stop you using variable parameters to pass input values into a procedure, and then using the same parameters to pass information back from the procedure. The only thing to remember is that if a parameter to a procedure is a variable parameter then any contents it may have before the procedure call can be overwritten and lost during the execution of the procedure.

A return statement can be used at any place in the body of a function, and its effect is to terminate the function immediately and return to the calling program with the value indicated in the return statement. It is also possible to terminate a procedure at any point in the procedure body, by the use of another form of return statement.

Procedures cannot return values, so the return statement used to terminate a procedure does not specify a return value. Here is an example of such a use of RETURN, although we will say later why it is not usually considered good programming style:

```
PROCEDURE Guess(number : INTEGER);
(* Ask the user to guess the given number, and continue asking until
guessed correctly. Indicates whether the guess is too high or too
low.
Pre-condition: number contains the number to be guessed.
Post-condition: writes out the guessed number. *)

VAR
   try : INTEGER;
```

```
BEGIN
   WriteString("Guess a number:  ");
   LOOP
      ReadInt(try);
      WriteLn;
      IF try < number THEN
         WriteString("Too small, try again!);
         WriteLn;
      ELSIF try > number THEN
         WriteString("Too large, try again!);
         WriteLn;
      ELSE (* Try equals number *)
         WriteString("That's the number!");
         WriteLn;
         RETURN;
      END;
      WriteString("Enter another number!   ");
   END; (* LOOP *)
END Guess;
```

Guess is a continuous loop, which keeps asking the user to guess a number, until it is eventually guessed correctly. When the right number is guessed a suitable message is printed out and the RETURN statement is executed. This causes control to be returned immediately to the calling program, jumping out of the loop, without any further statements being executed. You can put a RETURN statement anywhere in the main body of a procedure, and it will act as a terminator for the procedure, stopping it as soon as the statement is reached.

Almost invariably you will find that a loop like this can be rewritten in a such a way that the RETURN statement is not needed at all, and the procedure can run through to the END statement and then return control to the calling program. We can do it for Guess by using a REPEAT-UNTIL loop, which will be left only when the correct number is typed in:

```
Prompt user to enter a guess
Repeat the following
   Read in user's guess
   If guess is too low or too high then
      Tell user to try again
   Endif
Until guess is correct
Tell user guess is correct
```

In Modula-2:

```
PROCEDURE Guess(number : INTEGER);
(* Ask the user to guess the given number, and continue asking until
guessed correctly. Indicates whether the guess is high / low.
Pre-condition: number contains the number to be guessed.
Post-condition: none. *)
VAR
   try : INTEGER;
BEGIN
   WriteString("Guess a number:  ");
   REPEAT
      ReadInt(try);
      WriteLn;
      IF try < number THEN
         WriteString("Too small, try again!);
         WriteLn;
      ELSIF try > number THEN
         WriteString("Too large, try again!);
         WriteLn;
      END;
      WriteString("Enter another number!   ");
   UNTIL try = number;
   WriteString("That's the number!");
   WriteLn;
END Guess;
```

Good programming practice means that it is usually better to write a procedure (or indeed a function) in such a way that you don't have to jump out of the middle of it by a RETURN statement, when returning to the calling program. It is usually easier to see what is going on in a procedure when you don't have RETURN statements causing it to exit from several places. It is also easy to forget an intended RETURN statement, and cause strange errors when your procedure doesn't return from the intended point.

For example, if you forget the RETURN statement in the first version of Guess then the procedure will never return control to the calling program, because there is no EXIT statement for the LOOP and so no way of getting out of it, even by guessing the correct number!

3.4.3 Declaring procedures in program modules

We have seen how to define or *declare* a complete procedure in Modula-2. Now we need to be able to use such procedures in our program modules. A procedure declaration is not a compilation unit of Modula-2. That is, we can't give the compiler a procedure declaration on its own, the compiler can only recognise and compile complete modules. To use our procedures we must declare them inside modules.

The simplest place to declare procedures is inside a program module (later we will see how procedures can be more useful if declared inside library modules). A program module can be looked at as having two sections; the declaration section at the top, where all the imports, constants, types and variables are declared, and the main body, between the BEGIN and END statements, where the statements making up the algorithm go.

Not altogether surprisingly, if we want to declare a procedure to use in the main body of a program module then its declaration goes in the declaration part of the module. Procedures are the last things to be declared, coming just before the BEGIN statement marking the start of the main body.

For example, consider a program which reads in a character and tells the user whether or not it is an alphabetic character:

```
Read in character
Check if character is alphabetic
Write out result
```

We already have predefined procedures from InOut, for reading in a character and writing out a message, but we can define a function for checking the character in our program module:

```
MODULE CharacterTest;
(* Read a character from the input and tell user whether or not it is an
alphabetic character. *)

VAR
   ch : CHAR;

PROCEDURE IsAlpha(c : CHAR): BOOLEAN;
(* Pre-condition: none.
Post-condition: the value returned is TRUE if c is in the range
"a".."z" or "A".."Z", otherwise FALSE. *)

BEGIN
   RETURN ((c >= "a") AND (c <= "z")) OR ((c >= "A")
      AND (c <= "Z"));
END IsAlpha;
```

```
BEGIN (* Module. *)
   WriteString("Enter character:  ");
   Read(ch);
   IF IsApha(ch) THEN
      WriteString("Character is alphabetic");
   ELSE
      WriteString("Character is non-alphabetic");
   END;
   WriteLn;
END CharacterTest;
```

Often we may want to put the headers derived from our specifications into a module for compiling, to check that we have got the syntax correct, before we've written the complete implementation for each procedural abstraction. Consider the header for CalculateCharge given earlier:

```
PROCEDURE CalculateCharge(call : CallLog): Charge;
(* Pre-condition: call must contain a valid call logged by LogCall.
Post-condition: Returns the charge for a single call, by finding the
length of the call in minutes, and then multiplying by the appropriate
charge rate for the time of day the call started. The rates are: started
before 8.00am 10p per minute, started from 8.00am to 6.00pm, 25p
per minute. *)
```

This header will not compile on its own even if we put it into a program module. The compiler expects a function to have a BEGIN, an END and somewhere inside these a RETURN statement. If we want to make CalculateCharge compilable we make it a valid Modula-2 function and put it into a module. How can we make CalculateCharge a valid function without implementing it completely? We can provide a partial implementation of CalculateCharge rather than a complete implementation. Here is one possible partial implementation of CalculateCharge:

```
PROCEDURE CalculateCharge(call : CallLog): Charge;
(* Pre-condition: call must contain a valid call logged by LogCall.
Post-condition: Returns the charge for a single call, by finding the
length of the call in minutes, and then multiplying by the appropriate
charge rate for the time of day the call started. The rates are: started
before 8.00am 10p per minute, started from 8.00am to 6.00pm, 25p
per minute. *)
VAR
   c : Charge;
BEGIN
   c := 0.0;
   RETURN c;
END CalculateCharge;
```

We call this a *stub* because it provides a correct implementation for one particular set of inputs (in this case, a call of zero duration will have zero charge) without having to implement the entire algorithm. The RETURN statement is necessary because CalculateCharge is defined as a function, and must return a value to be valid Modula-2. The important point about a stub is that it shouldn't be as complicated as a full implementation, which must be correct for all inputs that meet the pre-conditions, but should just deal with one circumstance for the function. In Chapter 10 we will see how stubs can be used for testing a software system as it is being built.

If we now put this function stub into a program module we can produce a valid compilation unit (that is a part of a program which can be compiled separately from other parts – modules are the compilation units of Modula-2):

```
MODULE Logger;
FROM LUTypes IMPORT DateTimeRec;
(* Getting the system time will vary from computer to computer and
implementations of Modula-2. This version will work for Metrowerks
Modula-2 on the Apple Macintosh. *)

TYPE
   CallLog = RECORD
               start : DateTimeRec;
               end : DateTimeRec;
               instigator : CARDINAL;
            END;
   Charge = REAL;

VAR
   call : CallLog;

PROCEDURE CalculateCharge(call : CallLog): Charge;
(* Pre-condition: call must contain a valid call logged by LogCall.
Post-condition: returns the charge for a single call, by finding the
length of the call in minutes, and then multiplying by the appropriate
charge rate. Rates: calls started before 8.00am 10p per minute,
started from 8.00am to 6.00pm, 25p per minute. *)

VAR
   c : Charge;
BEGIN
   c := 0.0;
   RETURN c;
END CalculateCharge;

BEGIN
   (* Body of module Logger. *)
END Logger.
```

In order to obtain a compilation unit we have had to put the function into a program module, and add the type declarations for the parameters of CalculateCharge. Most implementations of Modula-2 will provide some way of getting the current time from the computer's built-in clock, although it will vary between implementations. The above version is written for Metrowerks Modula-2 on the Apple Macintosh.

3.4.4 Declaring procedures within procedures

We have shown that a Modula-2 procedure is very similar to a program module, in that it subdivides into two main parts: the declaration section and the main body. From this we might draw the conclusion that there is nothing to stop us declaring another procedure in the declaration section of a procedure. This is indeed the case, Modula-2 allows us to declare procedures within procedures.

We may need to declare a procedure within a procedure when a task which fits neatly into a procedural abstraction, has a subtask which is very specific to the original task, unlikely to be used elsewhere and complicated enough to warrant a separate function.

Consider implementing Simpson's Rule, which finds the area under a curve. For a curve F(x) between x=a and x=b, the integral

$$\int_a^b F(x)\,dx$$

can be approximated by Simpson's Rule. F(x) might be a curve of the form shown below, with the area under the curve divided into an even number of segments of width h:

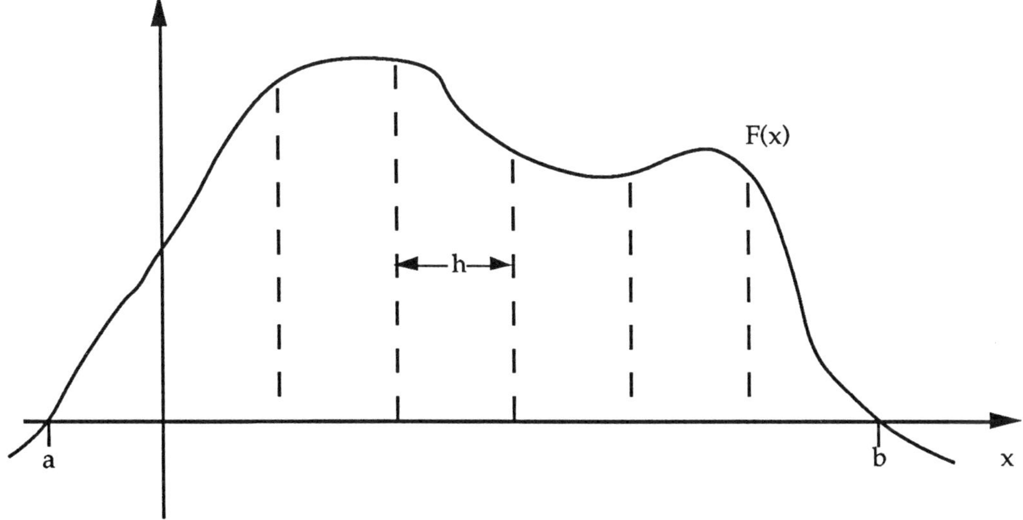

Simpson's Rule is given by:

$$\int_a^b F(x)\,dx \approx \sum \frac{h}{3}\left(F(x) + 4F(x+h) + F(x+2h)\right)$$

where the sum is over all pairs of segments.

We can implement Simpson's rule as a function, say Simpson, with the function F(x) defined inside Simpson as a *sub-procedure.*

Let's see how this will work. First, here is an incomplete implementation of Simpson, without F(x) implemented:

```
PROCEDURE Simpson(a, b: REAL; n : CARDINAL): REAL;
(* Precondition: a and b are the limits for the integration, n is the
number of segments to divide the area into.
Postcondition: the value returned is the area under the curve F(x)
between x=a and x=b. *)

VAR
    x : REAL;
    h : REAL; (* Width of each segment. *)
    s : REAL;
    i : INTEGER;

BEGIN
    s := 0.0;
    h := (b-a) / FLOAT(n);
    FOR i := 0 TO n-1 BY 2 DO
        x := a + (h * i);
        s := s + (F(x) + 4.0 * F(x + h) + F(x + 2.0 * h)) / 3.0;
    END;
    RETURN s * h;
END Simpson;
```

We can declare the function F(x) within function Simpson. Let's assume that F(x) is the following function:

$$x^2 + 4x - 2$$

Here is Simpson again, with F(x) declared within it, and Simpson itself declared inside a program module, to provide a complete implementation:

```
MODULE SimpsonsRule;

FROM InOut IMPORT WriteString, WriteLn, WriteReal, ReadReal;
(* Some versions of Modula-2 will not have real number routines in
the InOut library, but in a library called RealInOut. *)

VAR
   lowerBound, upperBound : REAL;
   steps : REAL;

PROCEDURE Simpson(a, b : REAL; n : CARDINAL): REAL;
(* Precondition: a and b are the limits for the integration, n is the
number of segments to divide the area into.
Postcondition: returns the area under the curve F(x) between x=a
and x=b. *)

VAR
   x : REAL;
   h : REAL;     (* Width of each segment. *)
   s : REAL;     (* Intermediate store. *)
   i : INTEGER;  (* Loop control variable. *)

PROCEDURE F(x): REAL;
(* Calculate F(x) = x*x + 4*x - 2. *)
BEGIN
   RETURN (x*x) + (4.0 * x) - 2.0;
END F;

BEGIN
   s := 0.0;
   h := (b - a) / FLOAT(n);
   FOR i := 0 TO n-1 DO
      x := a + (h * i);
      s := (s + F(x) + 4.0 * F(x + h) + F(x + 2.0 * h)) / 3.0;
   END;
   RETURN s * h;
END Simpson;

BEGIN (* Module SimpsonsRule. *)
   WriteString("Find the area under the curve x*x + 4*x - 2");
   WriteLn;
   WriteString("between x = a and x = b.");
```

```
    WriteLn; WriteLn;
    WriteString("Enter a (as a real number, for example 1. or 2.3): ");
    ReadReal(lowerBound);
    WriteLn; WriteLn;
    WriteString("Enter b (real number too):                      ");
    ReadReal(upperBound);
    WriteLn; WriteLn;
    WriteString("Enter the number of segments to use:     ");
    ReadCard(steps);
    WriteLn; WriteLn;
    WriteString("The result is    ");
    WriteReal(Simpson(lowerBound, upperBound, steps),10, 10 );
    WriteLn;
END SimpsonsRule.
```

Do you think that we could call function F from outside Simpson (that is, in the program module's main body)? Try putting a call to F in the body of the program module and see what error your compiler reports. The problem is one of *visibility* and is discussed in detail in the next section

3.4.5 The visibility of identifiers

An identifier is simply a valid name for some item in a program, and when we talk about *visibility* we mean the section of a program in which any particular identifier can be used. That is, the area over which the identifier is valid. Visibility has been implicit in our programs so far; when we declare imports, constants, types and variables at the top of a program module the visibility of these items is across the module. For example, consider the following program module:

```
MODULE VisOne;
FROM InOut IMPORT WriteCard;
CONST
   FieldWidth = 3;
VAR
   count : CARDINAL;
BEGIN
   count := 999;
   WriteCard(count, FieldWidth);
END VisOne.
```

The visibility of the identifiers declared in the declaration section, WriteCard,

FieldWidth and count, is the program module in which they have been declared. That is, the whole of VisOne. The first rule of visibility in Modula-2 is:

1. An identifier is visible inside the entire module or procedure in which it is declared, including any inner procedures.

An identifier declared at the top of a module or procedure is said to be *global* to that module or procedure.

This rule is not sufficient to cope with all circumstances however, and will need some further clarification. Consider the following program module, which has a procedure declared in it:

```
MODULE VisTwo;
FROM InOut IMPORT WriteInt;
VAR
   x : CARDINAL;

PROCEDURE Example;
VAR
   x, y : CARDINAL;
BEGIN
   x := 100;
   y := 10;
END Example;

BEGIN (* VisTwo. *)
   x := 30;
   WriteInt(x, 3);
   Example;
END VisTwo.
```

Example declares a local variable with the same name as the global variable of VisTwo, x. The assignment x := 30, in the main body of VisTwo, sets the global variable x (the one declared at the top of VisTwo) to 30. But what about the assignment in Example, x := 100, which x will it refer to, the one declared locally inside Example, or the one declared at the top of VisTwo? The second rule of visibility modifies the first rule to take account of such situations:

2. If an existing identifier is re-used (that is re-declared) inside an inner procedure, the original declaration of the identifier is not visible inside this procedure, only the local declaration is visible.

There is one more rule illustrated by VisTwo, and this concerns the variable y, which is a local variable of procedure Example. Do you think that y should be visible outside Example? The visibility rules of Modula-2 state that locally declared identifiers (be they constants, variables, types or procedures) are not visible outside the procedure in which they are declared. Thus, in the program module given above, variable y is not visible outside procedure Example. The final rule is therefore:

3. An identifier is not visible outside the procedure or program module in which it is declared.

Now we know the rules of visibility of identifiers, let's look at another example, and see how the rules apply.

```
MODULE VisThree;
VAR
   a, b, c : CARDINAL;

PROCEDURE P1;
VAR
   a, y : INTEGER;

   PROCEDURE P2;
   VAR
      a, b, y : REAL;
   BEGIN
      (* Body of P2. *)
   END P2;

BEGIN
   (* Body of P1. *)
END P1;

BEGIN
   (* Body of VisThree. *)
END VisThree.
```

Things are now beginning to look quite complicated, with all these variables being declared and redeclared all over the place, so we will define a way of describing each identifier so that we know which particular instance of that identifier we are talking about.

In the example given above variable a declared at the top of VisThree will be called VisThree.a, the a declared in procedure P1 will be P1.a, and the a declared in procedure P2 will be P2.a.

Identifier	Visibility of identifier
VisThree.a	In the body of VisThree, but not in P1 or P2 (Rule 2).
VisThree.b	In the body of VisThree, and in P1, but not in P2 (Rule 2).
VisThree.c	In the body of VisThree, in P1 and in P2 (Rule 1). P1.a In P1 only (Rule 3). Overrides VisThree.a.
P1.y	In P1 only (Rule 3).
P2.a	In P2 only (Rule 3). Overrides VisThree.a
P2.b	In P2 only (Rule 3). Overrides VisThree.b.
P2.y	In P2 only (Rule 3).

Later on, when we look at library modules and local modules we will meet a further set of visibility rules, which deal specifically with visibility in these types of module.

3.4.6 Procedures as parameters

The example of the Simpson's rule calculation in section 3.4.4 leads us to a useful concept in procedural abstraction, which is implemented in Modula-2. Function Simpson has one major drawback, it only calculates the area under one particular curve, which is given in function F, declared inside Simpson. If we wanted to calculate the area under a different curve we would have to change Simpson by altering function F. We really need to be able to pass Simpson the function we wish it to use for F, because the method of finding the area under a curve remains the same, no matter what curve we choose. The concept of being able to give a procedural abstraction as a parameter to another procedural abstraction is very powerful and extremely useful. In this particular case it will allow us to make the Simpson function general enough to find the area under any given curve.

Modula-2 allows the use of procedures and functions as parameters to other procedures and functions by declaring *procedure types*. Remember that all objects manipulated in a program must have a known type (such as REAL, INTEGER etc). If we want to use procedures as parameters we must be able to distinguish them by their type, or rather, by the types of their parameters. To see how we declare and use procedures as parameters, let's return to the Simpson rule problem and declare a function as a parameter to Simpson:

```
MODULE SimpsonsRule;

FROM InOut IMPORT WriteString, WriteLn, ReadCard, HoldScreen;
FROM RealInOut IMPORT WriteReal, ReadReal;

TYPE
   CurveFunc = PROCEDURE(REAL): REAL;

VAR
   lowerBound, upperBound : REAL;
   steps : CARDINAL;

PROCEDURE SomeFunction(x : REAL): REAL;
(* Calculate SomeFunction(x) = x*x + 4*x - 2. *)
BEGIN
   RETURN (x*x) + (4.0 * x) - 2.0;
END SomeFunction;

PROCEDURE Simpson(F : CurveFunc; a, b : REAL; n : CARDINAL):
REAL;
(* Precondition: a and b are the limits for the integration, n is the
number of segments to divide the area into.
Postcondition: returns the area under the curve F(x) between
x=a and x=b. *)

VAR
   x : REAL;
   h : REAL;    (* Width of each segment. *)
   s : REAL;
   i : INTEGER;

BEGIN
   s := 0.0;
   h := (b-a) / FLOAT(n);
   FOR i := 0 TO n-1 DO
      x := a + (h * FLOAT(i));
      s := s + (F(x) + 4.0 * F(x + h) + F(x + 2.0 * h)) / 3.0;
   END;
   RETURN s * h;
END Simpson
```

```
BEGIN
   (* Module SimpsonsRule. *)
   WriteString("Find the area under a curve between ");
   WriteString("x = a and x = b,  using Simpson's Rule.");
   WriteLn; WriteLn;

   WriteString("Enter a (as a real number, for example, 1. or 2.3): ");
   ReadReal(lowerBound);
   WriteLn; WriteLn;

   WriteString("Enter b (real number again):                    ");
   ReadReal(upperBound);
   WriteLn; WriteLn;

   WriteString("Enter the number of segments to use:    ");
   ReadCard(steps);
   WriteLn; WriteLn;

   WriteString("The result is    ");
   WriteReal(Simpson(SomeFunction, lowerBound,
   upperBound, steps), 10, 10);
   WriteLn;
END SimpsonsRule.
```

In this version of SimpsonsRule we have declared a procedure type called CurveFunc:

```
TYPE
   CurveFunc = PROCEDURE(REAL): REAL;
```

This states that a function of type CurveFunc takes one REAL parameter, and returns a REAL value as its result. Note that this will match many functions, not just function F from Simpson, just so long as the function has one REAL parameter and returns a REAL result. In the function header for Simpson we have added an extra parameter, F, which is of type CurveFunc. That is, F must be a function taking one REAL parameter and returning a REAL result. Inside Simpson every reference to F is a reference to the function F, which has been passed to Simpson as a parameter. In the call of Simpson in the surrounding module, SimpsonsRule, we pass it the appropriate function just as if we were passing a variable. If we alter the body of SomeFunction, so that it gives a different curve, this will be passed to Simpson instead.

We can declare a procedure type and can pass a parameter which is a procedure. This implicitly suggests that we can also declare variables which have a procedure type. For example, we can declare a variable of type CurveFunc:

```
VAR
   curve : CurveFunc;
```

Now, assume we declare two curve functions in module SimpsonsRule:

```
PROCEDURE Quadratic(x : REAL): REAL
(* A simple quadratic equation. *)

BEGIN
   RETURN x*x + 2.0*x - 6.0;
END Quadratic;

PROCEDURE Cubic(x : REAL): REAL;
(* A simple cubic equation. *)

BEGIN
   RETURN x*x*x + 3.0*x*x - 4.0*x + 5.0;
END Cubic;
```

Now we can replace the WriteReal statement by the following code:

```
(* Find out if user wants a quadratic or cubic equation. *)
WriteString("Quadratic or cubic equation?  (q/c)  ");

REPEAT
   (* Can't get out of this loop until one of the two possible
   responses is typed!  *)

   Read(response);
   WriteLn;
   response := CAP(response);

   IF response = "Q" THEN
      curve := Quadratic;
   ELSIF response = "C" THEN
      curve := Cubic;
   ELSE
      WriteString("Please answer 'q' or 'c' ");
   END;
UNTIL (response = "Q") OR (response = "C");

(* Now call Simpson with the appropriate curve function, and write
out the result. *)
WriteReal(Simpson(curve, lowerBound, upperBound, steps,10,10);
```

In this way Simpson gets either the Quadratic procedure or the Cubic procedure, depending on which response is given by the user.

An important use of procedure parameters is in the implementation of *generic data types*, which are explored in Chapter 6.

3.5 Recursion

Recursion is a fundamental concept in both computer science and mathematics. The simplest definition may be stated as follows: *a procedure is recursive if it calls itself either directly or indirectly.* An example of this definition is:

```
PROCEDURE f(x : REAL);
BEGIN
    .
    .
    f(x * x)
END f;
```

This simple definition of recursion is not sufficient to achieve a computable result. A procedure which always calls itself will never stop. To complete the definition we need a stopping condition.

Definition: A recursive procedure is one which calls itself either directly or indirectly until stopped by a terminating condition.

Most of the specifications you meet will exhibit either direct or indirect recursion in their definition. For example, in Section 2.3.2 the set abstraction used a recursive operation to build the set {2, 9}, thus

```
Insert(Insert(New, 2, -9)
```

and in Section 2.3.3 the queue abstraction used a recursive operation to build the queue

```
Front 4 3 1 2 Rear
```

from the recursive expression

```
AddQ(AddQ(AddQ(AddQ(NewQ, 4), 3), 1), 2)
```

These are examples of explicit recursion; each recursive operation is explicitly stated in the expressions. In each example the stopping condition is trivial as the recursive terminates naturally when the series of operations are completed.

Recursion is a natural way to express problems that have similar characteristics to those of the simple specification examples and, therefore many of the implementations in later chapters are expressed in this way. But recursion is not always the best way of preceding with a solution.

The following examples illustrate both the power of recursion, and it exorbitant cost when applied to inappropriate problems.

Factorial example

Let us derive a mathematical recursive relationship. The factorial n! is defined as follows:

$$n! = n \times (n-1) \times (n-2) \times (n-3) \times \ldots\ldots \times 3 \times 2 \times 1$$

This is easily converted into a recursive definition:

$$n! = n \times (n-1)! \text{ for } n > 1, \text{ with } 0! = 1.$$

In this example, the recursive relation $n! = n \times (n-1)!$ obviously calls itself; the terminating condition is $0! = 1$.

Expand this relation with $n = 3$, then:

$$\begin{aligned} 3! &= 3 \times (3-1)! \\ &= 3 \times (2 \times (2-1)!) \\ &= 3 \times (2 \times (1 \times (1-1)!)) \\ &= 3 \times 2 \times 1 \times 0! \end{aligned}$$

Using the terminating conditions $0! = 1$

$$= 3 \times 2 \times 1 \times 1$$

As a recursive procedure, we would write this example as follows:

```
PROCEDURE Factorial(n : CARDINAL): CARDINAL;
(* Calculate factorial n by recursion. *)

BEGIN
   IF n = 0 THEN RETURN 1
      ELSE RETURN n * Factorial(n-1);
   END; (* IF *)
END Factorial;
```

let us trace the execution stages of this procedure for n = 3.

Execution: n = 3

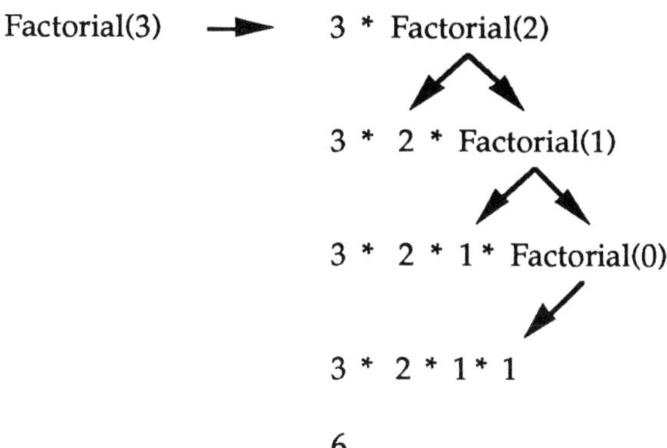

RETURN 6

The original procedure call, plus three recursive procedure calls, were required to evaluate the factorial product.

Many programmers use recursion wherever possible, as they believe it is the most expressive way of representing programs with the characteristics of these problems. It is certainly true that many problems are more naturally represented in this way, however it must be remembered that recursion can be costly to execute. In the previous example, it required four procedure calls to evaluate this simple function. The computational overhead for procedure calls is quite high, alternative methods such as using iteration or stacks can be far less costly to execute.

Fibonacci sequence example

Another well known function that may be expressed as a recursive procedure is the Fibonacci sequence:

1, 1, 2, 3, 5, 8, 13, 21, 34, 55, ...

where each term after 1, 1 is the sum of the previous two terms. Written as a recursive function we obtain:

$$F_n = F_{n-1} + F_{n-2},$$

where n indicates the n'th term in the sequence, starting from n = 0. The termination condition is needed for the zero'th and first term of the sequence, $F_0 = F_1 = 1$. Writing the recursive function as a recursive procedure we obtain:

```
PROCEDURE Fibonacci(N: CARDINAL): CARDINAL;
(* Calculate the Fibonacci sequence by recursion. *)

BEGIN
   IF n < 2 THEN
      RETURN 1;
   ELSE
      RETURN (Fibonacci(n-1) + Fibonacci(n-2));
   END; (* IF *)
END Fibonacci;
```

Again, we will trace the execution of the recursive procedure; evaluating the 5'th term in the sequence.

Execution: n = 5

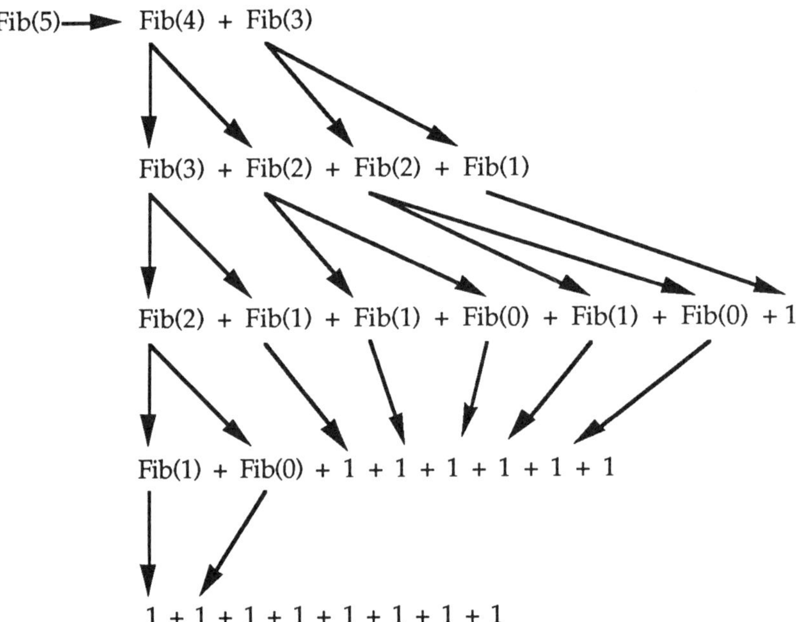

RETURN 8.

Fourteen recursive procedure calls were required to evaluate the 5'th term. This example clearly demonstrates that recursion should not be applied blindly, as fifteen procedure calls in total does seem a little excessive.

If we analyse the number of procedure calls, C_n, required for calculating the n'th stage of the sequence we get:

$$C_0 = 1$$
$$C_1 = 1$$
$$C_2 = C_1 + C_0 + 1$$
$$.$$
$$C_n = C_{n-1} + C_{n-2} + 1.$$

The number of procedure calls needed to calculate F for each value of n also fits a Fibonacci sequence. The number of calls required quickly become excessive, for example:

C_{10} = 177 calls, C_{15} = 1973 calls.

This is an example of an algorithm with exponential time complexity, the characteristics of which have been studied for many years. The growth of terms in a Fibonacci sequence is well understood and is known to behave as the function G^n, where G, the golden section constant, has the approximate value 1.618. Therefore, it is quite obvious that recursion is not always an appropriate method for solving problems. We will study the complexity of algorithms in greater detail in Chapter 11.

Order of recursive calls

The order in which recursive procedure calls are carried out is not always obvious. To illustrate the sequence of action in a non trivial example of recursion, we will use a recursive procedure to mark vertical lines on a measuring scale as follows:

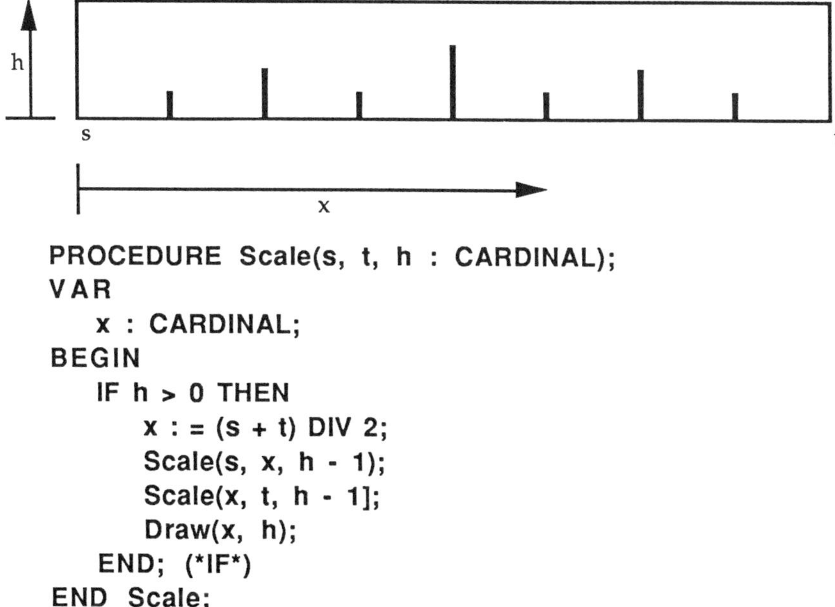


```
PROCEDURE Scale(s, t, h : CARDINAL);
VAR
   x : CARDINAL;
BEGIN
   IF h > 0 THEN
      x : = (s + t) DIV 2;
      Scale(s, x, h - 1);
      Scale(x, t, h - 1];
      Draw(x, h);
   END; (*IF*)
END Scale;
```

We assume we have available a procedure Draw(x, h) which draws a mark of height h at the point x on the line s to t. We will now follow the order of procedure call starting with Scale(0,8,3):

```
1.   Scale(0, 8, 3) call Scale
       x = 4
2.     Scale(0, 4, 2) call Scale
         x = 2
3.       Scale(0, 2, 1) call Scale
           x = 1
4.         Scale(0, 1, 0) call Scale (h = 0)
5.         Scale(1, 2, 0) call Scale (h = 0)

D1.        Draw(1, 1) draw first mark
```

Return to the statement after call (2), using x = 2 from (5), and l = 4 from (2)

```
         x = 2
6.       Scale(2, 4, 1) call Scale
           x = 3
7.         Scale(2, 3, 0) call Scale (h = 0)
8.         Scale(3, 4, 0) call Scale (h = 0)

D2.        Draw(3, 1) draw second mark
```

Return to the statement after call (1), using x = 4 from (8) and l = 8 from (1)

```
       x = 4
9.     Scale(4, 8, 2) call Scale
         x = 6
10.      Scale(4, 6, 1) call Scale
           x = 5
11.        Scale(4, 5, 0) call Scale (h = 0)
12.        Scale(5, 6, 0) call Scale (h = 0)

D3.        Draw(5, 1) draw third mark
```

Return to the statement after call (9), using x = 6 from (12), and l = 8 from (9)

```
         x = 6
13.      Scale(6, 8, 1) call Scale
           x = 7
14.        Scale(6, 7, 0) call Scale (h = 0)
15.        Scale(7, 8, 0) call Scale (h = 0)

D4.        Draw(7, 1) draw fourth mark
```

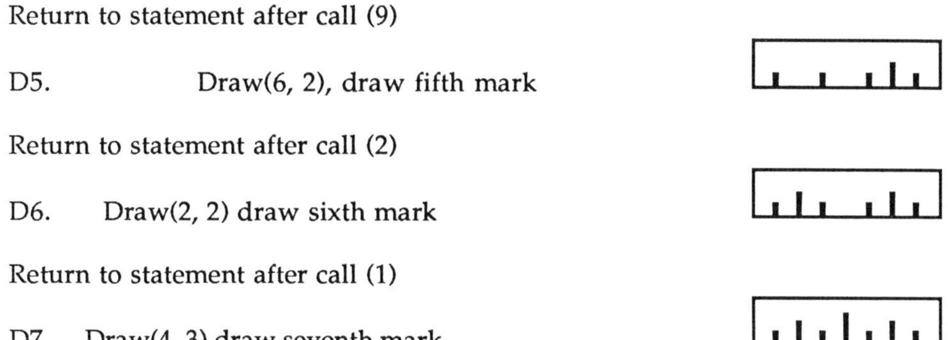

Return to statement after call (9)

D5. Draw(6, 2), draw fifth mark

Return to statement after call (2)

D6. Draw(2, 2) draw sixth mark

Return to statement after call (1)

D7. Draw(4, 3) draw seventh mark

In the above example the lifetime of each recursive procedure call is strictly nested within the lifetime of its parent call. This nesting of calls within the parents lifetime makes the unwinding of the call difficult to trace. The following diagram complements the call sequence given above to directly illustrate the parent and child relationships of the recursion:

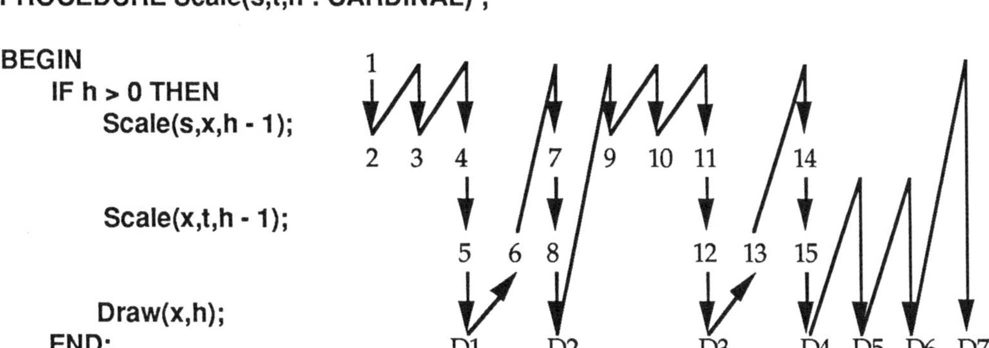
PROCEDURE Scale(s,t,h : CARDINAL) ;
BEGIN
IF h > 0 THEN
Scale(s,x,h - 1);
Scale(x,t,h - 1);
Draw(x,h);
END;
END Scale;
1
2 3 4 7 9 10 11 14
5 6 8 12 13 15
D1 D2 D3 D4 D5 D6 D7

Sierpinski curve example

The following example illustrates the power of recursion by constructing what appears to be a very complex pattern. Assume we have a procedure DrawBox(a,b,t) to draw a box of side 2t, centred at the point (a, b) then the Sierpinski pattern is given by the following procedure procedure:

```
PROCEDURE Pattern(a, b, t : CARDINAL);
(* Draw a pattern. *)

BEGIN
   IF t > 0 THEN
      Pattern(a - t, b + t, t DIV 2);
      Pattern(a + t, b + t, t DIV 2);
      Pattern(a - t, b - t, t DIV 2);
      Pattern(a + t, b - t, t DIV 2);
      DrawBox(a,b,t);
   END; (* IF *)
END Pattern;
```

The effect is to draw a series of boxes which halve in size and progressively shift the drawing centre to give the following:

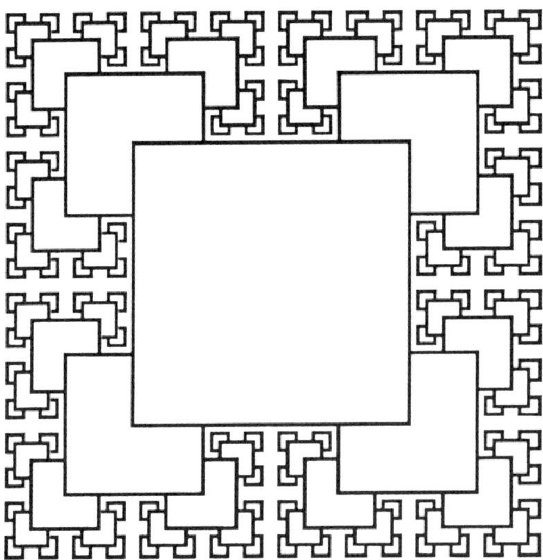

3.5.1 Removing recursion

It is sometimes necessary to remove recursion and particularly so when the cost is high, as in the Fibonacci example. If the recursive call is the last executable statement in a procedure it is easy to remove. This form of recursion is called tail recursion and is automatically removed by some compilers at compile time to improve the efficiency of the program's execution.

To remove tail recursion replace the IF statement by a WHILE loop and change the recursive procedure calls to assignment statements which explicitly evaluate the parameter list of the recursive procedure calls.

For example the tail recursive procedure in the following example can easily be removed. Assume that we have available three functions, A, B, C, then:

```
PROCEDURE TailRecursion(n : CARDINAL; b: BOOLEAN):
                                            CARDINAL;
VAR
   x, y : CARDINAL;

BEGIN
   IF b THEN
      x := A(n);
   ELSE
      b := B(n);
      y := C(n);
      x := TailRecursion(y, b);
   END;
   RETURN x;
END TailRecursion;
```

Using the method described above for removing tail recursion we obtain:

```
PROCEDURE NonRecursion(n : CARDINAL; b : BOOLEAN):
                                                       CARDINAL;
VAR
   x, y : CARDINAL;

BEGIN
   WHILE NOT b DO
      b := B(n);
      y := C(n);
      n := y;
   END;
   RETURN A(n);
END NonRecursion;
```

When the procedure is not tail recursive a little extra work may be needed to remove the recursion.

The factorial example in non recursive form becomes:

```
PROCEDURE Factorial(n : CARDINAL): CARDINAL;
VAR
   f, i : CARDINAL;
BEGIN
   f := 1;
   FOR i := 1 TO n DO
      f := f * i;
   END; (* FOR *}
   RETURN f;
END Factorial;
```

Similarly, the procedure for the Fibonacci number becomes:

```
PROCEDURE Fibonacci(n : CARDINAL): CARDINAL;
VAR
   f, f1, f2, i : CARDINAL;
BEGIN
   f1 := 1;
   f2 := 1;
   FOR i := 2 TO n DO
      f := f1 + f2;
      f2 := f1;
      f1 := f;
   END; (* FOR *}
   RETURN f;
END Fibonacci;
```

3.6 Functions or procedures?

Throughout this book our specifications have mainly used procedural abstractions which return single values. The only reason given so far is that this allows algebraic specification of these abstractions. However, once we start implementing our abstractions in a concrete programming language, such as Modula-2, another reason becomes apparent.

3.6.1 Procedures – programming with side-effects

A procedure in Modula-2 (and most other procedural programming languages, such as C and Pascal) may provide more than one value for the calling program by altering its input parameters or global variables. Such a procedure is said to have *side-effects* because it alters the values of variables which do not *belong* to the procedure (that is, they are not declared within the procedure).

A function which returns a value, and does not alter any input parameters or global variables, has no side-effects. In the calling program, all that happens is that the function call is replaced by the value evaluated by the function. No variables outside the function will be changed by it. However, Modula-2 will allow you to declare a function with variable parameters, or use a function to alter a global variable. But this is extremely bad practice.

If you need variable parameters for some reason or you have to alter a global variable, then use a procedure, not a function. Functions implemented in a programming language should act like mathematical functions and return single values, without altering anything else. The user of a function will not expect the function to alter any of its parameters.

We try to avoid side-effects when designing programs because they make a program far harder to reason about, and therefore harder to check for correctness. Side-effects also provide pitfalls for the unsuspecting programmer to fall into.

Consider the following (slightly contrived) example. Imagine we have a function called Cube, which cubes any given positive integer. The procedure header will be:

```
PROCEDURE Cube(c : CARDINAL): CARDINAL;
```

So we might call Cube like this:

```
answer := Cube(number);
```

If number equals 3 then answer will be 27.

We might assume, given the name and description of this function, that the following would be true:

```
Cube(x) - Cube(x) = 0
```

But now let's say that Cube has been written so that number is passed to it as a variable parameter, and the function actually assigns the cubed value back to this parameter, overwriting the original contents. The procedure header will look like this:

```
PROCEDURE Cube(VAR c : CARDINAL): CARDINAL;
```

When Cube returns, not only does it pass back the cubed number 27, to be substituted into the expression, but it has also altered the value of number, also to 27. In these circumstances the above expression certainly doesn't hold.

The user of Cube may not realise that the function is in fact altering its parameters, simply because it is usual practice to avoid variable parameters in functions.

Problems such as this one with Cube are caused because procedural languages, like Modula-2, are not *referentially transparent.* In solving an equation such as $2x - 3y = 4x + y$ we know that x has the same value at each position in the equation, and throughout the proof. In a programming language which is not referentially transparent we can only know the current value of x by looking back through the program to see what value was last assigned to it.

For a programming language to be referentially transparent there can be no assignment statements, to prevent items having their values changed throughout the program, and to prevent side-effects. Functional programming languages, such as Miranda and SASL, have been designed to be without side-effects, and so in theory should not have assignment statements. However, in practice there is usually a way of assigning a value to a variable, although in functional programming languages the programmer should avoid using them as much as possible.

There are certainly some cases where we do find ourselves using procedures, and when side-effects are useful. For example, most of the operations in the InOut library are written as procedures. These procedures have non-variable input parameters, but they do have side-effects. The most obvious is that they set a global variable called Done, which is also exported from InOut, to indicate whether or not the operation was successful.

Side-effects could have been avoided by making each operation a function which returns a Boolean value to indicate success or failure. This would have two consequences, firstly that the operations would not have side-effects, and secondly that the user of the operation might be more inclined to check for success or failure. For example, calling the existing version of WriteInt will look like this:

```
WriteInt(i, field);
```

If the user has imported Done, then it can be tested, but a separate statement will be required, for example

```
IF Done THEN
   (* Continue with program. *)
ELSE
   (* Report error. *)
END;
```

However, if WriteInt was a function returning a Boolean, where TRUE means success and FALSE means failure, we have to do something with the returned value. We can no longer have a simple procedure call. Instead we can use the returned value directly in the IF statement, like this:

```
IF WriteInt(i, field) THEN
   (* Continue program. *)
ELSE
   (* Report error. *)
END;
```

The input operations in InOut are also written as procedures. A variable parameter is used to pass back the value read in, for example:

```
PROCEDURE ReadCard(VAR c : CARDINAL);
```

This is a valid use of a procedure rather than a function. All input and output procedures have another type of side effect. Not only do they read in or write out the given information, but they also change the read/write position in the input/output stream (see Chapter 7).

3.6.2 Programming functionally

Functions can provide a fair degree of referential transparency in our software. However, the implementation of such functions must be strictly functional! That is, zero or more value input parameters (whose values therefore cannot affect the corresponding variables outside the function) and a return value. Most procedural programming languages, including Modula-2, allow variable parameters to functions, even though we shouldn't use them.

In most of our examples we have used functions to implement procedural abstractions because they best match the way these abstractions are defined. Consider the Set data abstraction from Chapter 2, remember each operation of a data abstraction is implemented as a procedural abstraction. The syntactic specification of the Set operations were given as follows:

```
New: → Set
Insert: Set, Integer → Set
Delete: Set, Integer → Set
IsIn: Set, Integer → Boolean
IsEmpty: Set → Boolean
```

The input parameters to these operations only supply values needed for the particular operation, and each operation returns one and only one item. There is a direct correspondence between this syntactic specification of an operation and an implementation using a Modula-2 function. For example,

```
New: → Set
```

becomes

```
PROCEDURE New(): Set;
```

and

```
Insert: Set, Integer → Set
```

becomes

```
PROCEDURE Insert(s : Set; i : INTEGER): Set;
```

If you are using functions defined by someone else (perhaps in a library module, as part of an abstraction) remember that there is no guarantee that the function has no side-effects. Even if the input parameters are defined as value parameters the function can still change any global variables in the library module in which it is defined. Additionally, as we mentioned earlier, any function which uses i/o operations will definitely have side-effects, because it will alter the current position of the read/write stream.

The onus is on the author of a function to ensure that it does not break the rules for functions, that is:

- A function should not alter any global variables.
- A function should not have variable input parameters.

If you need variable input parameters as a means of returning more than one value, use a procedure, not a function. Most i/o operations are also better implemented as procedures because they cannot avoid altering the i/o stream. However, in general try to stick to using functions to implement procedural abstractions, to ensure that your implementation is as near to the formal specification as possible.

Summary

Procedural abstractions are the building blocks of data abstractions, with each operation in a data abstraction corresponding to a single procedural abstraction.

Procedural abstractions can be implemented in Modula-2 as functions or procedures, although the specifications we have used lend themselves best to a functional implementation.

A function returns a single value, via a RETURN statement. The type of the value to be returned is declared at the end of the function header. A function should never have variable formal parameters.

A function must contain at least one RETURN statement. The function terminates as soon as a RETURN statement is reached.

A procedure cannot return a value via a RETURN statement.

A procedure can use a simple RETURN statement (with no return value) to terminate the procedure at any point in the procedure body. In the absence of any RETURN statements the procedure terminates when the final END statement is reached.

The parameters declared in a procedure or function header are called *formal parameters*. The parameters used in a call to a procedure or function are called *actual parameters*.

Formal parameters can be either *value parameters* or *variable parameters*.

A value parameter is given a copy of the corresponding actual parameter, so any changes made in the procedure or function to the value parameter have no effect on the corresponding actual parameter. A variable parameter works by renaming the corresponding actual parameter to the name of the variable parameter. Any changes to the variable parameter in the procedure are therefore made directly to the (renamed) actual parameter.

An identifier is visible inside the entire module or procedure in which it is declared, including any inner procedures, unless it is re-declared in such an inner procedure. In this case the original declaration of the identifier is not visible inside this procedure, only the local declaration is visible.

An identifier is not visible outside the procedure or program module in which it is declared.

Recursion is a fundamental property of many algorithms. A procedure (or function) is recursive if it calls itself (either directly or indirectly). The use of recursion can lead to simple implementations, but these may be expensive to compute.

Tail recursion (when the recursive call is the last executable statement in a procedure) can be easily transformed into a non recursive implementation.

Procedures with variable parameters produce a style of programming called *programming by side-effects*. It is hard to reason mathematically about such programs because of the way input parameters in a procedure can have their values changed during the course of the procedure.

Functions, strictly defined with only value parameters and not using any global variables, do not produce side-effects, because they do not alter any parameters except their local parameters. This makes it easier to reason mathematically about the correctness of a program.

Selected reading

Every Modula-2 book will contain a section on procedures and functions, so it is worth looking through a few to find if one has a treatment of the subject which you prefer.

Harrison, R
Abstract data types in Modula-2
J. Wiley and Sons, 1989
This book uses functions extensively in the implementation of data abstractions. It shows very clearly how functions may be used to produce side-effect free implementations, and discusses the reasons for using functions whenever possible.

4 Modules for abstraction

4.1 Introduction

So far we have only touched on modules as a means of decomposing problem solutions. The concept of the module is intimately tied up with the design and implementation of abstractions. Abstraction separates what something does from how it does it, which means that unnecessary information (such as how the Set abstraction Insert operation is actually implemented) can be hidden away, and necessary information (such as what Insert does to a set) can be made available to a user. The module concept provides a means of implementing abstractions to allow this *data hiding.*

The more modern programming languages, such as Modula-2, provide modules as a major part of the language. In Modula-2 there are program modules (modules which contain complete Modula-2 programs) and library modules. Library modules provide reusable resources for program modules and other library modules, and at the simplest level can be thought of as a lending library from which other modules can *borrow* software resources. More importantly from our point of view, library modules also provide the means to implement abstractions.

4.2 Module specification

When specifying data abstractions and procedural abstractions we made sure that the specifications contained a sufficient level of detail for someone to use the abstraction, giving the syntax and semantics of each operation, without any details on how the operations were implemented or how the data being modelled was actually represented. In any form of abstraction we are trying to hide away unimportant details such as implementation, and only deal with the concepts of how a structure such as a queue actually works.

If we want to use our data abstractions in a complete software solution they have to be implemented as concrete data structures, procedures and functions in some programming language. However, if we wish to retain the abstract nature of a data abstraction, even at the implementation level, we must still avoid the user seeing implementation details.

In Chapter 2 the modularisation technique found data abstractions (and sometimes functional abstractions) which provided individual modules in a problem solution. So we weren't just finding data abstractions, at the same time we were splitting the problem solution into modules. To preserve this modular structure in any implementation we must implement each abstraction as a module (in some cases we may need to modularise further, decomposing one module into several, simpler modules).

4.2.1 Properties of modules

A module for abstraction must provide several important things:

- A means of splitting the specification of the abstraction (what it does) from its actual implementation (how it does it).

  Effectively this means we want to have one part which contains similar information to our written specifications, and one part containing all the code to implement the data structures and operations defined in the specification part.

- The hiding of implementation details from the user, physically preventing the user from altering the implementation.

  This means a strictly controlled interface between the specification and implementation parts of a module. The only level of user access to a module containing an abstraction should be via the specification part (note that the 'user' may be another module). The user can therefore only access an abstraction via the named operations in the specification part, preventing illegal or incorrect usage of an abstraction.

  For example, a simple counter abstraction which counts up or down in steps of one, might have three operations, Reset, Increment and Decrement, where Reset sets the counter to zero, Increment adds one, and Decrement subtracts one.

  If access to the counter is only via the specification part of the module there is no chance of incorrectly adding more than one to the counter in one operation or resetting to some value other than zero. In a properly controlled interface the counter value can only be altered by the three defined operations.

4.2.2 Providing an interface specification

The *interface specification* of a module controls access to the implementation part of a module, allowing access to the module only through the definitions given in the specification. The interface specification for any module must state:

- Module name, usually corresponding to an abstraction name, so it can be identified and used.
- Any resources provided by other modules which are needed in the interface specification.
- The resources offered by the module itself.

There are several ways of classifying modules which offer different types of resources:

- Data abstraction module which specifies and implements a specific data abstraction (for example, Queue, CarWashers, Set).
- Functional abstraction module which contains procedural abstractions to perform related tasks, but does not define a data abstraction.
- Name abstraction module (you haven't met name abstractions before) which provides a new set of names for resources defined in other modules.

4.2.3 Data abstraction modules

If we are using a module to represent a data abstraction then the resource descriptions given by the interface specification will consist of

- The names of any data types or data structures defined by the abstraction.
- The name and syntax of each valid operation on the abstraction.
- The semantics of each operation. Pre- and post-conditions may have to be accepted.

In practise the module interface specifications in existing programming languages cannot include the semantics of an operation, because most programming languages have no formal means of describing semantics (other than by the user adding semantic information in a comment. At the abstract level, we need not worry about such problems, we can just assume that there is some way of describing the semantics.

A data abstraction module should define a data type or data structure (with perhaps some auxiliary types required by the user of the abstraction) in which data can be stored, and the allowed operations on the data stored in the defined way. For example, the simple Queue abstraction will provide an operation for removing an item from the front of a queue and adding an item to the back of a queue, but won'tprovide an operation for removing an item from the middle of a queue, as this is not a valid operation on a simple queue.

4.2.4 Functional abstraction modules

A functional abstraction is a collection of related operations, for example, the Requests abstractions from the car pool of Chapter 2. Functional abstractions don't define data types or structures, but may use one or more existing data abstractions to define a set of higher-level operations on the abstractions. This is exactly what Requests does in Chapter 2, using the Car and CarPool data abstractions and providing a new set of operations acting on a car pool.

Functional abstractions therefore tend to be used to add more *functionality* (that is usability) to existing abstractions, by providing algorithms to perform higher-level tasks. Again consider the Requests abstraction; Requests supplies two operations for reserving and unreserving a specific car from the car pool. The Car data abstraction provides operations for changing the reservation attribute of a particular car record, and the CarPool abstraction provides operations for adding, removing and finding car records. The Request abstraction uses operations from both Car and CarPool to define new operations which can make a particular car from the car pool either reserved or unreserved.

The information required in an interface specification for a functional abstraction will consist of

- The names of the data abstractions being used by the functional abstraction.
- The name and syntax of each higher-level operation on the data abstractions.
- The semantics of each operation. Pre- and post-conditions are usually given.

As with data abstraction interface specifications the operations' semantics may be difficult to describe in most module-based programming languages. In addition, it is often difficult to describe the operations in a functional abstraction in axiomatic form, so the semantics are best described by giving the pre- and post-conditions for each operation.

4.2.5 Name abstraction modules

Name abstraction modules provide new names for resources in existing modules. In other words a name abstraction module collects together resources for a particular task, and gives these resources new names more suited to the circumstances in which they are being used.

This may seem relatively pointless, but consider the implementation of the CarQueue abstraction (Chapter 2). This abstraction represents the queue of cars waiting to be washed, and the operations map directly to the Queue abstraction, although the operations' names are different, and provided the Queue implementation can deal with queues of Car records. CarQueue would not need to be implemented from scratch but could just be a name abstraction module, renaming the types and operations of the Queue abstraction. For example, the AddQ operation would be renamed AddCarToQueue, the FrontQ operation renamed FirstCar, and the type Item (the items stored in the Queue) would be renamed Car.

The interface specification for a name abstraction module will consist of:

- The new name of any type being renamed.
- The new name and syntax of each operation being renamed.
- The semantics of each operation. Pre- and post-conditions are usually given.

The renaming is transparent to the user of a name abstraction module, as only the new names will be given in the interface specification. The actual task of connecting the new names to the existing operations from other abstractions is done in the implementation part of the module.

This is another example of data hiding, the name abstraction hides the underlying data abstraction(s) or functional abstraction(s). The user of the abstraction does not need to know if the abstraction is simply a renaming of an existing abstraction, or a completely new abstraction.

4.3 Module implementation

The implementation part of a module must provide the actual implementation of the resources specified in the module's interface specification. Whilst the interface specification has to be available to the user of a module (otherwise they cannot know what resources are offered or how to use these resources) the implementation can be completely hidden.

The implementation of an interface specification can change without affecting the specification, and, therefore without affecting any user of the module (because access is only via the specification). For example, an operation which sorts a list of words may be specified as follows:

Sort: WordList → WordList
Pre-condition: none.
Post-condition: returns the list sorted in ascending alphabetical order.

The user of the Sort operation will only see this specification, and does not see how the sort is implemented. There are many ways of sorting a list, some methods are better than others, with some depending on how sorted the original list is (see Chapter 11). The implementation of the sort can be changed to different methods without altering the specification, because the operation still turns a list into a sorted list, **how** it does this isn't part of the specification.

Whilst the implementation of an operation can change its algorithm and the implementation of a data type can change the representation of that type, there are restrictions on how much an implementation can change. For example, the implementation of the Sort operation cannot change to such an extent that an extra parameter is required or the name of the operation or its parameter types has to be altered.

In practice the implementation can change anything except the names of types and operations, and the parameters of operations, which are defined in the interface specification. Usually the implementation changes involve substituting one algorithm for another or one data type representation for another, which won't have any effect on the interface specification. The implementation parts of modules for data abstractions and functional abstractions will contain procedures implementing each operation in the abstraction and representations of the types defined by the abstraction.

Name abstractions are slightly different and usually don't have much code in the implementation part of the module, because they are simply renaming resources implemented in other modules.

For example if we return to CarQueue, which we have already said can be implemented as a name abstraction, each operation of CarQueue is a renamed operation of the Queue abstraction, and the algorithms to implement these operations already exist in the Queue module. So to implement a CarQueue operation, AddCarToQueue say, we must simply provide the appropriate Queue operation, which is AddQ, with the appropriate parameters.

4.4 Software engineering concepts of module use

Modules are now used quite extensively in software engineering, especially where large software systems are being developed. There are many reasons for using modules, not just their usefulness for implementing abstractions, and we will look at some of these reasons in the following sections.

4.4.1 Problem decomposition

One of the most obvious reasons for using modules is that they allow us to divide up a large program into a number of smaller units. Each smaller unit is a smaller program to design, implement and test, making the overall design and implementation easier.

At this superficial level using modules is like using a number of files, each file containing a different part of the program. The majority of programming languages allow the programmer to split their programs amongst multiple files, but the split is very artificial, the compiler makes no attempt to check consistency between files or to control access to the code in the files.

Such languages do not provide modules in the true sense because the module concept involves the properties of separating specification from implementation, information hiding (hiding the implementation details) and controlled access. Whilst the first may be possible with files, the others will not be because file access is controlled by the operating system.

4.4.2 Preserving the structure of the problem solution

Most approaches to problem solving involve subdividing the problem into smaller, more easily solvable units. Modularisation and other object-oriented techniques do just this. If we have a problem solution which is divided into modules the implementation of that solution is far simpler if we can implement it with modules.

4.4.3 Data hiding

A module has a well-defined interface, which is the only part of the module visible (that is accessible) to a program importing resources from this module. It is also possible to prevent the programmer from seeing how the resources are implemented or from changing them in any way, by withholding the uncompiled implementation module, and providing only the compiled version (which will not be stored as readable text).

Having two separate parts to a library module gives us data hiding, with implementation details separate from specification details. The user of a library module is forced to use the resources via the definition part of the module. Implementations can be changed (so long as the specification remains unaltered) without affecting the user of the module, and indeed, without the user being aware of any changes.

4.4.4 Simplified testing

In any software system it is far easier to test individual parts of the system separately from each other, rather than to test the complete system as a whole. If we have a system implemented as a number of separate modules each module can be thoroughly tested before it is integrated with any other modules. We discuss module testing in more detail in Chapter 10.

4.4.5 Localised maintenance

Since each part of a library module is a compilation unit we can compile the parts separately from each other. This also leads to localised recompilation when individual modules are changed. Often we only need to recompile the module that was altered. Recompilation will only involve other modules if we have to alter the definition part of a library module. If the definition changes we are changing the module's interface to the outside world, and any module which uses this interface (that is imports resources from the module) must also be recompiled, so that the compiler can check that the external references are still correct.

4.4.6 Software re-use

A direct result of implementing software resources in a module is that these resources can be used by many programs and by other modules. This is software re-use – the same code being used again and again in differing circumstances. Think of all the programs you have written which reuse the resources in the InOut module.

4.4.7 Division of labour

Another advantage of using library modules relates directly to software systems which are designed and built by teams of software engineers. By breaking a software system down into modules, and deciding upon the interface specifications of these modules, we can then give individual modules to different people to implement. Of course, this is very simplistic view of division of work amongst a team but the important point is that once the interface specifications are written (the definition modules if we are using Modula-2), everyone knows how to use the resources in each module. They can get on with implementing their own module safe in the knowledge that where they have to use resources in someone else's module the interface to that module is fixed.

4.4.8 Portability of implementation

One aspect we have not yet mentioned is portability. This is the problem of moving software implemented on one type of computer onto another type of computer. The commonest reason for software being non-portable is low-level access to the computer hardware – different types of computer are built very differently. The processing chip in an Apple Mac is very different to the processing chip in an IBM PC, and they will run completely different machine code. Even things such as the word size (that is number of bits in a computer word) can vary between different types of computer. So a program which looks at the value of the last bit in a word on an Apple Mac SE/30 must look at the thirty-second bit, but on an IBM XT the last bit is the eighth bit.

Once we get down to low-level access of memory, registers and input/output ports we instantly run into portability problems. It is very unlikely that such low-level code will be portable. If we keep any low-level, non-portable code in several, well-defined modules, then only these modules need to be altered and recompiled if we have to move the software to a different type of computer.

Keeping low-level code restricted to one or two modules is also an example of using modules to group together related items. This is exactly how modules are used when implementing abstractions.

4.5 Library Modules in Modula-2

Modula-2 is one of the programming languages which provides a concrete implementation of modules for program building. There are several types of module defined in Modula-2, the first being the program module, which is the basis of all Modula-2 programs. You have already used program modules extensively. For abstraction, the most important type of module is the *library module*, library modules have the properties required for implementing abstractions. In the preceding sections the conceptual modules discussed for abstraction correspond directly to Modula-2 library modules.

We have already been using resources from library modules in our programs, although we didn't say where these resources came from. For example, most of your programs will contain imports of input/output operations from the InOut library module (which, in fact, is an implementation of the Stream data abstraction).

A library module consists of two parts (these are also called modules, which can be somewhat confusing):

- The *definition module*, which provides the interface specification of the module.

- The *implementation module*, which provides the implementation of the module.

Each part is compiled separately from the other, and separately from any program module which imports resources from the library module.

On the subject of separate compilation, Modula-2 has three types of compilation unit. A *compilation unit* is a block of code which the compiler can compile (unless it contains syntax errors, of course). The compilation units of Modula-2 are:

- Program modules.

- Definition modules.

- Implementation modules.

Other blocks of code, such as procedures, cannot be presented separately to the compiler, but must be inside a compilation unit.

4.5.1 The definition module

The definition part of a library module is really a specification of the software resources the library module provides for the outside world (other library module and program modules). It is the interface specification for the module because it provides the user with an interface to the software resources in the library module. Any module which imports resources from a library module can only access the definition part of the library module; the implementation part is hidden from it.

The definition module is often the only part of a library module to be published in a commercial software library. The corresponding implementation module can be provided in compiled form as an *object file*. An object file is simply the compiled version of a module – it is not a text file, and is not readable. This prevents a buyer from seeing how the implementation has been done whilst providing the interface specification to show what the library provides and how to use it. Some Modula-2 implementations provide the definition modules of the standard library modules in readable form, but do not allow access to the implementation modules.

Since the definition module provides the interface specification for a library module, and may be the only part of the library module visible to the user, it is always necessary to comment it fully. This means providing the following information:

- A comment at the top of the module, which describes its functionality (what the module aims to provide).
- Any constants, types, and variables declared in the module should be commented to indicate their function.
- Each procedure should have a comment fully describing its purpose and any parameters it uses. This comment should include the procedure's pre-conditions and post-conditions.

Program 4.1 is a definition module which provides procedures for finding the average, minimum, maximum, and total of an array of integers, and a procedure for printing out such an array.

Program 4.1 ArrayUtilities definition module

```
DEFINITION MODULE ArrayUtilities;
(* Procedures for finding the average, minimum, maximum and total of
integers in an array of MAXSIZE entries.  Also a procedure for displaying
such an array. *)

(* EXPORT QUALIFIED IntArray, MaxSize, ArrayMax, ArrayMin,
ArrayTotal, ArrayAverage, ArrayDisplay; *)
```

```
CONST
   MaxSize = 20;

TYPE
   IntArray = ARRAY [1..20] OF INTEGER;

PROCEDURE ArrayMax(a : IntArray): INTEGER;
(* Given an array of MaxSize integers, return the largest integer in the
array.
Pre-condition:  none.
Post-condition: the value returned is the largest integer in the array. *)

PROCEDURE ArrayMin(a : IntArray): INTEGER;
(* Given an array of MaxSize integers, return the minimum integer in a.
Pre-condition:  none.
Post-condition: the value returned is the smallest integer in a. *)

PROCEDURE ArrayTotal(a : IntArray): INTEGER;
(* Given an array of MaxSize integers, return the total of all the integers
in a.
Pre-condition:  none.
Post-condition: the value returned is the sum of all the integers in a. *)

PROCEDURE ArrayAverage(a : IntArray): REAL;
(* Given an array of MaxSize integers, return the average of the integers
in the array.
Pre-condition:  none.
Post-condition: the value returned is the average of all the integers in
the array. *)

PROCEDURE ArrayDisplay(a : IntArray);
(* Given an array of MaxSize integers print out the integers it contains in
a suitable format.
Pre-condition:  none.
Post-condition: prints out the integers in a, from lowest to highest
index, with spaces between each integer, on the standard output. *)

END ArrayUtilities.
```

The first line of Program 4.1 indicates that this is the definition part of a library module called ArrayUtilities. The EXPORT QUALIFIED line states the software resources the library module is making available to the outside world. In this case there are seven items – IntArray, MAXSIZE, MaxArray, MinArray, TotalArray,

AverageArray, and PrintArray. The EXPORT QUALIFIED statement is now no longer in Wirth's definition of the Modula-2 language, nor in the BSI's standardisation efforts. Instead of this statement, everything declared in a definition module will be automatically exported. However, many compilers on the market at the time of writing still require explicit export statements in definition modules. We will include the export list as a comment in our definition modules.

It may be necessary to import some software resources into a definition module for use in declaring the resources the module offers. This would be done with an import statement, just the same as in a program module. Program 4.1 doesn't need any imports, but Program 4.2 is a definition module which needs to import from ArrayUtilities.

Program 4.2 ArrayExtras definition module

```
DEFINITION MODULE ArrayExtras;
(* Adding and subtracting pairs of integer arrays. *)

FROM ArrayUtilities IMPORT IntArray;

(* EXPORT QUALIFIED AddArrays, SubtractArrays; *)

PROCEDURE AddArrays(a1, a2 : IntArray; VAR a3 : IntArray);
(* Add the arrays a1 and a2, putting the result in a3.
Pre-condition: none.
Post-condition: a3[n] = a1[n] + a2[n], for n from 0 to MaxSize-1. *)

PROCEDURE SubtractArrays(a1, a2 : IntArray; VAR a3 : IntArray);
(* Subtract array a2 from a1, putting the result in a3.
Pre-condition: none.
Post-condition: a3[n] = a1[n] - a2[n], for n from 0 to MaxSize-1. *)

END ArrayExtras.
```

In Program 4.2 because the procedures AddArrays and SubArrays need parameters of type IntArray, this type must be imported into the definition module from definition module ArrayUtilities.

The main body of the definition module is a specification of the resources it offers, and this follows the EXPORT statement. The specification may contain declarations of variables, constants, types procedures, and function procedures. Definition module ArrayUtilities exports one constant, MAXSIZE, and one type, IntArray. Any module which imports IntArray can declare variables to be of this type. ArrayUtilities also exports four functions. The specification of a procedure or function in a definition module consists only of a procedure header or *stub* containing the procedure name, the names and binding mechanisms (value or reference) of any formal parameters, and the return type (if a function).

Each header must have a corresponding procedure in the associated implementation module. The names, binding mechanisms and return type must be exactly the same in the definition module and the implementation module. Some of the commonest compile-time errors stem from a failure to get an exact correspondence between headers in the two parts of library module, so check them carefully!

The final line of a definition module is the same as in a program module, and terminates with a full stop.

4.5.2 The implementation module

An implementation module provides full implementations of any software resources specified in the corresponding definition module. Implementation modules are very similar to program modules, differing only in the addition of the reserved word IMPLEMENTATION. Program 4.3 shows the implementation module for ArrayUtilities.

Program 4.3 ArrayUtilities implementation module

```
IMPLEMENTATION MODULE ArrayUtilities;

FROM InOut IMPORT WriteInt, Write;

PROCEDURE ArrayMin(a : IntArray): INTEGER;

VAR
   c : CARDINAL; (* Loop index. *)
   min : INTEGER; (* Minimum integer so far. *)

BEGIN
   (* Set min to first entry in array. *)
   min := a[1];

   (* Find minimum and assign to min. *)
   FOR c := 2 TO MaxSize DO
      IF a[c] < min THEN
         min := a[c];
      END;
   END;
   RETURN min;
END ArrayMin;
```

```
PROCEDURE ArrayMax(a : IntArray): INTEGER;

VAR
   max : INTEGER; (* Maximum integer so far. *)
   i : CARDINAL; (* Loop index. *)

BEGIN
   (* Set max to first entry in array. *)
   max := a[1];
   (* Find maximum and assign to max. *)
   FOR i := 2 TO MaxSize DO
      IF a[i] > max THEN
       max := a[i];
      END;
   END;
   RETURN max;
END ArrayMax;

PROCEDURE ArrayTotal(a : IntArray): INTEGER;

VAR
   i : CARDINAL; (* Loop index. *)
   total : INTEGER; (* Running total of array. *)

BEGIN
   total := 0; (* Add each element to total. *)
   FOR i := 1 TO MaxSize DO
         total := total + a[i];
   END;
   RETURN total;
END ArrayTotal;

PROCEDURE ArrayAverage(a : IntArray): REAL;

VAR
   i : CARDINAL; (* Loop index. *)

BEGIN
   RETURN (FLOAT(ArrayTotal(a)) / FLOAT(MaxSize));
END ArrayAverage;
```

```
PROCEDURE ArrayDisplay(a : IntArray);
VAR
   i : CARDINAL; (* Loop index .*)
BEGIN
   FOR i := 1 TO MaxSize DO
         WriteInt(a[i], 7);
   END;
END ArrayDisplay;

BEGIN (* Main body of module. *)
   (* No initialisation code needed. *)
END ArrayUtilities.
```

The first line of the implementation module states that it is the implementation of ArrayUtilities.

It is often necessary to include an import list in an implementation module – ArrayUtilities needs to import WriteInt and Write from standard library module InOut. In addition, software resources which are imported into a definition module are **not** automatically imported into the corresponding implementation module. Usually, the implementation module will require the same resources as the definition module, plus some extras, so the definition module's import list will need to be duplicated in the implementation module. For example, the implementation of ArrayExtras (Program 4.4) will need to import IntArray from ArrayUtilities, and will also need to import MaxSize.

Program 4.4 ArrayExtras implementation module

```
IMPLEMENTATION MODULE ArrayExtras;

FROM ArrayUtilities IMPORT IntArray, MaxSize;

PROCEDURE AddArrays(a1, a2 : IntArray; VAR a3 : IntArray);
VAR
   i : CARDINAL;
BEGIN
   FOR i := 1 TO MaxSize DO
      a3[i] := a1[i] + a2[i];
   END;
END AddArrays;
```

```
PROCEDURE SubtractArrays(a1, a2 : IntArray; VAR a3 : IntArray);
VAR
   i : CARDINAL;

BEGIN
   FOR i := 1 TO MaxSize DO
      a3[i] := a1[i] - a2[i];
   END;
END SubtractArrays;

BEGIN
   (* No initialisations. *)
END ArrayExtras.
```

Implementation modules may contain global declarations of constants, types and variables not declared in the definition module, which are needed by the exported resources. However, these items are not available outside the implementation module. Any constants, types and variables declared in the definition module are automatically available in the implementation (this differs from the definition's imports, which are not automatically available). Such declarations do not need to be redeclared in the implementation. Thus, in the implementation of ArrayUtilities, (Program 4.4) IntArray and MaxSize do not need to be redeclared.

If the library module's definition has been correctly designed it should be possible to change all parts of the implementation (except the procedure headers, which must remain the same) without needing to alter the definition at all. This means that the library module's interface to the outside world remains the same, so other modules which use the interface are not affected in any way, whilst the implementation can be changed to make it faster or better in some way.

The separation of definition and implementation parts of a library module corresponds directly to the concept of a separate interface specification and implementation for a module. This gives us the data hiding we need for true abstraction. The advantages of library modules are given below:

- The specification (definition module) may be seen by the user of the abstraction so that
  - the user can see what the abstraction does and how to use it,
  - the user can only access the abstraction by the operations given in the specification.

- The implementation (implementation module) can be withheld from the user so that
  - the user cannot see how the abstraction is actually implemented,
  - the user cannot change how the abstraction is implemented (for example, add operations, data types etc).
- The abstraction is available for use by many programs (including by other library modules), who can import resources from it.
- Since the parts of a library module are separate and compile separately
  - the specification can be checked for syntactic correctness before the implementation has been written,
  - anyone implementing a program which will use the abstraction implemented by the library module can be given the definition part before the implementation part has been written, so that they know how to access the abstraction's operations. This allows parallel development by several different people.
- Since the library module is a separate entity it can be tested separately from other modules, needing only a program module to import and use its resources so that they can be tested.

4.5.3 Initialisation code

An implementation module contains a module body section just like a program module. The body starts at the BEGIN statement after all the declarations. None of our examples have contained any statements in the module body, simply because the modules do not require any initialisation. Initialisation code can be used to set up global variables used in the module or open files, write messages etc, and so give the correct initial conditions for the module. For example, in standard library module InOut the initialisation code is used to set up the initial input and output files to be the keyboard and the screen.

Since we have said that the initialisation code can be used to set up global variables and open files to get the correct initial conditions, it follows that the code must be executed before any of the module's software resources are used. So how is the initialisation code actually handled?

The initialisation code for each library module used by a program is only run *once*, this is when the import statement importing from that library is executed. Since the libraries are imported in the order of the import statements in the program module, the initialisations will be run one after the other, in the same order, before the declarations or the main body of the program are entered. So the initialisations will be completed before any use can be made of the imported resources.

4.5.4 Compilation units and separate compilation

We have mentioned that the two parts of a library module can be compiled separately – this is because the definition and the implementation modules are *compilation units.* A compilation unit is simply a compilable piece of code, in other words a piece of code which can be given to the compiler, and which the compiler will compile (as long as it has no syntax errors). When a module is compiled the compiler produces an object file containing a machine code version of the module.

As we mentioned earlier, Modula-2 has three types of compilation unit:

- Program module – you have been using these extensively.
- Definition module – the definition part or interface specification of a library module.
- Implementation module – the implementation part of a library module.

All modules can import resources from library modules, so obviously one library module may import resources from another library module. In a software system we may have a large number of library modules importing resources from each other. Each individual module will contain references, such as procedure calls, to the resources it is importing.

Many Modula-2 systems require an extra phase after compilation, called *linking.* Linking can be thought of as simply collecting together all the required imports from other modules.

What happens at compile-time

At compile time the compiler builds up a table of all external references (often called the *symbol table*), that is all references to software resources imported from library modules, for example:

Resource name	Address
WriteString	????
WriteLn	????

The table will contain the name of each external reference and a space for its address in memory. The address column of the table will initially be set to a special value to indicate that the addresses are currently unknown (we have put in question marks to show un unknown address). Eventually the addresses must be filled in (this is done by the linker at link-time) to show where each reference is to be found.

Whilst building the table, the compiler also checks that the external references are being used correctly, by checking them against the appropriate (compiled) definition modules. Specifically, this means that for references to external procedures and functions, all actual parameters must agree with the formal parameters in type, mode and number. Any incorrect or non-existent external references will cause a compilation error, and the compilation will fail.

What happens at link-time

By the linking stage the compiler must have already provided a table containing all external references in the program. The task of the linker is to resolve these references by filling in the addresses, which indicate where each resource is to be found in the appropriate compiled implementation modules. The compiled code for a module is put in an *object file*, so the object file of an implementation module contains the compiled code which implements its software resources. All the required object files will be pulled together to provide (along with the filled-in reference table) an executable file. The addresses provided by the linker will not be the final addresses used when the program is loaded into memory to be run; instead an appropriate offset will be added to all the addresses, to give their true position in memory at run time.

Some programming languages (such as Fortran) provide independent compilation. Independent compilation is similar to separate compilation, in that program units can be compiled separately and then joined together to make a complete program. However, compilers for languages providing independent compilation do not check the correctness of any external references, but assume them to be correct.

This can easily cause problems. For example, the programmer can refer to a non-existent variable or procedure in a program, and the compiler will not give any error messages, assuming that the item is defined externally somewhere. Such errors are spotted later at link-time or at run-time (which is even worse).

4.5.5 Order of compilation

Modula-2 does not allow the modules belonging to a software system to be compiled in any order. Instead there are certain rules about compilation order, which we must follow to compile a related group of modules successfully.

In the previous discussion on compilation units and separate compilation there was one particular section which is directly relevant to compilation order:

> the compiler also checks that the external references are being used correctly, by checking them against the appropriate (compiled) definition modules.

Since the Modula-2 compiler must check for correct usage against compiled definition modules, any module which imports from a library module can only be compiled after that library module's definition has been compiled. For example, if a program module imports from library module InOut, then the definition of InOut must have been compiled previously. If InOut imports from another library module, that module's definition needs to be compiled before InOut's definition. A module importing resources from a library module is called a *client* of the library module. Thus, the program module will be a client of InOut.

Once the appropriate definition modules have been compiled their associated implementation modules can be compiled in any order. It is also usual to compile the program module last of all, although this is not strictly necessary (it can, in fact, be compiled at any time after the definition modules). The rules of compilation order can be stated simply as follows:

- A definition module must be compiled before its clients (those modules which import resources from it).

- An implementation module can only be compiled after its corresponding definition module, *and* after any definition modules of which it is a client.

- A program module can only be compiled after any definition modules of which it is a client.

We can see how these rules work in practice by considering an example of a small software system consisting of several modules. Program 4.5 consists of a program module CompilationOrder, and two library modules Lib1 and Lib2.

Program 4.5 Example showing compilation order of modules

```
MODULE CompilationOrder;
(* A sample program to show compilation order. *)

FROM Lib1 IMPORT Proc1, Type1;
FROM Lib2 IMPORT Proc2;

VAR x : Type1;

BEGIN
   x := 30;
   Proc1(x);
   Proc2(x);
END CompilationOrder.


DEFINITION MODULE Lib1;
(* EXPORT QUALIFIED Proc1, Type1; *)
TYPE
   Type1 = CARDINAL;
PROCEDURE Proc1(VAR c : Type1);
END Lib1.
```

```
IMPLEMENTATION MODULE Lib1;
PROCEDURE Proc1(VAR c : Type1);
   BEGIN
      INC(c, 2);
   END Proc1;
BEGIN
END Lib1.

DEFINITION MODULE Lib2;
FROM Lib1 IMPORT Type1;
(* EXPORT QUALIFIED Proc2; *)
PROCEDURE Proc2(VAR c : Type1);
END Lib2.

IMPLEMENTATION MODULE Lib2;
FROM Lib1 IMPORT Type1;
PROCEDURE Proc2(VAR c : Type1);
   BEGIN
      INC(c, 2);
   END Proc2;
BEGIN
END Lib2.
```

In what order should we compile the modules in Program 4.5? The program module, CompilationOrder, is a client of both Lib1 and Lib2, since it imports resources from them. So, from our rules we know that the definition modules of Lib1 and Lib2 must be compiled before CompilationOrder. Can we compile these library modules' definitions in any order? No, because Lib2 is a client of Lib1 (Lib2 imports Type1 from Lib1), thus Lib1 must be compiled before Lib2. The implementations can be compiled in any order once their associated definitions have been compiled. Here are two possible compilation orders for Program 4.5:

Order 1	Order 2
Lib1 definition	Lib1 definition
Lib2 definition	Lib1 implementation
Lib1 implementation	Lib2 definition
Lib2 implementation	Lib2 implementation
CompilationOrder	CompilationOrder

4.5.6 When and what to recompile

A large software system may consist of many modules. How much of the system do we need to recompile if we alter one line in one module? If we had to recompile all the modules in a software system each time we changed a single module, it would be very time-consuming. Luckily this is not the case.

Remember that the compiler only *sees* the definition part of any library modules imported into the module it is compiling. This means that an implementation module can be altered and recompiled without affecting any other modules, as long as the corresponding definition module remains unchanged. However, if we alter a definition module we have altered the library module's interface to the outside world, so not only will this module have to be recompiled (followed by its implementation) but also any clients of the library module (called the library module's *clients*). After all the appropriate modules in a system have been recompiled we have to link the main program module to obtain an executable file. Here are some guide-lines for recompilation:

- If an implementation module is altered, only this module needs to be recompiled.
- If a definition module is altered, not only must this module be recompiled, but all client modules must be recompiled too. In a large system this will lead to a cascade of recompilations, as clients of clients will have to be recompiled, and so on.
- If the program module is altered, only this module needs to be recompiled (a program module can't have any clients).

4.5.7 Library module variables

It is possible, and sometimes necessary, to declare variables inside an implementation module. Note that we are not talking about the local variables of any procedures declared in the implementation module. Such variables are called *global variables*, as they are available throughout the entire module (just in the same way as variables declared in a program module).

Not only does a global variable retain its value across separate uses of the implementation module (calls of the procedures exported by the definition module), but it is only visible inside the implementation module. A global variable cannot be visible outside the implementation module because it is only declared in this module, and therefore not exported by the definition module. Such a variable can only be altered by the procedures of the module or in the initialisation code of the module body. So the variable cannot be corrupted by external sources in the software system.

4.6 Case study – computer call logger

In Chapter 3 we specified the procedural abstractions for a computer call logger; now we'll build a simple library module to implement the call logger. We have already defined the interface specification for each abstraction, and shown them as Modula-2 procedure headers. It is a relatively simple task to turn this information into the definition part of a library module. Remember that the definition part of a library module is a specification (in Modula-2) of the resources offered by the module.

Program 4.6 gives the definition module for our call logger example.

Program 4.6 Call Logger definition module

```
DEFINITION MODULE CallLogger;

FROM LUTypes IMPORT DateTimeRec;
(* How and where the time is stored will be system dependent. The
above import will work on an Apple Macintosh, running Metrowerks
PSE. *)

TYPE
   CallLog = RECORD
               start : DateTimeRec;
               end : DateTimeRec;
               instigator : CARDINAL;
             END;

   Charge = REAL;

PROCEDURE GetUserId(): CARDINAL;
(* Pre-condition: none.
Post-condition: returns a user id, which is a cardinal number read in
from standard input. *)

PROCEDURE LogCall(i : CARDINAL; VAR log : CallLog);
(* Pre-condition: a call must be starting.
Post-condition: returns a log of the call, giving the start and
finish times and the instigator of the call.
This procedure is the heart of the simulation. Once the start time has
been recorded in the call log LogCall simply waits for the user to press
<return>, to indicate the end of the 'call', at which point the finish time
is recorded in the call log. *)
```

```
PROCEDURE CalculateCharge(call : CallLog): Charge;
(* Pre-condition: call must contain a valid call logged by LogCall.
Post-condition: returns the charge for a single call, by finding the
length of the call in minutes, and then multiplying by the appropriate
charge rate for the time of day the call started. The rates are: started
before 8.00am 10p per minute, started from 8.00am to 6.00pm, 25p per
minute. *)

PROCEDURE BillForCall(amount : Charge; call : CallLog);
(* Pre-condition: call must contain a valid call.
Post-condition: send electronic mail to the instigator of the given call,
indicating how much the call has cost. We will simulate this by simply
sending the message to a file, whose name must be entered by the
user. *)

PROCEDURE ShowBill(amount : Charge; call : CallLog);
(* Pre-condition: call must contain a valid call.
Post-condition: writes the bill for the given call, with the given charge,
to the current output stream. *)

END CallLogger.
```

As you can see, the definition module for CallLogger is quite simple – most definition modules are simple, because they contain only the interface specification, and therefore none of the implementation details are given. There is one exception to this – the type declarations are really implementation details, because they show how the types used in the operations are implemented in Modula-2. We should not really have this level of implementation detail in the interface specification, and we can avoid it by using *opaque type* declarations, which are introduced in Chapter 5. However, for this example we will leave the type declarations as they are shown above.

The only other point to note about the above definition module is the change in header for LogCall. In Chapter 3 we showed the header as a function header returning a value of type CallLog. In definition module CallLogger we have declared the header for LogCall as a procedure with a single variable parameter of type LogCall. Although newer versions of Modula-2 allow functions to return structured types such as records (of which type CallLog is an example) many existing compilers will not allow it, so we have made LogCall return the call log via a variable parameter.

Remember that a definition module is a valid compilation unit in Modula-2, so we can compile the above module to check that we have typed in the interface specification correctly, and so that we are ready to write the corresponding implementation module.

The implementation part of library module CallLogger must contain the actual implementations of the operations specified in the definition module. Remember that the procedure headers need to match those in the definition module exactly.

Program 4.7 gives the implementation module for CallLogger.

Program 4.7 Call Logger implementation module

```
IMPLEMENTATION MODULE CallLogger;
(* Simulation of a computer call logger. *)

(* Implemented using Metrowerks Modula-2 PSE on an Apple Macintosh
LC. *)

FROM LUTypes IMPORT DateTimeRec;
FROM Utilities IMPORT GetTime, Date2Secs;
FROM InOut IMPORT WriteLn, WriteInt, WriteString, Write, OpenOutput,
                  WriteCard, ReadCard, CloseOutput, WriteReal,
                  Read, EOL, HoldScreen;
FROM Terminal IMPORT BusyRead;

(* Forward declaration. Some compilers need these when a procedure
is called in a module before its definition. *)

PROCEDURE WaitForEOL(); FORWARD;

PROCEDURE GetUserId(): CARDINAL;
VAR
   c : CARDINAL;

BEGIN
   ReadCard(c);
   (* Throw away the return typed by the user. *)
   WaitForEOL();
   RETURN c;
END GetUserId;

PROCEDURE LogCall(i : CARDINAL; VAR log : CallLog);
(* Refer to Chapter 3 where CallLog is given as TYPE RECORD. *)
VAR
   date : DateTimeRec;
   c : CHAR
```

```
BEGIN
   (* Indicate call is starting, and record start time in call log. *)
   WriteString("Call starting....press <return> key to finish....");
   WriteLn;
   GetTime(date);
   log.start := date;
   log.instigator := i;
   (* Wait for user to press return to finish the call. *)
   WaitForEOL();
   (* Indicate call has finished, and record finish time in call log. *)
   WriteString("Call finished");
   WriteLn;
   GetTime(date);
   log.end := date;
END LogCall;

PROCEDURE CalculateCharge(call : CallLog): Charge;
CONST
   StartHigh = 8; (* High rate starts at 8.00am, *)
   EndHigh = 18; (* and finishes at 6.00pm, *)
   CheapRate = 0.10; (* 10p per minute, *)
   HighRate = 0.25; (* 25p per minute. *)

VAR
   rate : REAL; (* Charge rate for call, depends on start time. *)
   startSecs, endSecs : LONGINT; (* Start and finish time in
                seconds. Date2Secs returns a LONGINT. *)
BEGIN
   WITH call DO
      (* Convert start and finish time to seconds. *)
      Date2Secs(start, startSecs);
      Date2Secs(end, endSecs);
      (* Find out which rate applies, depending on start time. *)
      IF (start.hour < StartHigh) AND (start.hour > EndHigh)
      THEN
         rate := CheapRate;
      ELSE
         rate := HighRate;
      END;
      (* Calculate the charge as: length of call in minutes * rate. *)
      RETURN (FLOAT(endSecs - startSecs) / 60.0) * rate;
   END;
END CalculateCharge;
```

```
PROCEDURE BillForCall(amount : Charge; call : CallLog);
BEGIN
   (* Get the name of the bill file. *)
   WriteString("Name of file to send bill to?  ");
   (* Open the file (the null string indicates an empty filename
   extension). Any output will now be written to this file, not to
   the computer screen, so the information displayed by ShowBill
   goes directly into the bill file. *)

   OpenOutput("");
   ShowBill(amount, call);

   (* Close the file. Subsequent output will be written to the
   screen again. *)
   CloseOutput;
END BillForCall;


PROCEDURE ShowBill(amount : Charge; call : CallLog);
BEGIN
   WriteLn;
   WriteLn;
   WriteString("Customer reference number:    ");
   WriteCard(call.instigator,6);
   WriteLn;
   WriteLn;

   WITH call.start DO
      WriteString("The following call took place on:   ");
      WriteInt(day,1); Write(":");
      WriteInt(month, 1); Write(":");
      WriteInt(year, 1);
      WriteLn;
      WriteString("The start time was:  ");
      WriteInt(hour,1); Write("."); WriteInt(minute,1);
      WriteLn;
   END;
   WITH call.end DO
      WriteString("The finish time was:  ");
      WriteInt(hour,1); Write("."); WriteInt(minute,1);
      WriteLn;
   END;
```

```
    WriteString("The charge for the call is:  ");
    Write("£");
    WriteReal(amount, 1, 3);
    WriteLn;
    WriteLn;
END ShowBill;

(* Internal procedure, not exported from the library module. *)

PROCEDURE WaitForEOL();
(* Pre-condition: None.
Post-condition: EOL has just been read off the keyboard.
This procedure simply performs read operations until the <return>
character is typed at the keyboard. (BusyRead reads a character
from the keyboard and returns it (in variable c). If no character is
typed it returns the null character). *)

VAR
    c : CHAR;
BEGIN
    REPEAT
        BusyRead(c);
    UNTIL c = EOL;
END WaitForEOL;

BEGIN
    (* No initialisation code required. *)
END CallLogger.
```

This library module alone will not provide us with a working call logger. We have only produced the operations for the call logger. Now we need to implement the algorithm which simulates the call logger in a program module, and use the operations to drive the simulation. We suggested the following algorithm for the logger in Chapter 3:

```
    Loop forever
        Log call
        Calculate charge
        Bill for call
    Endloop
```

This can be implemented in a program module which imports the required operations from library module CallLogger.

Program 4.8 Program module for call logger simulation

```
MODULE LoggerSim;

FROM CallLogger IMPORT CallLog, GetUserId, LogCall,
CalculateCharge, BillForCall, ShowBill;
FROM InOut IMPORT WriteLn, WriteString, ReadCard, HoldScreen;

VAR
   caller : CARDINAL;
   call : CallLog;

BEGIN (* Main program. *)
   (* Announce the simulator! *)
   WriteString("Call logger simulation");
   WriteLn;
   WriteString("----------------------");
   WriteLn; WriteLn;
   (* Get user identifier, that is call instigator. *)
   WriteString("Enter user identifier (positive integer):  ");

   (* Simulate the call and log it. *)
   LogCall(GetUserId(), call);
   BillForCall(CalculateCharge(call), call);
   ShowBill(CalculateCharge(call), call);

   WriteLn;
   WriteString("Press any key to finish simulation");
   HoldScreen;
END LoggerSim.
```

To run the call logger the definition module CallLogger must be compiled first, then the implementation module and the program module.

4.7 Case study – a simple elevator simulation

The problem is to simulate an elevator moving up and down a building in response to passenger requests to go to particular floors of the building. The building has 6 floors: car park, basement, ground floor, mezzanine, top floor and roof. The elevator can reach all of these floors. When responding to a request to go to a particular floor the elevator announces each floor as it is reached (including intermediate floors). On reaching the requested floor the elevator also rings a bell. So, for example, on a trip from the roof to the basement the announcements will be:

```
Top Floor
Mezzanine
Ground Floor
Basement
```

and the bell will be rung on arrival at the basement. Assume that the elevator can only accept one request at a time, and that this request is carried out before another request can be accepted.

4.7.1 Problem specification

The description given above is insufficient as a complete problem definition. We need details about what input is required from the user, and a more formal description of the output to be given by the program.

For input it is easier if the user can give the number of the floor required, rather that having to type in all or part of its name. Giving a floor number is also more akin to pressing a numbered button in a real elevator. We can number the floors in several ways, starting at 1 for the car park and going up to 6 for the roof; starting at 0 and going up to 5; starting at -2 and going up to 3. The most obvious is probably to make the ground floor 0, the basement -1, the mezzanine 1 and so on.

There are several other points which need to be considered in the specification. First of all we need to say what floor the elevator starts from when the program is run – the most obvious would probably be the ground floor. The second point is implicit in the original problem definition and in our understanding of how elevators work – when the elevator arrives at one floor in response to a request it should then wait for another floor to be requested and then travel from the floor it is currently on to the newly requested floor. We therefore don't want the program to exit after a single request, otherwise we will always have the ground floor as our starting position. Instead, we want the user interface to the program to request a new floor every time it finishes a previous request, but there must still be a means for the user to stop the program from running.

Final Specification

Specification for a program to simulate a simple elevator moving up and down the floors of a building in response to user requests.

- The user gives a floor request to the elevator as a number from -2 to 3, where the numbers correspond to the floors as follows:

-2 CarPark
-1 Basement
0 Ground Floor
1 Mezzanine
2 Top Floor
3 Roof

- The prompt for input should consist of a list of the names and numbers of the available floors, and a request for the user to enter one of these numbers. The user interface will provide a prompt which looks like this:

```
Floors: -2 Car Park, -1 Basement, 0 Ground,
1 Mezzanine, 2 Top, 3 Roof.
Enter required floor number:
```

- If an incorrect number is entered it will not be accepted, an error message will be given, and the user will be prompted again to enter a correct number.

- In response to a request the program outputs the name of each floor it passes to reach the requested floor. On arrival at the requested floor the floor name is announced and the bell is rung.

- For the first request when the program is run, the elevator is always started from the ground floor (number 0). For subsequent requests the starting floor is the finishing floor for the previous request. After each request has been carried out the user is asked to give another floor number. The user must respond by typing a single character. If the response is *n* or *N*, the simulation will finish. If any other character is typed the simulation will continue.

4.7.2 Initial design

The initial problem solution will give us the information we need to consider how we can modularise the solution. The simulation must consist of a loop which continually gets a floor request from the user, and moves the elevator to that floor. Before the loop is entered the elevator must be set up to start from the ground floor.

```
Put elevator on ground floor
Repeat the following
    Ask user to enter floor number
    Read in floor number
    Move elevator to floor number
    Ask user if s/he wants to continue
    Read in response
Until response is "n" or "N"
```

There are very few objects in this problem, only the building's floors and the elevator itself. We will call these abstractions Floor and Elevator respectively.

4.7.3 Defining the abstractions

Let's define the Elevator abstraction first. The operations we need for an elevator are: to start the elevator from the ground floor in the first instance, to find out which floor the user wants to go to, and to move the elevator to that floor. The operations and their names are given below:

- Start – Start the elevator from the ground floor.
- Pressed – Find out which floor the user wants the elevator to move to.
- Move – Move the elevator from the floor it is at to the requested floor, announcing each floor by name.

The syntax for these operations is given below:

Start: → Elevator
Pressed: from input → Floor
Move: Elevator, Floor → Elevator

Elevator is more like a functional abstraction than a data abstraction. The operations do not obviously divide into constructors, modifiers and observers, making axiomatic specification difficult. We will therefore define Elevator as a functional abstraction, giving only the interface specification with pre- and post-conditions rather than axioms. The specification for Elevator is given in Specification 4.1.

Specification 4.1 Interface specification for the Elevator abstraction

Types provided: Elevator

Other abstractions used: Floor

Start: → Elevator
Pre-condition: none
Post-condition: elevator is at ground floor

Pressed: from input → Floor
Pre-condition: none
Post-condition: returns a valid floor, read from the standard input

Move: Elevator, Floor → Elevator
Pre-condition: the elevator is at a valid floor
Post-condition: the elevator is at the floor given by the second input parameter

---

Before we give the Modula-2 definition module for Elevator consider how an elevator is to be represented. In fact the representation of an elevator is very simple; we can represent an elevator by the *floor* it is currently on. This means that the type Elevator, defined by the Elevator abstraction can be represented as type Floor, defined by the Floor abstraction.

The definition module showing this representation of Elevator is given in Program 4.9.

Program 4.9 Elevator abstraction definition module

```
DEFINITION MODULE Elevator;
(* Elevator abstraction. Providing the functionality to start a lift, get a
floor request from the user, move the elevator to the chosen floor. *)

FROM Floor IMPORT Floor;
(* EXPORT QUALIFIED Elevator, Start, Pressed, Move; *)

TYPE
   Elevator = Floor;

PROCEDURE Start(): Elevator;
(* Start elevator at ground floor.
Pre-condition: none.
Post-condition: returns with elevator at the ground floor. *)

PROCEDURE Pressed(): Floor;
(* Find out which floor the user wants the elevator to go to.
Pre-condition: none.
Post-condition: returns a valid floor. *)

PROCEDURE Move(lift : Elevator; newFloor : Floor): Elevator;
(* Move the elevator (lift) to the given floor.
Pre-condition: lift is at a valid floor.
Post-condition: returns with the elevator at the new floor. *)

END Elevator.
```

The Floor abstraction is needed by the Elevator abstraction as the representation for an elevator, but it must also provide a number of operations to implement the operations of Elevator. The operations we need for the Floors abstraction are given below:

- Ground – Return the ground floor.
- Top – Return the top floor.
- Bottom – Return the bottom floor.
- GetFloor – Read in a valid floor number.
- Above – Is one floor above another floor?
- Below – Is one floor below another floor?
- NextUp – Return the floor above the given floor.
- NextDown – Return the floor below the given floor.
- WriteFloor – Write out the name of the given floor.

Perhaps surprisingly we can give a full specification for Floor, including the axioms, without too much difficulty, even though we have the (now familiar) problem of no obvious constructors for the abstraction. The specification is shown below in Specification 4.2.

Specification 4.2 The Floor data abstraction

Types provided: Floor

Other abstractions used: Boolean, Integer

Operations:

Ground: → Floor
Top: → Floor
Bottom: → Floor
Above: Floor, Floor → Boolean
Below: Floor, Floor → Boolean
NextUp: Floor → Floor
NextDown: Floor → Floor
GetFloor: from input → Floor
WriteFloor: Floor → tooutput

```
Axioms:
    Ground = 0
    Top = 3
    Bottom = -2
    Above(f1, f2) = If f1 > f2 then true otherwise false
    Below(f1, f2) = If f1 < f2 then true otherwise false
    NextUp(f) = If f < Top then f + 1 otherwise Top
    NextDown(f) = If f > Bottom then f - 1 otherwise Bottom
```

There are several interesting things to note in the above specification. First, the specification states that we are using type Integer in the Floor abstraction, and (from the axioms) you can see that a subrange of Integer is indeed used to represent the floors of the building. The assumption that type Integer will be available as a built-in type of whichever programming language we choose for implementing Floor is probably quite safe!

Second, notice how we are using operations of type Integer to define the axioms for Above, Below, NextUp and NextDown (specifically the operations >, <, + and -).

The Modula-2 interface specification for the Floor abstraction is given below in Program 4.10.

Program 4.10 Floor abstraction definition module

```
DEFINITION MODULE Floor;

(* EXPORT QUALIFIED Floor, Ground, Top, Bottom, GetFloor, Above,
Below, NextUp, NextDown, WriteFloor; *)

TYPE Floor = INTEGER;

PROCEDURE Ground(): Floor;
(* Return the ground floor number.
Pre-condition: none.
Post-condition: returns the ground floor, which is value 0 in type
Floor. *)

PROCEDURE Top(): Floor;
(* Return the top floor number.
Pre-condition: none;
Post-condition: returns the number of the top floor, which is the
highest value of type Floor allowed by GetFloor. *)
```

```
PROCEDURE Bottom(): Floor;
(* Return the bottom floor number.
Pre-condition: none.
Post-condition: returns the number of the bottom floor, which is the
lowest value of type Floor allowed by GetFloor. *)

PROCEDURE GetFloor(): Floor;
(* Prompt user to enter a floor number. Return this number. Will not
accept a number outside the range -2 to 3.
Pre-condition: none.
Post-condition: returns a floor read in as an integer from the standard
input. *)

PROCEDURE Above(f1, f2 : Floor): BOOLEAN;
(* True if f1 is above f2, false if it isn't.
Pre-condition: f1 and f2 are valid floors.
Post-condition: returns TRUE if f1 is above f2, FALSE if below or equal.
*)

PROCEDURE Below(f1, f2 : Floor): BOOLEAN;
(* True if f1 is below f2, false if it isn't.
Pre-condition: f1 and f2 are valid floors.
Post-condition: returns TRUE if f1 is below f2, FALSE otherwise. *)

PROCEDURE NextUp(f : Floor): Floor;
(* Gives the number of the floor above f.
Pre-condition: f is a valid floor.
Post-condition: returns the next floor up, unless f is the top floor in
which case returns f. *)

PROCEDURE NextDown(f : Floor): Floor;
(* Gives the number of the floor below f.
Pre-condition: f is a valid floor.
Post-condition: returns the next floor down, unless f is the bottom
floor, in which case returns f. *)

PROCEDURE WriteFloor(f : Floor);
(* Print the name of the given floor (not its number).
Pre-condition: f is a valid floor.
Post-condition: writes the name of the floor to the standard output. *)

END Floor.
```

4.7.4 Implementing the informal solution

At this stage we can write the informal solution as a program module, which calls the appropriate resources from the library modules Floor and Elevator. Then we can start to implement each of the library modules. Program 4.11 gives the program module for our elevator simulation.

Program 4.11 Program module for the elevator simulation

```
MODULE SimulateElevator;

FROM Floor IMPORT Floor;
FROM Elevator IMPORT Elevator, Start, Pressed, Move;
FROM InOut IMPORT WriteString, WriteLn, Read;

VAR
   lift : Elevator;
   newFloor : Floor;

PROCEDURE Continue(): BOOLEAN;
(* Check if user wants to carry on. *)
VAR
   ch : CHAR;

BEGIN
   REPEAT
      WriteLn;
      WriteString("Enter another request? (y/n):  ");
      Read(ch);
   UNTIL (CAP(ch) = "N") OR (CAP(ch) = "Y");
   RETURN CAP(ch) = "Y";
END Continue;

BEGIN
   lift := Start();
   REPEAT
      newFloor := Pressed();
      lift := Move(lift, newFloor);
   UNTIL NOT Continue();
END SimulateElevator.
```

4.7.5 Implementing the abstractions

We will start with the lowest level abstraction, Floor. First, consider the data representation. The floors are numbered from -2 to 3, and any other floor number is invalid. We can either simply declare a floor as being of type INTEGER or use a subrange of type INTEGER, for example,

```
TYPE
    Floor = [-2..3];
```

Using a subrange might seem a good idea because any attempt to assign a value outside this subrange to a variable of type Floor will result in the program halting immediately. However, this is not a very graceful way for the program to deal with an incorrect floor number! It will be far better if we ourselves include a section of code specifically to deal with the problem of incorrect floor numbers, and the easiest way to allow this is by using type INTEGER for Floor **without** using a subrange of INTEGER.

We have represented Floor by type INTEGER in the definition module for just this reason – it will give us far more flexibility for dealing with errors in the user's input to the simulation.

The operations of Floors are all simple, and Ground is the simplest of all, just returning the number of the ground floor, 0. Above and Below are equally simple, just comparing two floor numbers and return a Boolean value. NextUp and NextDown return the number of the floor above or below the current floor respectively.

The implementation of these operations is given in Program 4.12.

Program 4.12 Floor abstraction implementation module

```
IMPLEMENTATION MODULE Floor;

FROM InOut IMPORT WriteInt, WriteLn, WriteString, ReadInt, Read;

CONST
    GroundFloor = 0;
    LowestFloor = -2;
    HighestFloor = 3;
```

```
PROCEDURE Ground(): Floor;
(* Return the ground floor number, which is defined as a constant
above.
Pre-condition: none.
Post-condition: returns the ground floor, from which the lift is to
start. *)
BEGIN
   RETURN GroundFloor;
END Ground;

PROCEDURE Top(): Floor;
BEGIN
   RETURN HighestFloor;
END Top;

PROCEDURE Bottom(): Floor;
BEGIN
   RETURN LowestFloor;
END Bottom;

PROCEDURE GetFloor(): Floor;
(* Prompt user to enter a floor number. Return this number. Will not
accept a number outside the range -2 to 3.
Pre-condition: none.
Post-condition: returns a floor read in as an integer from the standard
input. *)
VAR
   nextFloor : INTEGER;
   done : BOOLEAN;
   eol : CHAR; (* Need to throw away the return the user types after the
                floor number. *)

PROCEDURE PromptForFloor();
BEGIN
   WriteLn;
   WriteString("Floors: -2 Car Park, -1 Basement, 0 Ground, ");
   WriteLn;
   WriteString("1 Mezzanine, 2 Top, 3 Roof");
   WriteLn; WriteLn;
   WriteString("Enter floor number required: ");
END PromptForFloor;
```

```
BEGIN
   done := FALSE;

   REPEAT
      (* Prompt user to enter floor number. *)
      PromptForFloor();
      ReadInt(nextFloor);
      Read(eol); (* Throw away end of line. *);

      IF (nextFloor <= HighestFloor) AND (nextFloor >= LowestFloor)
      THEN
         done := TRUE;
      ELSE
         WriteLn;
         WriteString("Floor number must be from -1 to 3");
         WriteLn;
         PromptForFloor();
      END;
   UNTIL done;
   RETURN nextFloor;
END GetFloor;

PROCEDURE Above(f1, f2 : Floor): BOOLEAN;
(* True if f1 is above f2, false if it isn't.
Pre-condition: f1 and f2 are valid floors.
Post-condition: returns TRUE if f1 is above f2, FALSE if below or
equal. *)
BEGIN
   RETURN f1 > f2;
END Above;

PROCEDURE Below(f1, f2 : Floor): BOOLEAN;
(* True if f1 is below f2, false if it isn't.
Pre-condition: f1 and f2 are valid floors.
Post-condition: returns TRUE if f1 is below f2, FALSE if above or
equal. *)
BEGIN
   RETURN f1 < f2;
END Below;
```

```
PROCEDURE NextUp(f : Floor): Floor;
(* Gives the number of the floor above f.
Pre-condition: f is a valid floor.
Post-condition: returns the next floor up, unless f is the top floor in
which case returns f. *)

BEGIN
   IF f = HighestFloor THEN
      RETURN f;
   ELSE
      RETURN f+1;
   END;
END NextUp;

PROCEDURE NextDown(f : Floor): Floor;
(* Gives the number of the floor below f.
Pre-condition: f is a valid floor.
Post-condition: returns the next floor down, unless f is the bottom
floor, in which case returns f. *)

BEGIN
   IF f = LowestFloor THEN
      RETURN f;
   ELSE
      RETURN f-1;
   END;
END NextDown;

PROCEDURE WriteFloor(f : Floor);
(* Print the name of the given floor (not its number).
Pre-condition: f is a valid floor.
Post-condition: writes the name of the floor to the standard output. *)
BEGIN
   WriteInt(f, 3);
END WriteFloor;

BEGIN (* Module body. *)
   (* No initialisation needed. *)
END Floor.
```

The first operation of Elevator, Start is so simple we can implement it directly. The only change we will make is to write it as a procedure rather than as a function.

```
PROCEDURE Start(VAR f : Floor);
BEGIN
    RETURN Ground();
END Start;
```

The Pressed operation must return the value for the floor the user wants the elevator to go to, which must be read in from the keyboard. The Elevator abstraction doesn't know how a floor is represented (type Floor is an opaque type in abstraction Floor), and so cannot read a floor value in directly. The Floor abstraction provides a GetFloor operation, to read in a floor; without it there would be no way of reading in a floor value. The description of GetFloor states that it will only return a valid floor number, so Pressed simply needs to call GetFloor:

```
PROCEDURE Pressed(): Floor;
BEGIN
    RETURN GetFloor();
END Pressed;
```

The final operation for Elevator is Move. This is the most complex of the three. Move expects to be given a new floor, to which the elevator must be moved.

```
If new floor above current floor then
    Move elevator up to new floor
Otherwise if new floor below current floor then
    Move elevator down to new floor
Otherwise
    Must be the same floor, do nothing
Endif
Ring door bell to show we have arrived
    Return current floor
```

To refine this further we need to refine *Move elevator up to new floor* and *Move elevator down to new floor*:

```
While new floor above current floor do
    Set current floor to next floor up
    Print out the name of the current floor
Endwhile

While new floor below current floor do
    Set current floor to next floor down
    Print out the name of the current floor
Endwhile
```

Now we can go straight into the final Modula-2 version:

```
PROCEDURE Move(newFloor, currentFloor): Floor;
BEGIN
   IF Above(newFloor, currentFloor) THEN
      (* Move elevator up. *)
      WHILE Above(newFloor, currentFloor) DO
           currentFloor := NextUp(currentFloor);
           WriteFloor(currentFloor);
           WriteLn;
      END;
   ELSIF Below(newFloor, currentFloor) THEN
      (* Move elevator down. *)
      WHILE Below(newFloor, currentFloor) DO
         currentFloor := NextDown(currentFloor);
         WriteFloor(currentFloor);
         WriteLn;
      END;
   END;
   Write(bel);
END Move;
```

The procedure call Write(bel) causes the computer's bell to ring once. The ASCII character *bel* is imported from the ASCII standard library. The full implementation of Elevator is shown in Program 4.13.

Program 4.13 Elevator abstraction implementation module

```
IMPLEMENTATION MODULE Elevator;

FROM Floor IMPORT Floor, Ground, GetFloor, Above, NextUp, Below,
NextDown, WriteFloor;
FROM InOut IMPORT WriteString, WriteLn, Write;

PROCEDURE Start(): Floor;
BEGIN
   RETURN Ground();
END Start;

PROCEDURE Pressed(): Floor;
BEGIN
   RETURN GetFloor();
END Pressed;
```

```
PROCEDURE Move(newFloor, currentFloor : Floor): Floor;
CONST
   BEL = 7; (* ASCII number for the terminal bell. *)
BEGIN
   IF Above(newFloor, currentFloor) THEN
      (* Move elevator up. *)
      WHILE Above(newFloor, currentFloor) DO
           currentFloor := NextUp(currentFloor);
           WriteFloor(currentFloor);
           WriteLn;
      END;
   ELSIF Below(newFloor, currentFloor) THEN
      (* Move elevator down.*)
      WHILE Below(newFloor, currentFloor) DO
         currentFloor := NextDown(currentFloor);
         WriteFloor(currentFloor);
         WriteLn;
      END;
   ELSE (* Must have asked for the same floor again. *)
      WriteString("You are already at the  ");
      WriteFloor (currentFloor);
   END;
   Write(CHR(BEL));
END Move;
BEGIN
   (* No initialisation code. *)
END Elevator.
```

The complete simple elevator simulation is implemented by program module SimulateElevator, and library modules Elevator and Floors.

Summary

A module must provide the means to separate the specification of an abstraction from its implementation – this allows *data hiding*.

Data hiding prevents the user of an abstraction from:

- seeing how it is actually implemented, misusing the abstraction, altering the implementation,

whilst allowing the user to see the interface specification which specifies the abstraction.

Data abstraction modules specify and implement data abstraction, consisting of a type and a number of operations valid for that type. Functional abstraction modules specify and implement higher level operations for other modules; they do not usually define their own types.

Name abstraction modules rename resources already implemented in one or more other modules.

The interface specification is the part of a module which specifies the resources offered by the module, so that a user can access those resources in the correct manner. This part of a module is usually visible to a user.

The implementation part of a module implements the resources specified in the module's interface specification. This part of a module may be hidden from the user if data hiding is required. The implementation of a module may change without affecting the interface specification, and therefore without the knowledge of any users of the module, who can only see the interface specification.

Modules provide the following useful attributes for software engineering:

- allow problem decomposition
- allow division of labour in group work
- preserve the structure of a problem solution
- allow data hiding for abstraction
- simplify testing and maintenance
- aid software re-use
- aid portability of code.

Modula-2 library modules provide reusable resources for program modules and other library modules.

A library module has two parts, the definition module and the implementation module, which are compiled separately from each other. The definition module provides the interface specification, specifying the resources offered by the library module to the outside world. Importing modules only *see* the definition part of a library module. The implementation module implements the resources specified in the definition module.

Initialisation code, in the module body of an implementation module, can be used to set initial conditions for the resources in the library module (for example, setting global variables, opening files). It is executed once, when the first import statement from the library is executed.

Compilation of a module (separate compilation) – the compiler builds a table of external references (that is, imported software resources) and checks them for correctness.

Linking a module – the linker fills in the address of each external reference in the table built by the compiler. Some compilers link automatically after compilation, so linking is not an obvious phase in the compilation process.

In separately compiled languages (for example, Modula-2) the external references are checked for correctness by the compiler. In independently compiled languages (for example, C, Fortran) there are no checks on external references and you won't find out if you've used any incorrectly until you run your program!

The order of compilation of modules in Modula-2 is very important, and follows strict rules:

- A definition module must be compiled before its clients. An implementation module may only be compiled after its definition module and after any definition modules of which it is a client. A program module may only be compiled after any definition modules of which it is a client.

Recompilation of modules when code is altered may be necessary:

- If a program module is altered only this module needs to be recompiled. If an implementation module is altered only this module needs to be recompiled. If a definition module is altered this module, its implementation module and all client modules must be recompiled.

Selected reading

Ford, G and Wiener, R.
Modula-2, a software development approach
J. Wiley and Sons, 1985
Contains a good introduction to the use of library modules, and their properties, particularly from the point of view of good software engineering practice.

Lins, C
Modula-2 software component library, Volumes 1, 2, and 3
Springer-Verlag, 1989
The contents of this book make it very suitable for those interested in implementing data abstractions. It contains lots of examples of library modules and is a good example of the usefulness of library modules for building a software library.

5 Standard data abstractions

5.1 Introduction

Data abstractions, as we already know, are a means of defining data types without reference to any details of how the type is represented, or how the operations are implemented on a computer. The chapter on Modularisation showed how data abstractions can be used as a method of problem solving, and how such abstractions can be defined in a formal manner.

Knowing how to specify and define data abstractions, and how to use them in problem solving is not very useful, unless we can turn our abstractions into concrete implementations in a programming language. Without writing implementations we cannot produce programs to solve the problems we have looked at.

You have effectively been using implemented data abstractions in your Modula-2 programs. Modula-2 provides a number of built-in data types (example, INTEGER, REAL, CARDINAL) which can be used (in the majority of cases) without the programmer needing to know how the types are represented on the computer or how the operations (example, addition, subtraction, etc.) are implemented by the language.

The important point to remember is that we can use a data abstraction without needing to know how the type (or types) in the abstraction are represented or how the operations are implemented. We know that the data abstractions we defined earlier are usable without knowing these details, because we have already specified and used these abstractions in problem solving, although we have not yet implemented either the abstractions or the problem solutions.

5.2 Data hiding

We looked briefly at implementing data abstractions back in Chapter 2, saying only that an implementation of a data abstraction requires (i) a way of representing the data type(s) in the abstraction, and (ii) a procedure or function to perform each operation. Rather than the user of a data abstraction simply not looking at the abstraction's implementation, we may wish to go one stage further and hide the details of the implementation from the user. Why would we wish to actively prevent the user of a data abstraction from accessing that abstraction's implementation? If the user cannot access the implementation of an abstraction then:

- The user cannot change the implementation. This may prevent the user from making changes to the implementation which would make it incorrect.

- The implementation can be changed (perhaps for a better or faster implementation) without the user of the abstraction having to know about it.

The enforced hiding of the implementation of an abstraction from the user of the abstraction is called *data hiding*, the data being the implementation details of the abstraction. If we hide the implementation of an abstraction from the user we must still allow the user to see the specification or definition of the abstraction, so that they know what types and operations are offered by the abstraction.

Whether or not we can hide the implementation of an abstraction to ensure the two properties given above depends on the programming language we use for the implementation. Modula-2 has features specifically designed to allow data hiding and to aid the implementation of abstractions. You may have already guessed that these special features are library modules. Library modules are excellent for data hiding and data abstraction, with the definition module providing the specification of the abstraction and the implementation module containing the actual implementation. The use of opaque types in library modules also assists in the task of data hiding, as we will see in the following sections.

5.3 Library modules for data hiding

We have already used library modules as a way of grouping together related routines to provide resource libraries of useful software. The standard libraries of Modula-2 provide input/output resources, mathematics resources, system resources etc. We have also seen that if such resources are implemented using library modules the author can withhold the implementation part of the library module and only give the user of the resource the definition part. The user can find out all the functionality of the resource, but cannot find out how it has been implemented. However, library modules are far more important for software design than simple repositories for groups of procedures; they provide a means of data hiding which can be used to implement data and procedural abstractions.

Data hiding for data abstraction requires that the user of an abstraction has only sufficient detail to use the abstraction, but no detail at all on how the abstraction is implemented. For most data abstractions sufficient detail means the names of the types and the headers of the procedures, which are the types and operations of the abstraction. As an example we'll look at a simple counter abstraction. We will assume that the counter can be initialised (to zero), incremented by one and decremented by one.

Specification 5.1 shows the formal specification for our counter abstraction.

Specification 5.1 The Counter data abstraction

Types provided: Counter

Other abstractions used: none

Operations:

Init: → Counter
Inc: Counter → Counter
Dec: Counter → Counter

Axioms:

Dec(Init) = Error
Inc(Dec(x)) = x
Dec(Inc(x)) = x

Where:

x is of type Counter

Program 5.1 shows an implementation of a simple counter abstraction. The user of this abstraction will only see the definition module. At first glance you may think that this provides complete data hiding for the abstraction, but look again.

Program 5.1 Counter library module

```
DEFINITION MODULE Counter;

TYPE
   Counter = CARDINAL;

PROCEDURE Initialise(): Counter;
(* Set counter to zero. *)

PROCEDURE Increment(c : Counter): Counter;
(* Increase the value of c by 1. *)

PROCEDURE Decrement(c : Counter): Counter;
(* Decrease the value of c by 1. *)

END Counter.


IMPLEMENTATION MODULE Counter;

FROM InOut IMPORT WriteString;

PROCEDURE Initialise(): Counter;
(* Pre-condition: none.
Post-condition: returns 0. *)

VAR
   c : Counter;
BEGIN
   RETURN 0;
END Initialise;

PROCEDURE Increment(c : Counter): Counter;
(* Pre-condition: none.
Post-condition: returns the counter incremented by 1. *)

BEGIN
   RETURN c + 1;
END Increment;
```

```
PROCEDURE Decrement(c : Counter): Counter;
(* Pre-condition: none.
Post-condition: returns the counter decremented by 1. *)
BEGIN
   IF c > 0 THEN
      RETURN c - 1;
   ELSE
      WriteString("Can't decrement, counter is zero");
      HALT;
   END;
END Decrement;

BEGIN
   (* No initialisation required. *)
END Counter.
```

Although the implementations of the operations (the procedures) are completely hidden, the implementation for the type Counter is visible. We can see that Counter is implemented as a CARDINAL. This allows us to access Counter without using the operations defined on it. Program 5.2 shows some examples of such access to variables of type Counter.

Program 5.2 IllegalCounter program module

```
MODULE IllegalCounter;

FROM Counter IMPORT Counter, Initialise, Increment, Decrement;
FROM InOut IMPORT WriteCard, HoldScreen;

VAR
   c1, c2 : Counter;

BEGIN
   c1 := Initialise();
   c2 := 100;
   WHILE c1 < c2 DO
      c1 := Increment(c1);
      c2 := Decrement(c2);
   END;
   c1 := c1 * c2;
   WriteCard(c1, 3);
   HoldScreen();
END IllegalCounter.
```

The type representation for Counter, CARDINAL, is visible in the definition module for the Counter abstraction. The compiler therefore *knows* that Counter is the same type as CARDINAL, and will accept not only the intended operations of Counter (Initialise, Increment and Decrement), but also the operations of CARDINAL (*, DIV, + and -).

In the example program the assignments c2 := 100 and c1 := c1 * c2 are accepted, even though they are not defined as operations of the Counter abstraction and were not intended as operations by the author of the abstraction.

Having recognised this as a problem we need to consider how we would like to avoid it. Perhaps the most obvious way is not to give the representation type for Counter in the definition module, but to hide it in the implementation module. If we hide the entire type definition in the implementation module, we won't be able to use Counter in the definition module itself – this rather prevents us from defining Init, Inc and Dec with parameters of type Counter! The user of Counter won't be able to declare any variables of type Counter, as it doesn't appear in the definition module.

We really want to be able to state only the name of the Counter type, Counter, in the definition module, and leave the representation, CARDINAL, in the implementation module, where it is hidden. Modula-2 provides the concept of *opaque types* to do exactly this.

5.3.1 Hiding type information

The declaration of type Counter in our Counter abstraction definition module is *transparent*. By this we mean that the user of Counter can see the way that Counter is implemented, because the full definition appears in the definition module. To declare a type as *opaque* we only state its name in the definition module, so the declaration of an opaque Counter would look like this:

```
TYPE
    Counter;
```

Now we cannot tell if Counter is implemented as a CARDINAL or an INTEGER or any other type; there is simply no information available about Counter's implementation.

Of course, we have to state somewhere how Counter is actually implemented, and the obvious place to do this is in the associated implementation module along with the implementations of Counter's operations.

We might think that this is simply done by stating the type declaration in full, so we declare Counter = CARDINAL. If you try to do this and then compile the implementation module (remember to have compiled the new definition module first), the compiler will object to this type declaration.

Our problem is this:

- We don't want to put the full type definition Counter = CARDINAL into the definition module, because this will enable the user and compiler to see the representation type of Counter, thus preventing data hiding, and true data abstraction.

- If we don't put the full type definition into the definition module the compiler will be unable to tell how much memory to reserve for any variables of type Counter used in other modules.

In order to solve this problem we need a special data type, called the *pointer*.

5.3.2 Memory addresses and pointers

Every individual location in a computer's memory has a unique address. Most data items used in our programs tend to be stored in a number of consecutive memory locations. For example, a single character may be stored in one location, but a single integer may require four locations.

The high level abstraction of the memory address, which is usually used in programming languages, is called the *pointer*. You can visualise a pointer as an arrow directing you towards something.

Modula-2, and most high-level programming languages provide some kind of pointer type. The pointer type is not really a single type, but a *type constructor*, like the record, array and set types, and must be used with other data types to build a data structure. For example, an array must be an array of integers, or an array of characters, etc. Here is an example of a pointer type declaration in Modula-2:

```
TYPE
    NewType = POINTER TO SomeType;
```

In this example the type pointed to by the pointer, called SomeType, is the *base type* of pointer type NewType. The pointer type can only point to objects which are of the given base type. Thus a variable of type NewType can only point to an object of type SomeType.

All pointer types have one special value in common, the constant NIL. NIL is the nil or null pointer, that is a pointer which isn't pointing to anything at all. It is very important to remember that a pointer set to NIL is **not** the same as an undefined pointer. An undefined pointer is one which has not been set either to NIL or to the address of an object of the pointer's base type. Such a pointer may very well contain an address, but it will not be a valid one.

Just being able to point to a particular location in memory is not very useful! We also need to be able to get at the value of the object stored in that location. There is a special operation for doing this, which is sometimes called the *dereferencing operation*. The symbol for this operation is the up arrow ↑ or the hat ^ . We can look upon dereferencing a pointer as following the pointer to the value that it is pointing to.

Let's declare a pointer type and a variable of that type.

```
TYPE
   Strange = POINTER TO CARDINAL;
VAR
   first : Strange;
   card : CARDINAL;
```

Strange is a user-defined type (we have just defined it!) which is a pointer type. The base type of Strange is CARDINAL, so variables of type Strange are only allowed to point to (that is, contain the addresses of) CARDINAL values. The only exception to this is that a variable can be set to the special value NIL – so that it isn't pointing anywhere at all.

Variable first is of type Strange, so it can only point to CARDINAL values. Variable card can contain only CARDINAL values. If we want to put the value 99 into card we simply assign it:

```
card := 99;
```

What happens if we try exactly the same assignment on first?

```
first := 99;
```

Remember that first is a pointer type and that a pointer contains the address of a location in memory. The above assignment has put the value 99 into first, so first now points to location 99 in the computer's memory. If we actually want to put the value 99 in the location that first points to we have to dereference the pointer in the assignment statement, or *follow* it to the location it points to.

```
first^ := 99;
```

This assignment has put the value 99 in the memory location that first points to, which happens to be at memory address 99 (this was done by the original assignment).

The dereferenced pointer first^ is also a variable, and must therefore have a type. The type of such a variable is always the base type of the pointer type to which the pointer belongs. So first^ is of type CARDINAL. Thus

```
first^ := 123
```

is a valid assignment, but

```
first^ := -24
```

is invalid, because -24 is an INTEGER not a CARDINAL.

We say that the variable represented by first^ is an *anonymous variable*, because it is not declared anywhere, nor does it have a name; it can only be accessed through the pointer variable *first*.

We need a quick aside here to remind us of what happens at compilation time. The compiler checks each line of code for being correct Modula-2, and translates it into machine code or assembler, so that the program can actually be run on the computer. The compiler also allocates space in the computer's memory for storing all the constants and variables declared in the program. However, the compiler has no way of knowing about the undeclared, anonymous variables in the program. It therefore cannot allocate space for such variables; this must be done explicitly in the program by calling a special procedure called ALLOCATE.

ALLOCATE comes from the Storage library. It reserves memory space for anonymous variables. When a program is running the memory of the computer is divided up into sections, each of which the program can use for a particular purpose. One part is reserved for data which has not been specifically declared in the program, such as anonymous variables. The ALLOCATE procedure can allocate space in this part of memory for anonymous variables, then the variable can be used like any other to store data of the appropriate type. The programmer does not have to know the actual address of the space allocated by ALLOCATE for the variable.

The DEALLOCATE procedure can be used to *free* the memory used by an anonymous variable, once it is no longer needed. If the space is not freed after use, the memory may become full and cause the program to crash. Normally, declared variables are looked after for you by the system software when the program is run, and their space is allocated and freed when appropriate, so you don't have to worry about them. But anonymous variables must be managed entirely by the programmer.

The following piece of code uses ALLOCATE to allocate space for first, then stores the value 72 at the memory location pointed to by first, prints it out, and then deallocates the memory.

```
ALLOCATE(first, SIZE(CARDINAL));
first^ := 72;
WriteCard(first^, 2);
DEALLOCATE(first, SIZE(CARDINAL));
```

ALLOCATE needs to be given two things to perform its task of reserving space for an anonymous variable. First, ALLOCATE must be given the pointer variable (first in this example) which is to point to the anonymous variable. Second, we have to explicitly state how much memory we want ALLOCATE to reserve for the anonymous variable. We know that the pointer first can only point to anonymous variables which are of type CARDINAL, so we want to reserve sufficient space to store a CARDINAL. This is the purpose of SIZE(CARDINAL). SIZE is a built-in function which, given the name of a type, returns the number of bytes required to store a variable of that type. Thus, SIZE(CARDINAL) gives the number of bytes required to store any CARDINAL value.

The call to ALLOCATE has two consequences, one being that we reserve memory space for an anonymous variable of type CARDINAL, and the other being that first now contains the address of that reserved memory. Now that first points to reserved memory we can store something in it, so we dereference first (go to the memory address stored in it), and store the value 72 in this memory.

To free the memory used by the anonymous variable (that is, throw the variable away) we use the DEALLOCATE procedure. DEALLOCATE must be given the memory address where the anonymous variable is stored (which is, of course, stored in first), and the number of bytes of memory to be freed (given by SIZE(CARDINAL) again).

You must allocate and deallocate memory in this way for every anonymous variable you use in a program. The possibilities are endless for making mistakes when handling pointers and memory, and such mistakes usually cause very obscure bugs in your programs. You must be very careful that you *tell* ALLOCATE and DEALLOCATE the correct number of bytes to be reserved/freed. If you reserve too little then the data you try and store may overwrite another variable. If you free more memory than you originally reserved you may free memory belonging to another variable, which is still in use. Such errors cannot be spotted by the compiler, and may only appear when the program runs.

5.3.3 Declaring opaque types

Can you see the connection between pointers and opaque types? With an opaque type declaration in a definition module the compiler can't determine variable size. This would suggest that in the implementation module we can declare our type fully as

```
TYPE    Counter = POINTER TO CARDINAL;
```

and then add a new line to the Init operation, to call ALLOCATE to allocate space for a variable of type Counter.

This is, in fact, exactly what we must do. If the compiler sees an opaque type in a definition module, when it comes to compile the appropriate implementation module it will only accept the opaque type being declared as a pointer type.

It is important to remember that all variables of pointer types must have their storage space allocated by a call to the ALLOCATE procedure. Library modules which export opaque types should always provide a *create* or *setup* operation, which calls ALLOCATE to allocate memory for a variable of the opaque type.

It is not just a matter of declaring the opaque type as POINTER TO sometype, and calling ALLOCATE to allocate space. Remember that a pointer contains a memory address which gives the location of a variable in memory. To access the variable itself we need to dereference or *follow* the pointer, using the ^ operation. For example, the body of Initialise in Counter would become:

```
ALLOCATE(c, SIZE(CARDINAL));
c^ := 0;
```

The call to ALLOCATE sets up space for an anonymous variable of type CARDINAL and puts the address of the reserved space into c. The assignment stores the value 0 at this memory address. Program 5.3 shows the counter abstraction using an opaque type declaration.

Program 5.3 Opaque Counter library module

```
DEFINITION MODULE Counter;

EXPORT QUALIFIED Counter, Initialise, Increment, Decrement;

TYPE Counter;

PROCEDURE Initialise(): Counter;
(* Set counter to zero. *)

PROCEDURE Increment(c : Counter): Counter;
(* Increase the value of c by 1. *)

PROCEDURE Decrement(c : Counter): Counter;
(* Decrease the value of c by 1. *)

END Counter.


IMPLEMENTATION MODULE Counter;

FROM Storage IMPORT ALLOCATE;
FROM InOut IMPORT WriteString;

TYPE
   Counter = POINTER TO CARDINAL;
```

```
PROCEDURE Initialise(): Counter;
VAR
   c : Counter;
BEGIN
   ALLOCATE(c, SIZE(CARDINAL))
   c^ := 0;
   RETURN c;
END Initialise;

PROCEDURE Increment(c : Counter): Counter;
BEGIN
   c^ := c^ + 1;
   RETURN c;
END Increment;

PROCEDURE Decrement(c : Counter): Counter;
BEGIN
   IF c^> 0 THEN
      c^ := c^ - 1;
      RETURN c;
   ELSE
      WriteString("Can't decrement, counter is zero");
      HALT;
   END;
END Decrement;

BEGIN
   (* No initialisation required. *)
END Counter.
```

If we try to compile IllegalCounter using this version of the Counter abstraction, the compiler will report errors in the following code fragments:

```
c2 := 100
c1 < c2
c1 := c1 * c2
WriteCard(c1, 3)
```

These are all operations of type CARDINAL, which are no longer valid, because Counter is opaque and the compiler doesn't know that it's a CARDINAL, and so won't allow these operations to be used on counter variables.

5.4 Choosing data representations

Before we can produce an implementation of a data abstraction in any programming language we need to consider how to represent the data objects of the abstraction, using the data representation facilities provided by the chosen programming language. Choice of programming language for a particular software system is often determined by the presence of certain data representation facilities. For example, if we were writing software which used lists extensively for all data objects then we might choose a language with a built-in list data representation (LISP is an example of such a language).

Most programming languages provide a number of built-in data types for representing common data objects such as integer numbers, character etc. We have already discussed the built-in types provided by Modula-2 (in Appendix A). Most languages also allow the user to build his own data representations out of existing ones.

How do we decide which representations to use for a particular data abstraction? We will use the Car Pool Reservation System as a case study for this problem, but first there are some basic questions we need to bear in mind when choosing data representations:

- Does the target programming language already provide any suitable representations, or can we use another language which does? In some cases we will have no choice of target language (here for example!), and in others we will be able to choose the most suitable language for the software system.

- Is the representation easily searched and updated? This is important for allowing us to access and alter the data, although in some cases it is possible that the data only needs to be accessed, and is never updated after its initial entry.

- Does the representation use excessive amounts of storage space? Although storage is often unrestricted for all but the largest applications, it may be necessary to store data economically. Additionally, excessive use of storage may indicate a poor choice of representation, and in these circumstances you should think about other possible representations for comparison of storage usage.

- Can we access the representation at an intermediate stage in the task the data is being used for? In some applications it may be helpful to see intermediate results which are stored in our data representation.

We can sum all this up in one question:

Is the data representation a good model for the data abstraction?

There are a number of data abstractions which are commonly used throughout computing. We have already looked at two such abstractions, the Set and the Queue, but other common data abstractions are List, Stack, and BinaryTree. All of these provide very different ways of storing and accessing data, although their equational specifications are not dissimilar. We shall spend some time discussing and specifying the List, Stack and BinaryTree data abstractions, because they are needed so frequently in implementing problem solutions.

5.5 The Stack data abstraction

How can we best describe a stack? An English description of a stack is:

> An ordered collection of items, where new items can be inserted and items can be removed from one end, which is called the *top* of the stack.

The first example which comes to mind is the automatic plate stack in a self-service restaurant, where the customer takes a plate off the top of the plate stack and the whole stack moves upwards to present the next customer with a plate. The plates can only be removed from the top of the plate stack, as all other plates in the stack are hidden under the counter top. The second example is the in-tray you might find on a desk. Many people seem to operate their in-trays on the stack principle, where any new work which arrives is put onto the top of the existing work in the in-tray. When we want to deal with the items in the tray we remove the top item and deal with that, then remove the next item and deal with that, and so on. Of course, these people would be much better off organising their in-trays as queues!

More formally, the properties of a stack mean that items are arranged so that given any two items in the stack, one item is *higher* than the other item. This higher item must have been added to the stack after the item below it, and will be removed from the stack before the item below it. Figure 5.1 shows us a stack at various stages in its growth.

Figure 5.1 Stages in the growth of a stack

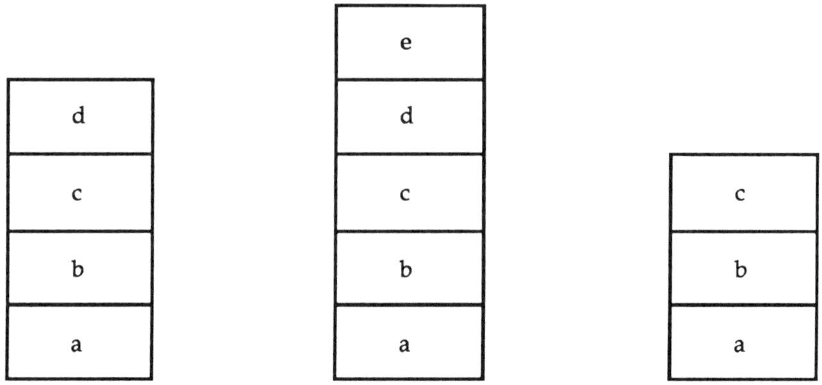

If we look at items b and c in in the first snapshot of the stack we see that c is higher up the stack than b, and must therefore have been put onto the stack more recently than b. Item d is higher than item c and is at the *top* of the stack. If we add a new item, e, to the stack it will get placed above d. This is the situation shown in the second snapshot. We say that we have *pushed* the item onto the stack, to indicate that the new item has effectively moved or *pushed* all the existing items further away from the top of the stack.

If we remove or *pop* an item from the stack we will get the last item pushed onto the stack, item e, and item d becomes the new top of the stack. If we remove another item we get item d, and item c becomes the new top of the stack.

The third snapshot shows the stack after two pops have been performed. You will notice that the stack grows and shrinks with the number of items stacked; it is a further example of a dynamic data structure.

Although we have shown a side-on view to illustrate how a stack changes with additions and deletions from the stack, in reality we look down on a stack, so that only the top item is visible. Figure 5.2 shows how the stack in Figure 5.1 appear when viewed from above.

Figure 5.2 The normal view of a stack

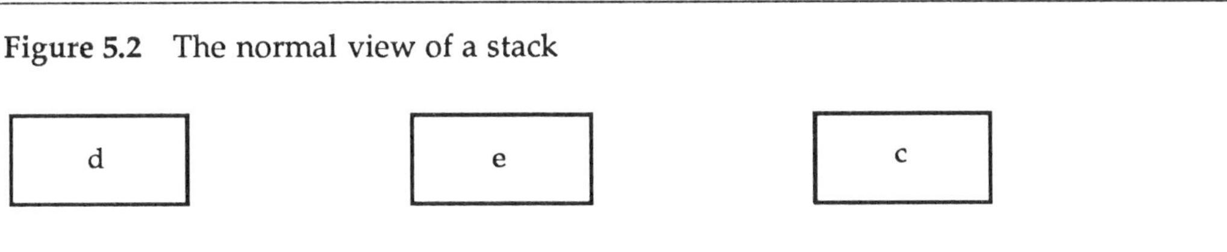

You will find that stacks are frequently described as *last-in, first-out* or LIFO data structures, because the last item pushed onto the stack is always the first item to be popped off the stack.

5.5.1 Specifying the Stack data abstraction

The preceding description of a stack has already provided us with two operations. The Push operation puts items onto the top of a stack, giving a new stack with one more item, and is therefore a *constructor* of the Stack abstraction. The Pop operation removes items from the top of a stack, giving a stack with one less item, and is therefore a *modifier* of the Stack abstraction.

In Chapter 2 we found that we required a constructor to create new examples of a data abstraction, so we need such a modifier for stacks; let's call it Create. Do we need any observers for the Stack? An observer which tells us whether or not the stack is empty will be needed so that we can make sure we never try to remove an item from an empty stack – IsEmpty will be this observer. The only other observer we might need will allow us to look at the item on the top of the stack without removing it from the stack – this is the Top observer. Top can be simulated if the abstraction doesn't provide it – it is a Pop operation followed by a Push operation to put the popped item back onto the stack.

Here are all the operations needed for the Stack abstraction:

- Create – create a new, empty stack.
- Push – add an item onto the top of the stack.
- Pop – remove the item at the top of the stack.
- Top – look at the item on the top of the stack, but don't alter the stack.
- IsEmpty – return True if the stack is empty and False if it isn't.

Now we have the operations and a brief English description of how they work we need to specify them more formally. As in Chapter 2, we must specify both the syntax and the semantics of the operations. Remember that to specify the semantics we must construct a general empty stack and a general non-empty stack using the constructors, and apply each modifier and observer to these examples. The empty stack is represented by

Create

and the non-empty stack is represented by

Push(s, i)

where s is a stack and i is an item. Note that the stack described by this Push operation is guaranteed to be non-empty, even if s is an empty stack (s will no longer be empty once i is pushed onto it).

Specification 5.2 gives the full specification for our Stack abstraction.

Specification 5.2 The Stack data abstraction

Types provided: Stack

Other abstractions used: Item, Boolean

Operations:

Create: → Stack
Push: Stack, StackItem → Stack
Pop: Stack → Stack
Top: Stack → StackItem
IsEmpty: Stack → Boolean

Axioms:

```
Pop(Create) = Create
Pop(Push(s, i)) = s
Top(Create) = Error
Top(Push(s, i)) = i
IsEmpty(Create) = True
IsEmpty(Push(s, i)) = False
```

Where:

```
s is of type Stack,
i is of type Item.
```

Let's look at some of these axioms in more detail. First, take

```
Pop(Create) = Create
```

If we Pop something off an empty stack we will be left with an empty stack (take nothing from nothing, and you are left with nothing!). In some cases we might wish to define Pop(Create) to return an error.

If we pop something off a non-empty stack

```
Pop(Push(s, i))
```

we pop the item at the top of the stack, that is the last item put onto the stack. So the Pop operation removes i and leaves us with the stack *before* i was pushed onto it, that is s.

Finding the top item on an empty stack is clearly an error. Top is expected to return an item, which

```
Top(Create)
```

cannot. Therefore we make Top return an error in these circumstances.

Finding the top item on a non-empty stack is very simple. The top item is always the last item pushed onto a stack. Thus, with

```
Top(Push(s, i))
```

we know that the last item pushed onto the stack is i, and this is what Top must return.

5.5.2 Implementation of the Stack abstraction – static stacks

First we need to consider the representation we will use for our stacks. In this chapter we are dealing only with static implementations, so we need a static data structure that can hold a number of elements of the same type. The obvious choice for this is the array.

A Modula-2 array is a static data structure, whose size is determined by its type definition. Storage for the entire array is allocated at compilation time. Given the following variable declaration,

```
VAR
    charArray : ARRAY [1..20] OF CHAR;
```

the compiler will allocate space for twenty characters. The user does not have to use all this space, and can store less than 20 characters in the array, but he cannot store more than 20, without changing the size of the array, which cannot be done dynamically whilst the program is running. We can use an array as the underlying representation for a Stack if we choose a sensible maximum size for the array. A *sensible* size will depend on the target application.

There are two ways we can represent a stack in an array, either with the stack starting at the highest index and growing down towards the lowest index, or with the stack starting at the lowest index and growing up towards the highest index. We'll use the latter approach and grow the stack up from lowest to highest index. Here is one possible type definition for representing a stack of characters:

```
CONST
    MaxStack = 100;

TYPE
    Stack = ARRAY [1..MaxStack] OF CHAR;
```

But before you rush off and use this representation consider this – how do we know where in the array the top of the stack currently is? The main property of a stack is that items can only be added to or removed from the top of the stack. In an array, how do we know where the top of the stack is? Our Stack representation should let us keep a record of the index for the current top of the stack, so we need a representation which will allow us to store two types of information, the stack itself and the index of the stack top; a record is the obvious choice:

```
TYPE
    Stack = RECORD
                stack : ARRAY [1..MaxStack] OF CHAR;
                top : [0..MaxStack];
            END;
```

Note that we have decided to use a subrange for the index – top. This is a safety device, so that top can only take valid values. If top is set to 0 this indicates that the stack itself is empty, otherwise the value of top will always be the index for the current top of stack. Any attempt to set top to a value outside the declared range will cause a fatal error when the program is run.

Now we can get on with implementing the operations of the Stack abstraction. In the preceding discussion of representations for a stack we allowed the operations to *drive* the direction of the representation choice, so that we have arrived at a representation which is suitable for implementing all the operations of the Stack abstraction.

First we will look at the simplest constructor of the Stack abstraction. Create has to set the top of the stack to 0, as this is the indicator of an empty stack, and a newly created stack must be empty. The algorithm for this is so simple that we can go straight into the Modula-2 declaration of the procedure:

```
PROCEDURE Create(VAR s : Stack);
(* Pre-condition: none.
Post-condition: s is an empty stack. *)
BEGIN
    s.top := 0;
END Create;
```

Note that we have had to implement Create as a procedure rather than a function because a stack is a structured type, and in most versions of Modula-2 functions cannot return values of structured types.

We don't need to do anything to s.stack, the array which will hold the stack items, however we must remember that the observer IsEmpty must check only the value of s.top to decide whether or not the stack is empty. IsEmpty is also very simple and can be implemented now:

```
PROCEDURE IsEmpty(s : Stack): BOOLEAN;
(* Pre-condition: none.
Post-condition: returns TRUE if the stack s is empty, and FALSE if it
isn't. *)
BEGIN
    RETURN s.top = 0;
END IsEmpty;
```

Note that we have not used an IF-statement to return the values TRUE or FALSE, but have simply used the RETURN statement to return the Boolean value of the expression s.top = 0.

Having implemented the two simplest operations of the stack abstraction we can now turn to the other constructor, Push, which puts an item onto an existing stack (that is, a stack already created by the Create constructor). In our array implementation of stacks this means adding an item to the array at the next free location, which will be at s.top + 1. Thus to push an item onto a stack takes two stages:

```
INC(s.top);
s.stack[s.top] := i;
```

where item i is being pushed onto stack s. First we add one to the top of stack index, s.top, so that it indexes the next free location in the array s.stack. Then we put i into the array at this index position. We could use the Modula-2 WITH statement to make the references to the record elements shorter:

```
WITH s DO
   INC(top);
   stack[top] := i;
END;
```

This has exactly the same effect as the previous piece of Modula-2.

Can you see any problems with this implementation of Push? Remember that we are representing a stack, which is a dynamic data structure, with an array, which is a static data structure.

If we keep adding items to the stack we will eventually fill up the array in which the stack is stored (when we reach MaxStack items). If we attempt to add a further item to the stack we will cause a *stack overflow* error, as we try to put an item into a piece of memory which does not belong to the array. The run-time effect of this will be that the program will crash as soon as we try to add too many items, and the operating system will report a *memory overflow* error (or something similar). We should avoid leaving the operating system to report such an error as the system report will not indicate what the problem is in the context of the program.

The Push implementation must check to see if the stack has filled the array before it attempts to add another item, and not add the item if the array is full. We really need to have some way of indicating an unsuccessful push operation to the user, so we can modify Push to have a variable parameter *overflow*, which is set to TRUE if an attempt is made to add an item to a full stack.

```
PROCEDURE Push(VAR s : Stack; i : StackItem; VAR overflow :
   BOOLEAN);
(* Pre-condition: none.
Post-condition: If s is not full then a new item, i, is put onto the top
of s, and overflow is set to FALSE. Else overflow is set to TRUE. *)
BEGIN
   overflow := FALSE;
   WITH s DO
      IF top < MaxStack THEN (* Stack isn't full yet. *)
         INC(top);
         stack[top] := i;
      ELSE (* Stack is full - can't push. *)
         overflow := TRUE;
      END;
   END;
END Push;
```

The stack abstraction has only one modifier, Pop, which removes an item from the top of a stack. In the specification of Pop it returns the stack it is given minus the top item, but doesn't return the item which has been removed. Our equational specifications cannot allow two return values, although we can implement Pop as a procedure with variable parameters. The observer Top will allow us to find out the value of the item currently at the top of a stack, and it can then be removed by a Pop operation.

There is one more thing to be considered for the Pop operation. What happens if we try to pop an item off an empty stack? This situation is called *stack underflow*. If Pop does not prevent such a situation from occurring the program will crash at run-time when we try to pop an item from an empty stack. The operating system will report with a similar message to the stack overflow. We can give Pop another variable parameter, called *underflow*, which is set to TRUE if there is an attempt to pop from an empty stack, and FALSE if the stack is not empty.

```
PROCEDURE Pop(VAR s : Stack; VAR i : StackItem; VAR underflow :
BOOLEAN);
(* Pre-condition: none.
Post-condition: if s is not empty, the top item is removed and
underflow is set to FALSE. If s was empty and no item could be
popped underflow is set to TRUE. *)

BEGIN
   underflow := FALSE;
   IF NOT IsEmpty(s) THEN
      (* Stack isn't empty. *)
      WITH s DO
         i := stack[top];
         DEC(top);
      END;
   ELSE
      (* Stack is empty - can't pop. *)
      underflow := TRUE;
   END;
END Pop;
```

We have used the stack observer IsEmpty to test whether or not the stack is empty, before popping an item off it. This tests if s.top = 0.

The remaining observer of the stack abstraction, Top, returns the value of the item at the top of the stack, but does not remove that item from the stack. It is similar to Pop except that it does not move s.top. Top also has similar problems to Pop – what happens if we ask for the top item on an empty stack? Again we need a Boolean variable to indicate whether or not a stack underflow is occurring:

```
PROCEDURE Top(s : Stack; VAR i : StackItem;
                         VAR underflow : BOOLEAN);
(* Pre-condition: none.
Post-condition: if s is not empty the top item is removed and put into
i, underflow is set to FALSE. Otherwise if s is empty underflow is
set to TRUE. *)
BEGIN
   underflow := FALSE;
   IF NOT IsEmpty(s) THEN
      i := s.stack[s.top];
   ELSE
      underflow := TRUE;
   END;
END Top;
```

We have now implemented all the operations in the Stack abstraction, although we have had to alter the actions and parameters of some operations to take account of error conditions and usefulness to the user. The implementation should be done in a library module, so that the stack abstraction will be available to all programs we write. A library module will also allow us to hide the implementation of the stack and its operations from the user, so that it cannot be misused. The user will see only the definition part of the library module, which is shown in Program 5.4.

Program 5.4 Static Stack definition module

```
DEFINITION MODULE StaticStack;
(* An implementation of the Stack data abstraction, which provides
stacks of CARDINALs. The implementation is static, and stacks cannot
grow above MaxStack items. *)

(* EXPORT QUALIFIED Stack, StackItem, MaxStack, Create, Push, Pop,
Top, IsEmpty; *)

CONST
   MaxStack = 100;

TYPE
   Stack;
   StackItem = CARDINAL;

PROCEDURE Create(VAR s : Stack);
(* Pre-condition: none.
Post-condition: s is an empty stack. *)
```

```
PROCEDURE Push(VAR s: Stack; i : StackItem; VAR overflow :
   BOOLEAN);
(* Pre-condition: none.
Post-condition: if s is not full then a new item, i, is put onto the top of s,
and overflow is set to FALSE.  Otherwise if s is full overflow is set to
TRUE. *)

PROCEDURE Pop(VAR s: Stack; VAR i : StackItem; VAR     underflow :
BOOLEAN);
(* Pre-condition: none.
Post-condition: if s is not empty, the top item is removed and underflow
is set to FALSE.  If s was empty and no item could be popped underflow
is set to TRUE. *)

PROCEDURE Top(s : Stack; VAR i : StackItem; VAR underflow :
   BOOLEAN);
(* Pre-condition: none.
Post-condition: if s is not empty the top item is removed and put into i,
underflow is set to FALSE.  Otherwise if s is empty underflow is set to
TRUE. *)

PROCEDURE IsEmpty(s : Stack): BOOLEAN;
(* Pre-condition: none.
Post-condition: returns TRUE if the stack s is empty, and FALSE if it
isn't. *)

END StaticStack.
```

In the definition module we have made the Stack type opaque, to prevent the user from seeing how the type is implemented, and from accessing the type incorrectly. The implementation module must therefore contain the full type definition of Stack, which must now be a pointer to a record rather than simply a record:

```
StackRecord = RECORD
                  stack : ARRAY [1..MaxStack] OF StackItem;
                  top : [0..MaxStack];
              END;

Stack = POINTER TO StackRecord;
```

All references to the fields of the record are now incorrect. For example s.top is invalid, because s is not a record any more, it is a pointer (although it does point to a record). We have to indicate that we want to access what s points to, rather than s itself, and we do this in Modula-2 with the ^ operation. So s.top becomes s^.top, that is we want the top field of what s is pointing to. In addition we now have to ask for memory space for the record ourselves. The compiler will only reserve space for the pointer. The ALLOCATE procedure from the Storage module will do this. If we allocate space and change all such invalidated references in our procedures we obtain the implementation module shown in Program 5.5.

Program 5.5 Static Stack implementation module

```
IMPLEMENTATION MODULE StaticStack;
(* Static implementation of the stack data abstraction. *)

FROM Storage IMPORT ALLOCATE;

TYPE
   StackRecord = RECORD
                  stack : ARRAY [1..MaxStack] OF StackItem;
                  top : [0..MaxStack];
                 END;

   Stack = POINTER TO StackRecord;


PROCEDURE Create(VAR s : Stack);
(* Create could be declared as a function (in definition as well) because
functions can return pointer types and Stack is now a pointer type. We
have left it as a procedure for consistency with Push, Pop and Top. *)

VAR
   newStack : Stack;

BEGIN
   ALLOCATE(newStack, SIZE(StackRecord));
   s^.top := 0;
END Create;


PROCEDURE IsEmpty(s : Stack): BOOLEAN;

BEGIN
   RETURN s^.top = 0;
END IsEmpty;
```

```
PROCEDURE Push(VAR s : Stack; i : StackItem; VAR overflow :
   BOOLEAN);
BEGIN
   overflow := FALSE;
   WITH s^ DO
      IF top < MaxStack THEN (* Stack isn't full yet. *)
         INC(top);
         stack[top] := i;
      ELSE (* Stack is full - can't push. *)
         overflow := TRUE;
      END;
   END;
END Push;

PROCEDURE Pop(VAR s : Stack; VAR i : StackItem; VAR underflow :
   BOOLEAN);
BEGIN
   underflow := FALSE;
   WITH s^ DO
      IF NOT IsEmpty(s) THEN (* Stack isn't empty. *)
         i := stack[top];
         DEC(top);
      ELSE  (* Stack is empty - can't pop. *)
      underflow := TRUE;
      END;
   END;
END Pop;

PROCEDURE Top(s : Stack; VAR i : StackItem; VAR underflow :
   BOOLEAN);
BEGIN
   underflow := FALSE;
   IF NOT IsEmpty(s) THEN
      i := s^.stack[s^.top];
   ELSE
      underflow := TRUE;
   END;
END Top;

BEGIN
END StaticStack.
```

There are many problems with a static implementation of a stack, such as having to declare the array sufficiently large to hold the largest stack we think we might need in our program. Although we want our stack implementation to be opaque to the user it is probably a good idea to indicate that the implementation is static, and give the maximum number of items the stack can hold, otherwise the user may be expecting a dynamic implementation.

5.6 The List data abstraction

The List data abstraction is probably the single most used and most useful data abstraction of all. It is possible to use the list abstraction to implement other abstractions such as Stack and Queue. Lists are very widely used in programs and they occur all the time in the real world.

A list is a linear sequence of an arbitrary number of items.

Unlike the stack abstraction we have not said anything about how the list is accessed. There are many different versions of the List abstraction, which all vary on how the list may be accessed. We will look at two versions.

5.6.1 Specification of the List data abstraction

The first version is the classic description of a list, although not very similar to those we might meet in everyday life.

Specification 5.3 The Simple List data abstraction

Types provided: List

Other abstractions used: Item, Boolean

Operations:

```
Create: → List
Cons: List, Item → List
Head: List → Item
Tail: List → List
IsEmpty: List → Boolean
```

Axioms:

```
Tail(Create) = Create
Tail(Cons(l, i)) = l
Head(Create) = Error
Head(Cons(l, i)) = i
IsEmpty(Create) = True
IsEmpty(Cons(l, i)) = False
```

```
Where:
    l is of type List,
    i is of type Item.
```

Look closely at Specification 5.3. Does it perhaps bear more than a passing resemblance to the Stack abstraction? The Create operation of List maps directly to the Create operation of Stack, and the Cons operation is exactly the same as Push, because the new item gets put on the head of the list. Head, Tail and IsEmpty correspond to the Stack operations Top, Pop and IsEmpty respectively.

5.6.2 The Ordered List data abstraction

The lists that we meet in everyday life are usually less restrictive than the Simple List. If we write a shopping list we may go back and insert forgotten items into the middle of the list; we can look through an entire list to see what items are in it, and we are more likely to want to add items to the end of the list rather than to the top. The specification for a more general list is obviously more complicated, but it will provide us with a far more useful Ordered List abstraction.

Specification 5.4 The Ordered List data abstraction

```
Types provided: OrderedList

Operations:
    Create: → OrderedList
    Cons: OrderedList, Item → OrderedList
    Insert: OrderedList, Item → OrderedList
    Remove: OrderedList, Item → OrderedList
    Tail: OrderedList → OrderedList
    Head: OrderedList → Item
    IsEmpty: OrderedList → Boolean
    IsIn: OrderedList, Item → Boolean

Axioms:
    Insert(Create, i) = Cons(Create, i)
    Insert(Cons(l, j), i) = if Equal(i, j) then Cons(l, j)
        else if Greater(i, j) then Cons(Cons(l, j), i)
        else Cons(Insert(l, i), j)
    Remove(Create, i) = Create
    Remove(Cons(l, j), i) = if i = j then l
        else Cons(Remove(l, i), j)
    Tail(Create) = Create
    Tail(Cons(l, i)) = l
```

```
Head(Create) = Error
Head(Cons(l, i)) = i
IsEmpty(Create) = True
IsEmpty(Cons(l, i)) = False
IsIn(Create, i) = False
IsIn(Cons(l, j), i) = If i = j then True
   else IsIn(Cons(l, j), i)
```

Where:

l is of type OrderedList,
i, j are of type Item.

In Specification 5.4 we have used two operations which are not defined within the Ordered List abstraction, Greater and Equal. We will assume that these are operations of the Item abstraction, with the following syntax:

```
Greater: Item, Item → Boolean
Equal: Item, Item → Boolean
```

In general we can consider Greater(i, j) to return True if item i is greater (according to whatever definition of Greater we are using) than item j, and False if it isn't. Similarly Equal(i, j) will return True if i and j are the same, and False if they aren't.

Note that we have included the operations from the Simple List abstraction in the Ordered List. This is not strictly necessary, we could just have indicated that Simple List was to be used in defining the Ordered List abstraction

Inserting items into an Ordered List

Let's take a closer look at the Insert operation of Ordered List. If we insert an item into an empty list

```
Insert(Create, i)
```

Then the result can only be the list created by consing i to the the empty list, that is

```
Cons(Create, i).
```

There is only one item in this list, so the ordering is meaningless.

If we insert an item into a non-empty list,

```
Insert(Cons(l, j), i)
```

we now have to worry about putting i into the correct position in the list Cons(l, j). To find the correct position we have to work down the list, comparing each item with the one we wish to insert. The item will be inserted ahead of all lesser items, and behind all greater items.

First consider the situation where we want to insert the item a into the list represented by

```
Cons(Create, b),
```

that is the list with only one item, b. The insert will look like this:

```
Insert(Cons(Create, b), a)
```

We will assume that the ordering we are imposing on this list states that item a is greater than item b, and so must be inserted ahead of it in the list Cons(Create, b). The cons operation adds items to the head or front of the list, so

```
Insert(Cons(Create, b), a) = Cons(Cons(Create, b), a)
```

Now consider the case where we want to insert an item c into the list, where c is less than a. The insert operation is as follows:

```
Insert(Cons(Create, b), c)
```

This time we have to invert the order of the list, so that c becomes the tail of the list, and b becomes the head of the list, being higher in the ordering than c. Thus we have to insert c into the empty list, and then cons b onto the front of the list so created, that is

```
Insert(Cons(Create, b), c) = Cons(Insert(Create, c), b)
```

Now we need to perform the Insert(Create, c) operation, for which we have a separate axiom – inserting something into an empty list is the same as consing something onto the empty list, thus

```
Insert(Create, c) = Cons(Create, c)
```

Putting this back into the original equation:

```
Insert(Cons(Create, b), c) = Cons(Cons(Create, c), b)
```

which is the list (b, c), where b is the head of the list and (c) is the tail of the list.

A similar sequence of operations is needed for inserting into a list with more than one item already in it. It is simply a matter of unwinding the Cons operations which make up the list, and re-ordering them, so that the new item is consed into the list at the correct position.

Removing an item from an Ordered List

If we try to remove an item from the empty list, we just get the empty list again, that is

```
Remove(Create, i) = Create
```

If the list is non-empty there are two possibilities:

1. The item we want to remove is at the head of the list, so we can just return the tail of the list as the result of removing the item.

2. The item isn't at the head, so we have to look for the item in the tail of the list.

The axiom for these circumstances is

```
Remove(Cons(l, j), i) = if i = j then l
                        else Cons(Remove(l, i), j)
```

Note that we have to rebuild the list as we work our way down it, this is exactly the same as the Delete operation of the Set abstraction in Chapter 2.

Finding an item in an ordered list

The IsIn operation is not very dissimilar to the Remove operation, except that when it finds the required item it returns a Boolean TRUE, rather than deleting the value from the list!

Obviously, if we are looking for an item in an empty list it can't possibly be there, so IsIn must return False:

```
IsIn(Create, i) = False
```

If the list is non-empty we must look at each item in turn and see if it is the item we want. So, like Remove, if the item isn't at the head of the list we must look for it in the tail of the list:

```
IsIn(Cons(l, j), i)) = if i = j then True else IsIn(l, i)
```

Note that we don't need to rebuild the list as we search down it, because IsIn is only an observer, and is not changing the list in any way.

5.6.3 Implementing the Simple List data abstraction – static lists

Before we start considering a suitable representation for List, it is useful to know some of the properties of a list:

- A list can grow and shrink in size as required, depending on the number of objects in the list.

- An item in a list is accessed by traversing the list from the beginning. This is very different to accessing an array, where the nth item can be reached in one operation, whereas a list will need n operations, as the first n-1 items must be discarded first.

- It is easy to insert items into and delete items from a list, and this does not involve disturbing the other items in the list. With an array, to insert an item into the middle all the items at and after the insertion position must be moved up the array by one position to leave room for the new item. Deleting from an array causes similar problem, as some items must be moved down the array by one position.

Lists are among the simplest and most useful dynamic data structures. Many real world situations are naturally represented by lists, for example, a telephone directory is a list of names and phone numbers.

Modula-2 does not provide any built-in dynamic data structures which we could use for representing a list. Instead we will have to make do with a static list implementation using an array, similar to the static Stack implementation. Later we will show how the Modula-2 type POINTER can be used to build dynamic lists, and other dynamic data structures.

Consider the operations we need to perform for the list abstraction: Create, Cons, Head, Tail, Size, IsEmpty. All these operations must be implementable using our chosen representation type, and their implementation is highly dependent on this type. Ideally we would have used a list representation which did not involve using a static data structure like an array – remember that a static data structure has all its space allocated at compilation time, and cannot grow or shrink in size whilst the program is running. A list is really a dynamic data structure, which can grow or shrink as necessary depending on the number of items it contains – thus for a dynamic implementation of a list the Create operation is required to allocate some space for a new list (whilst the program is running), but in the static implementation the space is already allocated, so Create would seem to be superfluous.

Now consider the Cons operation, which is supposed to Cons an item onto the list. The item will be added to the top of the list – so it becomes the first item on the list. Since we are using a static data structure for the list, any implementation of Cons must first check that there is room in the array for the new item, alternatively it could be allowed to overwrite an existing item. The problem is to know when the array is full – IsEmpty should allow us to do this, as it will return FALSE when the array is full. So we can implement a safe Cons, which does not overwrite existing items in the list, if we know (i) if there is room left in the array, and (ii) where that room is.

If we tackle the first problem we must look at how IsEmpty can be implemented. There are two possibilities:

- Keep track of the last used array location.

- Initially set up the array with values which indicate that an array location is not in use.

The second possibility may be problematical because it depends on there being an obvious value of ItemType which can be used to indicate an unused array location. The first option is much easier to implement and independent of ItemType. It can be done by defining the List type to be a record containing the array storing the list items and an index value indicating the last used array location (just like the Stack representation):

```
TYPE
   List = RECORD
             items : ARRAY [1..MaxSize] OF ItemType;
             index : [0..MaxSize];
          END;
```

The Create operation for List must indicate that the list is empty, so we can simply have it store the value 0 in the index field of the record (remember that the array is indexed from 1, so a 0 in index can be used to represent an empty list). The observer IsEmpty is now trivial to implement, and just needs to check to see if index is set to 0.

```
PROCEDURE Create(VAR l : List);
(* Pre-condition: none.
Post-condition: l is an empty list. *)
BEGIN
   l.index := 0;
END Create;

PROCEDURE IsEmpty(l : List): BOOLEAN;
(* Pre-condition: none.
Post-condition: returns TRUE if l is empty, FALSE if it isn't. *)
BEGIN
   RETURN l.index = 0;
END IsEmpty;
```

The Cons operation is also relatively simple. The index field must contain the last used array location; a new item is added at location index + 1, unless the array is full (in this case index will be MaxSize).

The algorithm is:

```
if the list isn't full then
   move index to next free location in array
   store new item
otherwise
   report error
endif
```

In Modula-2:

```
PROCEDURE Cons(VAR l : List; i : ItemType);
(* Pre-condition: none.
Post-condition: item i has been added to the head of l. *)
BEGIN
   WITH l DO
      IF index < MaxSize THEN
         INC(index);
         items[index] := i;
      ELSE
         WriteString("List.Cons: Can't add, list is full.");
         WriteLn;
      END;
   END;
END Cons;
```

Head, Tail and Size are relatively trivial to implement using the array representation, once the problems of Create, Cons and IsEmpty have been solved.

```
PROCEDURE Head(l : List): ItemType;
(* Pre-condition: list is not empty.
Post-condition: returns the item at the head of l. *)
BEGIN
   IF NOT IsEmpty(l) THEN
      RETURN l.items[l.index];
   ELSE
      WriteString("List.Head: No head, list is empty.");
      HALT;
   END;
END Head;
```

Note that the implementation of Head given above will only be acceptable if ItemType is a simple, unstructured type. If ItemType is a structured type such as an array or record you will have to pass its value back via a variable parameter to Head.

```
PROCEDURE Tail(VAR l : List);
(* Pre-condition: none.
Post-condition: l has one item less (the head item). *)
BEGIN
   IF NOT IsEmpty(l) THEN
      DEC(l.index);
   END;
END Tail;
```

Tail is very simple: if the list is empty nothing needs doing, otherwise it effectively throws away the current head of the list by moving the index back one array location. There is no need to actually remove the unwanted item from the array, it will simply get overwritten later when the list grows again.

Program 5.6 gives the definition module for the implementation of the List abstraction. The implementation module will simply contain the full implementation of each list operation.

Program 5.6 List data abstraction definition module

```
DEFINITION MODULE StaticList;
(* Static implementation of the Simple List data abstraction.  This
version implements lists of INTEGERs. *)


TYPE
   ItemType = INTEGER;

   List = RECORD
             items : ARRAY [1..MaxSize] OF ItemType;
             index : [0..MaxSize];
          END;

PROCEDURE Create(VAR l : List);
(* Pre-condition: none.
Post-condition: l is an empty list. *)

PROCEDURE Cons(VAR l : List; i : ItemType);
(* Pre-condition: none.
Post-condition: item i has been added to the head of l. *)

PROCEDURE Tail(VAR l : List);
(* Pre-condition: none.
Post-condition: l has one item less (the head item). *)

PROCEDURE IsEmpty(l : List): BOOLEAN;
(* Pre-condition: none.
Post-condition: returns TRUE if l is empty, FALSE if it isn't. *)

END StaticList.
```

5.7 The Binary Tree data abstraction

Trees are an extremely important class of data structures, and are named because of the branching structure they display. Examples of trees in the real world are family tree showing ancestors and descendants and hierarchies for representing the relationships between various classes of life form. Trees are a hierarchical arrangement of items, and are always depicted upside down with the root item at the top and the remainder of the tree arranged below.

Figure 5.3 A simple tree

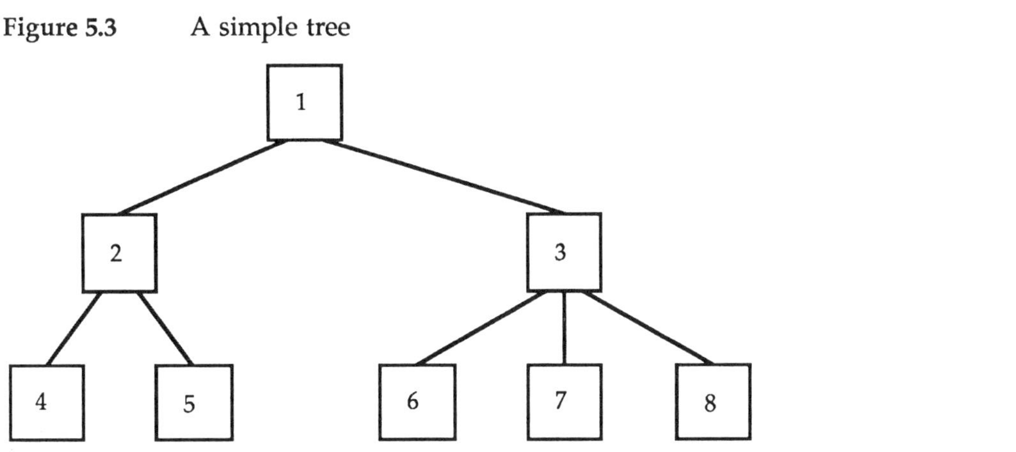

There is an entire set of words associated with tree data structures, the meanings of which are not always obvious. Figure 5.3 gives the tree which we will use to provide the examples for the following definitions:

- The points in the tree where the data is stored are called *nodes*. For example, 1, 2, 3, 4, 5, 6, 7 and 8.
- The first or top node in the tree is called the *root* node, For example, 1
- A node can have *offspring* or *descendants*, which are those nodes directly below, connected by lines to the higher node. The higher node is the *parent* node for its descendants. For example, node 2 is the parent of nodes 4 and 5, who are, in turn, the descendants of node 2.
- The lines emanating from a node, connecting it to its descendants, are called *branches*. For example, the line connecting node 3 to node 7.
- If we move down the tree, following branches from node to node we are *traversing* the tree. For example, one possible traversal is 1 to 2 to 4; another is 1 to 3 to 8.

- The nodes at the ends of all the paths down the tree, which do not have any descendants are the *leaves*. For example, 4, 5, 6, 7 and 8.
- Nodes with the same parent are called *siblings* or *brothers*. For example, 4 and 5 are brothers, so are 2 and 3, so are 6, 7 and 8.
- Each branch of the tree leads to a *subtree*, which, when looked at in isolation, consists of a root node, with further subtrees. For example, the left branch from node 1 leads to a subtree with root 2; the right branch leads to a subtree with root 3. The left branch from node 3 leads to a subtree with root 6, and no descendants.

There are many different types of tree, some variations are based on the number of descendants allowed from any node in the tree. We will be looking at a type of tree structure which only allows a maximum of two descendants from any node in the tree – this is called a *binary tree*. Figure 5.4 shows an example of a binary tree.

Figure 5.4 A simple binary tree

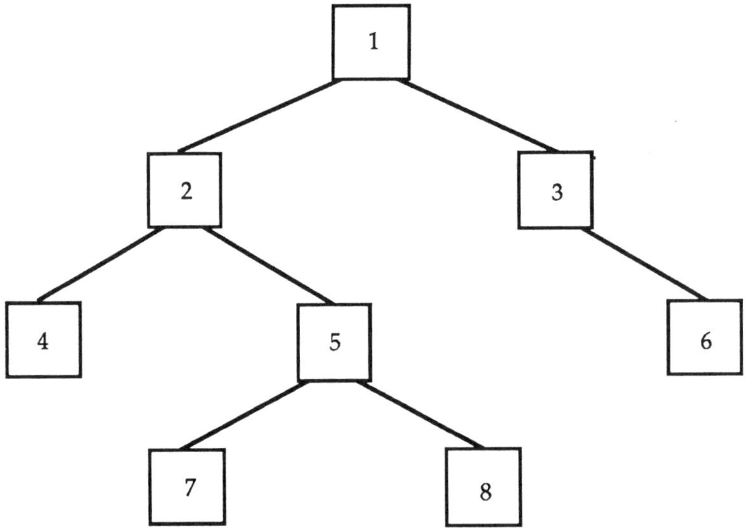

The binary tree is the simplest type of tree to implement and use, and is the basis for many more complex tree structures. The concepts involved in binary trees are similar to those for other types of tree. There are a few more words specifically for describing binary trees:

- Each descendant of a node is either a *left descendant* or a *right descendant*, for example, in Figure 5.4, 4 is a left descendant of node 2, and 5 is a right descendant.

- A subtree is either a *left subtree* or a *right subtree*. For example, the subtree with root 2 is a left subtree, and the subtree with root 3 is a right subtree.

In the simplest binary tree abstraction new nodes are always added at the root of the tree, so that the new node becomes the root. Specification 5.5 gives the operations and axioms for a simple binary tree.

Specification 5.5 The Binary Tree data abstraction

Types provided: Tree

Other abstractions used: Item, Boolean

Operations:

```
NewTree: → Tree
AddTree: Tree, Item, Tree → Tree
Root: Tree → Item
Left: Tree → Tree
Right: Tree → Tree
IsEmpty: Tree → Boolean
```

Axioms:

```
Root(NewTree) = Error
Root(AddTree(l, i, r)) = i
Left(NewTree) = NewTree
Left(AddTree(l, i, r)) = l
Right(NewTree) = NewTree
Right(AddTree(l, i, r)) = r
IsEmpty(NewTree) = True
IsEmpty(AddTree(l, i, r)) = False
```

Where:

l and r are of type Tree,
i is of type Item.

The AddTree operation is the one which puts nodes into non-empty trees. The new node must become the root, so the rest of the tree must move down to become either a left subtree or a right subtree, or be split in some other way. For example, consider the following tree:

```
AddTree(Empty, i, Empty)
```

this is a tree with one node (which must therefore be the root!). If we now want to add another node, j for example, to this tree we have several ways of building the new tree. Two possibilities would be:

```
AddTree(AddTree(Empty, i, Empty), j, Empty)
```

which gives the following tree,

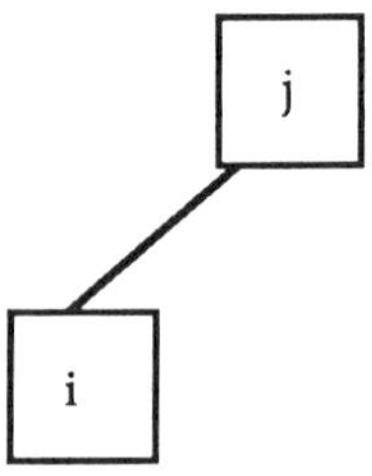

and

```
AddTree(Empty, j, AddTree(Empty, i, Empty))
```

which can be represented pictorially as

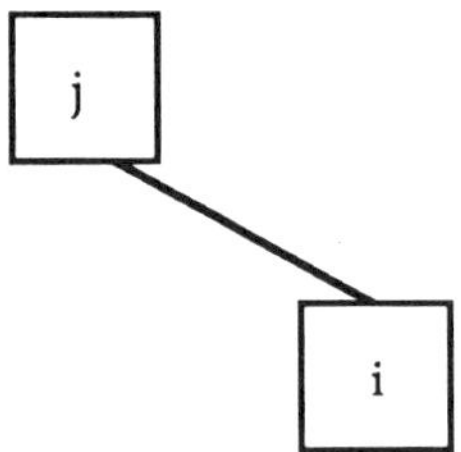

5.7.1 The Binary Search Tree data abstraction

There is another class of binary trees which are a modification of the simple binary tree we have given above, called binary search trees. The concept behind binary search trees is similar to that behind ordered lists – the nodes in the tree are ordered with respect to each other. Taking any individual node in a binary search tree, all the nodes in its left subtree will have values less than that node, and all the nodes in its right subtree will have values greater than that node.

To specify a binary search tree we need all the operations of the simple Binary Tree and five more operations, one to allow us to add a node to the correct position in a tree (not just at the root), one to allow us to remove a node from anywhere in the tree, one to allow us to search for a particular item in the tree, and one each to enable us to search through a tree for the greatest and smallest items. We will call these operations Insert, Remove, IsIn, Greatest and Smallest respectively. Specification 5.6 gives the specification for a binary search tree.

Specification 5.6 The Binary Search Tree data abstraction

```
Types provided: Tree

Other abstractions used: BinaryTree, Item

Operations:
   Insert: Tree, Item → Tree
   Remove: Tree, Item → Tree
   IsIn: Tree, Item → Boolean
   Greatest: Tree → Item
   Smallest: Tree → Item
Axioms:
   Insert(NewTree, i) = AddTree(NewTree, i, NewTree)
   Insert(AddTree(l, j, r), i) = if Equal(i, j) then AddTree(l, i, r)
      else if Less(i, j) then AddTree(Insert(l, i), j, r)
      else AddTree(l, j, Insert(r, i))
   Remove(NewTree, i) = NewTree
   Remove(AddTree(l, j, r), i) =
      if Equal(i, j) then
         if IsEmpty(l) then r
         else if IsEmpty(r) then l
         else AddTree(l, Smallest(r), Remove(r, Smallest(r)))
      else if Less(i, j) then AddTree(Remove(l, i), j, r)
      else AddTree(l, j, Remove(r, i))
   IsIn(NewTree, i) = False
   IsIn(AddTree(l, j, r), i) = if Equal(i, j) then True
      else if Less(i, j) then IsIn(l, i)
      else IsIn(r, i)
   Greatest(NewTree) = Error
   Greatest(AddTree(l, i, r)) = if IsEmpty(r) then i
      else Greatest(r)
   Smallest(NewTree) = Error
   Smallest(AddTree(l, i, r)) = if IsEmpty(l) then i
      else Smallest(l)
Where:
   i and j are of type Item
   l and r are of type Tree
```

Note how we have included the simple Binary Tree abstraction, rather than redefining all its operations within the Binary Search Tree specification. The operations Less and Equal are assumed to belong to the Item abstraction, and have the following syntax:

```
Less: Item, Item → Boolean
Equal: Item, Item → Boolean
```

where Less(i, j) = True if i is less than j, and Equal(i, j) = True if i and j are the same.

Let's take a detailed look at how binary search trees work and how these axioms represent such trees.

Inserting into a binary search tree

Consider the problem of storing the words from this sentence in a binary search tree. The words are put into the tree in the order in which they appear in the sentence. The first word, "consider" will be put into an empty tree, so the first Insert axiom will apply, that is

```
Insert(NewTree, i) = AddTree(NewTree, i, NewTree)
```

which makes "consider" the root of the tree, with empty left and right subtrees, represented by the expression

```
AddTree(NewTree, "consider", NewTree)
```

The next word can be inserted in three possible ways:

1. if it's equal to the root node, it isn't inserted at all

2. if it's alphabetically less than the root node, it is inserted to the left of the root

3. if it's alphabetically more than the root node, it is inserted to the right of the root.

The next word in the sentence is "the", which therefore gets inserted to the right of the subtree, the particular Insert axiom which applies is therefore:

```
Insert(AddTree(l, j, r), i) = AddTree(l, j, Insert(r, i))
```

where l, r = NewTree, j = "consider" and i= "the", giving the expression

```
AddTree(NewTree, "consider", Insert(NewTree, "the"))
```

Now we have to insert "the" into the empty right subtree, which is simply the first Insert axiom again:

```
Insert(NewTree, "the") = AddTree(NewTree, "the", NewTree)
```

Substituting this, we get the following expression for our tree:

```
AddTree(NewTree, "consider", AddTree(NewTree, "the",
                                              NewTree))
```

The pictorial representation of this tree is:

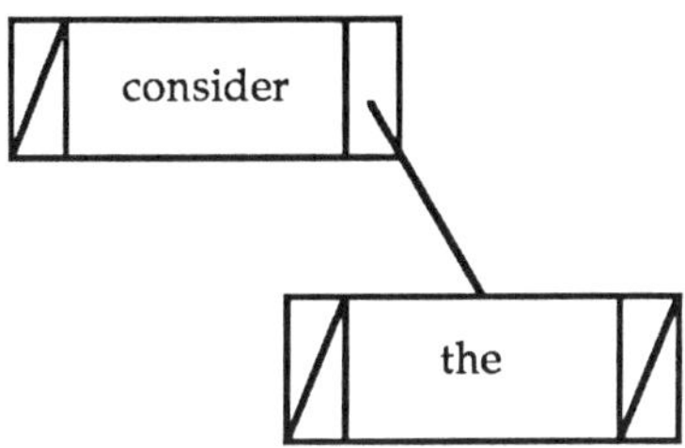

We will go through the axioms for inserting once more. The next word we have to insert is "problem", since the tree is not empty (we know it's got two words in already). The second Insert axiom must be applied first:

```
Insert(AddTree(l, j, r), i) = if Equal(i, j) then AddTree(l, i, r)
        else if Less(i, j) then AddTree(Insert(l, i), j, r)
        else AddTree(l, j, Insert(r, i))
```

The tree we are inserting into is

```
AddTree(NewTree, "consider", AddTree(NewTree, "the",
                                              NewTree))
```

so mapping this to the left hand side of the axiom, we have l = NewTree, j ="consider" and r = AddTree(NewTree, "the", NewTree).

Thus the first part of the right hand side

```
if Equal(i, j) then AddTree(l, i, r)
```

doesn't apply since "problem" is not the same as "consider". The second part of the right hand side,

```
if Less(i, j) then AddTree(Insert(l, i), j, r)
```

doesn't apply either, since "problem " is alphabetically greater than "consider". So the final part

```
AddTree(l, j, Insert(r, i)
```

must apply, which inserts the new word "problem" into the right subtree of the existing tree. Substituting the various parts of this expression we obtain the following description of the tree:

```
AddTree(NewTree, "consider", Insert(AddTree(NewTree, "the",
                                    NewTree), "problem")
```

Now we have to try to insert "problem" into the right subtree

```
Insert(AddTree(NewTree, "the", NewTree), "problem")
```

Since "problem" is alphabetically greater than "the" it must be inserted in the right subtree, which is empty,

```
AddTree(NewTree, "the", Insert(NewTree, "problem"))
```

becoming

```
AddTree(NewTree, "the", AddTree(NewTree, "problem",
                                         NewTree))
```

Substituting this back into the original tree, we obtain the following expression:

```
AddTree(NewTree, "consider", AddTree(NewTree, "the",
             AddTree(NewTree, "problem", NewTree)))
```

If you can't follow the expression here is its pictorial representation!

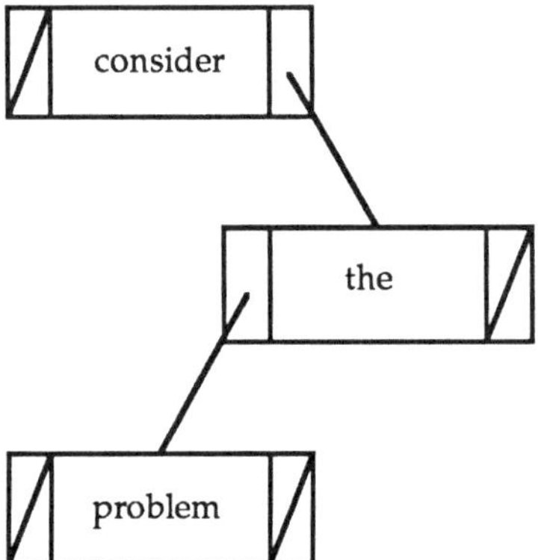

Further words are added to the tree in a similar manner, but we won't go through the axiom applications, because they are getting rather long and difficult to follow! The next word "of" is greater than "consider", so we try to insert it into the right subtree. It is less than "the", so we try to insert in the left subtree; it's less than "problem", so we try to insert into the left subtree which is empty, so "of" goes there giving the tree:

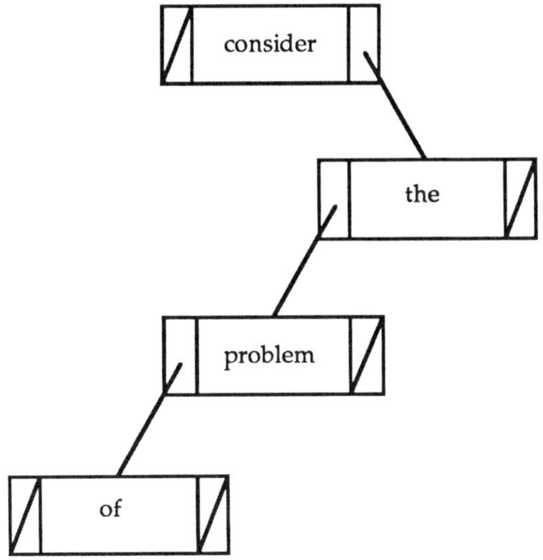

The next word, "storing" is greater than consider, less than "the" and greater than "problem", so gets inserted to the right of "problem" giving the tree:

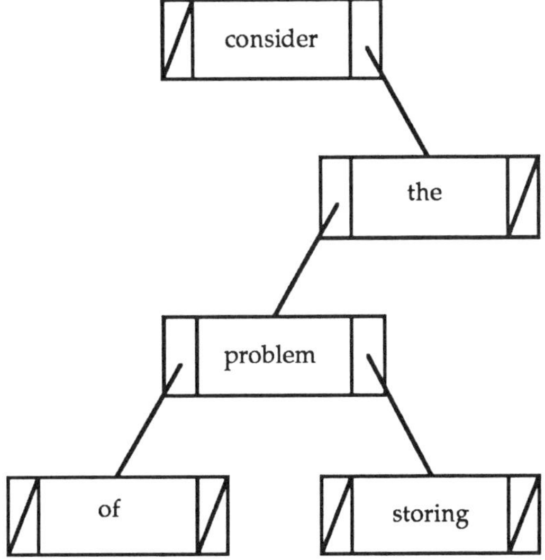

Finding items in a binary search tree

The IsIn operation is not unlike the Insert operation in the way it searches through a binary tree, although it is much simpler because it doesn't have to alter the tree in any way. Here are the IsIn axioms again:

```
IsIn(NewTree, i) = False
IsIn(AddTree(l, j, r), i) = if Equal(i, j) then True
    else if Less(i, j) then IsIn(l, i)
    else IsIn(r, i)
```

The case when the tree is empty is simple, the item can't possibly be in an empty tree, so we return False. When the tree is not empty there are three possibilities (just like Insert) for finding the item, i:

1. Item i is the root of the tree, in which case return True.

2. Item i is less than the root of the tree, so we must look for it in the left subtree.

3. Item i is greater than the root of the tree, so we must look for it in the right subtree.

For example, consider searching the tree we built in the Insert example, for the word "problem". The tree is not empty so the second axiom must apply:

```
IsIn(AddTree(l, j, r), i) = if Equal(i, j) then True
    else if Less(i, j) then IsIn(l, i)
    else IsIn(r, i)
```

First we check to see if the root is the node we are looking for. Since Equal("problem", "consider") is false, we must try the next part of the axiom. This time Less("problem", "consider") will be false too, so we must apply the final part of the axiom IsIn(r, i) where r is the right subtree with root "the", and i is the word we are looking for, that is "problem".

We apply Insert again with these parameters, and this time Less("problem", "the") will be true so we must apply IsIn to the left subtree of "the". The root of the left subtree is "problem", so Equal("problem", "problem") will return True, and the item has been found.

What happens if we try to search the tree for an item which isn't in it. Consider searching the tree for the word "with". Obviously "with" isn't at the root, so we look in the right subtree("with" > "consider"), "with" isn't at the root of this tree either (the root is "the"), so we look right again ("with" > "the"), but this subtree is empty. So the first axiom applies

```
IsIn(NewTree, i) = False
```

so "with" isn't in the tree and the axiom returns False.

Deleting from a binary search tree

The axioms for deleting from a binary search tree look rather more complicated than any we have met so far. To see why these axioms have to be complicated consider two different deletions from our sentence tree.

First, deleting the word "of"; this is easy, we just remove the node and the rest of the tree is unchanged. Now, what about deleting the word "problem"? This certainly is a problem, because the "problem" node has two subtrees, which have to remain part of the tree. The parent node of "problem", "the", can't have two left subtrees, instead we have to rearrange the tree so it looks like this:

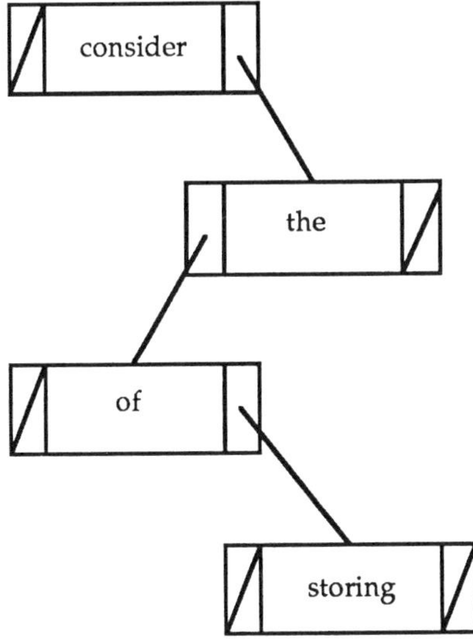

Since the Remove axioms have to perform this rearrangement it's not surprising that they are so complicated! Can you see how the rearrangement of the two subtrees of "problem" has happened?

The left subtree of "problem" has become the left subtree of "the" (it must be less than "the" because "problem" was the left subtree of "the" too). The right subtree of "problem" has become the right subtree of "of".

Let's see how the axioms provide this rearrangement. First, if the tree is empty we can just return the empty tree:

```
Remove(NewTree, i) = NewTree
```

If the item we want to remove is actually at the root of the tree there are three possibilities for removing it:

1. The right subtree is empty, so just return the left subtree, that is

   ```
   Remove(AddTree(l, i, NewTree), i) = l
   ```

2. The left subtree is empty, so just return the right subtree, that is

   ```
   Remove(AddTree(NewTree, i, r), i) = r
   ```

3. Neither subtree is empty, this case is rather more complicated. Remember that everything to the left of the root is smaller than the root itself, and everything to the right of the root is larger than the root. We have to find a node in the subtrees which has the same properties as the root we want to remove. The smallest item in the right subtree will have these properties, so we make this item the root, that is

```
Remove(AddTree(l, i, r), i) =
        AddTree(l, Smallest(r), Remove(r, Smallest(r)))
```

   Note, that if we make the smallest item in the right subtree the root, we have to remove that item from the right subtree, that is

```
Remove(r, Smallest(r))
```

Finally, if the item we want to remove isn't at the root we must try to remove it from the appropriate subtree, that is

```
Remove(AddTree(l, j, r), i) =
                if Less(i, j) then AddTree(Remove(l, i), r)
                else AddTree(l, j, Remove(r, i))
```

This gives us the complete set of axioms for Remove:

```
Remove(NewTree, i) = NewTree
Remove(AddTree(l, j, r), i) =
      if Equal(i, j) then
         if IsEmpty(l) then r
         else if IsEmpty(r) then l
         else AddTree(l, Smallest(r), Remove(r, Smallest(r)))
      else if Less(i, j) then AddTree(Remove(l, i), j, r)
      else AddTree(l, j, Remove(r, i))
```

Finding the greatest and smallest items in a tree

These are two relatively simple operations, after Insert and Remove. Bigger items are inserted to the right of the root, so if the right subtree is empty then the root node is the greatest item, otherwise we look for the greatest item in the right subtree:

```
Greatest(NewTree) = Error
Greatest(AddTree(l, i, r)) = if IsEmpty(r) then i
      else Greatest(r)
```

The smallest item is found by looking in the left subtree:

```
Smallest(NewTree) = Error
Smallest(AddTree(l, i, r)) = if IsEmpty(l) then i
      else Smallest(l)
```

Static implementation of a binary search tree

We will not consider the static implementation of any form of tree data abstraction. Hierarchical structures do not easily lend themselves to implementation using linear data representations (such as arrays), and static tree implementations are time-consuming and fiddly.

5.8 Case study – finding data representations

When we start to consider data representations for the data abstractions in a modularised problem solution, it is best to start with the lower abstractions in the abstraction hierarchy. That is, those which are dependent upon other abstractions. There are several reasons for this, but the important one for the moment is that it should allow us to build up our implementation incrementally out of library modules. We can roughly relate each abstraction in a design to a single library module, so, if we remember the rules about compilation order, library modules at the bottom of the hierarchy (those used by other library modules) must be compiled first. If we start with the lowest abstractions we can incrementally build a compilable set of library modules.

5.8.1 The Car data abstraction

In the Car Pool abstraction hierarchy the Car data abstraction is the lowest in the hierarchy, and is needed by most of the remaining abstractions. This abstraction is therefore a good place to start for considering data representations. In our design in Chapter 2 we stated that the data for a particular car in the car pool should be stored in a record structure, which we called Car (giving it the same name as the abstraction it is defined in). This record structure must allow us to access each field in the record individually, and to build up a new record from a set of appropriate information.

We will look first at whether or not Modula-2 provides any suitable data representation for Car. Modula-2 does, of course, provide its own record type, RECORD, which can be defined by the user to contain many different data objects, under one main data structure. We have already met RECORD, and seen that the use of the dot operation (such as s.top) allows us to access individual fields in a record, and the use of assignment statements allows us to build up a new record. Here is a possible representation of Car, using RECORD:

```
TYPE
   Car = RECORD
            registration : Reg;
            employeeId : Id;
            status : status;
         END;
```

Note that each field in Car must have a representation – we named these in Chapter 2, and must now consider how each of these data objects is represented.

Registration number

A car registration number is usually a mix of letters and digits, up to a maximum of seven characters (for a UK number). For example: UXE758Y, A583TGT, FAB1. We can use an array to store such a string of characters; the Modula-2 type definition for this is:

```
CONST
    MaxReg = 7;
TYPE
    Reg = ARRAY [1..MaxReg] OF CHAR;
```

Employee number

Employee numbers are often strings of digits such as 427, 031, 4173, so we will assume that the employee ids for our company are positive integers. We can restrict the possible range of integers, to catch erroneous employee ids, by using a Modula-2 subrange:

```
CONST
    MaxEmployees = 200;
TYPE
    Id = (1..MaxEmployees);
```

Thus the id numbers can run from 1 to MaxEmployees (which is 200) giving 200 possible employee ids. We can change this by altering the value of MaxEmployees.

Reservation status

We need to represent two possibilities: a reserved car and an unreserved car. We could use a Boolean value:

```
TYPE
    status = BOOLEAN;
```

We would then have to decide if TRUE represented a reserved car, and FALSE an unreserved car (or vice versa), and then use these value consistently. The representational values of TRUE and FALSE do not have any definitive connection with the values we wish to represent, "Reserved" and "Unreserved". Modula-2 provides us with the enumeration type for defining a type with only a small, set number of values:

```
TYPE
    status = (Reserved, Unreserved);
```

Now the names of the values of the type mean that mistakes in usage are less likely. There is also an added bonus in an enumeration representation – if we want to represent the third possibility, UnderRepair, say, we can simply add it to the type:

```
TYPE
    status = (Reserved, Unreserved, UnderRepair);
```

We could not extend a Boolean representation to cope with a third possibility.

Suitability of representation for Car

It is quite possible that the chosen representation is not easily usable. To avoid running into problems at the implementation stage we need to look in some detail at how this representation will work in our implementation.

First we will look at accessing and updating the data representation. The access operations provided by the Car abstraction, GetReg, GetId and GetStatus are designed to allow us to access each individual slot in a car record. At this stage we are not interested in the detailed implementation of these operations, only in seeing if their implementation is feasible. As we know, Modula-2 allows us to access a field in a record by the syntax <record-name>.<field-name>, so it is clearly possible to implement GetReg, GetId and GetStatus using this method. Similarly we can implement PutReg, PutId, and PutStatus, using the method provided by the language.

GetReg etc. could be looked upon as superfluous, since Modula-2 provides the facilities to access and/or update a field in a record directly, without the need for us to write our own access operation. Instead of the call:

```
newid := GetId(car1);
```

we use

```
newid := car1.id;
```

Are there any good reasons for keeping the operations given in the Car abstraction? Consider the possibility that we decide to alter the representation for car records after implementing the whole reservation system.

1. If our implementation is using the Modula-2 access operations for a car record, every one of these operations must be changed as they are specifically for accessing the Modula-2 RECORD representation of Car.

2. If our implementation is using the operations GetReg, etc., for accessing the records, all that needs to be changed is the implementation of the Car abstraction itself – no other code will need altering.

Obviously, situation 2 is highly desirable, and situation 1 needs to be avoided if possible. We should therefore use the operations from Car, as they provide a level of abstraction above specific representational details, which will allow later modifications to be localised.

There is some overhead in the record representation, which arises when a car's status is Unreserved thus making the employeeId field unnecessary. Space will still be reserved for employeeId in each record, even though it will be unused in some cases. We will assume that this storage overhead is acceptable.

A record of type Car can have its field accessed at any time, even before they have been set up by the BuildCarRec operation. This happens because a variable in Modula-2 exists as soon as it is declared in a VAR statement. Such a variable is certain to contain rubbish as soon as it is declared, and there is no means of making the act of declaration produce an empty variable of the appropriate type. It is up to the programmer to ensure that a variable is not used before the appropriate value (or values) have been assigned to it.

5.8.2 The CarPool data abstraction

Determining the representation type for CarPool is very simple – in fact we decided in Chapter 2 that a car pool may be represented by a list of car records, although we had only seen an informal description of a list at this point.

```
TYPE CarPool = List;
```

We must remember however that our list needs to be a list of Car records. We will see why later on.

Suitability of representation for CarPool

The operations of the CarPool abstraction (defined in Chapter 2) are:

- NewCarPool – Create a new, empty car pool.
- AddCar – Put a car into the car pool.
- RemoveCar – Remove a particular car from the car pool.
- IsCarPoolEmpty – True if the car pool has no cars in it, false otherwise.
- FindCar – Find a particular car in the car pool.

These operations will only map into the List abstraction if our implementation of List is tailored to items of type Car. AddCar will map directly into Cons if this is the case, but the other operations are more complicated. FindCar could be implemented using Head and Tail operations to search through a list until the correct record is found. RemoveCar also needs to use Head and Tail, and IsCarPoolEmpty maps directly onto the list IsEmpty operation. Actually, CarPool will map even more easily onto the OrderedList data abstraction – try for yourself!

If we had found that the List abstraction would not be a suitable representation type for the CarPool, we would have had to go back and try to find another abstraction or group of abstractions which might be suitable. In fact, we would probably need to go back and re-modularise all or part of our problem solution. This is an important point to remember – software engineering and problem solving are not strictly top-down. You cannot always work from the highest level of abstraction down to the lowest level, which provides the implementation of the problem solution, in one attempt. It is frequently necessary to backtrack when design choices which seemed sensible at the beginning start to cause problems later on in the design. Each individual step in the design may be top-down, but designing one step may cause you to go back and redesign an earlier step. If the problem to be solved is large, or if the problem solver is a novice, backtracking is more likely to be necessary.

Summary

Data abstractions must be turned into concrete implementations in a programming language if we are to use them in our programs. The built-in data types of Modula-2, such as INTEGER, REAL etc, are implemented data abstractions. We use them without any knowledge of implementation details.

Library modules provide the means to separate the specification of a data abstraction from its implementation so the user has sufficient details to use the abstractions but not to alter it. For complete abstraction when using library modules the types of the abstraction must be declared as opaque in the definition module. This means only giving the name of the type, and hiding its representation in the implementation module where the user of the abstraction cannot see it.

In Modula-2, opaque types must be declared using type constructor POINTER TO, and the implementor of the type must handle all the storage allocation and deallocation for variables of the type.

To implement a data abstraction in we must choose a representation for the data objects described by the abstraction. Most programming languages provide a number of built-in data types and allow the user to build new data representations out of combinations of existing types. When choosing a data representation for a data abstraction the following questions must be raised and answered:

- Does the target programming language provide a suitable type? Can we use another programming language which does? Is the representation suitable for the abstractions' operations? Can the data be accessed and altered easily?

The so-called *standard* data abstractions include: stacks, queues, lists and trees.

A stack is a linear ordered collection of items, where new items can be inserted and items can be removed from the top of the stack. The newest item in a stack will be the first to be removed. The stack is an example of a last-in, first-out data structure.

A queue is a linear ordered collection of items, where items are inserted at the rear of the queue, and items are removed from the other end, the front of the queue. This is an example of a first-in, first-out data structure, and is often called a *fair data structure.*

A list is a linear sequence of items. Some types of list have their items ordered on some criterion. Access to a simple list is allowed only at one end (rather like the stack). Access to an ordered list is allowed at any point within the list.

Trees are a hierarchical arrangement of items. The points of a tree where data is stored are called nodes. Each node may have a number of descendants. A binary tree is a restricted tree where each node may have a maximum of two descendants.

Selected reading

Harrison, R
Abstract data types in Modula-2
J. Wiley and Sons, 1989
Very useful for the large number of equationally specified abstractions it contains.

Lins, C
Modula-2 software component library, Volumes 1, 2, and 3
Springer-Verlag, 1989
Enormous number of specifications and implementations of data abstractions.

6 Implementing dynamic data structures

6.1 The need for dynamic data structures

As we saw in Chapter 5, using static data structures, such as Modula-2 arrays, sets and records, is often inappropriate. Static data structures, by their very nature, cannot change in size to meet the demands of varying amounts of data – the maximum memory required for each static data structure is allocated and fixed at compilation time. So they may waste large amounts of memory when far larger than is necessary for the required data. Conversely, they may fail to be sufficiently large if the data is larger than the programmer realised.

Most of the data abstractions we have met so far have been dynamic in nature. For example, the company car pool should be able to change in size as cars are added to it or removed from it. The stack and list abstractions are also dynamic; their specifications make no mention of the number or size of the items allowed in stacks or lists, but we have been forced to impose restrictions when we chose their data representations to be static.

Ideally, we would like to remove all restrictions on maximum (and minimum) size of such data abstractions, and dynamic data structures give us the means to do just this. However, it is worth remembering that even dynamic data structures will be limited by the size of the memory available on the computer.

6.2 Dynamic storage allocation

We have already used dynamic storage allocation when implementing data abstractions with opaque types. Remember that an opaque type in Modula-2 must always be implemented as a pointer to some other type. So an opaque record type will be declared as:

```
TYPE
   MyRecord;
```

in the definition module, and as

```
TYPE
   MyRecord = POINTER TO RECORD
                            field1 : CARDINAL;
                            field2 : REAL;
                         END;
```

in the corresponding implementation module.

It is worth dwelling again on why this is so. When we compile a module which imports an opaque type from some library module, the compiler only looks at the library module's interface to the outside world – the definition module. The definition module contains only the name of the opaque type, and does not provide any information on how this type is represented. Thus the compiler is unable to allocate memory space for variables of the opaque type. In such circumstances the compiler assumes that the type is declared as a pointer type – it *knows* how much memory a single pointer takes up (usually one word) and so allocates this amount for each variable of the opaque type. When we compile a library module whose definition part contains an opaque type declaration the compiler insists that the type is declared in the implementation part as a pointer type.

In fact, in some implementations of Modula-2, an opaque type does not have to be a pointer type, and can instead be any type which fits into a single word of memory. For example, a CARDINAL or an INTEGER. However, most implementations stick to the pointer type rule. A simple experiment with the opaque counter described in Chapter 5 will show you what your implementation of Modula-2 will accept, if you cannot find it documented.

Opaque type variables have their memory allocated dynamically by the ALLOCATE procedure (in the Storage library module). The programmer of an abstraction containing opaque types must always provide an initialisation operation, such as the Initialise operation of the Counter abstraction, which must use ALLOCATE to allocate the required amount of memory. For example, given our record type

MyRecord, we can allocate memory for a variable, *rec* say, of this type, by the following call:

```
ALLOCATE(rec, SIZE(MyRecord));
```

Remember that the SIZE function passes ALLOCATE the number of bytes to be allocated for rec.

All dynamic data structures must have their memory allocated by a call to the ALLOCATE procedure. Remember that dynamic data structures are meant to grow and shrink in size. ALLOCATE allows us to ask for more memory when we want a structure to grow, but we also need to use the procedure DEALLOCATE (also found in Storage) to *free* memory when the data structure shrinks in size.

We can assume that an area of memory is reserved for use by all the dynamic data structures in a program. This area is often called the *heap*. Calls to ALLOCATE take appropriate sized chunks of memory from the heap, decreasing the memory available for dynamic data allocation. Eventually we will run out of memory and then even our dynamic data structures will be unable to grow any larger. To avoid this it is important to return chunks of memory that are no longer needed by a dynamic data structure to the heap, so that they can be reused. This is exactly what the DEALLOCATE procedure does.

6.2.1 How to make a data structure dynamic

In many cases it is impossible to know when writing a program, the size of the data which the program will be expected to handle when it is run. An unsatisfactory solution is for the programmer to try and guess the maximum size of data and ensure that all appropriate data structures are declared large enough to cope with this. This is unsatisfactory, firstly because it wastes a great deal of space if the data subsequently turns out to be much smaller than allowed for, and secondly because it is always possible for the data to be larger than was allowed for by the programmer.

For those situations where we are unsure of the sizes of expected data we can use *dynamic data structures*. Dynamic data structures can grow and shrink in size to store as much or as little data as is required. The very nature of dynamic data structures suggests that we cannot know when we write our programs, how much data is to be stored in them, and so the compiler cannot allocate memory space for dynamic variables. Instead the programmer must deal with allocating space for such variables.

A static data structure, such as an array or record, has its elements stored in memory adjacent to each other, giving a wonderfully simple method of accessing each element, because if we know the address of the memory location where the data structure starts, and we know the size of the elements in the data structure, we can calculate the address of any element. Let's look at an example of this. Consider the following record type declaration.

```
TYPE
   Various = RECORD
                number : CARDINAL;
                character : CHAR;
                chars : ARRAY [1..5] OF CHAR;
             END;
```

Modula-2 records are static data structures, and it is impossible to change the number or types of the fields in a record whilst the program is running. Assuming we have a variable of type Various, at compilation time the compiler works out how much memory space is needed for the record variable. The storage space required for any particular type depends on the processor on which you are running Modula-2. For a standard 16-bit processor, such as in an IBM PC or similar, the sizes of the record fields will be as follows:

number (CARDINAL) = 2 bytes
character (CHAR) = 1 byte
chars (ARRAY [1..5] OF CHAR) = 5 bytes

Note that the array takes n times the size of a single location, where n is the number of locations in the array. So variable chars takes 5 * 1 byte. The total storage needed for a variable of type Various is the sum of the storage required for its fields, that is 8 bytes.

Knowing the starting address, if we want to get the CARDINAL value we look at the two bytes at starting-address and starting-address + 1. If we want to reach the second character in the array we look at the byte at starting-address + 4. Of course, all this is totally transparent to the programmer, because it is handled by the Modula-2 compiler and run-time system.

Accessing a static data structure therefore depends entirely on the fact that the structure is allocated adjacent memory locations. A dynamic data structure, on the other hand, will not necessarily be allocated adjacent memory locations, in fact this is highly unlikely to be the case. Dynamic data structures need to be able to make use of non-contiguous memory locations, to enable them to grow in size when necessary. If this is the case, we cannot use the previous method of adding appropriate offsets to the starting address of the data structure, to access a particular element. What is needed is for each element of the data structure to contain the address of the next element, as well as the data it is meant to store.

We therefore end up with a structure spread out across the available memory, with each element linked to the next one by a pointer (remember that pointers are the high-level abstraction of memory addresses in Modula-2).

To build such a dynamic data structure, we need to allocate storage space for each new element of the structure. This new element must then be linked into the appropriate place in the data structure (not necessarily at the end of the structure, as we will see).

These are the requirements for all dynamic data structures. In the following sections we will see how dynamic data structures can be implemented in Modula-2.

6.3 Dynamic List implementation

In Chapter 5 we saw the formal specification of the List data abstraction. A list is conceptually a dynamic data structure, growing in size as elements are added and shrinking again as they are removed. It would therefore seem natural to implement a list as a dynamic data structure.

First we need to consider how we are going to represent a list. Remember that each element in a dynamic data structure must store both the required data and a pointer to the next element in the data structure. We therefore need to store two things of differing types in one data item. A record would seem to be the obvious choice for this task. At this point it is worth mentioning a convention used when discussing dynamic data structures – because an element of a dynamic data structure contains an extra piece of information (a pointer to the next element) we call it a *node* of the data structure.

Consider the following representation for a node in a list:

```
TYPE
   List = POINTER TO ListNode;

   ListNode = RECORD
                 item : ListItem;
                 next : List;
              END;
```

This may look somewhat strange at first glance! However it does represent our English description of a dynamic data structure, where each node, of type ListNode in this case, has a pointer to the next node in the structure.

The data representation we choose for any data abstraction should, as far as possible, aid in the implementation of the abstraction's operations, and assist data hiding. List can be declared as an opaque type and variables of type List can be returned by functions in any version of Modula-2. It is also going to be simple to represent an empty list, we just set the list pointer (of type List) to NIL. So Create will look like this:

```
PROCEDURE Create(): List;
(* Pre-condition: none.
Post-condition: returns a new, empty list. *)
BEGIN
   RETURN NIL;
END Create;
```

The IsEmpty procedure is now:

```
PROCEDURE IsEmpty(l : List): BOOLEAN;
(* Pre-condition: none.
Post-condition: returns TRUE if l is empty, FALSE if it isn't. *)

BEGIN
   RETURN l = Create();
END IsEmpty;
```

Now let's look at the basic Cons operation, remembering that the Insert operation is defined in terms of Cons in the specification.

Figure 6.1 shows a non-empty list with three nodes, and we will consider adding an item to the head of this list.

Figure 6.1 A simple list

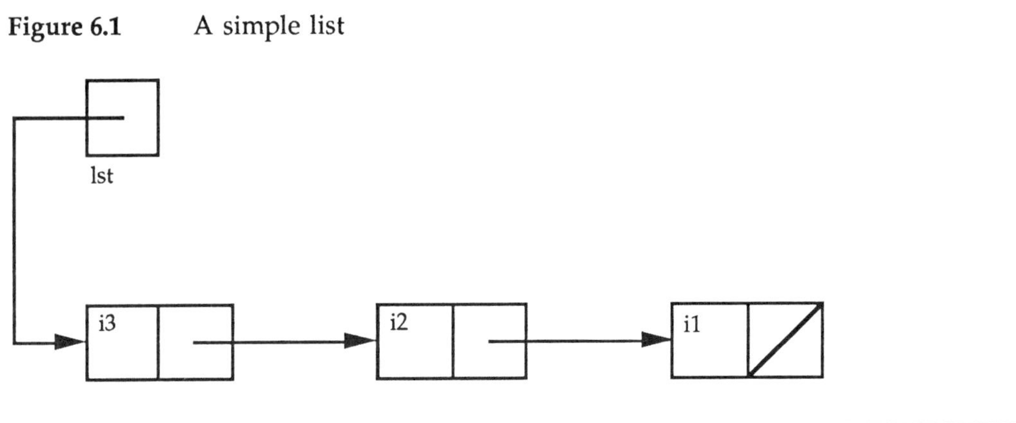

We could use the old list pointer and alter it to point to the new head of the list (which will be newNode) but doing this would make our implementation have the side effect of changing the original list. Since side effects should be avoided as far as possible we get round the problem by using a new list pointer.

The new pointer, tempL, is set to point to newNode, which itself points to the old head of the list.

Figure 6.2 shows how the list will look after the addition of the new node, i4. Note that the original list, with list pointer lst, is unchanged and we have a new list pointer tempL to point to the new node, which in turn points to the old head node in the list.

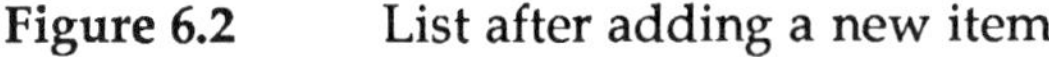

Figure 6.2 List after adding a new item

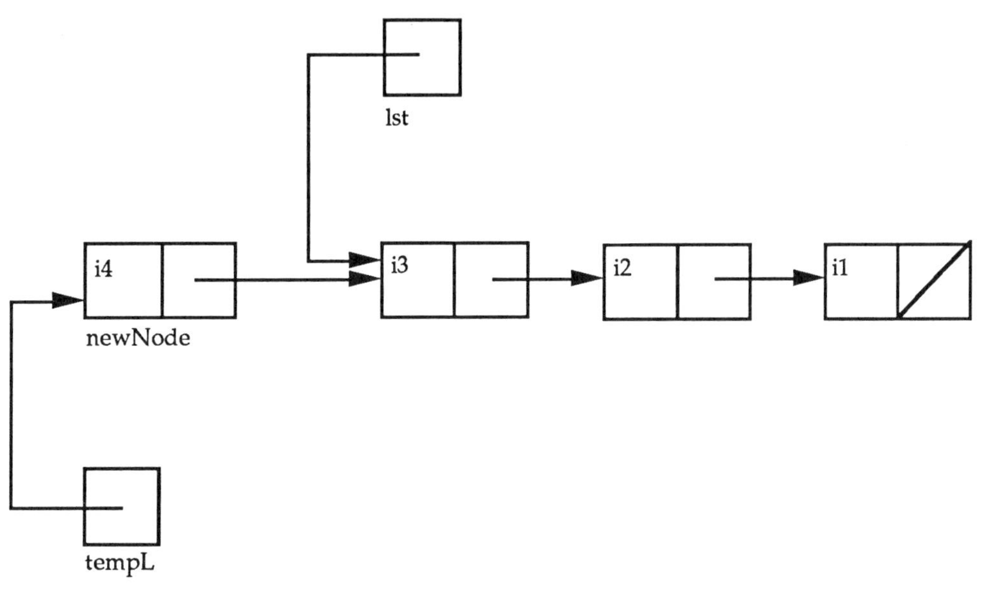

The algorithm for the Cons operation can be written as follows:

```
Allocate space for the new list node
Store the data item in the node
Set the node's next pointer to point to the head of the original list
Return the new list
```

The Modula-2 implementation of Cons is quite simple:

```
PROCEDURE Cons(l : List; i : ListItem): List;
(* Pre-condition: none.
Post-condition: returns list l with item i added to the head. *)
VAR
    tempL : List;

BEGIN
    (* First we must allocate space for the whole list node. *)
    ALLOCATE(tempL, SIZE(ListNode));

    (* Now store i in the node. *)
    tempL^.item := i;
```

```
        (*Set up the node's next pointer to point to the head of the
        original list, and then return this node, so we are returning
        a new list with the new node at the head. *)
        tempL^.next := l;
        RETURN tempL;
    END Cons;
```

The Tail operation must return the list minus its head item. It's so simple we'll go straight to the Modula-2 function:

```
    PROCEDURE Tail(l : List): List;
    (* Pre-condition: none.
    Post-condition: returns the tail of l. *)

    BEGIN
        IF IsEmpty(l) THEN
            WriteString("Error - Tail of empty list");
            HALT;
        ELSE
            RETURN l^.next;
        END;
    END Tail;
```

Similarly, the Head operation:

```
    PROCEDURE Head(l : List): ListItem;
    (* Pre-condition: l is not empty.
    Post-condition: returns the item at the head of the list. *)

    BEGIN
        IF IsEmpty(l) THEN
            WriteString("Error - Head of empty list");
            HALT;
        ELSE
            RETURN l^.item;
        END;
    END Head;
```

The extra operations required for implementing the Ordered List data abstraction (given in Chapter 5) are Insert, which inserts an item at any position in the list, Remove which removes an item from anywhere in the list, and IsIn which searches for a given item in the list.

The Insert operation is defined in terms of Cons and Create, and follows the axiom very closely.

The algorithm for Insert is:

```
If the list is empty then
   make the item the head of the list

otherwise (the list is non-empty)
   if the item is the same as the head of the list then
      just return the original list

   otherwise if the item is greater than the head of the list
      make the item the new head of the list

   otherwise
      try to insert the item in the tail of the list
   endif
endif
```

and in Modula-2:

```
PROCEDURE Insert(l : List; i : ListItem): List;
(* Pre-condition: item i is not in the list.
Post-condition: returns list l with item i inserted into the correct
position in the list. *)

BEGIN
   IF IsEmpty(l) THEN
      RETURN Cons(Create(), i);
   ELSE

      (* List is non-empty. *)
      IF Equal(Head(l), i) THEN
         (* Already in list - don't add it. *)
         RETURN l;

      ELSIF Greater(i, Head(l)) THEN
         RETURN Cons(l, i);
      ELSE
         RETURN Cons(Insert(Tail(l), i), Head(l));
      END;
   END;
END Insert;
```

The Remove operation is also implemented in terms of Cons and Create,

```
If the list is empty then
   return the empty list again
otherwise if the item is at the head of the list then
   return the tail of the list
otherwise
   try to remove the item from the tail of the list
endif
```

and in Modula-2:

```
PROCEDURE Remove(l : List; i : ListItem): List;
(* Pre-condition: item i is in the list.
Post-condition: returns list l with item i removed from it. *)

BEGIN
   IF IsEmpty(l) THEN
      RETURN l;
   ELSE
      IF Equal(Head(l), i) THEN
         RETURN Tail(l);
      ELSE
         RETURN Cons(Remove(Tail(l), i), Head(l));
      END;
   END;
END Remove;
```

The final operation of OrderedList is IsIn.

The algorithm for IsIn is:

```
if the list is empty then
   return false
otherwise if the item is at the head of the list then
   return true
otherwise
   look for the item in the tail of the list
endif
```

In Modula-2:

```
PROCEDURE IsIn(l : List; i : ListItem): BOOLEAN;
(* Pre-condition: none.
Post-condition: returns TRUE if i is in l, FALSE if it isn't. *)
BEGIN
   IF IsEmpty(l) THEN
      RETURN FALSE;
   ELSE
      IF Equal(Head(l), i) THEN
         RETURN TRUE;
      ELSE
         RETURN IsIn(Tail(l), i);
      END;
   END;
END IsIn;
```

Note how only the simple List operations, Create, Cons, Head, and Tail need to deal with the underlying data representation of the list. The Insert, Remove and IsIn operations are all defined in terms of Create, Cons, Head, Tail and IsEmpty. Operations such as Insert, Remove and IsIn are *higher-level operations* of the List abstraction, because they can be implemented with only the basic operations of the List abstraction.

Bear in mind that the implementation of Remove does not free the memory used by an unwanted node. In the next section we will implement a remove operation for the Queue abstraction showing how we free the memory used by an unwanted queue node.

Program 6.1 gives the definition module for the dynamic List implementation.

Program 6.1 Definition module for dynamic List implementation

```
DEFINITION MODULE DynamicList;
(* Dynamic implementation of the Ordered List abstraction. This version
builds list of characters. *)

TYPE
   ListItem = CHAR
   List;

PROCEDURE Create(): List;
(* Pre-condition: none.
Post-condition: returns a new, empty list. *)
```

```
PROCEDURE Cons(l : List; i: ListItem): List;
(* Pre-condition: none.
Post-condition: returns list l with item i added to the head. *)

PROCEDURE Head(l : List): ListItem;
(* Pre-condition: l is not empty.
Post-condition: returns the item at the head of the list. *)

PROCEDURE Tail(l : List): List;
(* Pre-condition: none.
Post-condition: returns the tail of l. *)

PROCEDURE IsEmpty(l : List): BOOLEAN;
(* Pre-condition: none.
Post-condition: returns TRUE if l is empty, FALSE if it isn't. *)

PROCEDURE Insert(l : List; i : ListItem): List;
(* Pre-condition: item i is not in the list.
Post-condition: returns list l with item i inserted into the correct position
in the list. *)

PROCEDURE Remove(l : List; i : ListItem): List;
(* Pre-condition: item i is in the list.
Post-condition: returns list l with item i removed from it. *)

PROCEDURE IsIn(l : List; i : ListItem): BOOLEAN;
(* Pre-condition: none.
Post-condition: returns TRUE if i is in l, FALSE if it isn't. *)

END DynamicList.
```

The implementation module for the dynamic List implementation must contain the full type declaration for List, and full implementations for each List operation, as well as the two comparison operations Equal and Greater for comparing two list items.

6.4 Dynamic Queue implementation

We saw the formal specification of the Queue back in Chapter 2. Just like the List, the Queue is a naturally dynamic data structure, growing in size as items are added to one end and shrinking again as they are removed from the other.

Bearing in mind that we would like Queue to be dynamic, we need a representation similar to the dynamic list, linking nodes in the queue by pointers. Consider the following representation for a node in the queue:

```
TYPE
  QueueNode = RECORD
                element : CHAR;
                next : POINTER TO QueueNode;
              END;
```

The type QueueNode only defines a single node in a queue. The queue itself consists of a number of such nodes, where two of these nodes have special importance – the node at the front where items are removed from the queue, and the node at the rear where items are added to the queue. A data representation for a whole queue (rather than a single node) could therefore consist of a record containing a pointer to the front node in the queue and a pointer to the rear node in the queue. Since each node is individually defined as having a pointer to the next node in the queue, this will describe a complete queue. In Modula-2 we can define a queue as follows:

```
Queue = RECORD
          front : POINTER TO QueueNode;
          rear : POINTER TO QueueNode;
        END;
```

Where the declaration of type QueueNode is the same as given previously. Figure 6.3 shows a pictorial description of this queue representation.

Figure 6.3 A simple queue representation

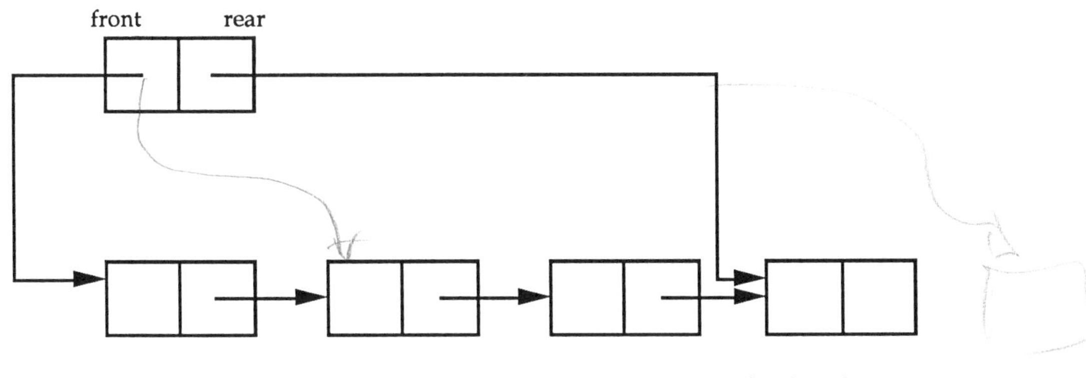

Is this representation for Queue sufficient? If we want to have the Queue type declared as opaque in the definition module when we implement it then the representation isn't sufficient. Opaque types have to be POINTER TO some type, so we have to declare Queue as:

```
Queue = POINTER TO RECORD
                     front : POINTER TO QueueNode;
                     rear : POINTER TO QueueNode;
                   END;
```

We can make this declaration of Queue look a lot tidier if we declare a type for the record and then make Queue a pointer to this type. Here is the complete declaration of the the Queue data representation, using all the above points:

```
TYPE
   QueuePtr = POINTER TO QueueNode;

   QueueNode = RECORD
                 item : QueueItem;
                 next : QueuePtr;
               END;

   QueueSentinel = RECORD
                     front : QueuePtr;
                     rear : QueuePtr;
                   END;

   Queue = POINTER TO QueueSentinel;
```

Note that we have also given a type name to the pointers which point to queue nodes (QueuePtr).

This representation for a queue gives easy access to the front of the queue for the FrontQ operation and to the rear of the queue for the AddQ operation. It is also going to be simple to represent an empty queue – the front and rear pointers can be set to NIL in these circumstances.

We will start by implementing the NewQ constructor which must return a new, empty queue. We have just said how an empty queue may be described in this data representation, so the operation is very simple:

```
PROCEDURE NewQ(): Queue;
(* Pre-condition: none.
Post-condition: returns a new, empty queue. *)
VAR
   tempQ : Queue;
BEGIN
   ALLOCATE(tempQ, SIZE(QueueSentinel));
   tempQ^.front := NIL;
   tempQ^.rear := NIL;
   RETURN tempQ;
END NewQ;
```

In order to return an empty queue NewQ must allocate storage space for the record containing the front and rear queue pointers (of type QueueSentinel), which is why we need the call to ALLOCATE. Once we have allocated space we can set the two pointers to NIL, indicating that the queue is empty.

The next best operation to implement is invariably the IsEmptyQ operation – we can tell if a queue is empty if either the front pointer is NIL:

```
PROCEDURE IsEmptyQ(q : Queue): BOOLEAN;
(* Pre-condition: none.
Post-condition: returns TRUE if q is empty, FALSE if it isn't. *)
BEGIN
   RETURN q^.front = NIL;
END IsEmptyQ;
```

Alternatively, we could test for the rear pointer being NIL.

Now let's consider the more complicated operations, starting with the constructor AddQ, which must add an item to the rear of the queue. Putting it simply, AddQ must create a new node for the item, and make this node the last node in the queue. We will give the algorithm and implementation of AddQ and then discuss this implementation.

```
Allocate space for new queue node
Allocate space for new queue sentinel node.
Set new queue node next pointer to point to previous rear node.
Set new queue sentinel to point to current front node and new rear
node.
Return new queue sentinel.
```

The Modula-2 implementation is:

```
PROCEDURE AddQ(q : Queue; i : QueueItem): Queue;

(* Pre-condition: none.
Post-condition: returns the queue formed by adding i to the
rear of q. *)

VAR
   tempQ : Queue;
   newNode : QueuePtr;

BEGIN
   ALLOCATE(newNode, SIZE(QueueNode));
   newNode^.item := i;
   newNode^.next := NIL;

   ALLOCATE(tempQ, SIZE(QueueSentinel));
   IF NOT IsEmptyQ(q) THEN

      q^.rear^.next := newNode;
      tempQ^.front := q^.front;
   ELSE

      (* The queue is empty. *)
      tempQ^.front := newNode;
   END;

   tempQ^.rear := newNode;

   RETURN tempQ;
END AddQ;
```

Figure 6.4 shows a typical queue containing three items,

Figure 6.4 A simple queue

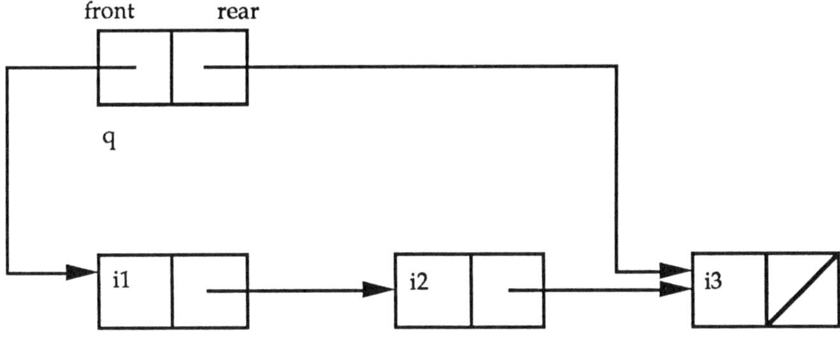

Variable q points to the node containing pointers to the front and rear of the queue. Item i3 is at the rear of the queue and must have been the most recently added; item i1 is at the front of the queue and must be the oldest item in the queue.

Our implementation first creates a new queue node, newNode, stores the appropriate data item in it and sets its next pointer to NIL.

As before with the implementation of the List abstraction, the Queue operations should be as side effect free as possible. This leads to a similar form of adding nodes, where we create a new sentinel node, tempQ, and leave the old queue sentinel alone.

The new sentinel, tempQ, is set to point to the front of the queue (which is unchanged) and the new queue node, newNode. If the old rear node, i3, is made to point to newNode we then have the scenario shown in Figure 6.5.

Figure 6.5 Queue after adding an item

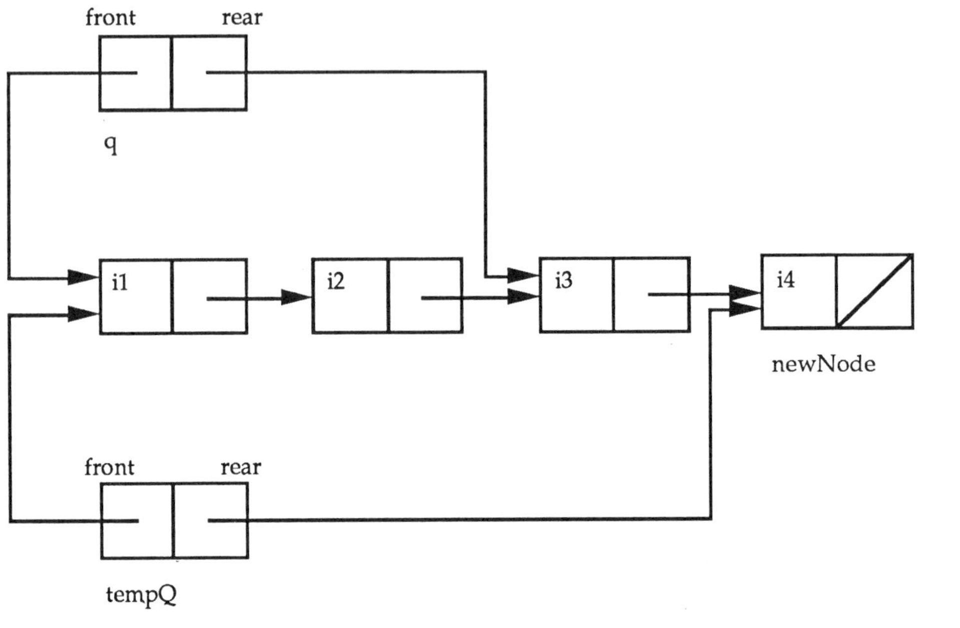

Note that the original queue, q, is completely unaffected by the addition of a new queue node, and the queue we return, tempQ, is effectively sharing nodes i1 to i3 with the original queue.

Now consider the implementation of the modifier RearQ, which, given a queue, returns the queue formed removing the front item from the original queue. We can use a similar approach to AddQ, when it comes to avoiding side-effects and can leave the original queue intact.

As before we create a new queue sentinel, tempQ, which is set to point to the rear of the original queue, q, and to the new front of the queue.

Figure 6.6 gives the scenario we want to implement in RearQ.

Figure 6.6 Queue after removing an item

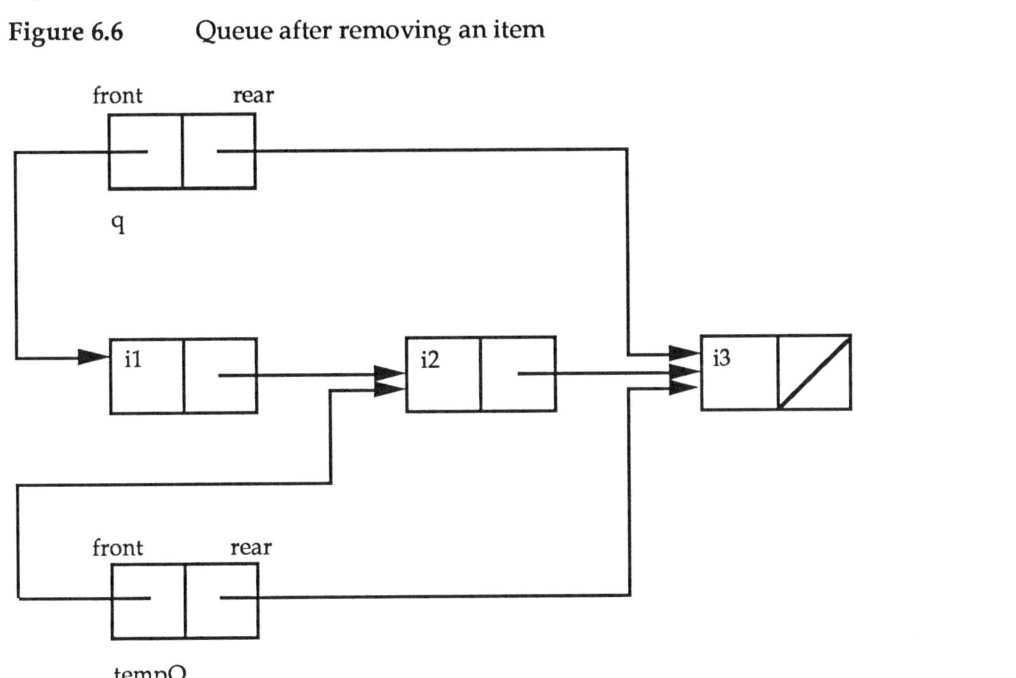

The new front of the queue will be the node behind the front of the original queue. If we return tempQ we are returning the rear of the original queue, as required, and the original queue has not been affected in any way.

Modelling this in the implementation, here is a simple algorithm for RearQ:

```
If the queue is empty then
   print out error message and halt
Otherwise
   If the queue has only one item then
      return the empty queue
   otherwise
      set up a new queue sentinel
      make sentinel point to rear of original queue and node
      next to front node
   endif
   return new queue sentinel
endif
```

In Modula-2, we have

```
PROCEDURE RearQ(q : Queue): Queue;
(* Pre-condition: the queue is non-empty.
Post-condition: returns the queue formed by taking the front item
off q. *)

VAR
   tempQ : Queue;

BEGIN
   IF IsEmptyQ(q) THEN
      WriteString("RearQ: the queue is empty.");
      HALT;

   ELSE
      IF q^.front = q^.rear THEN
         (* Only one item in queue. *)
         tempQ := NewQ();
      ELSE
         ALLOCATE(tempQ, SIZE(QueueSentinel));
         tempQ^.front := q^.front^.next;
         tempQ^.rear := q^.rear;
      END;
      RETURN tempQ;
   END;
END RearQ;
```

Note that this operation doesn't free any memory used by old front queue node, so that we don't affect the original queue.

If memory space is a problem we may have to stop worrying about side-effects and deallocate memory for nodes which are no longer needed.

Here is an operation, we'll call it DelQ, which deletes the top node on a queue:

```
PROCEDURE DelQ(q : Queue): Queue;
(* Pre-condition: the queue is non-empty.
Post-condition: returns the queue formed by taking the front item
off q, and deallocates the space used by this item, thus altering q. *)

VAR
   tempNode : QueuePtr;
```

```
BEGIN
   IF IsEmptyQ(q) THEN
      WriteString("DelQ: Queue is already empty");
      HALT;
   ELSE
      IF q^.front = q^.rear THEN
         (* Only one item in queue. *)
         DEALLOCATE(q^.front, SIZE(QueueNode));
         q^.front := NIL;
         q^.rear := NIL;
      ELSE
         tempNode := q^.front;
         q^.front := q^.front^.next;
         DEALLOCATE(tempNode, SIZE(QueueNode));
      END;
   END;
   RETURN q;
END DelQ;
```

The general idea of this operation is to change the front queue node pointer to the next node down the queue, then free the memory used by the old front node. We have split the operation into two cases, one for when the list only has one item in it, and one for when the list has more than one item in it. In the first case we deallocate the memory location that q^.front points to (which is the same memory location pointed to by q^.rear) and then set both the queue pointers to NIL, giving an empty queue. In the second case we have to be more careful. We can't start by deallocating the current front node because we would then lose our only pointer to the rest of the queue. This is why we use variable tempNode, which is given a copy of q^.front, so that we can still reach the rest of the queue. Then we deallocate the first node pointed to by tempNode.

This operation has the side-effect of changing the original queue. Remember that even though q is passed as a value parameter all this means is that we can't alter the value of q itself (which is a pointer to the queue sentinel) because the procedure only receives a copy of q. However, any changes we make in what q points to are not made to copies but to the originals. Since DelQ may alter q^.front (and possibly q^.rear) we are altering the original queue, as well as passing back a pointer to it.

The final operation is the observer FrontQ which returns the item currently at the front of the queue (that is, the oldest item in the queue). FrontQ must deal with the case where the queue is empty and there is no valid item to return, but other than this it is very simple. In this example we have implemented FrontQ to print a message and halt the program when it is used on an empty queue, which is similar to the way in which the other operations deal with error conditions.

```
PROCEDURE FrontQ(q : Queue): QueueItem;
(* Pre-condition: the queue is non-empty.
Post-condition: returns the item at the front of q. *)
BEGIN
   IF IsEmptyQ(q) THEN
      WriteString("FrontQ: no items, queue is empty.");
      HALT;
   ELSE
      RETURN q^.front^.item;
   END;
END FrontQ;
```

Program 6.2 gives the complete library module for the dynamic implementation of the Queue abstraction. This implementation builds queues of integers.

Program 6.2 Dynamic implementation of the Queue data abstraction

```
DEFINITION MODULE DynamicQueue;

TYPE
   Queue;
   QueueItem = INTEGER;

PROCEDURE NewQ(): Queue;
(* Pre-condition: none.
Post-condition: returns a new, empty queue. *)

PROCEDURE AddQ(q : Queue; i : QueueItem): Queue;
(* Pre-condition: none.
Post-condition: returns the queue formed by adding i to the rear of q. *)

PROCEDURE RearQ(q : Queue): Queue;
(* Pre-condition: the queue is non-empty.
Post-condition: returns queue formed by taking the front item off q. *)

PROCEDURE FrontQ(q : Queue): QueueItem;
(* Pre-condition: the queue is non-empty.
Post-condition: returns the item at the front of q. *)

PROCEDURE IsEmptyQ(q : Queue): BOOLEAN;
(* Pre-condition: none.
Post-condition: returns TRUE if q is empty, FALSE if it isn't. *)

END DynamicQueue.
```

```
IMPLEMENTATION MODULE DynamicQueue;

FROM Storage IMPORT ALLOCATE;
FROM InOut IMPORT WriteString;

TYPE
   QueuePtr = POINTER TO QueueNode;

   QueueNode = RECORD
                 item : QueueItem;
                 next : QueuePtr;
               END;

   QueueSentinel = RECORD
                     front : QueuePtr;
                     rear : QueuePtr;
                   END;

   Queue = POINTER TO QueueSentinel;


PROCEDURE NewQ(): Queue;
VAR
   tempQ : Queue;

BEGIN
   ALLOCATE(tempQ, SIZE(QueueSentinel));
   tempQ^.front := NIL;
   tempQ^.rear := NIL;
   RETURN tempQ;
END NewQ;


PROCEDURE AddQ(q : Queue; i : QueueItem): Queue;
VAR
   tempQ : Queue;
   newNode : QueuePtr;

BEGIN
   ALLOCATE(newNode, SIZE(QueueNode));
   newNode^.item := i;
   newNode^.next := NIL;

   ALLOCATE(tempQ, SIZE(QueueSentinel));
```

```
   IF NOT IsEmptyQ(q) THEN
      q^.rear^.next := newNode;
      tempQ^.front := q^.front;
   ELSE (* The queue is empty. *)
      tempQ^.front := newNode;
   END;
   tempQ^.rear := newNode;
   RETURN tempQ;
END AddQ;

PROCEDURE RearQ(q : Queue): Queue;
VAR
   tempQ : Queue;
BEGIN
   IF IsEmptyQ(q) THEN
      WriteString("RearQ: the queue is empty.");
      HALT;
   ELSE
      IF q^.front = q^.rear THEN
         (* Only one item in queue. *)
         tempQ := NewQ();
      ELSE
         ALLOCATE(tempQ, SIZE(QueueSentinel));
         tempQ^.front := q^.front^.next;
         tempQ^.rear := q^.rear;
      END;
      RETURN tempQ;
   END;
END RearQ;

PROCEDURE FrontQ(q : Queue): QueueItem;
BEGIN
   IF IsEmptyQ(q) THEN
      WriteString("FrontQ: no items, queue is empty.");
      HALT;
   ELSE
      RETURN q^.front^.item;
   END;
END FrontQ;
```

```
PROCEDURE IsEmptyQ(q : Queue): BOOLEAN;

BEGIN
   RETURN q^.front = NIL;
END IsEmptyQ;

BEGIN
   (* No initialisation code. *)
END DynamicQueue.
```

6.5 Dynamic Binary Tree implementation

In Chapter 5 we had a brief introduction to the binary tree data abstraction, and described its formal specification. We said then that a static implementation of binary trees is very time consuming and not really worth the effort if you can implement them dynamically. So here we will show a dynamic implementation of the Binary Search Tree data abstraction, as this is more useful than the simple Binary Tree.

First we need to consider the data representation. A binary tree is a hierarchical data structure, where each node may point to up to two other nodes (in a queue or list each node may only point to at most one other node, giving a linear data structure). Each node may therefore have a left descendant and a right descendant. This suggests we need two pointers in each node, to point to the descendants.

Here is a possible data representation for a binary tree, bearing all the above in mind:

```
TYPE
   Tree = POINTER TO TreeNode;

   TreeNode = RECORD
                 item : TreeItem;
                 left : Tree;
                 right : Tree;
              END;
```

This is very similar to List, except that we have two pointers in each node, which we have called left and right, for obvious reasons.

Figure 6.7 shows a pictorial representation of a binary tree defined in this way.

Figure 6.7 Simple representation of a binary tree

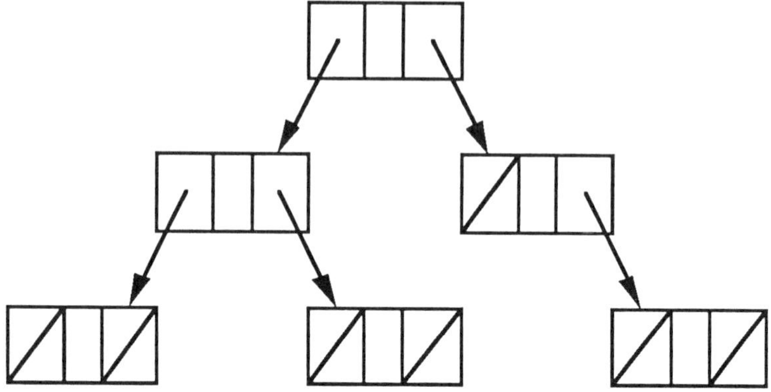

This is a perfectly acceptable representation for a binary tree, so we can now start implementing the operations. First, as usual, let's implement the constructor which returns an empty version of the data structure, NewTree in this case.

```
PROCEDURE NewTree(): Tree;
(* Pre-condition: none.
Post-condition: an empty tree is returned. *)
BEGIN
   RETURN NIL;
END NewTree;
```

The IsEmpty operation follows directly from this:

```
PROCEDURE IsEmpty(t : Tree): BOOLEAN;
BEGIN
   RETURN t = NewTree();
END IsEmpty;
```

With these operations implemented consider the AddTree operation. AddTree takes two trees and an item and builds a new tree with the item at the root, and the two trees as the left and right subtree. This is the basic constructor for the binary tree.

The algorithm for AddTree is very simple:

```
Allocate space for new tree node.
Store data item in this node.
Set left and right subtrees of node to given trees.
Return the new node, which is the root of the tree.
```

In Modula-2:

```
PROCEDURE AddTree(left : Tree; i : TreeItem; right : Tree): Tree;
(* Pre-condition: none.
Post-condition: returns a tree with i as root, l as left subtree and r as
right subtree. *)
VAR
   newTree : Tree;
BEGIN
   (* Allocate space for new tree node. *)
   ALLOCATE(newNode, SIZE(TreeNode));
   (* Set up tree. *)
   newTree^.left := left;
   newTree^.right := right;
   newTree^.item := i;
   RETURN newTree;
END AddTree;
```

The Insert operation must insert the given item into the correct position in the given tree. This position will depend on how the tree is ordered. The operation's implementation is very similar to the axioms describing Insert in the earlier specification of the binary search tree, that is

```
Insert(NewTree, i) = AddTree(NewTree, i, NewTree)
Insert(AddTree(l, j, r), i) = if Equal(i, j) then AddTree(l, i, r)
        else if Less(i, j) then AddTree(Insert(l, i), j, r)
        else AddTree(l, j, Insert(r, i))
```

Here is the Modula-2 implementation:

```
PROCEDURE Insert(t : Tree; i : TreeItem):Tree;
(* Pre-condition: none.
Post-condition: returns tree formed by inserting i into the correct
position in t. *)
BEGIN
   IF IsEmpty(t) THEN
      RETURN AddTree(NewTree(), i, NewTree());
   ELSIF i < Root(t) THEN
      RETURN AddTree(Insert(Left(t), i), Root(t), Right(t));
   ELSIF i > Root(t) THEN
      RETURN AddTree(Left(t), Root(t), Insert(Right(t), i));
   ELSE (* Item i is already in the tree, leave it alone. *)
      RETURN AddTree(Left(t), Root(t), Right(t));
   END;
END Insert;
```

The IsIn operation is very similar to the Insert operation, except that it doesn't have to rebuild the tree as it searches through (simply because it doesn't alter a tree, but returns a Boolean value instead).

```
PROCEDURE IsIn(t : Tree; i : TreeItem): BOOLEAN;
(* Pre-condition: none.
Post-condition: returns TRUE if i is in t, FALSE if it isn't. *)
BEGIN
   IF IsEmpty(t) THEN
      RETURN FALSE;
   END;
   IF i < Root(t) THEN
      RETURN IsIn(Left(t), i);
   ELSIF i > Root(t) THEN
      RETURN IsIn(Right(t), i);
   ELSE (* i = Root(t) *)
      RETURN TRUE;
   END;
END IsIn;
```

The Remove operation is also very similar to its axioms, that is

```
Remove(NewTree, i) = NewTree
Remove(AddTree(l, j, r), i) =
      if Equal(i, j) then
         if IsEmpty(l) then r
         else if IsEmpty(r) then l
         else AddTree(l, Smallest(r), Remove(r, Smallest(r)))
      else if Less(i, j) then AddTree(Remove(l, i), j, r)
      else AddTree(l, j, Remove(r, i))
```

and in Modula-2:

```
PROCEDURE Remove(t : Tree; i : TreeItem): Tree;
(* Pre-condition: none.
Post-condition: returns the tree formed by removing i from t. *)
BEGIN
   IF IsEmpty(t) THEN
      RETURN t;
   ELSIF i = Root(t) THEN
      IF IsEmpty(Left(t)) THEN
         RETURN Right(t);
      ELSIF IsEmpty(Right(t)) THEN
         RETURN Left(t);
      ELSE
```

```
        RETURN  AddTree(Left(t),  Smallest(Right(t)),
           Remove(Right(t),  Smallest(Right(t))));
     END;
  ELSE
     IF i < Root(t) THEN
        RETURN  AddTree(Remove(Left(t),  i),  Root(t),  Right(t));
     ELSE
        RETURN  AddTree(Left(t),  Root(t),
           Remove(Right(t),  i));
     END;
  END;
END  Remove;
```

Note how Insert and Remove do not depend how the tree is implemented at all. They would be exactly the same if the implementation was static, because they don't manipulate the representation themselves, but use the other tree operations (such as NewTree and AddTree). The same is true of the remaining binary tree operations, Left, Right, Root, Greatest and Smallest which are implemented below.

The implementations of the Left, Right and Root operations are very simple, so we will give them directly in Modula-2

```
PROCEDURE  Left(t  :  Tree):  Tree;
(*  Pre-condition:  none.
Post-condition: returns the left subtree of t.  Note that the left
subtree of an empty tree is an empty tree. *)
BEGIN
   IF  IsEmpty(t)  THEN
      RETURN  NewTree();
   ELSE
      RETURN  t^.left;
   END
END  Left;

PROCEDURE  Right(t  :  Tree):  Tree;
(*Pre-condition:  none.
Post-condition: returns the right subtree of t. Note that the right
subtree of an empty tree is an empty tree. *)
BEGIN
   IF  IsEmpty(t)  THEN
      RETURN  NewTree();
   ELSE
      RETURN  t^.right;
   END;
END  Right;
```

```
PROCEDURE Root(t : Tree): TreeItem;
(* Pre-condition: t must be non-empty.
Post-condition: returns the data item in the root node of t. *)

BEGIN
   IF IsEmpty(t) THEN
      WriteString("Root: error, tree is empty.");
      HALT;
   ELSE
      RETURN t^.item;
   END;
END Root;
```

It only remains to implement the Greatest and Smallest operations. The Greatest and Smallest operations must return the largest and smallest items in the tree respectively. Since a binary search tree is built by adding items smaller than the root to the left subtree and items larger than the root to the right subtree, the smallest item is the leftmost item, and the largest item is the rightmost item in the tree.

The algorithm for finding the smallest item is therefore:

```
If the left subtree is empty then
   return the root item (which must be the smallest)

otherwise
   find the smallest item in the left subtree
endif
```

in Modula-2:

```
PROCEDURE Smallest(t : Tree): TreeItem;
(* Pre-condition: none.
Post-condition: returns the smallest item in the tree. *)

BEGIN
   IF IsEmpty(Left(t)) THEN
      RETURN Root(t);
   ELSE
      RETURN Smallest(Left(t));
   END;
END Smallest;
```

The algorithm for the Greatest operation is very similar to this:

```
If the right subtree is empty then
    return the root item (which must be the largest)
otherwise
    find the largest item in the right subtree
endif
```

and in Modula-2:

```
PROCEDURE Greatest(t : Tree): TreeItem;
(* Pre-condition: none.
Post-condition: returns the greatest item in the tree. *)
BEGIN
    IF IsEmpty(Right(t)) THEN
        RETURN Root(t);
    ELSE
        RETURN Greatest(Right(t));
    END;
END Greatest;
```

Note that when Left and Right are given an empty tree they simply return an empty tree. However, Root reports an error and halts the program if it is given an empty tree, because there is no valid data item that can be returned as the root of an empty tree.

Traversing a binary search tree

We have defined how to build a binary tree, search it for various items and remove items, we haven't defined any operations for traversing the entire tree, looking at each node in turn. There are several ways of traversing a binary tree, all of which are well known by their names: preorder, inorder and postorder.

Preorder tree traversal involves visiting the root before visiting the left and right subtrees. Inorder traversal involves visiting the root in between visiting the left and right subtrees. Postorder traversal involves visiting the root after visiting the left and right subtrees.

Here is the algorithm for a preorder tree traversal:

```
If the tree isn't empty then
    process the item in the root
    traverse the left subtree by preorder
    traverse the right subtree by preorder
endif
```

This gives a deceptively simple Modula-2 procedure:

```
PROCEDURE PreOrder(t : Tree);
(* Pre-condition: none.
Post-condition: applies the operation ProcessItem on every item in
the tree. *)
BEGIN
   IF NOT IsEmpty(t) THEN
      ProcessItem(Root(t));
      PreOrder(Left(t));
      PreOrder(Right(t));
   END;
END PreOrder;
```

The algorithm for inorder traversal is simply:

```
If the tree isn't empty then
   traverse the left subtree by inorder
   process the item in the root
   traverse the right subtree by inorder
endif
```

and in Modula-2:

```
PROCEDURE InOrder(t : Tree);
(* Pre-condition: none.
Post-condition: applies the operation ProcessItem on every item in
the tree. *)
BEGIN
   IF NOT IsEmpty(t) THEN
      InOrder(Left(t));
      ProcessItem(Root(t));
      InOrder(Right(t));
   END;
END InOrder;
```

The algorithm for the postorder tree traversal is:

```
If the tree isn't empty then
   traverse the left subtree by postorder
   traverse the right subtree by postorder
   process the item in the root
endif
```

giving the Modula-2 procedure

```
PROCEDURE PostOrder(t : Tree);
(* Pre-condition: none.
Post-condition: applies the operation ProcessItem on every item in the
tree. *)

BEGIN
        IF NOT IsEmpty(t) THEN
        PostOrder(Left(t));
        PostOrder(Right(t));
        ProcessItem(Root(t));
    END;
END PostOrder;
```

To see the different effects of these three tree traversal let's look at traversing the following binary tree:

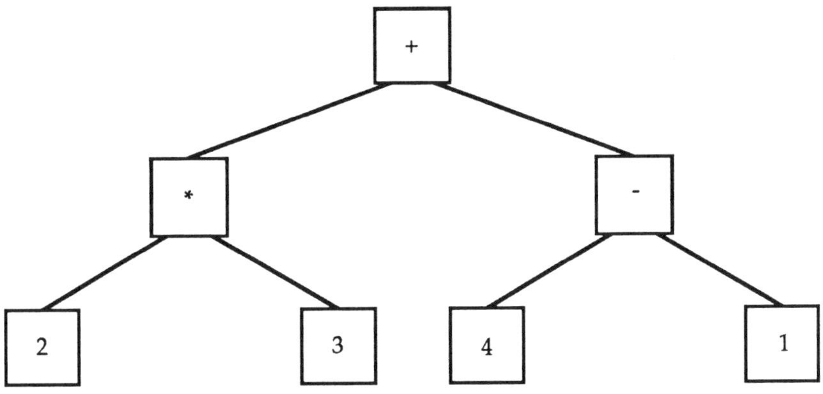

First the preorder traversal, which visits the root before each subtree:

+ * 2 3 - 4 1

Now the inorder traversal, which visits the root in between each subtree:

2 * 3 + 4 - 1

Finally the postorder traversal, which visits the root after each subtree:

2 3 * 4 1 -+

Program 6.3 gives the complete dynamic implementation of the Binary Search Tree abstraction:

Program 6.3 Dynamic implementation of the Binary Search Tree abstraction

```
DEFINITION MODULE DynamicTree;

TYPE
   TreeItem = CHAR;
   Tree; (* opaque type declaration *)

PROCEDURE NewTree(): Tree;
(* Pre-condition: none.
Post-condition: an empty tree is returned. *)

PROCEDURE IsEmpty(t : Tree): BOOLEAN;
(* Pre-condition: none.
Post-condition: returns TRUE if t is empty, FALSE if it isn't. *)

PROCEDURE AddTree(left : Tree; i : TreeItem; right : Tree): Tree;
(* Pre-condition: none.
Post-condition: returns a tree with i as root, l as left subtree and r as
right subtree. *)

PROCEDURE Insert(t : Tree; i : TreeItem): Tree;
(* Pre-condition: none.
Post-condition: returns tree formed by inserting i into the correct
position in t. *)

PROCEDURE IsIn(t : Tree; i : TreeItem): BOOLEAN;
(* Pre-condition: none.
Post-condition: returns TRUE if i is in t, FALSE if it isn't. *)

PROCEDURE Remove(t : Tree; i : TreeItem): Tree;
(* Pre-condition: none.
Post-condition: returns the tree formed by removing i from t. *)
```

```
PROCEDURE Left(t : Tree): Tree;
(* Pre-condition: none.
Post-condition: returns the left subtree of t. Note that the left subtree
of an empty tree is an empty tree. *)

PROCEDURE Right(t : Tree): Tree;
(*Pre-condition: none.
Post-condition: returns the right subtree of t. Note that the right
subtree of an empty tree is an empty tree. *)

PROCEDURE Root(t : Tree): TreeItem;
(* Pre-condition: t must be non-empty.
Post-condition: returns the data item in the root node of t. *)

PROCEDURE Smallest(t : Tree): TreeItem;
(* Pre-condition: none.
Post-condition: returns the smallest item in the tree. *)

PROCEDURE Greatest(t : Tree): TreeItem;
(* Pre-condition: none.
Post-condition: returns the greatest item in the tree. *)

PROCEDURE PreOrder(t : Tree);
(* Pre-condition: none.
Post-condition: applies the operation ProcessItem on every item in the
tree. *)

PROCEDURE InOrder(t : Tree);
(* Pre-condition: none.
Post-condition: applies the operation ProcessItem on every item in the
tree. *)

PROCEDURE PostOrder(t : Tree);
(* Pre-condition: none.
Post-condition: applies the operation ProcessItem on every item in the
tree. *)

END DynamicTree;
```

```
IMPLEMENTATION MODULE DynamicTree;

FROM Storage IMPORT ALLOCATE;
FROM InOut IMPORT WriteString;

TYPE
   Tree = POINTER TO TreeNode;

   TreeNode = RECORD
                   item : TreeItem;
                   left : Tree;
                   right : Tree;
                END;


PROCEDURE NewTree(): Tree;

BEGIN
   RETURN NIL;
END NewTree;


PROCEDURE IsEmpty(t : Tree): BOOLEAN;

BEGIN
   RETURN t = NewTree();
END IsEmpty;


PROCEDURE AddTree(left : Tree; i : TreeItem; right : Tree): Tree;
VAR
   newTree : Tree;

BEGIN
   (* Allocate space for new tree node. *)
   ALLOCATE(newNode, SIZE(TreeNode));
   (* Set up tree. *)
   newTree^.left := left;
   newTree^.right := right;
   newTree^.item := i;
   RETURN newTree;
END AddTree;
```

```
PROCEDURE Insert(t : Tree; i : TreeItem): Tree;
BEGIN
   IF IsEmpty(t) THEN
      RETURN AddTree(NewTree(), i, NewTree());
   ELSIF i < Root(t) THEN
      RETURN AddTree(Insert(Left(t), i), Root(t), Right(t));
   ELSIF i > Root(t) THEN
      RETURN AddTree(Left(t), Root(t), Insert(Right(t), i));
   ELSE (* Item i is already in the tree, leave it alone. *)
      RETURN AddTree(Left(t), Root(t), Right(t));
   END;
END Insert;

PROCEDURE IsIn(t : Tree; i : TreeItem): BOOLEAN;
BEGIN
   IF IsEmpty(t) THEN
      RETURN FALSE
   END;
   IF i < Root(t) THEN
      RETURN IsIn(Left(t), i);
   ELSIF i > Root(t) THEN
      RETURN IsIn(Right(t), i);
   ELSE (* i = Root(t). *)
      RETURN TRUE;
   END;
END IsIn;

PROCEDURE Remove(t : Tree; i : TreeItem): Tree;
BEGIN
   IF IsEmpty(t) THEN
      RETURN t;
   ELSIF i = Root(t) THEN
      IF IsEmpty(Left(t)) THEN
         RETURN Right(t);
      ELSIF IsEmpty(Right(t)) THEN
         RETURN Left(t);
      ELSE
         RETURN AddTree(Left(t), Smallest(Right(t)),
            Remove(Right(t), Smallest(Right(t))));
      END;
```

```
   ELSE
      IF i < Root(t) THEN
         RETURN AddTree(Remove(Left(t), i), Root(t),
            Right(t));
      ELSE
         RETURN AddTree(Left(t), Root(t),
            Remove(Right(t), i));
      END;
   END;
END Remove;

PROCEDURE Left(t : Tree): Tree;
BEGIN
   IF IsEmpty(t) THEN
      RETURN NewTree();
   ELSE
      RETURN t^.left;
   END
END Left;

PROCEDURE Right(t : Tree): Tree;
BEGIN
   IF IsEmpty(t) THEN
      RETURN NewTree();
   ELSE
      RETURN t^.right;
   END;
END Right;

PROCEDURE Root(t : Tree): TreeItem;
BEGIN
   IF IsEmpty(t) THEN
      WriteString("Root: error, tree is empty.");
      HALT;
   ELSE
      RETURN t^.item;
   END;
END Root;
```

```
PROCEDURE Smallest(t : Tree): TreeItem;
BEGIN
   IF IsEmpty(Left(t)) THEN
      RETURN Root(t);
   ELSE
      RETURN Smallest(Left(t));
   END;
END Smallest;


PROCEDURE Greatest(t : Tree): TreeItem;
BEGIN
   IF IsEmpty(Right(t)) THEN
      RETURN Root(t);
   ELSE
      RETURN Greatest(Right(t));
   END;
END Greatest;


PROCEDURE PreOrder(t : Tree);
BEGIN
   IF NOT IsEmpty(t) THEN
      ProcessItem(Root(t));
      PreOrder(Left(t));
      PreOrder(Right(t));
   END;
END PreOrder;


PROCEDURE InOrder(t : Tree);
BEGIN
   IF NOT IsEmpty(t) THEN
      InOrder(Left(t));
      ProcessItem(Root(t));
      InOrder(Right(t));
   END;
END InOrder;
```

```
PROCEDURE PostOrder(t : Tree);
BEGIN
   IF NOT IsEmpty(t) THEN
      PostOrder(Left(t));
      PostOrder(Right(t));
      ProcessItem(Root(t));
   END;
END PostOrder;

BEGIN
   (* No initialisation code. *)
END DynamicTree.
```

6.6 Generic implementations of data abstractions

If we are implementing one of our data abstractions it is preferable that the implementation fully implements the given specification. We have seen how a static implementation of a data abstraction, such as a list, cannot be a full implementation of the specification because it restricts the size of the list. The specification of the List abstraction contains no restrictions on size. A dynamic implementation of List removes this size restriction, limiting the size of a list only to the available memory size. This brings our List implementation closer to the specification.

The operations of List are just as applicable to a list of integers as to a list of characters or a list of records. It is the way in which the items in the list relate to each other which makes the data structure a list, the type of each individual item is unimportant. The List abstraction describes a list of any type of item, we just gave the item type an arbitrary name, ListItem.

If our Modula-2 implementation of the List abstraction could be made the same as the specification in this respect, we would be able to use this one implementation to build and manipulate lists of integers, list of characters, lists of strings, lists of lists etc. We call such an implementation a generic implementation, because it can describe a whole class of lists, rather than just one (that is lists of INTEGER in the dynamic implementation of List given earlier).

6.6.1 Generic implementation of the Queue abstraction

First, let's consider in more detail exactly what we want to achieve with a generic implementation of a data abstraction. We will look at the implementation of a generic queue. We want to end up with a library module, implementing the Queue data abstraction, which provides operations for building and using queues containing any type of item. So, for example, given the following variables,

```
VAR
    q1, q2 : Queue;
    c1 : CHAR;
    i1 : INTEGER;
```

the AddQ constructor from the QueueADT library module should be usable in both the following cases:

```
    q1 := AddQ(q1, c1);
    q2 := AddQ(q2, i1);
```

Here we are using AddQ to put a CHAR onto queue q1, and an INTEGER onto queue q2.

Note: it is normal to assume that data abstractions such as queues, lists, trees etc are homogeneous, that is all the individual data items in any instance of the data abstraction are of the same type. So, for example, a particular queue may contain items which are all CHAR, or items which are all CARDINAL, but it won't contain a mixture of the two.

There are a number of questions to be answered if we want to be able to define a generic queue. First, how do we declare and implement the operations of Queue to accept any type of data item to store in a queue? Second, how do we declare the data representation of a QueueNode when we don't know what type of item is to be stored in it? To answer these two questions we need to look briefly at open array parameters and the low-level data abstractions WORD and BYTE.

Open array parameters

Whenever we declare an array variable or an array type in a module or procedure we have to state the type of its items and its size (the number of items which can be stored in the array). The size is stated by giving the index range of the array, for example, a variable of

```
ARRAY [-2..5] OF CHAR
```

can store 8 characters, and a variable of

```
ARRAY [3..103] OF INTEGER
```

can store 101 integers.

However, operations which have to handle arrays (particularly one-dimensional arrays like the ones shown above) are very common, so Modula-2 provides a way of passing array parameters without stating their size. The advantage of this is that a procedure which, say, finds the maximum value in an array of 50 integers, can, if the array parameter is declared without any size, also find the maximum in an array of any arbitrary dimension.

An array parameter to a procedure (or function) which is declared without its size in the procedure header is called an open array parameter. We can only use one-dimensional arrays as open array parameters. As an example, here is the header of procedure ArrayMax from Chapter 4, with the array declared as an open array parameter:

```
PROCEDURE ArrayMax(a : ARRAY OF INTEGER): INTEGER;
```

If the body of ArrayMax is implemented suitable we can make it find the maximum value in any size of integer array.

The problem you might have spotted with open array parameters is simply, how do we know how big the array is so that we can index it, since the size isn't stated in the parameter declaration? Modula-2 provides a special function, called HIGH, which, given the name of an open array parameter, will return a value one less than the size of the array. The reason it returns one less than the size is that HIGH assumes the array is indexed from 0 and so is returning the highest index value. In an array [0..5] the highest index value is 5, and the actual size is 5+1, because the array starts at 0.

WORD and BYTE

Every Modula-2 system should provide the data type WORD (usually found in the SYSTEM module), which is directly equivalent to a binary word. Some Modula-2 systems (particularly the newer ones) will also provide the data type BYTE, which is equivalent to a binary byte.

These two data types allow us low-level access to data stored by our programs. Every data item on a computer is stored in a number of binary words, and hence in a number of binary bytes (a binary word is made up of two or more bytes, depending on the type of computer you are using). Every data item can, at a very low-level, be accessed as an array of words or as an array of bytes.

For example, on a computer which has four bytes per word an integer is stored in

```
ARRAY [0..3] OF BYTE
```

Since arrays of bytes and words are compatible with **all** our data items, if we declared a procedure with an open array parameter of ARRAY OF BYTE, that procedure will accept **any** data item which can be stored in an array of bytes (which effectively means any data item) for the parameter.

With these two concepts in hand let's return to the problem of implementing a generic AddQ operation:

To get AddQ to accept an item of any type to store in the queue we can use an open ARRAY OF BYTE, which will be compatible with any data item we care to store in our queue. We can therefore declare the header of AddQ as:

```
PROCEDURE AddQ(q : Queue; item : ARRAY OF BYTE): Queue
```

Since the formal parameter item is an open ARRAY OF BYTE the corresponding actual parameter in any call to AddQ can be declared as any other type. So the calls

```
q1 := AddQ(q1, c1);
q2 := AddQ(q2, i1);
```

will be perfectly allowable because type INTEGER and type CHAR are all compatible with type ARRAY OF BYTE. We also need to be able to store any type of data item in a QueueNode. The current definition we have for a QueueNode is as follows:

```
QueueNode = RECORD
                data : QueueItem;
                next : QueuePtr;
              END;
```

The data item must be of type QueueItem, which is certainly not generic. You might think that this is the definition we need now:

```
QueueNode = RECORD
                data : ARRAY OF CHAR;
                next : QueuePtr;
            END;
```

but this is wrong! We can't use an open array descriptor, because they are only valid in procedure headers, neither can we define a fixed size array, because we don't know in advance how big the data item will be. Instead we have to find some other way of storing the data item.

Let's approach this problem from a slightly different point of view. What information do we have to have in order to be able to retrieve an unknown type of data item from memory? There are just two pieces of information:

- The starting address of the item.
- The number of bytes it is stored in.

Armed with this information we can retrieve any data item from memory. We don't even have to know what type of data item we are retrieving, because we can store it in an ARRAY OF BYTE which is compatible with all other types.

Here is a definition of QueueNode which contains the appropriate information to store any type of data item in memory:

```
QueueNode = RECORD
                data : ADDRESS;
                size : CARDINAL;
                next : QueuePtr;
              END;
```

The data we are now storing in a queue node is no longer the data item itself, because we don't know what type it will be, but a memory address, giving the starting address in memory of the data item. We also need an extra field to store the size of the data item in bytes, so that we know how much memory to look at when we go to the starting address of the item.

Type ADDRESS is compatible with all POINTER types; remember that a pointer variable is really the address of a single memory location, but we restrict a pointer to point to a particular data type. An ADDRESS variable is also just the address of a single memory location, but there is no restriction on what is stored at this memory location.

Remember how we added a new node onto a dynamic queue:

```
Allocate space for new queue node.
Store data item in queue node.
Set new queue node next pointer to point to previous rear node.
Allocate space for new queue sentinel node.
Set new queue sentinel to point to current front node and new rear
node.
Return new queue sentinel.
```

The first line of the algorithm allocates space for the new queue node, and at the same time allocates space for one data item of type QueueItem inside the queue node. The second line simply assigns the data item to the appropriate field in the node. In Modula-2 these two lines become:

```
ALLOCATE(newNode, SIZE(QueueNode));
newNode^.data := i;
```

where i is the data item being stored in the node.

Remember that our new definition of type QueueNode doesn't contain the data item itself, but only the address and size of the data item in memory. In such circumstances the above call to ALLOCATE will only allocate space for the address field, the size field and the pointer to the next node; it will not allocate space for the data item, we have to allocate the memory to store the data item separately.

We need to find the size of the data item in bytes, and give this and the variable to which the address is to be assigned to the ALLOCATE procedure. Here is how we do this in Modula-2:

```
newNode^.size := HIGH(i) + 1;
ALLOCATE(newNode^.data, newNode^.size);
```

Remember that HIGH is a built-in Modula-2 function which returns the highest array index used by the given variable (i in this case). To get the total number of bytes needed by i we must add one to the value returned by HIGH, remembering that open array parameters (and i is one!) are always indexed from 0. The address of the allocated memory is put into newNode^.data.

Our next problem is that we have to store the data item in this allocated memory. Unfortunately we can't do a simple assignment like before

```
newNode^.data := i;
```

because the data field contains the address of i, not i itself. Instead we have to copy each byte of i into memory, starting at the address stored in newNode^.data.

```
Set up a temporary pointer to point to the location where the current
byte of the item is to be stored in memory

For each byte in item
   copy the byte into memory at the current location
Endfor
```

in Modula-2:

```
location := newNode^.data;

FOR offset := 0 TO HIGH(i) DO
   location^ := i[offset];
   INC(location);
END;
```

And that's all we need to do to store a generic data item in our queue!

Once we have stored a data item in our queue the next problem is to retrieve it from memory. This is in fact quite simple, since we know where the item starts (the data field of the node stores its address) and we know how many bytes we have to read.

Once again we set up a pointer to the first location in which the data item is stored and copy each byte from memory back into an ARRAY OF BYTE, that is

```
location := q^.data;

FOR offset := 0 TO q^.size -1 DO
   i[offset] := location^;
   INC(location);
END;
```

where q is a Queue and i is the ARRAY OF BYTE in which the data item is to be returned.

The complete generic (and still dynamic) implementation of Queue is given below in Program 6.4 .

Program 6.4 Generic implementation of the Queue data abstraction

```
DEFINITION MODULE GenericQueue;
(* The Queue data abstraction, generic implementation. *)

FROM SYSTEM IMPORT BYTE;

TYPE
   Queue; (* This is declared as an opaque type. *)

PROCEDURE NewQ(): Queue;
(* Returns a new, empty queue.
Pre-condition: none.
Post-condition: a new, empty queue is returned. *)

PROCEDURE AddQ(q : Queue; i : ARRAY OF BYTE): Queue;
(* Adds an item to the front of a queue.
Pre-condition: none.
Post-condition: returns the queue by adding i to the rear of q. *)

PROCEDURE IsEmptyQ(q : Queue): BOOLEAN;
(* True if the queue is empty, false if it isn't.
Pre-condition: none.
Post-condition: returns TRUE if the queue is empty and FALSE if not. *)

PROCEDURE RearQ(q : Queue): Queue;
(* Return the queue minus its front item.
Pre-condition: q is non-empty.
Post-condition: returns the queue formed by removing the front item. *)

PROCEDURE FrontQ(q : Queue; VAR i : ARRAY OF BYTE);
(* Gives the item at the front of the queue, but doesn't remove it from
the queue.
Pre-condition: none, but if q is empty FrontQ will report an error.
Post-condition: i contains the item at the front of q, but q is left
unchanged. *)

END GenericQueue.
```

```
IMPLEMENTATION MODULE GenericQueue;

(* Generic implementation of the queue data abstraction.

The queue is implemented with a header/sentinel node, holding
pointers to the first and last nodes in the queue.  Each node in the
queue contains the address and size of a data item, and a pointer to the
next node in the queue. *)

FROM Storage IMPORT ALLOCATE;

FROM SYSTEM IMPORT ADDRESS, BYTE;

FROM InOut IMPORT WriteString, WriteCard, Write;

TYPE
   (* Pointer to an individual queue node. *)
   QueuePtr = POINTER TO QueueNode;

   (* Queue node, storing a data item, and a pointer to the next
   node in the queue. *)

   QueueNode = RECORD
                 data : ADDRESS;
                 size : CARDINAL;
                 next : QueuePtr;
               END;

   (* The sentinel/header node, storing pointers to the first and
   last nodes in the queue. *)

   QueueSentinel = RECORD
                     front : QueuePtr;
                     rear : QueuePtr;
                   END;

   (* A queue is a pointer to a sentinel node. *)
   Queue = POINTER TO QueueSentinel;

(* Implementations of the individual queue operations. *)
```

```
PROCEDURE NewQ(): Queue;
(* Returns a new, empty queue.
Note that we must allocate space for the sentinel node, because a
queue is a pointer to a sentinel, and so the compiler will not allocate the
space for us. *)

VAR
   tempQ : Queue;

BEGIN
   (* Allocate space for a sentinel node. *)
   ALLOCATE(tempQ, SIZE(QueueSentinel));

   (* Set up the sentinel to have nil pointers to the first and last
   items -- the queue is new, so it must be empty! *)

   tempQ^.front := NIL;
   tempQ^.rear := NIL;

   RETURN tempQ;
END NewQ;


PROCEDURE AddQ(q : Queue; i : ARRAY OF BYTE): Queue;
(* Adds an item to the front of a queue. *)

VAR
   tempQ : Queue;
   nodePtr : QueuePtr;  (* For setting up a new queue node to
                           hold i. *)
   offset : CARDINAL; (* Number of bytes needed to store i. *)
   location : ADDRESS; (* A memory address, used as the current
                          address at which a byte is to be stored. *)
BEGIN
   (* Allocate space for a new queue node. *)
   ALLOCATE(nodePtr, SIZE(QueueNode));
   nodePtr^.next := NIL;

   (* Find size of i and store in size field of queue node. *)
   nodePtr^.size := HIGH(i) + 1;

   (* Allocate the correct number of bytes to store i. *)
   ALLOCATE(nodePtr^.data, nodePtr^.size);
```

```
   (* Store i in memory at starting address nodePtr^.data, one byte
   at a time. *)
   location := nodePtr^.data;
   FOR offset := 0 TO HIGH(i) DO
      location^ := i[offset];
      INC(location);
   END;

   (* Allocate space for the new queue sentinel. *)
   ALLOCATE(tempQ, SIZE(QueueSentinel));

   IF NOT IsEmptyQ(q) THEN

      (* Make the last node in q point to the new node, which
      therefore becomes the last node in q. *)
      q^.rear^.next := nodePtr;
      (* Make the new queue sentinel point to the front of the
      queue. *)
      tempQ^.front := q^.front;
   ELSE
      (* The queue is empty so the new node is the first node in
      the queue. *)
      tempQ^.front := nodePtr;
   END;

   (* Whether or not the queue is empty, the new node must
   always become the last node in the queue, so set up the new
   queue sentinel appropriately. *)
   tempQ^.rear := nodePtr;
   (* Return the new sentinel. *)
   RETURN tempQ;

END AddQ;


PROCEDURE IsEmptyQ(q : Queue): BOOLEAN;
(* True if the queue is empty, false if it isn't. *)

BEGIN
   (* If there is no node at the front of the queue, then the queue
   must be empty. Note that IsEmptyQ relies on NewQ setting
   q^.front to nil when a new queue is created, and on RearQ
   setting q^.front to nil when it returns the rear of a queue with
   only one item. *)
   RETURN q^.front = NIL;
END IsEmptyQ;
```

```
PROCEDURE RearQ(q : Queue): Queue;
(* Return the queue minus its front item. *)

VAR
   newQueue : Queue;

BEGIN
   IF IsEmptyQ(q) THEN

      (* Stop if we have got an empty queue.  Note that RearQ
      could be implemented to return an empty queue in such
      circumstances. *)

      WriteString("Error - Rear of empty queue");
      HALT;

   ELSE
      (* The queue has at least one item. *)

      IF q^.front = q^.rear THEN

         (* Only one item in the queue, so the rear of this must
         be an empty queue, which is exactly what NewQ gives
         us. *)
         newQueue := NewQ();

      ELSE
         (* Allocate space for a new queue sentinel. *)
         ALLOCATE(newQueue, SIZE(QueueSentinel));

         (* Set the sentinel to point to the second item in the queue
         and the last item in the queue. *)

         newQueue^.front := q^.front^.next;
         newQueue^.rear := q^.rear;
      END;
      (* Return the new sentinel which gives us the original queue,
      minus its first item. *)

      RETURN newQueue;
   END;
END RearQ;
```

```
PROCEDURE FrontQ(q : Queue; VAR i : ARRAY OF BYTE);
(* Gives the item at the front of the queue, but doesn't remove it
from the queue. *)
VAR
   location : ADDRESS; (* Starting address of i. *)
   offset : CARDINAL; (* Number of bytes taken by i. *)

BEGIN
   IF IsEmptyQ(q) THEN
      (* Stop if the queue is empty.  There is nothing valid for
      FrontQ to return if the queue is empty. *)
      WriteString("Error - Front of empty queue");
      HALT;
   ELSE
      (* Return the data item stored in the node pointed to by the
      front pointer in the queue sentinel. *)
      location := q^.front^.data;

      (* Copy data from memory into i. *)
      FOR offset := 0 TO q^.front^.size-1 DO
         i[offset] := location^;
         INC(location);
      END;
   END;
END FrontQ;

BEGIN (* Main body of GenericQueue. *)
   (* No initialisation code needed. *)
END GenericQueue.
```

6.6.2 Generic implementation of the List data abstraction

The implementation of a generic list is very similar to the generic queue. The representation type for a list node must be altered to store the address and size of the data item, rather than the item itself, that is:

```
TYPE
   ListNode = RECORD
                 data : ADDRESS;
                 size : CARDINAL;
                 next : List;
              END;

   List = POINTER TO ListNode;
```

The operations Cons (equivalent to AddQ in the Queue data abstraction), and Head (equivalent to FrontQ) have to be altered to deal with the storage and retrieval of a generic data item. Here is the new Cons operation:

```
PROCEDURE Cons(l : List; i : ARRAY OF BYTE): List;
(* Add an item to the head of a list. *)

VAR
   new : List;
   byteCount : CARDINAL; (* Number of bytes needed to store
                            data item i. *)
   location : ADDRESS; (* Address of i. *)

BEGIN

   (* First we must allocate space for the whole list node. *)
   ALLOCATE(new, SIZE(ListNode));
   new^.size := (HIGH(i) + 1);

   (* Now allocate the correct number of bytes to store data item. *)
   ALLOCATE(new^.data, new^.size);

   (* Store data item in memory one byte at a time. *)
   location := new^.data;

   FOR byteCount := 0 TO HIGH(i) DO
      location^ := i[byteCount];
      INC(location);
   END;

   (* Set up the node's next pointer to point to the head of the
   original list, and then return this node. *)

   new^.next := l;

   RETURN new;
END Cons;
```

Here is the new implementation of Head, which retrieves a generic item from memory:

```
PROCEDURE Head(l : List; VAR i : ARRAY OF BYTE);
(* Set variable i to contain the data item stored in the head
of the list. *)
VAR
   byteCount : CARDINAL; (* Number of bytes taken by i. *)
   location : ADDRESS; (* Starting address of i. *)

BEGIN
   IF IsEmpty(l) THEN
      WriteString("Error - Head of empty list");
      HALT;
   ELSE
      (* Set location to the starting address of the data. *)
      location := l^.data;
      (* Now copy each byte into i. *)
      FOR byteCount := 0 TO l^.size-1 DO
         i[byteCount] := location^;
         INC(location);
      END;
   END;
END Head;
```

The other operations of the List abstraction, Create, IsEmpty and Tail do not need to be altered in any way from the implementations we gave for the dynamic list. Program 6.5 gives a complete implementation of the generic List abstraction.

Program 6.5 Generic implementation of the List data abstraction

```
DEFINITION MODULE GenericList;

FROM SYSTEM IMPORT BYTE;

TYPE
   List;

PROCEDURE Create(): List;
(* Pre-condition: none.
Post-condition: returns a new, empty list. *)

PROCEDURE Cons(l : List; i : ARRAY OF BYTE): List;
(* Pre-condition: none.
Post-condition: returns list l with item i added to the head. *)
```

```
PROCEDURE Head(l : List; VAR i : ARRAY OF BYTE);
(* Pre-condition: l is not empty.
Post-condition: i contains a copy of the item at the head of l. *)


PROCEDURE Tail(l : List): List;
(* Pre-condition: none.
Post-condition: returns the tail of l. *)


PROCEDURE IsEmpty(l : List): BOOLEAN;
(* Pre-condition: none.
Post-condition: returns TRUE if l is empty, FALSE if it isn't. *)

END GenericList.


IMPLEMENTATION MODULE GenericList;

FROM SYSTEM IMPORT ADDRESS, BYTE;

FROM Storage IMPORT ALLOCATE;

FROM InOut IMPORT WriteString;

TYPE
   ListNode = RECORD
                 data : ADDRESS;
                 size : CARDINAL;
                 next : List;
               END;

   List = POINTER TO ListNode;


PROCEDURE Create():List;

BEGIN
   RETURN NIL;
END Create;
```

```
PROCEDURE Cons(l : List; i : ARRAY OF BYTE): List;
(* Add an item to the head of a list. *)

VAR
   new : List;
   byteCount : CARDINAL; (* Number of bytes needed to store
                            data item i. *)
   location : ADDRESS; (* Address of i. *)

BEGIN
   (* First we must allocate space for the whole list node. *)
   ALLOCATE(new,  SIZE(ListNode));
   new^.size := (HIGH(i) + 1);

   (* Now allocate the correct number of bytes to store data item . *)
   ALLOCATE(new^.data,  new^.size);

   (* Store data item in memory one byte at a time. *)
   location := new^.data;

   FOR byteCount := 0 TO HIGH(i) DO
      location^ := i[byteCount];
      INC(location);
   END;

   (* Set up the node's next pointer to point to the head of the
   original list, and then return this node. *)
   new^.next := l;
   RETURN new;
END Cons;

PROCEDURE Head(l : List; VAR i : ARRAY OF BYTE);
(* Set variable i to contain the data item stored in the head of the list. *)
VAR
   byteCount : CARDINAL; (* Number of bytes taken by i. *)
   location : ADDRESS; (* Starting address of i. *)

BEGIN
   IF IsEmpty(l) THEN
      WriteString("Error - Head of empty list");
      HALT;
```

```
   ELSE
      (* Set location to the starting address of the data. *)
      location := l^.data;

      (* Now copy each byte into i. *)
      FOR byteCount := 0 TO l^.size-1 DO
         i[byteCount] := location^;
         INC(location);
      END;
   END;
END Head;


PROCEDURE Tail(l : List): List;
(* Return the list formed by removing the head of l. *)

BEGIN
   IF IsEmpty(l) THEN

      WriteString("Error - Tail of empty list");
      HALT;

   ELSE
      RETURN l^.next;
   END;
END Tail;


PROCEDURE IsEmpty(l : List): BOOLEAN;

BEGIN
   RETURN l = Create();
END IsEmpty;

BEGIN
   (* No initialisation code. *)
END GenericList.
```

Summary

Most data abstractions are dynamic by nature, that is a list has no fixed size, but grows and shrinks as items are added to it or removed from it.

Implementing data abstractions with static data representations is not very satisfactory. Static data structures cannot change in size to meet the demands of varying amounts of data, but dynamic data structures can.

Memory for dynamic data structures is allocated from the system heap, by calls to the ALLOCATE procedure (found in library module Storage), which must be performed by the program itself. The compiler and run-time system cannot allocate space for dynamic data structures.

Memory allocated from the heap is **not** contiguous, so a dynamic data structure cannot be accessed by adding an offset to the start of the data structure. Each element of a dynamic data structure must have the address of the next element in the structure, wherever it is stored in memory.

A dynamic data structure is therefore stored spread out across memory, with each element or node linked to the next one by a pointer (the high level abstraction of the memory address). To build a dynamic data structure we must allocate storage space for a new node and link it into the correct position in the data structure.

When a node of a dynamic data structure is no longer wanted the memory it uses can be returned to the heap for use by other items, by using the DEALLOCATE procedure (in Storage).

Deallocating unwanted nodes in a dynamic data structure may cause unwanted side effects in procedures that use the structure.

Dynamic list, queues, stacks, trees etc are all implemented in a similar way. Each individual item in the structure contains not only the data to be stored, but also one or more pointers to the other items in the structure.

A generic implementation of a dynamic data structure is one which allows any type of data item to be stored in the structure. Thus only one generic list implementation is needed to allow us to have lists of records, integers, arrays, strings etc.

Selected reading

Stubbs, D and Webre, N
Data structures with abstract data types and Modula-2
Brooks/Cole Publishing Company, 1987
A good introduction to data abstraction in Modula-2. Suitable for beginners and with plenty of examples of implementations. Good descriptions of the most common data abstractions.

Sincovec, R and Wiener, R
Data structures using Modula-2
J. Wiley and Sons, 1986
Another book full of implementations of data abstractions in Modula-2. Beginners may find it hard going, but the examples are very useful.

Ford, G and Wiener, R
Modula-2 a software development approach
J. Wiley and Sons, 1985
One of the best Modula-2 books around, but not suitable for beginners, as it assumes some previous programming experience. In particular, there are excellent chapters on using library modules, and dynamic and generic implementations of data abstractions. This should be on the bookshelf of every serious Modula-2 user.

7 Input/output abstractions

7.1 Introduction to i/o

From the earliest days of computing input and output (invariably abbreviated to i/o) has been of major importance to both computer designers and computer users. There is very little point in having the most powerful computers in the world if there is no way of getting information into or out of them! It may therefore seem surprising, since i/o is of such fundamental importance, that it is also one of the most problematical areas for programming language designers, as it is usually the richness of the programming language which provides the user with access to the operating system and the underlying computer.

In the early days of computing input of data might be done with a card reader, reading decks of punched cards, or, at the very beginning, by changing the positions of a set of switches on the front of the computer itself! Output was similarly primitive, and might consist of a stream of punched paper tape, or typed output on a printer. Luckily we have progressed a long way since then, and i/o devices range from simple video terminals to complex graphics terminals, light pens on sensitive screens and voice recognition systems.

7.1.1 Providing input and output capabilities

For any programming language to be useful it must have some means of providing i/o capabilities. There are two approaches to providing i/o, which are used by most programming languages. The first approach is to provide it as a defined part of the language; this means the language will contain special built-in procedures (as INC and DEC are built into Modula-2) using reserved words, to read in and write out data. If you consider the number of different types of i/o that might be wanted (characters, strings, integers, real numbers, formatted, files, i/o to devices such as printers and plotters etc.), you can see that to cover all possibilities a language would need a vast array of such built-in procedures. For example, the i/o for a video terminal would be very different to that for a voice-controlled door, whilst the scientist wanting to interface his computer to an experiment has very different needs to the business user wanting to type a report. Languages which take this approach tend either to provide too many such procedures, making the compilers and the language itself large and cumbersome (PL/1 is an example), or they provide only a small set of procedures, which can only satisfy a small percentage of users.

The alternative approach is to leave i/o out of the language definition, and allow each separate implementation of the language (for different machines and/or operating systems) to be tailored to the needs of the users. The problem with this approach is that programs written in the language can no longer be moved freely from one computer system to another, because the i/o is likely to be incompatible.

7.1.2 Input and output with Modula-2

The initial definition of Modula-2 tried to follow a method most similar to the second approach, by not providing i/o capabilities as a defined part of the language. Instead, all Modula-2 implementations were supposed to provide library modules containing procedures for performing such operations. However, the definition only stated that these libraries should exist, and provide the same i/o capabilities, not how these capabilities should be implemented, or what the various procedures should be called.

Unfortunately this doesn't completely avoid the problem of programs written on one Modula-2 implementation not running under a different implementation. The problem is somewhat alleviated because, since all implementations should provide the same capabilities, it should be possible to change the procedures for one implementation to those offering the same capabilities in the other implementation, to obtain the same results. However, to have to do this for a large program would be a time-consuming and frustrating task.

Wirth defined a possible i/o library module in *Programming in Modula-2*, called InOut. Luckily, this has become a de facto standard library module. That is, because of the large number of Modula-2 implementations which use InOut, it has become an honorary part of Modula-2, and you should find it available on the majority of Modula-2 systems. However, many of the Modula-2 implementations running under the Unix operating system do not have InOut in any recognisable form – if you are using such an implementation you will have to find out where your i/o varies from Wirth's InOut.

The BSI Standardisation Committee has been examining the provision of i/o capabilities in Modula-2 for some time, and are currently trying to define a suitable library to become a standard part of Modula-2. When this happens we should hope for all new compilers to follow the standard, although older compilers may not. We will look at the i/o capabilities provided by InOut (as defined by Wirth), and those provided by the proposed BSI standard library module.

7.2 The Stream abstraction

We have already said that there are many different types of i/o device available. We need some means of performing i/o for each type of device. If we had to develop the i/o capabilities for each device from scratch it would be a tremendous task, but the alternative is to consider whether or not there is an abstraction we can use to represent i/o for all devices.

7.2.1 The Sequence abstraction

If we take a look at the more common i/o devices (for example, terminals, files, disks) we can see some similarities. All these devices can have data written to them or read from them in a sequence, *a followed by b followed by c, ...,* and so on. The data usually has to be written or read in a particular order – just as we cannot write letters in any order if we want them to make sense as words and sentences.

Perhaps the easiest way of describing a sequence is to draw parallels with the way we read and write. If we write a number we start with the highest digit and move the pen to the right before writing each subsequent digit. Similarly, as we read a sentence we read the first word, second word, etc. After reading/writing we move our eye/pencil onto the next position ready to read/write the next item. Our eye or pencil therefore always *knows* the next position we should read from or write at. We can imagine that each sequence has a pointer which points to the current position in the sequence, for example:

Reading from an input sequence

Before anything is read the pointer is pointing to the first character in the sequence:

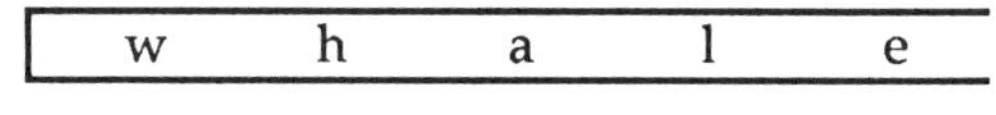

↑ Starting position

After reading the first character, "w", the pointer moves to the next character, "h", which is the next character that will be read.

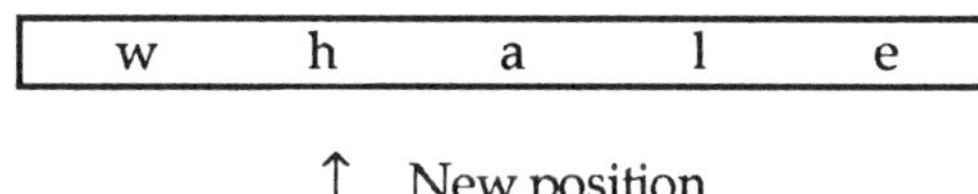

↑ New position

Writing to an output sequence

Before anything is written the sequence is empty, and the pointer points to the first location in the sequence.

```
|                                        |
 ↑ Starting position
```

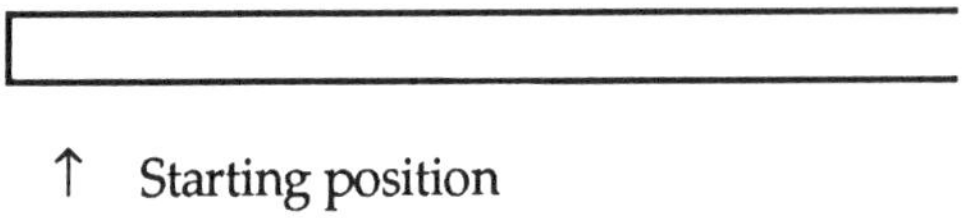

After writing "s" the pointer moves to the next free location in the sequence, which is where the next character will be written.

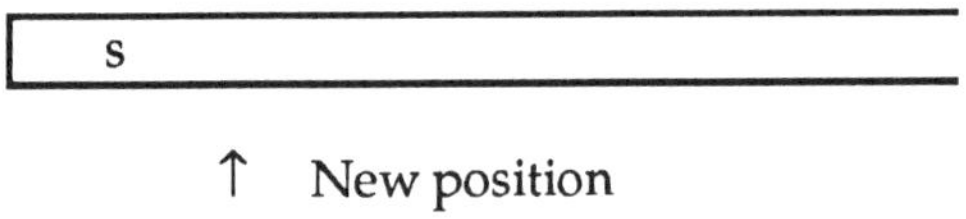

```
|  s                                     |
       ↑ New position
```

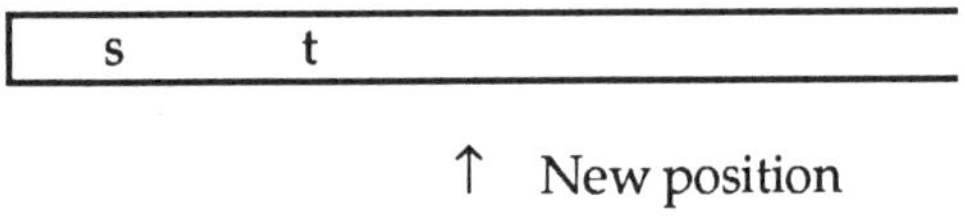

```
|  s       t                             |
                 ↑ New position
```

A word is a sequence of alphabetic characters, and a number is a sequence of digits. Similarly, we can look upon a file as being a sequence of bytes stored on a disk or in memory, as this is how it appears to us, although in reality the file may be stored split up on different parts of the disk. A terminal screen consists of a sequence of locations onto which we can write characters, and a keyboard provides a sequence of characters for the computer to interpret.

So, we can take many devices as being *sequential* in their i/o, and although this may not be true at the very lowest level in a device, this view of such devices provides us with an abstraction for representing their input and output. For a device to provide both input and output we need to associate two sequences with it, one for writing (the output sequence), and one for reading (the input sequence).

7.2.2 Defining the sequence abstraction

First we need to consider the functionality we want the abstraction to give us. There are two main functions required:

- To read an item from a device.
- To write an item to a device.

We can describe this functionality in two operations:

Read: Sequence → Item
Write: Sequence, Item → output item

where Read is given the name of the device to read from, and returns the item which it reads, and Write is given the name of the device to write to, and the item to be output on that device.

Each device can be viewed as a separate entity to the main computer. Most devices do not need to be accessed all the time, and some may be read-only (they can only be read from, not written to, for example an optical disk), others may be write-only (they may only be written to, not read from, for example a printer), some may need read and write access. We have already defined two types of sequence, the input sequence (for reading from a device), and the output sequence (for writing to a device). On this basis, some devices will need to be associated with an input sequence, some with an output sequence, and some with both, but not necessarily all the same time.

It follows from this that we need some means of controlling how we associate sequences with devices. One method of achieving this is to assume that each device must be specifically associated with an input or output sequence before it can be used for i/o. In computer-speak we call this *opening* a sequence for reading or writing. Looking at this from a different point of view, a sequence is *connected* to a device, to allow read or write access to that device. The phrases *input sequence* and *output sequence* are the shortened form of the phrases *input sequence for device x* and *output sequence for device x*:

OpenInput: Device → Sequence
OpenOutput: Device → Sequence

If we can set up a sequence to a device for input or output in such a way, it would also seem appropriate to be able to disconnect a sequence from a device, or *close* that device for input or output. We need two more operations:

CloseInput: Sequence → disconnect input sequence
CloseOutput: Sequence → disconnect output sequence

Now we have the operations for the Sequence abstraction we also need the equations, which define how these operations work and interact with each other. You should remember that there are five stages to finding the equations:

- Determine the constructors for the type we are defining. The constructors are the operations which can be used, by repeated application if necessary, to provide all possible examples of the type. In this case the constructors are OpenInput, OpenOutput, and Write. OpenInput and OpenOutput create new examples of Sequence, and Write adds an item to a sequence.

- Determine the modifiers. The modifiers change (or modify) examples of the type.

- Determine the observers. The observers are those operations which allow access to the type, so that we can find out what data it contains. We only have one observer so far: Read, which reads an item from a sequence.

However, we could introduce another observer, Length, which could give the number of items in a sequence at any given time:

```
Length: Sequence Cardinal
Length(Write(s, i)) = 1 + Length(s)
```

- Form the equations. Write the modifier and observer operations in terms of the constructors. If we take s as an occurrence of type Sequence, d as an occurrence of type Device, and i as an occurrence of type Item, then the equations will look like this:

```
Read(OpenInput(d)) = ERROR
Read(OpenOutput(d)) = ERROR
Read(Write(s, i)) = i
Length(OpenInput(d)) = 0
Length(OpenOutput(d)) = 0
Length(Write(s, i)) = 1 + Length(s)
```

Now let's put everything together, and see what we've come up with. The final set of operations is shown in Specification 7.1. You will notice that we have changed the name from Sequence to Stream, as we are not dealing with a sequence in the mathematical sense.

Specification **7.1** The Stream data abstraction

```
Types provided: Stream

Other abstractions used: Device, Item, Error

Operations:
   OpenInput: Device → connect input Stream (for reading).
   OpenOutput: Device → connect output Stream (for writing).
   CloseInput: → disconnect input Stream.
   CloseOutput: → disconnect output Stream.
   Read: Device → Item
   Write: Device, Item → output Item.

Axioms:
   Read(OpenInput(d)) = Error
   Read(OpenOutput(d)) = Error
   Read(Write(s, i)) = i
```

Where:
d is of type Device,
s is of type Stream,
i is of type Item.

We can also give a list of the properties a stream must have (after Wirth):

- A stream has no fixed length. The length at any given time is the number of data items in the stream at that time.

- A stream can only be accessed at one position – which is called the *current position*.

- A stream can only be accessed in two ways:

    1. Read – input operation. Accesses the item at the current position in the stream, and moves the current position up the stream by one item.

    2. Write – output operation. Appends an item to the end of the stream, which is always the current position for an output stream. The current position is moved up the stream by one item after a write operation.

- A stream must be *opened* before it can be accessed by read or write operations. By opening a stream we are effectively setting the current position to be:

    1. The start of the stream for a read/input stream.
    2. The first allowable position, for a write/output stream.

    The length of an output stream is set to zero when the stream is first opened, as no items can yet have been written to it.

- A stream must be *closed* when it has been accessed. After closing, the stream cannot be accessed by Read or Write operations, until another Open operation is performed on the stream.

7.2.3 Streams in Modula-2

Wirth defined the InOut library, which provides input and output capabilities for Modula-2, to be based on the Stream abstraction. Thus the operations of InOut bear a great similarity to the operations of the Stream abstraction. There are however some very obvious differences.

The first difference is that where the stream abstraction requires only one read operation and one write operation, the InOut implementation of it requires five read operations and five write operations, one to cope with each type of data:

```
ReadChar: Device → Char
WriteChar: Device, Char → output character
ReadInt: Device → Int
WriteInt: Device, Int → output integer
ReadCard: Device → Card
WriteCard: Device, Card → output cardinal
ReadString: Device → String
WriteString: Device, String → output string
```

Since i/o is unlikely to be completely error free in the real world (partly because humans are fallible), InOut must take this into account, so that the operations it provides are capable of dealing with errors. First of all, are there any obvious error conditions? What about the following?

- Performing a read and not finding anything valid to read. For example, trying to use ReadInt with the only available data as "hello".
- Performing a read and getting partially correct data. For example, ReadReal on the data 11.3a, will fail once it reaches the "a".
- Trying OpenInput/OpenOutput on a device which doesn't exist or is somehow or other invalid.
- Trying CloseInput/CloseOutput on a device which has not previously been opened for i/o.

After any read operations or open/close operations we want to be able to find out how successful the operation was. The method used by InOut is to have a variable parameter, called Done, which can be set to TRUE if an operation was successful, and FALSE if it fails for some reason. The parameter is shared by all the procedures in the library module, and so does not have to be passed as a parameter to each procedure.

In the InOut implementation of the Stream abstraction we are restricted to only two streams,

- The input stream – the one we read from.
- The output stream – the one we write to.

InOut provides default settings for these streams – they are both set to the terminal, so input comes, by default, from the keyboard, and output goes, by default, to the screen. The input and output streams are changed to other devices by use of the

OpenInput and OpenOutput operations, and when these connections are closed by CloseInput or CloseOutput, the streams return to the default – the terminal.

7.3 Text i/o in Modula-2

For i/o to be writable and readable by the user it must be character based – consisting of alphabetic characters, digits, spaces, punctuation etc. InOut provides procedures for reading in and writing out such data.

7.3.1 Single Character Data

The reading and writing of single characters is done with the use of the procedures Read and Write.

```
PROCEDURE Read(VAR ch : CHAR);
```

Procedure Read reads in a single character from the input device (by default this will be the keyboard in most systems), and stores it in variable parameter ch, which is of type CHAR. Read can read in any ASCII character, including the non-printing ones.

```
PROCEDURE Write(ch : CHAR);
```

Procedure Write writes a single character to the output device (by default this will be the terminal screen in most systems). The character is given in parameter ch. Write can write any valid character, including those which are non-printing.

7.3.2 Character strings

Single character data is very useful for some circumstances, such as reading a y/n response typed in by the user, but in many cases we would like be able to read and write strings of characters. InOut provides the procedures ReadString and WriteString for this purpose.

```
PROCEDURE ReadString(VAR string : ARRAY OF CHAR);
```

Procedure ReadString reads a string of characters into a character array. It will read characters from the input device until either it fills up the array, or it reads a terminator character. Each implementation of InOut will have its own defined set of terminators. The most common terminators are the carriage return and linefeed characters. The variable term ch which is exported by InOut contains the terminator character that ReadString met when reading in the string. ReadString will ignore all leading blanks, but once it has read a non-blank character it will include any blanks which occur inside the string.

```
PROCEDURE WriteString(string : ARRAY OF CHAR);
```

Procedure WriteString writes out a string of characters, given in parameter string.

It should be noted that although ReadString and WriteString appear in most implementations of InOut, they may behave slightly differently from implementation to implementation. In particular the WriteString procedure may only write out the given character string up to (but not including) the first terminator character it comes across. Wirth's definition of WriteString has the entire string being written out, no matter what its contents.

You will notice that Modula-2 does not provide a special string data type, but you may find that your particular implementation does provide one. Remember that if you use a special string type your programs will not be portable.

7.3.3 Cardinals, integers and real numbers

Although it is possible for us to write a procedure to read in a number as a character string, and convert it internally into the correct value, this is such a common necessity that InOut provides ready-made routines for doing it.

```
PROCEDURE ReadCard(VAR number : CARDINAL);
PROCEDURE WriteCard(number, width : CARDINAL);
```

ReadCard provides a means of reading in a cardinal number from the input device. The number is read in as ASCII characters and converted by ReadCard into the appropriate numeric value. ReadCard ignores leading blanks, and reads until a non-digit is met, or until the number is the maximum size for the particular implementation of Modula-2. A valid cardinal number must have at least one digit.

WriteCard is used to write cardinal values to the output device. The width parameter gives the minimum number of characters in which to write out the number. If the number is shorter than the minimum width, blanks are added preceding the number to bring it up to the minimum width. For example, if we have the following call to WriteCard:

```
WriteCard(1120, 6);
```

the output will be *padded out* with two spaces *before* the digits of the number are written.

If the number is larger than the given width it will simply overrun it to the right, for example,

```
WriteCard(98300, 2);
```

The whole of the number will be displayed, even though only two spaces were requested.

The procedures for integer i/o are very similar to those for cardinal i/o, the most obvious difference being that a number may start with a negation sign, -, or a plus sign, +.

```
PROCEDURE ReadInt(VAR number : INTEGER);
PROCEDURE WriteInt(number : INTEGER; width : CARDINAL);
```

ReadInt reads an integer number from the input device, as a string of ASCII characters, and converts the string into an integer number. It ignores leading blanks and will allow a + or - sign to immediately precede the digits of the number. ReadInt will read up to the first non-digit character. A valid integer must have at least one digit, but a sign is optional.

WriteInt writes out an integer value to the output device as a string of ASCII characters. If the number is negative it will be preceded by a - sign. As in WriteCard, the width parameter gives the minimum field width in which to output the number (including any sign). If the number is larger than the given width it will overrun to the right, if it is smaller blanks will be added to the left, preceding the number.

Input and output for real numbers is often a problem, as there are several ways of displaying real numbers (using ordinary notation or exponential notation), and adding the field width to allow formatted output makes things much harder. You will find that some implementations of Modula-2 simply do not provide procedures for real number i/o, but most will provide them in a library module called RealInOut.

```
PROCEDURE ReadReal(VAR number : REAL);
PROCEDURE WriteReal(number : REAL; width : CARDINAL);
```

ReadReal reads in a real number from the input device. There are two formats for a valid real number:

- Optional sign, digits, decimal point, digits. This allows real numbers of the form: -0.32 +12.4509 01.50 9.9

- Optional sign, digits, decimal point, digits, exponentiation (E), optional sign, digits. This allows numbers of the form: -12.4E3 3.89E-2

Note that in both cases the digits are not optional – there must be at least one digit in each position, even if that digit is 0.

WriteReal writes out a real number to the output device, using width as the minimum field width to write it in. If the number is shorter than the given width, it is padded with blanks; if longer, the width is ignored and the number is simply written out.

7.3.4 Boolean i/o

Modula-2 provides a built-in Boolean type, BOOLEAN, with two truth values, TRUE and FALSE. The InOut library does not provide any means of reading or writing Booleans, so it is up to the programmer to provide his own routines.

For BOOLEAN i/o we need two procedures – one for reading in BOOLEAN values and one for writing out BOOLEAN values. What design issues do we need to address for BOOLEAN i/o? Instead of taking the input and output procedures separately, look at them together. Is there anything we need these procedures to address? Look at ReadCard and its alter ego WriteCard – ReadCard can read cardinal numbers written out by WriteCard, and WriteCard can write out cardinal numbers successfully read in by ReadCard. The same is true of ReadInt/WriteInt and the other sets of i/o routines. Since we need to provide both input and output capabilities it is only sensible to ensure that they are compatible with each other.

In the case of Boolean i/o it would be easy to make the mistake of incompatibility – WriteBoolean could be expected to write out "TRUE" and "FALSE" in full, as this requires no effort from the user of the program, but ReadBoolean must read in data typed in by the user, who may not wish to have to type in the complete words "TRUE" and "FALSE". Looking at it from the user's point of view it would be easy to forget compatibility and make ReadBoolean accept single characters "t" and "f".

We will start with the easiest case – writing out a BOOLEAN value. Given a Boolean variable *finished* we cannot say:

```
WriteString(finished);
```

as WriteString can only be given parameters of the ARRAY OF CHAR type, and the compiler will spot this incompatibility of types and refuse to compile our program. Likewise, WriteInt, WriteCard and WriteReal are unable to help us directly. We can, however use WriteString to write out the appropriate string, "TRUE" or "FALSE" depending on the value of *finished*. This needs a conditional branching structure:

```
If finished is TRUE then
   WriteString("TRUE")
otherwise (* Finished must be FALSE. *)
   WriteString("FALSE")
endif.
```

We can translate this directly into Modula-2:

```
PROCEDURE WriteBoolean(bool : BOOLEAN);
BEGIN
   IF bool THEN
      WriteString("TRUE");
   ELSE
      WriteString("FALSE");
   END;
END WriteBoolean;
```

Procedure WriteBoolean takes a BOOLEAN value and writes out the string "TRUE" if the given value is TRUE and writes out "FALSE" if the given value is FALSE. Remember that there is no other possibility for writing out a Boolean value, since WriteBoolean can only accept a Boolean parameter. A call such as:

```
WriteBoolean(26);
```

will not be accepted by the compiler as 26 is of type CARDINAL or INTEGER, not type BOOLEAN.

We will accept that ReadBoolean should be able to read in a Boolean written out by WriteBoolean. This makes the ReadBoolean procedure equally simple:

```
Read in a word

If the word is "TRUE" then
   Set bool to TRUE

Otherwise if the word is "FALSE" then
   Set bool to FALSE
Endif
```

where bool is a BOOLEAN variable, in which the result of ReadBoolean is passed back to the calling program.

Can you see any problems implementing this algorithm in Modula-2? How about the comparison between the word read in and the strings "TRUE" and "FALSE"? As long as word is an ARRAY OF CHAR we will be able to compare the two items using the = operation. So the Modula-2 version will look like this:

```
PROCEDURE ReadBoolean(VAR bool : BOOLEAN);
VAR
   word : ARRAY [0..5] OF CHAR;

BEGIN
   ReadString(word);
   IF word= "TRUE" THEN
      bool := TRUE;
   ELSIF word = "FALSE" THEN
      bool := FALSE;
   END;
END ReadBoolean;
```

7.4 Files and the Random Access abstraction

Files are the operating system's tool for storing data on a computer. In our programs the variables and data structures we use to store information whilst a program is running disappear as soon as the program finishes. However, when you use some type of editor to type in a program in Modula-2 it is stored in a file. The file does not disappear when you leave the editor, and you can always get your program back if you want to look at it, edit it or compile it.

The files in which programs and other data are stored belong to the operating system of the computer. The programs which we write can create, access and modify files, but the way in which they can do this is dependent on the underlying operating system.

It is possible for a program to use files in two different ways (although to some extent this is dependent on the implementation of Modula-2 you are using). The simplest form of file access (and one which is invariably available in Modula-2 implementations) uses the operations in the InOut module. We have mainly used InOut operations to display information on the computer screen, or read information typed at the keyboard by the user. However, as we saw earlier, InOut does provide operations for connecting the input and output streams to devices other than the screen and keyboard – OpenInput and OpenOutput (and the equivalent for reconnecting to the screen and keyboard – CloseInput and CloseOutput).

Wirth's definition of OpenInput and OpenOutput was slightly strange, requiring the operations to be passed a file name extension, after which the user would be requested on standard output, to type in the name of the file to open (to which the extension would be added). Thus if OpenInput is passed the string "def" and the user types in "StaticStack" in response to the OpenInput prompt, the file "StaticStack.def" will be opened, if it exists, and created if it doesn't. This is certainly a problem if we don't want to ask the user for a filename.

The other restriction with using files via InOut is that it only allows one input stream and one output stream to be open at any time. So, if we have a program that wants to send its output to two files, every time we want to write something to both files we have to do the following:

```
Open first output file
Write data into it
Close first output file
Open second output file
Write the data into it
Close second output file
```

An easier alternative would be to open both files at once, perhaps at the start of the program, then we could write to either one as necessary:

```
Open first output file
Open second output file

Do some processing, including a number of writes of the form:
    Write to first file
    Write to second file

Close first output file
Close second output file
```

The first method, the one enforced by InOut is in fact much safer than the second method. We are less likely to write data into the wrong file when we must specifically ask for a file to be opened each time we want to write into it. However, the second method is sometimes preferable.

InOut has yet another problem which is inherent in the abstraction on which InOut is based – the Stream abstraction. Access to a stream is sequential, so if we connect the input stream to a file and want to append data to the end of the file, we must read sequentially through the file until we reach the end. If we are using the file to search for information the problem is similar, we have to read sequentially through each item in the file until we reach the one we want.

As we know, sequential search is very inefficient, and not really tenable for searching large data sets. Imagine searching sequentially through the telephone directory for a name beginning with "Z".

7.4.1 The Random Access abstraction

For the reasons given above (and some others we haven't mentioned) most operating systems allow a second kind of access to files. This type of access is called *random access*. Random access is the ability to go straight to any position inside a file **without** having to read sequentially through the file until we reach the required position.

File implementation, especially for random access, is dependent on the operating system and versions of Modula-2 running on different computers with different operating systems are likely to provide varying operations for random file access. A program which uses random file access operations on an Apple Macintosh is unlikely to run without alteration on a Sun Workstation, and so such programs become non-portable.

This in itself is a good reason for stopping with the sequential access operations provided by InOut! However, if you still wish to know the secrets of random file access we will continue. For our examples we will be using the random access operations provided by the Metrowerks Modula-2 compiler for the Apple Macintosh.

First we need to consider how files are actually stored by the operating system. Files are usually stored on disk, and they can be assumed, for our purposes, to be a sequence of bytes. In fact on some operating systems a file is a sequence of records rather than bytes, and on all operating systems files are rarely stored in a continuous sequence of bytes, but are dotted all over the disk where ever there is space available (in a similar way to how dynamic data structures are stored in memory). However, we can assume that a file is a continuous sequence of bytes, because the operating system will make it appear as such.

When a program opens a random access file the operating system gives the program a unique *file descriptor* by which the file can be accessed. Any operations performed on the file use the file descriptor to access the file. When a file is opened it has a *state* attached to it, this state tell us what sort of access we can make to the file. The three types of access allowed are:

- Read only.
- Write only.
- Read/write.

If a file is opened *read only* then it cannot be written to (unless we close it and reopen it with write access allowed), only read from. If a file is *write only* it cannot be read from, only written to. Not surprisingly, if a file is opened with *read/write* access we can read from it and write to it.

Note how different this is from the input/output abstraction provided by InOut. InOut allows us to connect one output stream to one output device (which may be a file) and one input stream to one input device. The random access abstraction provides as many output streams and input streams as we want (up to the limits allowed by the operating system).

Now we are ready to begin specifying the random access abstraction. Here is a basic set of random access operations:

- Open – get a file descriptor for a particular file, with the appropriate access state.
- Close – close the file attached to a particular file descriptor.
- Seek – move to a given offset from the start of the file.
- Length – return the total number of bytes in the file.

- ReadNBytes – read a given number of bytes from the current position in the file.
- WriteNBytes – write a given number of bytes to the current position in the file

Your implementation of Modula-2 should provide a similar set of random access operations, although probably under different names. Specification 7.2 gives the syntactic specification of these operations:

Specification 7.2 The Random Access abstraction

Types provided: FileDescriptor

Other abstractions used: Boolean, Address, LongInt, AccessType, FileName

Operations:

Open: FileName, AccessType → FileDescriptor
Close: FileDescriptor → Boolean
Seek: FileDescriptor, LongInt → LongInt
Length: FileDescriptor → LongInt
ReadNBytes: FileDescriptor, LongInt, Address → LongInt
WriteNBytes: FileDescriptor, LongInt, Address → LongInt

Let's examine the above operations in more detail. The Open operation needs a file name and the type of access required for the file (that is read only, write only or read/write). It must return a file descriptor to the opened file. In many implementations the file descriptor will be returned as -1 if the file could not be opened for some reason (for example, asking for write access to a file which can only allow read access). The Close operation takes a file descriptor and closes the file associated with the descriptor. It will return True if the file is closed successfully and False if it isn't.

The Seek operation needs the descriptor of the file and the offset (from the start of the file) to move to. File positions are usually given using long integers (on a computer, long integers have twice the range of ordinary integers, so we can use much larger numbers), because files are often many thousands of bytes long. Once we have done a seek to some position within a file we have effectively moved the start of the read or write stream to this point in the file. Seek returns the offset it managed to reach. If we try to seek past the end of the file, Seek returns a negative offset.

In order to avoid trying to seek past the end of a file we have the Length operation, which returns the size of the file in bytes.

ReadNBytes and WriteNBytes allows us to write data into the file, starting at the current offset from the start of the file, and read data from the file, starting at the current offset. At this level of file access we want our read and write procedures to be generic, that is to be able to read or write any type of data. Rather than passing an ARRAY OF BYTE (which is very Modula-2 specific) we pass instead an address. For ReadNBytes this gives the memory address at which to store the data read from the file. For WriteNBytes this gives the memory address at which to find the data to be written into the file. We have to pass ReadNBytes and WriteNBytes the number of bytes to be read or written (as an long integer), and they return the number of bytes that were successfully read or written.

7.4.2 An example file i/o using a random access abstraction

Let's use the Metrowerks Modula-2 PSE version of these file operations (in library module FileIO) to store a queue of cardinal numbers in a file, and then try to read back from the file by random access. Note that ReadNBytes and WriteNBytes are called ReadMany and WriteMany respectively in the FileIO module. Here is a simple algorithm for what we want the program to do:

```
Create a queue of cardinal numbers
Open file for writing
Write each queue item into the file
Close the file
Re-open the file for reading
Ask the user which item to seek to
Seek to the requested item
Read the item
Display it on the screen
```

The complete program is given below in Program 7.1. Have a look at it, and then we'll discuss it in detail.

Program 7.1 Demonstration of random file access

```
MODULE FileTest;
(* Testing writing to and reading from a file using the file access
operations from the FileIO library module of Metrowerks Modula-2 PSE,
on an Apple Macintosh.

The data is written into a file called QueueFile. If QueueFile already
exists it is truncated to zero length, so any data in it will be lost. *)

FROM FileIO IMPORT FileDescr, accessMode, accessPerm, direction,
Open, Close, Seek, ReadMany, WriteMany;
FROM SYSTEM IMPORT ADR; (* Returns the address of a variable. *)
```

```
FROM GenericQueue IMPORT Queue, NewQ, AddQ, RearQ, FrontQ,
                         IsEmptyQ;

FROM InOut IMPORT WriteString, WriteLn, WriteCard, WriteInt,
ReadCard, HoldScreen;

VAR
   item : CARDINAL; (* A queue item. *)
   i : CARDINAL; (* Loop index. *)
   n : CARDINAL; (* Which item to seek as far as. *)
   q : Queue;
   fd : FileDescr; (* The file descriptor. *)

BEGIN
   (* Create a small queue of cardinal numbers! *)

   q := NewQ();
   FOR i := 1 TO 10 DO
      item := 2 * i;
      q := AddQ(q, item);
   END;

   (* Open the file for writing, stop if it can't be opened, truncate
   it to zero length if it already exists. *)
   fd := Open("QueueFile", accessMode{create, trunc,
                                     writeOnly});
   IF fd < 0 THEN
      WriteString("Couldn't open file to write.  Press key to abort
program.");
      HoldScreen;
      HALT;
   ELSE
      WriteString("Saving queue in file....");
      WriteLn;
      (* File opened OK, so store each queue item in it. *)
      WHILE NOT IsEmptyQ(q) DO
         FrontQ(q, item);
         q := RearQ(q);
         (* Write out the item before we store it, so we can see
         that something is happening. *)
         WriteString("writing...   ");
         WriteCard(item,3);
         WriteLn;
```

```
         (* Write the item into the file, stop if we can't write for
         some reason. *)
         IF WriteMany(fd, ADR(item), SIZE(CARDINAL)) <
                     LONGINT(SIZE(CARDINAL)) THEN
            WriteString("Couldn't write data.  Press key to abort
program.");
            HoldScreen;
            HALT;
         END;
      END;

      (* Close the file, stop if we can't close it for some reason. *)
      IF NOT Close(fd) THEN
         WriteString("Couldn't close file.  Press key to abort
program.");
         HoldScreen;
         HALT;
      END;
   END;

   (* Now we'll reopen the file and try to read back one of the
   queue items. *)
   WriteString("Random access test");
   WriteLn;
   fd := Open("QueueFile", accessMode{readOnly});
   IF fd < 0 THEN
      WriteString("Couldn't open file to read.  Press key to abort
program.");
      HoldScreen;
      HALT;
   ELSE

      WriteString("Seek to which item? (1..10): ");
      ReadCard(n);

      IF n > 10 THEN
         WriteString("File doesn't contain that many items.");
         HALT;
      END;

      (* This will seek to the item that is placed in position n in the file.
      Note that we must subtract 1 from n, because the first item is at
      offset position 0. *)
```

```
      IF Seek(fd, LONGINT((n-1) * SIZE(CARDINAL)),
                          fromCurrent) < LONGINT(0) THEN
         WriteString("couldn't find data.  Press key to abort
program.");
         HoldScreen;
         HALT;
      ELSE

         (* Read data from file and write it out to screen. *)
         IF ReadMany(fd, ADR(item), SIZE(CARDINAL)) <
                          LONGINT(SIZE(CARDINAL)) THEN
            WriteString("Couldn't read data.  Press key to abort
program.");
            HoldScreen;
            HALT;
         ELSE
            WriteString("The data item is ");
            WriteCard(item, 3);
            WriteLn;
         END;
      END;
   END;

   WriteString("FileTest finished.  Press any key to exit
program.");
   HoldScreen;
END FileTest.
```

There are a number of interesting things to note in this program. First of all, it seems rather long because of the amount of print statements we have put in, and because every time a file operation is done, we have to test the result, and do something (halt the program) if an error has occurred.

The Open operation opens a file called "QueueFile":

```
   fd := Open("QueueFile", accessMode{create, trunc,
                                     writeOnly});
```

The actual parameter

```
   accessMode{create, trunc, writeOnly}
```

is the set of modes with which the file is to be opened, that is it is to be created if it doesn't exist, truncated to zero length if it does (so any data already in it is lost), and with write only access.

The WriteMany function writes a given number of bytes into the file we have just opened, from the given starting address:

```
IF WriteMany(fd, ADR(item), SIZE(CARDINAL)) <
                    LONGINT(SIZE(CARDINAL)) THEN
```

The ADR operation is imported from the SYSTEM module and returns the address of a variable. SIZE we have already met, it returns the size of a variable of the given type. We have put the WriteMany function in an IF statement so we can test the value it returns to see if the operation was successful or not.

Once all the queue items have been written into the file we close it and re-open it with read access (in fact we could have opened for read/write access in the first place, but this is slightly safer):

```
fd := Open("QueueFile", accessMode{readOnly});
```

The Seek operation must be given the offset to seek to, which is relative to the start of the file, and this is effectively the number of bytes from the start of the file:

```
IF Seek(fd, LONGINT((n-1) * SIZE(CARDINAL)),
                          fromCurrent) < LONGINT(0) THEN
```

The operation will seek up to the start of the n'th CARDINAL number in the file. Remember that the first number is at offset 0, which is why we have to subtract 1 from the variable n to establish the final term in the file.

Once we've found the correct position in the file we use ReadMany to read the correct number of bytes (given by SIZE(CARDINAL)):

```
IF ReadMany(fd, ADR(item), SIZE(CARDINAL)) <
                          LONGINT(SIZE(CARDINAL)) THEN
```

The bytes read are copied into memory at the starting address of item (given by ADR(item)).

Any type of data item can be stored in and retrieved from a random access file in a similar way to the above example.

Finally, remember that the preceding example is specific to the Metrowerks version of Modula-2 running on an Apple Macintosh. If you are using a different computer and a different Modula-2 compiler then you will almost certainly have to make major changes to the program to make it compile and execute. However, the concepts of random access discussed above are applicable to any operating system which provides random access facilities.

7.5 User interfaces

The cleverest, most complicated program or software package is wasted if its users find it hard to use. Software may be hard to use for many reasons (most usually for a combination of reasons): commands may have obscure names and syntax; responses from the system may be too terse or incomprehensible; the system may *crash* (stop working) without warning if the user does the wrong thing and so on.

The *user interface* is the part of a software package which allows the user to communicate with (and therefore, to use) that package. For example, the operating system on the computer you are using provides the user interface to the computer itself, thus allowing you to use the computer. All operating systems provide a set of commands which you can use to get the computer to perform various, basic tasks.

The MS-DOS operating system provides commands for listing the files in a directory, copying and removing files, running programs, and so on. You have probably been typing in your Modula-2 programs using an editor, a special package to allow you to type information into files on the computer. The editor will have a user interface - the set of commands it provides to help you put in information, such as indenting a line, saving the file being edited, deleting a character or word etc; and possibly some information on how to use the editor, which you can request to see at any time, if you get stuck or forget a command.

User interfaces vary greatly in their complexity and ease of use. Some types of interface use *menus* and a *mouse* (if the computer has one). Others use *windows*, or a simple *command line*; many interfaces use a combination of approaches. We will describe the various types of interface later, but the overall aim is the same in all of them – to allow the user to use the software package they belong to. It is becoming increasingly important for the developer of a software package to provide a good, easy-to-use user interface. We will look at some of the attributes we need to consider for the interface when we design a software package.

The basic rules are that an interface should be:

- Simple for the user to learn and use.
- Consistent in its approach.
- Follow any standard conventions for the type of package or the type of computer it is to be used on.

A good user interface which follows these rules is often described as *user-friendly*, to imply that the interface tries to make life as easy as possible for the user.

User-friendly software should display the following attributes:

- Easy to learn and use.
- Hard to crash.
- Helpful.

For an interface to be easy to learn it must be small (not too many commands) and simple (require only a few concepts to understand the interface). Often, we learn only a small subset of the available commands, which are suited to the tasks we most frequently perform. Consider the operating system on the computer you are using, and write down the commands that you know. Then go to the user guide or command reference manual and see how many commands there are that you don't know!

An interface is hard to crash if it prevents the user from causing the software to terminate abnormally, or to *hang*, refusing to accept any further input. If the user gives some form of illegal input or attempts an illegal operation, it is usually a mistake on the part of the user, but a malicious user may try to crash a system just to cause inconvenience to other users.

If the user types something wrong in response to a prompt, the software should not accept it, but neither should it crash. The error should be reported to the user (with some indication of why it was an error) and the incorrect input then ignored. If the user types at the wrong time, this too should be ignored, perhaps with an indication such as ringing the bell. A robust system must also cope with other failures, such as missing files, missing printer, no storage space etc., without crashing.

The interface will have to have extra parts to do all the error checking, which can add considerably to the size of the software. For example, consider the simple case of reading in a single character typed by the user in response to some yes/no question, where character "y" stands for "yes", and character "n" stands for "no". If we don't bother with error checking we could use the following algorithm:

```
Ask user to enter "y" or "n" in response to question
Read in the character entered
If character is "y" then
   Process as a "yes" response
Otherwise if character is "n" then
   Process as a "no" response
Endif
Continue processing
```

The problem here is that any response other than "y" or "n" will not get dealt with. A slightly different approach would be just to check for a "y" and let all other responses be taken as an "n". However, we want to ensure that we only ever get either a "y" or an "n" response, we need something like this:

```
Ask user to enter "y" or "n" in response to question
Repeat the following
   Read in the character entered
   If character is neither "y" nor "n" then
      Tell user response must be "y" or "n"
   Endif
Until character is a "y" or "n"
 (* At this stage character must be "y" or "n". *)
If character is "y" then
   Process as a "yes" response
Otherwise if character is "n" then
   Process as a "no" response
Otherwise (* This should never happen! *)
   Tell user there is a problem with the software
Endif
Continue processing
```

The second version is much longer, but after the loop we are guaranteed to have a correct value for the character. The final clause is added to the if statement to catch some catastrophic error causing the character to be corrupted between the end of the loop and the processing in the if statement, although this is very unlikely to occur. Adding clauses to the code, to cope with incorrect, unforeseen or apparently impossible circumstances, is called *defensive programming.*

If the user interface of a software package is to be helpful, then it must provide help for the user on several levels. Firstly, we need meaningful command names, clear prompts for input, informative error messages and understandable results from the package. In other words, all the attributes which make a package easy to learn and use. In addition a helpful system will display information about how to use the system on the screen, at any time the user requests it. Such information might include a short summary of commands, an overall description of the system etc. Some *help* systems are sophisticated enough to provide *context sensitive* help. For example, if you ask for help in the editor part of a software system, you are given information about the editor, in some cases you might get information about the specific editing command you are currently trying to use; if you ask for help in the file handling part of the system, then you get information about file handling, and so on.

Summary

There are two main approaches to providing i/o in a programming language:

- I/o operations are defined as part of the language. This can lead to very large languages with many i/o operations, in an attempt to satisfy as many users as possible.

- I/o is left out of the language completely. Each individual implementation of the language must provide i/o operations which can be tailored to the user's needs. This can lead to programs being non-portable, because each implementation's i/o operations are likely to be very different.

Modula-2 does not provide i/o facilities as part of the language, but all Modula-2 implementations should provide a library of basic i/o operations. These libraries usually follows Wirth's definition of the InOut i/o library.

Many i/o devices are sequential in nature, so i/o libraries tend to be based on the Sequence or Stream abstraction.

There are two types of stream, the input stream (for reading from a device) and the output stream (for writing to a device). The appropriate stream must be connected to a device if the device is to be read from or written to.

The properties of streams are:

- A stream has no fixed length. The length at any given time is the number of data items in the stream at that time.

- A stream can only be accessed at one position – which is called the *current position*.

- A stream can only be accessed in two ways:

    1. Read – input operation. Accesses the item at the current position in the stream, and moves the current position up the stream by one item.
    2. Write – output operation. Appends an item to the end of the stream, which is always the current position for an output stream. The current position is moved up the stream by one item after a write operation.

- A stream must be *opened* before it can be accessed by read or write operations. By opening a stream we are effectively setting the current position to be:

    1. The start of the stream for a read/input stream.

2. The first allowable position, for a write/output stream.

The length of an output stream is set to zero when the stream is first opened, as no items can yet have been written to it.

- A stream must be *closed* when it has been accessed. After closing, the stream cannot be accessed by Read or Write operations, until another Open operation is performed on the stream.

The Modula-2 InOut library is an implementation of the Stream abstraction. It provides read and write operations for common data types such as characters, integers, etc.

Files are used for long term data storage (usually on a disk). They belong to the operating system but may be created, accessed and modified by programs, thus providing a means of storing data used or built by a program.

The simplest form of file access is sequential access. The InOut library provides sequential file access facilities. To get to say the 100th item in a sequential file we must start at the beginning of the file and read each item in turn until we reach the 100th item. In a very large file sequential access can be very slow.

A faster form of access, but one which is dependent on the facilities offered by the operating system and the language implementation, is random access. To get to the 100th item in a random access file we can jump directly to the item in one operation. There is no need to read past the 99 items we aren't interested in.

To use a random access file a program is given unique file descriptor for the file. All operations on the file are performed via the file descriptor.

The user interface is the part of a software system which presents information to, and interacts with, the user of the system.

A user interface should be easy to learn and use, consistent, hard to crash and helpful. In two words – user friendly!

Selected reading

Most books on Modula-2 will contain a chapter on input and output, and this may be all that you need to use. Books on user interfaces are harder to find, although many operating systems books will contain sections about the user interfaces used in particular operating systems. If you are interested in the current state of research on user interfaces, computing journals are a good source of up to date papers on the subject.

Wirth, N
Programming in Modula-2, 4th Edition
Springer-Verlag, 1989
This contains the definitive description of the InOut and RealInOut library modules. At least until the British Standard version becomes widely used. Most compilers on the market at the time of writing follow the i/o descriptions given by Wirth.

8 Process abstraction

8.1 Concurrency

Most naturally occurring phenomena display some kind of concurrency in the way actions and interactions occur. For example, the whole of human society is based on a complex interplay of simultaneous events. To some degree this society depends on the global actions of others, and sometimes critically on the local actions of a smaller numbers of individuals. Even though there may be no direct communication between the majority of the members of the human race their actions are linked by politics, economics, education and many other social factors. In addition, natural phenomena such as climate, disease, and disasters such as earthquakes, can have important local and global effects on human society.

In any large project, such as major construction work, we would expect teams of people to cooperate to achieve some goal. At the site level the workers need to coordinate their actions, but still work as individuals to carry out their separate tasks as required. At the management level the workers' tasks need to be coordinated, but management must also respond to the instructions of government or some other high ranking body. In addition external factors can interact with local control.

All individual tasks are carried out sequentially, but mostly in parallel with other sequentially executed tasks. Some of these tasks need to be synchronized, with other tasks. Control of the whole project and the synchronisation of individual tasks requires a flexible and reliable communication system. Later we shall describe computer models where the equivalent of the workers, management and government become computational *processes*.

We may assume that most events, whether human, natural or abstract, exhibit some degree of concurrency. It seems quite sensible to expect any computer model of these events to embrace the same degree of concurrency.

The early years of computer programming were spent developing methodologies that mimicked the von Neumann model of a computer. This computer model was strictly sequential in its actions and, therefore very artificial barriers were created which, for many years, inhibited the sound development of concurrent programming methods. Even today, the common view is to treat concurrency as a special case.

We have seen that most phenomenon are naturally concurrent, therefore it seems reasonable to state that the correct stance for us to take is to treat concurrency as normal and sequentiality as the special, or degenerate case of concurrency. Let us clarify this statement: events are naturally sequential in nature, but the interaction of events are concurrent, and so the degenerate model of these events would be to design not only the events as sequential instances but also to impose a sequential structure on the interaction of events. Even though this approach to computing is possible, it is always going to be a special and very artificial solution, and as such is undesirable.

8.1.1 Concurrency in computing

Let us concentrate for the moment on reasons why we should be interested in concurrency in computing.

Firstly, there are many low cost and high speed computers, such as the Intel i860 and Inmos Transputer, that can be built into systems to work together on problems that require large amounts of computing power. Many problems in science, technology and commerce were until recently thought to be too expensive to compute. By splitting these problems into many subproblems they can be solved in parallel and then re-combined to give the final solution. One such problem is found in computer graphics, where the synthesis of a complex image may be divided into n equal parts and then shared between n processors in the hope of producing the finished image in *1/n th* of the time taken by one processor.

The division of a problem into many parts is not always as easy as that described above. If we refer back to the the construction problem, external forces frequently occur at the various organisational levels. For example, climate can have considerable influence on the efficiency of the workers and can cause subtle changes to the overall project. In computer terms, these events are known as data dependencies and can lead to errors in the solution if not modelled correctly. In general, we need to exercise care in accounting for related data that is being manipulated on some distant computer.

We cannot simply assume that distant calculations have no effect on the calculations that are being carried on the local computer. For example, if we wished to generate a high quality computer graphics image we would probably use a technique known as the radiosity method. This method has the ability to model the way in which the colour of neighbouring objects can have a subtle interaction with each other. The method uses the laws of radiation physics to compute the interactions of all the objects and surfaces within some environment. So simply dividing the tasks that are needed to create this image into *n* parts and distributing these parts to *n* computers, and then instructing these computers to carry out their tasks independently, would lead to an incorrect result. In this problem a particular section of the image is related in some way to all other parts of the image. In other words there are data dependencies which require every computer involved in solving this problem to inform every other computer of each intermediate solution that has been calculated.

Unfortunately, many problems in science and engineering have solutions with strong data dependencies. This phenomena causes some algorithms, that are frequently used on sequential computers, to simply not work on parallel computers. In addition, some computer configurations become inadequate as they cannot efficiently support the level of communication that is necessary for these problems. These difficulties, therefore lead to a restriction in the degree of freedom that is available to the hardware and software designers who wish to solve these problems.

Secondly, many problems, by their very nature, are better solved if they are distributed across a number of computers. If your bank has only one branch then you would expect one computer to be sufficient to handle all the customer transactions. Even if the bank had a large number of branches we could still argue that one large computer with remote terminals at each branch is the most satisfactory method of handling all customer transactions. But what if we were to consider a bank with branches that cross state, country and even continental boundaries? Then the single computer solution becomes far less attractive. The delays that would result from so many users trying to access a single computer would be unacceptable. In addition, the dangers resulting from so many interactions being dependent on one central computer are unacceptable.

A better solution for problems such as financial transactions between banks and individuals is to distribute the work between many computers. This distributed system should be connected by a network that allows individuals to access computers and also allows computers to communicate with each other. Another easily visualised distributed system is given by an interactive reservation network. These reservation networks often need concurrent access, sometimes on a world-wide basis (for example an airline reservation network).

Other distributed systems are hidden away from us but can critically affect our lives in many ways. For example, an aircraft navigation system computer may interact with the aircraft guidance system computers, which in turn may interact with the engine and wing control computers. At the same time there may be an interaction with the ground control computers which may also interact with other aircraft, all as a consequence of the the initial action of the navigation computer. All of these events are concurrent in their actions and would probably give rise to complex secondary interactions (feedback) between what are obviously distributed computers. For applications of this type the software and hardware of the computer system must be capable of immediately responding to real time events. A high degree of concurrency is obviously needed for an effective solution to this type of problem.

The third form of concurrency that interests us is restricted to a single processor. There are many activities beside executing a straight-forward program that need to be carried out on a processor. For example, an editor must interact with some data structure, possibly your program, and also receive information from the keyboard and display information to the screen, as shown in Figure 8.1

Figure 8.1 Concurrency

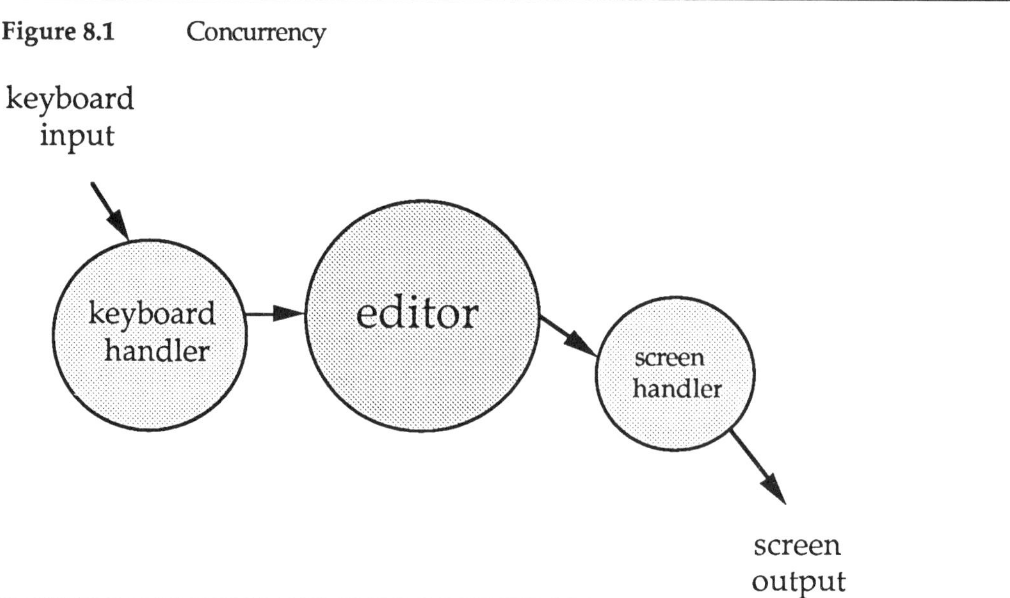

Although there appears to be a natural sequence of events shown in Figure 8.1, in reality the processor must be able to order these events in such a way as to enable the needs of many competing actions to be met. In fact, the computer operating system has to schedule demands for many competing functions such as: screen handling, disk access, memory access, executing the application program and perhaps handle external communications to and from other computers.

On a single processor the execution of various events cannot normally happen concurrently (except when special hardware support allows the overlapping of some of these requirements). Instead the events must be scheduled for action in some way to allow the efficient processing of all the separate functions. This implies that the *event scheduler* must be capable of starting an action, stopping an action, suspending an action that cannot be completed, and also being able to return to that action at a later time to complete the task. This event handling control system is obviously executed sequentially on a single processor, however the underlying software model must be concurrent to allow the scheduling of events to correctly occur in the time dependent environment in which the execution of the software takes place. Thus, there is a need for concurrency on a single processor, if only to enable the operating system to support our programming requirements.

In its present form Modula-2 does not support the kinds of concurrency that allows programs to use more than one processor to achieve its objectives. However, Modula-2 does fully support the third type of concurrency described above, whereby events can interact on a single processor.

The events that can be identified as concurrent among the elements shown in Figure 8.1 are normally referred to as processes. The process is a useful concept and we need to look at it in some detail.

8.2 The process model

The term *process* is used to describe a sequence of actions that can be performed concurrently with other processes, each of which describes other sets of actions. In general, the individual processes execute sequentially, and we will assume this to be the case for the remainder of this chapter.

Processes may be mutually independent, that is non-interacting, as shown in Figure 8.2.

Figure 8.2 Independent processors

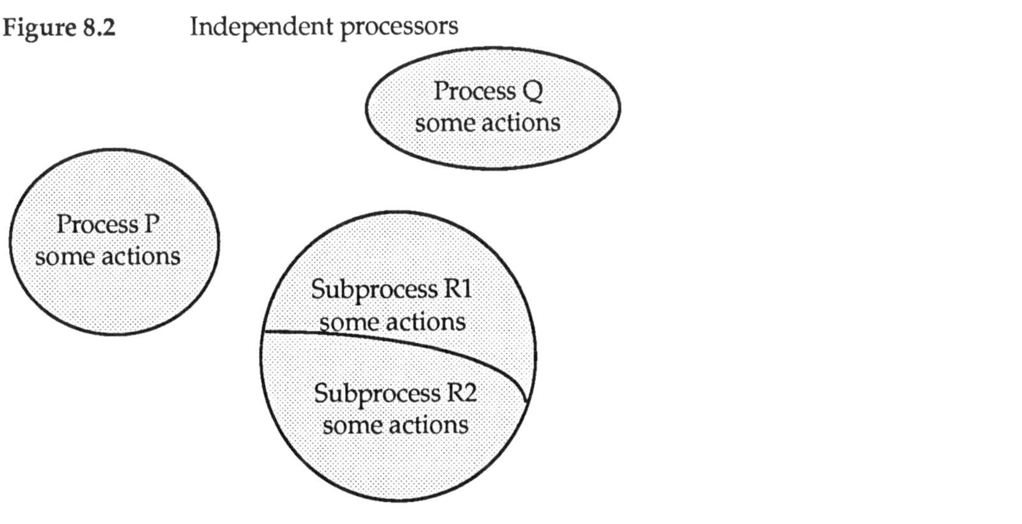

Here, processes P, Q and R are all independent of each other. The subprocesses R1 and R2 may for instance share some common features but they still act independently. Thus the execution of all these processes does not affect the internal actions of the other processes.

Alternatively, processes can be mutually dependent, and therefore, cooperate in some way, as given in Figure 8.3:

Figure 8.3 Process model

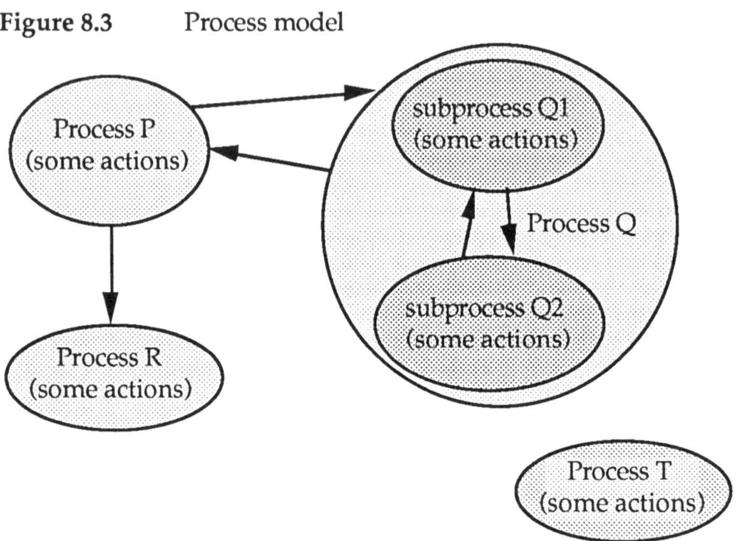

In the example shown in Figure 8.3 Process T is independent, Process P interacts with Process Q (which itself has two subprocesses). Process R is affected by Process P but does not itself affect Process P.

The execution of Process P will also affect the execution of Processes Q and R in some way. The effect on Process Q will in turn have a feedback on Process P. Programming this complex interaction of events must obviously be carefully specified and designed if we are to ensure that the computation carries out the desired set of actions at all times.

8.2.1 Process communication

Whether or not processes are confined to one processor or distributed between many processors, it is inevitable that some processes will need to communicate with other processes. In some cases this communication may be asynchronous, that is the order in which messages arrive may not be critical to the current execution of the processes. But this is not always the case as many other problems may depend on the strict synchronisation of communications between processes.

8.2.2 Independent and dependent processes

The *n* independent processes P1,.....,Pn may or may not have identical tasks to perform. This is simply a matter that must be accommodated in the overall program structure. However, what is important is that the independence implies that each process has quite separate and independent data structures. As an example, consider *n* processes being applied to a simple linear search. Here, divide the data evenly between the *n* processes and let each process search its portion of data. These processes are obviously independent, and perform the search on separate data. The order in which the processes are carried out and the degree of concurrency employed do not affect the final result.

When processes interact, that is they are interdependent, then they may share resources. We may ask the question *does this dependence present special problems*? The answer is yes as most shared resources need careful use. Consider the problem of aircraft traffic control. Aircraft flying in a certain direction have different resources allocated to them, namely, a length of airspace for their exclusive use. Similarly, aircraft flying in directions have different resources by being separated vertically in difference airspace. But what about the time when aircraft are landing and taking-off?

Let us suppose that only one airstrip is at our disposal (Hong Kong Airport is such an example) and must therefore be used by aircraft that are both landing and taking-off. It is obvious that this resource must be shared but with strict control to ensure that when one activity is underway then the other is excluded. In other words, the control mechanism ensures *mutual exclusion* of the shared resource. But note, the control mechanism itself is also a shared resource and is subject to *mutual exclusion* of its shared resources.

When a process is using a shared resource it is said to be operating in its *critical section.*

8.2.3 The critical section problem

Let two processes P and Q be executing concurrently. Each process contains a critical section where simultaneous entry of processes is not permitted. A simple example of a shared resource is a printer, to which access is given to one process at a time. An example of a shared data resource is the record of the cash recorded in your bank account. In this example, you would expect all access to this data to be correct at all times, therefore a process such as credit must block other processes, such as debit, until its actions are completed and it has left the critical section.

Before we consider an algorithm that satisfies the mutual exclusion principle, let us first consider the properties that must be satisfied to achieve a safe and efficient solution (remember, processes are either executing, waiting to execute or have been descheduled while awaiting some future event):

1. At any instant of time a critical section contains at most one process.

2. A process that is outside its critical section and is not attempting to enter its critical section must not prevent another process entering its critical section. A process that violates this condition is guilty of *blocking* or *livelock*.

3. A degree of *fairness* is applied to a number of processes that are waiting to execute their critical sections, and in particular no process is neglected for undue time.

4. Processes about to enter a critical section must not be allowed to block each other because of indecision on which process actually enters the critical section. Processes that violate this conditions are guilty of *deadlock*.

A correct solution to these conditions requires that the processes are always sequenced in the right order. However, unlike what occurs in a simple sequential program, the sequencing of the processes cannot be predetermined by the order of the statements in the program. Instead, the sequence of processes is controlled by the processes communicating with each other to enable the precise synchronisation of process event to occur as allowed by the four condition described above.

8.2.4 Process synchronisation

Whenever we as individuals combine with colleagues to solve some problem then it is most unlikely that we can make our individual contributions without a considerable amount of communication. We can expect concurrent processes to need communication facilities in the same way. Before parallel processing with many cooperating processors became a reality, the need for processes to interact was studied in great depth, particularly in the context of operating system use and design. The traditional synchronisation mechanism favoured by operating system designers, and early concurrent processor designers, was based on the use of shared variables. Consider two processes which have been placed on different processors as shown in Figure 8.4.

Figure 8.4 Shared Memory

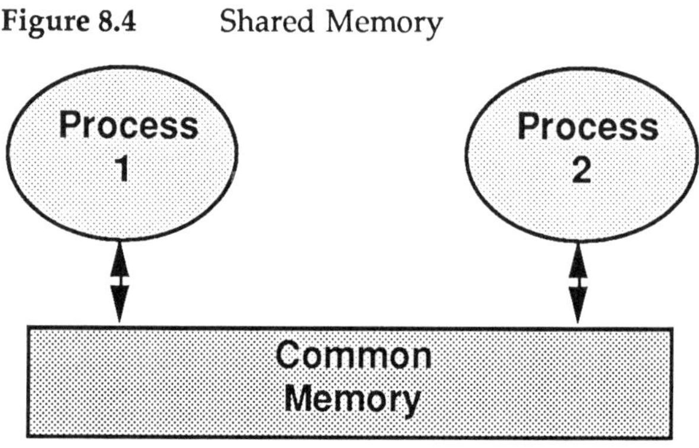

In this model of a computer system the memory has an address structure which is common to all processes, irrespective of processor. This is a situation in which the need for solving the critical section problem is immediately obvious. Although the processes are independent, the need to access and modify the same data structure by both of these processes during the normal course of execution could easily occur.

Although communicating via *common or shared memory* may appear to be the obvious way to implement a parallel system, it is by no means the only method used by system designers. In recent times, many systems have been implemented that distribute memory among the processors in such a way that each processor is responsible for a portion of private memory which is not made directly available to any other processor. This is an easy model for humans to appreciate as we function in precisely this way.

How do we communicate to achieve cooperation with each other? Obviously by visual or verbal messages. Distributed memory, or message passing systems as they are sometimes referred to, use the same model of communication as humans. Messages carry requests for data, or issues instructions to modify data. One major penalty incurred by this type of system which can significantly reduce the efficiency, is caused by needing copies of the same information stored in the private memory of different processors. A change to one copy of this information may result in needing to modify all the copies to ensure uniformity of data across many processors. The general system *architecture* is given in Figure 8.5.

Figure 8.5 Distributed memory processors

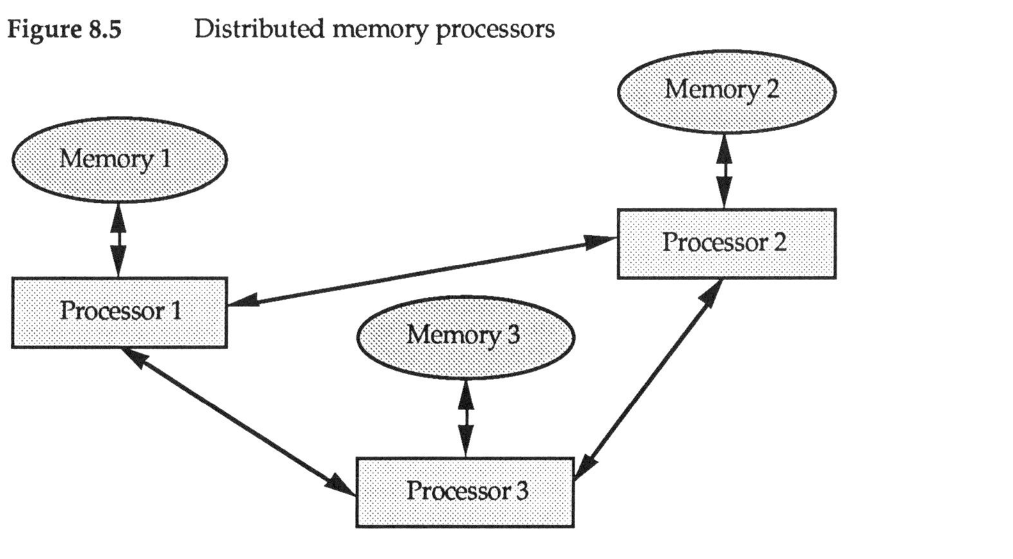

Access to the data stored in a private memory module from a distant processor is possible via a message request to the processor that controls the private memory.

Requests by more than one processor gives rise to an identical critical section problem as previously discussed for the shared memory model. However, due to the characteristics of the distributed memory model the solution will be somewhat different. In distributed systems of this type the use of messages for interprocess communication also becomes the basis of process synchronization.

As our primary interest is in the Modula-2 model of process abstraction we will restrict most of our discussions to the shared variable model of computation.

Let us examine some methods that will enable processes to synchronize their actions and therefore allow a solution to the critical section problem.

8.2.5 Semaphores

A powerful synchronization device called a semaphore was introduced by the Dutch computer scientist Dijkstra in 1965 to allow mutual exclusion to be applied to *n* processes.

A semaphore S is an integer variable that can be altered in one of two ways by the processes P(S) and V(S). These are defined as follows for the process Q that is attempting to enter its critical section:

P(S) IF S > 0 THEN S := S - 1; let Q enter its critical section ELSE the execution of the the process Q is suspended;

V(S) IF some process Q has been suspended by a call to P(S) on semaphore S THEN wake up Q ELSE S := S + 1;

The two operations P and V are derived from the Dutch words passeren (pass) and vrijgeven (release).

Modifications to the value of S are only allowed atomically, that is if a process is modifying S, then another process cannot modify the same semaphore. However, if two processes execute P(S) and V(S) then these processes will be executed sequentially in some arbitrary order.

When the variable S is restricted to the values 0 and 1 then the semaphore is called a binary semaphore. A general semaphore allows S to assume any cardinal value.

8.2.6 Using semaphores

Semaphores can be used to solve a number of problems of which the read/write and producer/consumer problems are typical. Let us start by examining the straight forward mutual exclusion problem.

Mutual exclusion

An n-process critical section problem can be solved using a general semaphore. Each process shares a common semaphore S, which is initialised to 1. Each critical section can then be safely dealt with by bracketing the critical section by P and V operations.

```
P(S);
   <critical section>
V(S);
```

We can illustrate this by using a binary semaphore to satisfy the mutual exclusion problem for the two concurrent processes Process1 and Process2, each with a critical section, which are required to be mutually exclusive.

For the moment, we will not discuss how to implement concurrent processes in Modula-2. The pseudo instructions COBEGIN and COEND will be used to indicate where processes should be executed concurrently.

Consider the following program fragment:

```
VAR S: semaphore;

PROCEDURE Process1;
BEGIN
   LOOP
      P(S);
         (* Critical section. *)
      V(S);
   END; (* Loop. *)
END Process1;


PROCEDURE Process2;
BEGIN
   LOOP
      P(S);
         (* Critical section. *)
      V(S);
         <statement>; (* Non-critical section. *)
   END; (* Loop. *)
END Process2;
```

```
BEGIN (* Main program. *)
   S: = 1; (* Initialise semaphore. *)
   COBEGIN (* Pseudo code. *)
      Process1;
      Process2;
   COEND;
END.
```

Using this example we can illustrates the simplicity and power of the semaphore:

Imagine that this problem describes a car wash which has a car park that is sufficiently large to allow all cars to wait on arrival. The car wash itself only allows one car to be present at a time, and use a signal go/stop at the door to admit or restrict entry from the car park.

Two types of drivers are present: those who require their car to be washed and waxed, CarWashWax, and those who require their car to be washed and immediately leave the premises, CarOnlyWash.

To allow the first car to enter, the signal is initially set to go. As the car enters the car wash the signal is set to stop. Any car arriving at the premises that attempts to enter the carwash is refused by the stop signal and must wait in the car park or leave. When a car leaves the car wash, say CarWashWax, the signal is reset to go and one of the waiting cars will now be successful in gaining entry, say CarOnlyWash, and the signal is reset to stop.

While CarOnlyWash is in the car wash, CarWashWax is concurrently waxed, as there is no restriction on this action because the waxing the car operation is not in a critical section. We are assuming that there are always sufficient resources available for waxing to be carried out on demand. This set of actions will continue until no further cars are waiting.

The specification of the Car Wash simulator given in Section 2.4 is still sufficient to specify the problem as described above. The only extra detail needed is to require that the operations MakeActive and MakeInactive are implemented with the binary semaphore operations P(S) and V(S). This requirement is, of course, completely hidden at the specification level. The procedural abstraction WaxTheCar is not guarded by semaphore operations, therefore it may be accessed by all values CarWashWax, of type Car, as they become available on exiting a car wash.

This car wash model is an accurate representation of the set of procedures described in the previous example.

You may ask what happens while the process is in P mode? In the example given above the process would be held, that is descheduled, until the other process exits the critical region. The held process would periodically *look* to determine if the value of the semaphore had changed, but otherwise no useful work would be undertaken by the held process. However, if the ordering of actions in the held process is unimportant and could be divided in some way, then subprocesses could be introduced which could be scheduled for processing while the held process waits to enter its critical section. Then:

```
VAR S : semaphore;

PROCEDURE Subprocess1a;
BEGIN
   LOOP
      <statements>
   END; (* Loop. *)
END Subprocess1a;

PROCEDURE Subprocess1b;
BEGIN
   LOOP
      P(S);
         write(data)
      V(S);
   END; (* Loop. *)
END Subprocess1b;

PROCEDURE Process2;
BEGIN
   LOOP
      P(S);
         Read(data) (* Critical section. *)
      V(S);
   END; (* Loop. *)
END Process1;

BEGIN
   S := 1; (* Initialise semaphore. *)
   COBEGIN (* Pseudo code. *)
      Process1;
      Subprocess1a;
      Subprocess1b;
   COEND;
END.
```

In this example, Subprocess1a does not have a critical section, therefore it is free to execute its code at all times. Subprocess1a and Process2 do, however have critical sections, and consequentially mutual exclusion must be applied to these processes.

Although one only of these mutually excluded processes may be executing at any instant of time, with the other suspended, each can be executing in parallel with Subprocess1a.

We will later describe Modula-2 constructs to carry out these pseudo parallel processing functions such as given by COBEGIN.

The bounded producer-consumer problem

Producer-consumer processes commonly appear in computing problems. For example, a graphics driver produces an image which is consumed by a display monitor. A more complete example starts with you typing at a keyboard. Your fingers produce output which must be consumed by the keyboard handler. This in turn produces output which may be consumed by an editor which will also produce output to be consumed by the memory manager, and so on until the series of events is completed.

This chain of actions is only possible if we ensure that the producer has a place to deposit its actions, and the consumer has a place from which to claim its requirements. In other words, we need an intermediate storage facility, a *buffer*. A pool of buffers that can be filled and emptied by the producer-consumer will allow these processes to execute concurrently, provided that they are properly synchronized. For example, we must ensure that the consumer does not attempt to consume items that have not yet been produced as this will lead to the consumer having to wait on the producer with an inevitable loss of efficiency. And also, we must ensure that the producer does not produce items that the consumer cannot accept because all the buffers have been previously filled, unless of course we have an endless supply of buffers.

In practical applications we would need to limit the number of buffers that are allocated to the producer-consumer problem. Then, the producer will have to stop production if all the buffers are full until the consumer has emptied a buffer, as shown in Figure 8.6.

Figure 8.6 Producer consumer-problem

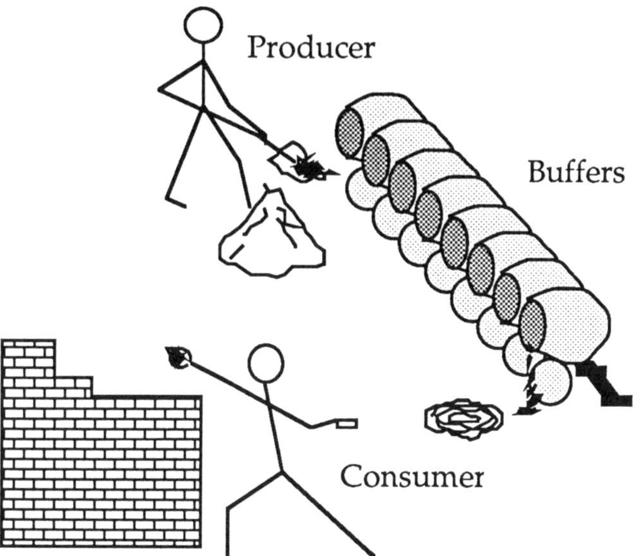

Assume that *n* buffers are available and that each buffer can hold one data item. Remember that the concurrent solution for the bounded buffer problem requires that the producer should wait when the buffers are full. A binary semaphore (S) will provide the control for mutual exclusion. In addition, general semaphores are required to indicate the filled buffers (filled), and then empty buffers (empty). Execution starts with S := 1, filled := 0 and empty := n, then:

```
VAR
   S : binarySemaphore;
   empty : semaphore;
   filled : semaphore;

PROCEDURE Producer;
BEGIN
   LOOP (* Produce an item. *)
      P(empty); (* This decrements the vacancy semaphore. *)
      P(S);
            (* Critical section. *)
            (* Add the item to the next buffer. *)
      V(S);
      V(filled); (* This increments the filled semaphore. *)
   END;
END Producer;
```

```
PROCEDURE Consumer;
BEGIN
   LOOP
      (* Ready to consume an item. *)
      P(filled); (* This decrements the filled semaphore. *)
      P(S);
            (* Critical section. *)
            (* Remove the item from the last buffer. *)
      V(S);
      V(empty); (* This increments the empty semaphore. *)
      (* Consume an item. *)
   END; (* Loop. *)
END Consumer;

BEGIN (* Main Program. *)
   (* Initialise. *)
   S : = 1;
   empty : = n;
   filled : = 0;
   COBEGIN
      Producer;
      Consumer;
   COEND;
END
```

In the consumer process, the operation P(empty) *guards* the producer from trying to fill buffers that are already full, that is when empty has the value 0 P(empty) → empty = 0 → deschedule producer process. The producer process must idle until the consumer process increments empty by the command V(empty).

When the value of the variables empty and filled are both greater than zero, then the guards P(empty) and P(filled) always allows access to the critical section. Mutual exclusion is assured in exactly the same way as in the earlier example.

The distributed read/write problem

Many distributed systems, such as a banking or airline reservation system, may need multiple access to a data record. Reading a record normally allows simultaneous access to all users of a system. However, changing a record by a write process must be mutually exclusive, denying access to all other processes until the write process has completed.

A simple solution would have the following properties:

- write processes are mutually exclusive.

- waiting read processes are given priority after a write process has completed.
- no read process should wait simply because a write process is waiting.

The write process is easily controlled by a binary semaphore S that has been initialised to 1:

```
PROCEDURE WriteProcess;
BEGIN
   P(S);
      <write to record>
   V(S);
END WriteProcess;
```

This process must be *guarded* to give the waiting read processes priority.

A further binary semaphore readexclude, and a read process counter, n, are needed to control the access to the read processes.

Initialise the semaphore readexclude to 1 and the counter n to 0. A solution is then given by:

```
PROCEDURE ReadProcess;
(* Remember many read processes may be calling this section
simultaneously. *)

BEGIN
   P(readexclude);
      n: = n + 1;
      if n = 1 then P(S);
   V(readexclude);
      <execute read instruction>
   P(readexclude);
      n : = n - 1;
      if n = 0 then V(S);
   V(readexclude);
END ReadProcess;
```

Let us examine the action of this process.

Suppose the write process is using its critical section, then S = 0.
The first read request enters the read process and increments the value of n → 1, executes P(S), that is P(S) → S = 0 → deschedule read process. This first read request is therefore suspended until the write critical section is exited and V(S) returns the value of S to 1. If read processes are waiting then one process is queued on semaphore S and the remaining n-1 read processes are queued on semaphore readexclude.

The suspension of the first read request is then lifted and the action of the read process continue. S is immediately reset to 0 which in turn blocks the write process. The remainder of the read requests now stream through the read process until n is returned to the value 0. At this point S is reset to 0 by V(S), thus allowing the next read or write request to access its respective process.

Note that this solution does not exclude the possibility of starvation, as either read or write calls would continuously deny each other access to its critical section.

8.2.7 Monitors

The mechanisms we have described in this chapter for controlling the synchronisation and mutual exclusion of parallel processes are dispersed throughout the program. This unstructured approach is not in keeping with the philosophy we have adopted on data abstraction and modularisation. To overcome this defect the *monitor* construct was introduced by Brinch Hansen in 1973 to allow the safe and efficient sharing of abstract data types among a set of processes. The monitor guarantees that only one process is active at any time, thereby assuring mutual exclusion.

A monitor is a module that hides shared variables. By ensuring that the shared variables have a scope only within the module and by restricting access to the monitor to one process at a time then we can ensure the integrity of the modules local data. The hidden data is only accessible through calls to the monitors exported subprograms. In other words, the critical sections have been removed from the processes and have been collected together as procedures of the monitor. If a process wishes to execute its critical section then it must make the appropriate procedure call to the monitor. The integrity of the critical section is preserved by only allowing one process access to the monitor at a time.

We can illustrate the monitor concept by expressing a binary semaphore as a monitor:

```
MONITOR BinarySemaphore;

VAR
   busy: BOOLEAN;
   ready: CONDITION; (* State variable. *)

PROCEDURE P;
BEGIN
   IF busy THEN wait(ready); END;
   busy := TRUE;
END;
```

```
PROCEDURE V;
BEGIN
   busy := FALSE;
   send(ready);
END;
BEGIN
   busy := FALSE;
END, (* BinarySemaphore. *)
```

Here we have represented the binary semaphore by a monitor with two procedures, P and V. Two alternatives are allowed, either P waits until V has left the monitor, or V waits until P has left the monitor. The usual semaphore state variable, S, has been replaced with the BOOLEAN variable *busy*. The CONDITION data type provides a queue of waiting processes which can be manipulated by wait and send operations to enable a process to be delayed and added to the queue, or rescheduled and removed from the queue. The wait(ready) operation suspends a process and appends it to the ready queue. In addition, the P operation releases the monitor exclusion condition, thus allowing other process to call the monitor procedures. The send(ready) operation causes the first processes on the ready queue to be released.

When the monitor is declared, the initialisation operation busy := FALSE is executed, thereafter the monitor is ready to receive calls from any of the processes running on the system. When the first call is made to the P procedure, the semaphore *busy* is set to TRUE. The monitor exclusion is then released to enable the monitor procedures to receive further calls. If any process makes further calls to the procedure P, then, upon finding the semaphore *busy* to be TRUE, the procedure call is placed on the queue associated with the condition variable ready and then the exclusion of the monitor is released. The queue of waiting processes is maintained until a release of the first process is signalled by a V procedure call being made by some active process. Then the semaphore *busy* is set to FALSE and the first process on the queue is awakened by the send(ready) operation. This newly active process resets the semaphore *busy* to TRUE and then releases the exclusion condition of the monitor.

We will discuss the implementation of wait and send operations later in this chapter.

As Modula-2 is implemented on a uniprocessor then every module can be viewed as a monitor. However, we can explicitly label a module to be a monitor by giving it a specific priority in the module heading:

```
MODULE Controller [1];
```

The constant expression 1 serves to label the module as a monitor. This label does not give any indication of the order of execution but is useful to specify a priority among a number of processes that are ready for execution.

8.3 The Coroutine abstraction

When a number of parallel processes are executing on a single processor they are referred to as coroutines. The execution of coroutines are, therefore quasi-concurrent and must be scheduled so that each gets its share of the processors central processing unit. This scheduling could be a simple queue in which *first come are first served* or there could be some ordering based on some form of priority. This description of the ordering of coroutines may sound, at a superficial level, simply like the ordering of procedure calls. However, there is one subtle difference that allows us to identify coroutines to be in the same class of events as described for concurrent process. If a simple procedure was abandoned for some reason, then the procedure call is *dead* as far as the remainder of the program is concerned. But when a coroutine is *suspended*, say because of mutual exclusion, then it may be *resurrected* at any later time. This re-scheduling can occur even when coroutines that were originally at the back of the queue have subsequently overtaken the suspended coroutine and have been executed. Thus the actions and conditions needed to control the coroutine are precisely those that we required for concurrent processes, except of course that only one central processing unit is available.

The coroutines abstraction is not very useful if we wish to distribute a single task as a set of subtasks, as these tasks can only be executed on one processor. But when we have many different tasks that need to interact with each other in an undetermined way then the single processor is not a restriction to the coroutine abstraction. The read/write problem is a typical example where the use of coroutines can satisfy all the interactive requirements of the tasks that control these processes.

8.3.1 Implementing coroutines

Coroutines are implemented in Modula-2 by the system dependent procedure named NewCoroutine. This procedure is imported from the module Coroutines and enables us to dynamically create coroutines in a program which may be run at any time and in an ordering which does not have to be predetermined. Coroutines that are created by a call to NewCoroutine satisfies all our requirements for coroutines. We can create new coroutines, terminate coroutines, execute coroutines, suspend coroutines and reinstate suspended coroutines. In addition control of a coroutine can be transferred to another coroutine by use of a procedure call to Transfer.

Perhaps, before proceeding we should comment on the conceptual difference between procedures and coroutines.

In Modula-2, a Procedure is a subprogram that is subordinate to some higher level program. In the normal course of events, when a procedure is called it starts executing at its first statement and continues to the end of the procedure or until a return statement is met. Then, the execution thread is passed back to the statement that originally invoked the procedure call. Therefore, there is an explicit hierarchy relationship between the high level program and the lower level subprograms. Coroutines on the other hand, can be viewed as having equal status to other parts of the program. They execute cooperatively rather than hierarchically, therefore when a coroutine regains control of execution it does not begin at the first statement, but continues from the point where it previously relinquished control.

8.3.2 Creating coroutines

Remember that the word *coroutine* describes a concept associated with the ideas of concurrency, therefore it is natural that it appears as a type in the Coroutines module. The software that is needed to execute coroutines is held in this system module. What must principally concern us, if we are to implement the ideas of coroutines, are the procedure calls to this low level software. But firstly, let us examine the way in which we structure the code for individual coroutines.

The code for a Modula-2 coroutine is written in the form of a parameterless procedure:

```
PROCEDURE Task;
local declarations
BEGIN
   Procedure Body
   Transfer control to next Task
END Task;
```

There are two ways in which we can use PROCEDURE Task. Firstly, as a single coroutine, or secondly as a template from which many coroutines may be created. Before we proceed to an example of using coroutines we need to examine all the mechanisms for creating and transferring coroutines. These mechanisms are contained in the definition module Coroutines:

Program 8.1 Coroutines

```
DEFINITION MODULE Coroutines;
TYPE Coroutine; (* Opaque type for the coroutine descriptor. *)
FROM SYSTEM IMPORT ADDRESS;

PROCEDURE InitCoroutines(MemoryPoolSize : LONGINT);
(* Reserves the memory pool on the stack. *)
PROCEDURE NewCoroutine(p : PROC; WorkSpaceSize : LONGINT;
                      VAR q : Coroutine);
(* Create a coroutine from a template procedure p. *)
PROCEDURE Transfer(VAR from, to : Coroutines);
(* Transfer control between coroutines. *)
END Coroutines.
```

This definition of the coroutine concept gives a clear specification for implementing the required procedures. However, many implementations use the PROCESS data type, imported from the SYSTEM module, to build coroutine abstractions. Using the PROCESS data type to support the coroutine abstractions is very ambiguous, as we are actually using coroutines to simulate processes as quasi-concurrency objects. Here, in this chapter, our main interest is to demonstrate the principles of coroutines and processes, with specific implementations being of secondary importance. Therefore, for consistency with the basic definitions and descriptions of coroutines and processes that are outlined in earlier sections of this chapter we will use the coroutine abstraction as the basic method for implementing quasi-concurrency.

For a description of the use of the PROCESS data type to implement coroutines you are referred to Wirth or Ford and Wiener.

InitCoroutines

Has the procedure heading:

```
InitCoroutines(MemoryPoolSize  :  LONGINT);
```

This procedure call reserves the memory pool on the processor stack that we need for creating coroutines. The call to InitCoroutines is made just once, but it must be the first executable statement in the body of the main module.

The parameter MemoryPoolSize gives the total amount of workspace that is needed by all coroutines, including coroutines that are imported from other modules.

NewCoroutine

Has the procedure heading:

```
NewCoroutine(CoroutineTemplate  :  PROC;
             WorkSpaceSize  :  LONGINT;
             VAR  coroutineName  :  Coroutine);
```

This procedure call will dynamically create a new coroutine as follows:

The parameter CoroutineTemplate is the parameterless procedure that contains the code that will form the basis of one or more coroutines. Each time NewCoroutine is invoked it creates an instance of a coroutine with code taken from the procedure CoroutineTemplate. The type PROC is pre-defined as:

```
TYPE  PROC  =  PROCEDURE;
```

The second parameter, WorkSpaceSize, gives the size of the workspace allocated from the memory pool to the new coroutine.

The final parameter, CoroutineName, gives the name by which the new coroutine will be known, as illustrated by the procedure call below:

```
NewCoroutine(Task, size, TaskOne);
```

Then the new coroutine has the name TaskOne, with code taken from the procedure Task, and has been allocated size bytes of workspace.

Transfer

This has the procedure heading

```
Transfer(VAR ThisCoroutine, NextCoroutine : Coroutine);
```

A call to this procedure will cause the transfer of control from ThisCoroutine to NextCoroutine. The parameters are obviously coroutines and are ordered in the direction we wish to transfer the control to activate a particular coroutine. Thus, the procedure call

```
Transfer(TaskOne, TaskTwo);
```

causes the coroutine TaskOne to stop execution and in its place TaskTwo becomes active.

This transfer call seems to cover all eventualities in our need to transfer control, except one. How do we start the sequence of transfers between coroutines? The answer is to take the main body of the program as a coroutine and to initiate the sequence by transferring control from the main body to the first coroutine, that is:

```
Transfer(MAIN, TaskOne);
```

After this initial procedure call all further transfer of control takes place from within coroutines.

8.4 Using coroutines

We will explore the use of coroutines with the aid of three simple examples. The first creates each coroutine from a separate template procedure, but the later examples use a single template procedure for creating multiple coroutines.

8.4.1 A producer-consumer example which uses coroutines

In the following example we use simple coroutines to pass control between a producer operation and a consumer operation. The producer procedure requests the user to type a cardinal number, after which control is passed to the consumer coroutine which writes the number to the screen. Typing zero stops the execution of the coroutines by passing control back to the main program, which is itself a coroutine.

Program 8.2 Producer-consumer

```
MODULE ProduceConsume;
(* Producer-Consumer example based on transfer of control between
coroutines. *)

FROM InOut IMPORT WriteString, WriteCard, ReadCard, WriteLn,
                                              HoldScreen;
FROM Coroutines IMPORT InitCoroutines, NewCoroutine, Transfer,
                                              Coroutine;

CONST
   MemoryPoolSize = 6000;
   CoroutineWorkSpace = 2000;

VAR
   MAIN, coroutineProducer, coroutineConsumer : Coroutine;
   (* Three coroutines declared. *)
   buffer : CARDINAL; (* Single element buffer. *)

PROCEDURE Producer;
(* Template procedure for the producer coroutine. *)
VAR
   x : CARDINAL;

BEGIN
   LOOP
      WriteString("Producer coroutine. - Type any cardinal > 0, or 0 to
stop?");
      WriteLn;
      ReadCard(x);
      IF x = 0 THEN
         Transfer(coroutineProducer, MAIN);
      END;
      (* x = 0, therefore stop all coroutines and return control to
   MAIN program. *)
      buffer := x; (* Producer insert x into buffer. *)
      Transfer(coroutineProducer, coroutineConsumer);
      (* Transfer to consumer coroutine and suspend producer
      coroutine. *)
   END;
END Producer;
```

```
PROCEDURE Consumer;
(* Template procedure for the consumer coroutine. *)
VAR
   y : CARDINAL;
BEGIN
   LOOP
      y := buffer; (* Consumer remove cardinal y from buffer. *)
      WriteString("Consumer coroutine - Your number is ");
      WriteCard(y, 3);
      WriteLn;
      Transfer(coroutineConsumer, coroutineProducer);
      (* Transfer to producer coroutine and suspend consumer
      coroutine.*)
   END;
END Consumer;

BEGIN
   (* We must first reserve the memory pool for all coroutine
   activity. *)
   InitCoroutines(MemoryPoolSize);

   (* Create the coroutines. *)
   NewCoroutine(Producer, CoroutineWorkSpace,
                             coroutineProducer);
   NewCoroutine(Consumer, CoroutineWorkSpace,
                                     coroutineConsumer);

   (* Transfer from the MAIN program to the first coroutine. *)
   Transfer(MAIN, coroutineProducer);

   WriteString("End of Program.");
   WriteLn;
   HoldScreen;
END ProduceConsume.
```

Program action for the set of cardinal values 2, 5, 0:

Producer coroutine - Type any cardinal > 0, or 0 to stop?
2
Consumer coroutine - Your cardinal is 2

Producer coroutine - Type any cardinal > 0, or 0 to stop?
5

Consumer coroutine - Your cardinal is 5

Producer coroutine - Type any cardinal > 0, or 0 to stop?
0

End of Program.

Let us examine the structure and actions of this program in some detail. The program consists of three coroutines:

- The main program coroutine – MAIN.
- The coroutine created from the producer procedure by the statement NewCoroutine(producer, CoroutineWorkSpace, coroutineProducer) – coroutineProducer.
- The coroutine created from the consumer procedure by the statement NewCoroutine(consumer, CoroutineWorkSpace, coroutineConsumer) – coroutineConsumer.

To start the sequence of actions control is passed from the the MAIN coroutine to the coroutine coroutineProducer by the transfer operation Transfer(MAIN, coroutineProducer). Thereafter, control is passed between coroutines by the transfer operation until control is finally passed back to the MAIN coroutine by the transfer operation Transfer(coroutineProducer, MAIN), in response to a zero being typed.

This program uses a very simple method to communicate information between coroutines. The variable *buffer* has a general scope, therefore *buffer* is in effect a shared variable which conveys information between coroutines. We shall return to this point when we consider process communication in Section 8.7.

It is easy for us to determine that a single thread of control permeates the action of the coroutines, and that this control depends entirely on the way that the coroutine transfer operation is implemented in the program. We may naively conclude that there is little or no difference between transferring control between coroutines and making procedure calls to achieve a similar end. The next example should demonstrate a clear difference between a set of procedure calls and what is possible by creating and transferring control between coroutines.

8.4.2 Using a single coroutine template procedure

In Program 8.3 we generate multiple coroutines from a single template procedure. Again we must use the transfer procedure to give control to another coroutine. Each of the coroutines prints a simple messages, indeed the coroutines are identical except for the message each writes to the screen. Executing the program gives the following stream of messages:

Number 1 task has been completed. Next task please.
Number 2 task has been completed. Next task please.
Number 3 task has been completed. Next task please.
Number 1 task has been completed. Next task please.
Number 2 task has been completed. Next task please.
Number 3 task has been completed. Next task please.
Number 1 task has been completed. Next task please.
Number 2 task has been completed. Next task please.
....
....
....
....

until the sequence of transfers between coroutines is broken by the use of an event handler (such as the use of a mouse), or by a similar method to that described in Program 8.2.

Program 8.3 Coroutines from a single template procedure

```
MODULE CoprocessTasks;
(* This module creates a set of coroutines from a single template
procedure. *)

FROM Coroutines IMPORT InitCoroutines, NewCoroutine, Transfer,
                                       Coroutine;
FROM InOut IMPORT writeString, WriteCard, WriteLn, HoldScreen;
FROM EventManager IMPORT Button;

CONST
   MemoryPoolSize = 8000; (* Total WorkSpace for all
                                    coroutines. *)
   CoroutineWorkSpace = 2000; (* WorkSpace for each instance
                                      of coroutine. *)
   coroutineCount = 3; (* Number of coroutines required. *)

VAR
   MAIN : Coroutine; (* Main program defined as a coroutine. *)

   (* This is the set of coroutines to be created. *)
   Task : ARRAY[1 .. Coroutinecount] OF Coroutine;

   coroutineTask : CARDINAL; (* Indicates the current instance
                                     of a coroutine. *)
```

```
PROCEDURE  SetOfTasks;
(* This is the parameterless template procedure for create coroutines. *)
VAR
   thisTask : CARDINAL; (* thisTask is used to record the
                                   current instance of the coroutines. *)
BEGIN
   LOOP
      thisTask : = coroutineTask;
      (* The body of the task statements would normally be placed
      here. *)
      (* . *)
      (* . *)

      (* The sequence of write statements given below records
      the current task number by writing it to the screen. *)
      WriteString("Number");
      WriteCard(coroutineTask);
      WriteString(" task has been completed.  Next task please.");
      WriteLn;

      (* Now set the next task in the repeated sequence
      1 , 2,........,coroutineCount. *)
      IF (coroutineTask < coroutineCount) THEN
      INC(coroutineTask);
      ELSE
         coroutineTask: =1;
      END;

      (* Transfer control to the next coroutine and suspend the
      current coroutine. *)
      Transfer(Task[ThisTask], Task[coroutineTask]);
   END;
END SetOfTasks;

BEGIN (* MAIN coroutine. *)
   (* We must first reserve the memory pool for all coroutine activity. *)
   InitCoroutines(MemoryPoolSize);

   (* Now create the coroutine instances using SetOfTasks as the
   template for coroutines:
   Task[1], Task[2], ...., Task[coroutineCount]. *)
```

```
FOR coroutineTask := 1 TO coroutineCount DO
   NewCoroutine(SetOfTasks, CoroutineWorkSpace,
      Task[coroutineTask]);
END;

(* All that now remains is to set the system off by transferring
control from the main body of the module to the first coroutine,
Task[1]. *)

(* Initialise the task index. *)
coroutineTask : = 1;

(* Transfer control to the first coroutine. *)
Transfer(MAIN, Task[coroutineTask]];

WriteString("End of Program.");
HoldScreen;
END CoprocessTasks;
```

By examining this program we observe that the FOR loop:

```
FOR coroutineTask := 1 TO coroutineCount DO
   NewCoroutine(SetOfTasks, CoroutineWorkSpace,
        Task[coroutineTask]);
END; (* For. *)
```

is used to create the three coroutines as array elements, with the names Task[1], Task[2] and Task[3], by making three separate calls to the procedure NewCoroutines. Each instance of a coroutine is taken from the template procedure SetOfTasks. Once the initial transfer of control from MAIN to Task[1] has taken place then all further transfer of control is made between the coroutines TASK[1], Task[2] and Task[3] by using the normal Transfer operation.

The template procedure SetOfTasks must, therefore carry all the program statements that are needed for each of the different coroutines. If very differing actions are required for each of the coroutines, we would need conditional statements in the coroutines to give the required actions. An obvious method would be to use the coroutine name (that is, the index) as a condition variable to enable the coroutine condition to be determined. Using this principle the producer-consumer procedures of Program 8.2 could be combined into one template procedure, as shown in Program 8.4.

Program 8.4 Producer-consumer

```
MODULE ProducerConsumer;
(* This module uses a single template procedure to create two
coroutines that execute as producers and consumers. *)

FROM InOut IMPORT WriteString, WriteCard, ReadCard, WriteLn,
                        HoldScreen;
FROM Coroutines IMPORT InitCoroutines, NewCoroutine,
                            Transfer,Coroutine;

CONST
   MemoryPoolSize = 6000;
   CoroutineWorkSpace = 2000;
   coroutineCount = 2;

VAR
   MAIN : Coroutine;

   (* Set of coroutines declared. *)
   TASK : ARRAY [1..coroutineCount] OF Coroutine;

   coroutineTask, buffer : CARDINAL; (* Single buffer element. *)

PROCEDURE ProducerAndConsumer;
(* This template procedure allows the creation of multiple coroutines,
with differing functionality. *)
VAR
   thisTask , x : CARDINAL;

BEGIN
   LOOP
      (* Set the current instance of the coroutine. *)
      thisTask := coroutineTask;

      IF thisTask = 1 THEN
         (* This is the producer function. *)
         WriteString("Producer process.  Type any cardinal > 0,
                    or 0 to stop?");
         WriteLn;
         ReadCard(x);
```

```
        IF x = 0 THEN
           Transfer(TASK[thisTask], MAIN);
           (* Stop all coroutines and return to MAIN coroutine. *)
        END;
        buffer := x; (* Producer insert x into buffer. *)

     ELSE
        (* This is the consumer function. *)
        x:= buffer; (* Consumer remove x from buffer. *)
        WriteString("Consumer process - Your number is ");
        WriteCard(x, 3);
        WriteLn;
     END;

     IF (coroutineTask < coroutineCount) THEN
        INC(coroutineTask);
        ELSE coroutineTask :=1;
        (* Cycle coroutineTask between 1 and coroutineCount. *)
     END;

     (* Transfer to next coroutine. *)
     Transfer(TASK[thisTask], TASK[coroutineTask]);
  END;
END ProducerAndConsumer;

BEGIN
  (* Main coroutine. *)
  InitCoroutines(MemoryPoolSize);

  (* Next loop creates the coroutinesTask[1]..Task[coroutineCount]. *)
  FOR coroutineTask := 1 TO coroutineCount DO
     NewCoroutine(ProducerAndConsumer,
                       CoroutineWorkSpace,TASK[coroutineTask]);
  END;

  (* Initialise the first coroutine index. *)
  coroutineTask := 1;

  (* Start the system off by transferring MAIN to the first coroutine. *)
  Transfer(MAIN,TASK[coroutineTask]);

  WriteString("End of Program.");
  HoldScreen;
END ProducerConsumer.
```

Two identical coroutines were created, namely Task[1] and Task[2]. The current task, indicated by the instance variable thisTask, is initialised to the value 1 and subsequently incremented on every execution cycle of the coroutine. As thisTask always gives the index of the current coroutine then this variable is an appropriate choice for the condition variable. An examination of the IF condition in the template procedure ProducerAndConsumer reveals that the appropriate condition, that is producer or consumer, is dependent on the value of the coroutine index being either 1 or 2. But note that the program supports multiple consumer coroutines by simply changing the parameters coroutineCount and memoryPool Size.

Of course, the choice of the coroutine index as the condition variable is appropriate for this example, but in general the choice of code to be executed in a coroutine could be based on any runtime variable, or combination of variables. Similarly the transfer of control to the next coroutine could be made dependent on a variety of runtime factors.

Before we complete this section we should again examine the fundamental differences between procedures and coroutines. Remember, that when a procedure is called we are always accessing the procedure body from the beginning. In contrast, when we restart a coroutine we begin at the point where the coroutine was previously suspended.

A coroutine type is clearly an abstraction which allows us to stop and restart the actions of an object, while a procedure call only allows a complete enactment of an object. If you refer back to the description of a process you will immediately realise that the ability to stop and restart an object is precisely the mechanism that is required to implement a process.

8.5 The Process abstraction

In Modula-2 a process is a parameterless procedure which must not be contained in any other procedure. A genuine process model is not possible in Modula-2, as the only construct the languages has available to implement processes is the coroutine type. However, it is possible to develop process abstractions that clearly illustrate the process interaction that would be achieved if we had the ability to execute concurrent programs, rather than being forced to simulate such concurrent process by sequential coroutines.

8.5.1 Creating a NewProcess

A NewProcess is implemented as the data type Coroutine, which is imported from the module Coroutines. Thus, as in Section 8.3.2, the creation of a NewProcess must be implemented by a module which uses the InitCoroutines and NewCoroutine procedures to allocate the the workspace that is needed and then dynamically create a new coroutine. The transfer of control between the coroutines explicitly uses the Transfer procedure.

The process type is, therefore a high level abstraction which uses coroutines at the implementation level. The mechanisms for suspending and restarting processes are hidden in the implementation, but we need further high level abstractions to enable process interactions to be achieved. Indeed, if we formulate the interactions of processes in such a way that they may be executed concurrently, when the support for genuine concurrency exists, then we are able to ensure that a single processor can support quasi-concurrency. Modula-2 allows the formulation of processes and their quasi-concurrent interaction on a single processor. We now need to develop the high level abstractions to control process interaction.

8.6 The process synchronisation abstraction

We need to build an abstraction that will allow the interaction of processes at the highest level without needing to specify the means by which the processes perform the act of suspension and resumption of their activities. Further, it is desirable that the abstraction is sufficiently powerful that a process need not have any explicit knowledge about the state or actions of any other process. This, of course, implies that the decision to reschedule a particular process must be external to that process. This particular process may simply be the first on a ready queue of processes, or may be one which has been assigned some priority over other processes. In summary, the abstraction that is needed must allow the processes to access shared data and provide the synchronisation primitives to enable the necessary scheduling and mutual exclusion operations to be carried out in all circumstances.

Shared variables can be used to transfer data among processes, provided that the processes observe the condition of mutual exclusion with only one process accessing the shared variables at any one time. A module which performs the function of a monitor is guaranteed to support the mutual exclusion of processes. However, if we are restricted to a single processor then every module can provide the functionality of a monitor. This fact will simplify the construction of modules in which processes interact with shared variables.

Previously, we noted that a condition variable is used to identify a queue of waiting processes within a monitor. Modula-2 provides a data type known as a Signal which provides the functionality of the condition variable, and through its use we are able to synchronise processes.

To enable process to be suspended and restarted the appropriate signals are delivered by the appropriate procedure call chosen from Wait(S) or Send(S). S is the Signal data type, which has no value, nor should a value be assigned to it at any time. It is used entirely for signalling and only supports three operations: an initialisation operation, InitSignals, and the Wait and Send operations.

The definition module Signals is given in Program 8.5.

Program 8.5 Definition module of Signals

```
DEFINITION MODULE Signals;
(* This module defines quasi-concurrent programming based on the
synchronisation of process. *)
TYPE Signal;
(* Opaque type for the signal descriptors.  Signals are the means of
process synchronisation. *)

PROCEDURE InitSignals(MemoryPoolSize : LONGINT)
(* This procedure reserves the memory pool on the processor stack. *)
PROCEDURE CreateSignal(VAR S : Signal);
(* Initialises a Signal object. *)
PROCEDURE StartProcess(P : PROC; size : LONGINT);
(* This starts a new process which executes the code given in
procedure P. *)
PROCEDURE Awaited(S : Signal): BOOLEAN;
(* This procedure tests for a waiting process. *)
PROCEDURE Send(VAR S : Signal);
(* This sends a signal from the current process. *)
PROCEDURE Wait(VAR S : Signal);
(* Wait for another process to send a signal. *)
END Signals.
```

This definition module gives us the procedures needed to implement the synchronisation primitives. Let us examine these properties a little more closely.

InitSignals

This procedure reserves the memory pool on the stack. It must reserve sufficient memory for all the processes created by the program, including processes imported from other modules. The parameter MemoryPoolSize indicates the size required for this workspace. The call to InitSignals is made just once, but it must be the first executable statement in the body of the main module.

CreateSignal

This procedure has the heading:

```
CreateSignal(VAR SignalName : Signal);
```

All objects of type Signal must be initialised by a call to this procedure before the Signal objects can be used by any other procedure in the module. For example, to create a signal Hello requires a call with Hello named as the parameter:

```
CreateSignal(Hello);
```

StartProcess

This has the procedure heading:

```
StartProcess(ProcessTemplate : PROC; WorkSpaceSize : LONGINT);
```

This procedure call will dynamically create a new process as follows:

The ProcessTemplate provides the code for each instance of the process that is created by a call to StartProcess. The parameter WorkSpaceSize gives the size of the workspace needed by the particular process instance. For example, a call to StartProcess:

```
StartProcess(FetchData, WorkSpaceSize);
```

will dynamically create the process FetchData, in the workspace reserved by WorkSpaceSize, and then pass control from the main module to the process FetchData.

Send

This procedure, with the heading

```
Send(VAR SignalName : Signal);
```

is used to send a signal SignalName to another process from the current process. For example, the procedure call

```
Send(Hello);
```

sends the signal Hello to another process. If no other process is waiting for the signal it is lost. Otherwise a process which is waiting for the signal will be given control and will resume its operations.

Wait

The procedure with heading

```
Wait(VAR SignalName : Signal);
```

gives the mechanism to suspend a process. The operation waits for another process to send a signal, such as Hello. Then the operation

```
Wait(Hello);
```

receives the signal and the process suspends its actions.

Awaited

This function procedure, with heading

```
Awaited(SignalName : Signal) : BOOLEAN;
```

is used to test if any process is waiting for the signal SignalName.

For example, the procedure call

```
Awaited(Hello);
```

returns the value TRUE if at least one process is waiting for the signal Hello, otherwise the returned value is FALSE.

At the time the signal SignalName is initialised by the procedure call to CreateSignal, the BOOLEAN value Awaited(SignalName) is initialised to FALSE.

8.6.1 Send and Wait operations

The measure of quality exercised on the control of processes by the synchronisation abstraction depends to a great extent on the attributes given to the Send and Wait operations. We need to consider these operations in some detail.

At the level of abstraction we are considering, a process should not be concerned with having to explicitly handle coroutine transfers. But as a process is actually a coroutine in Modula-2 we must find some way of solving this problem. By building the transfer mechanisms into the signal operators at the implementation level we are able to resolve the dilemma.

A Wait operation suspends the current process while it waits on a signal. Therefore, a transfer of control must occur at this point. However, a record of this event must somehow be maintained to enable the process to be resumed at some later time. A list or queue of suspended processes is the obvious way to maintain this record. So, when a process is suspended by a Wait(SignalName) operation, it is saved on the appropriate queue that is associated with the particular Signal SignalName. To ensure some degree of fairness the queue is best organised on a first come first served basis. If a number of processes are waiting for a signal and only one can be resumed on receipt of that signal, then the process indicated by the front of the signal queue is the obvious one to be resumed.

A Send operation has distinctly different properties. A Send operation is performed when the process has either completed its operations or when it has reached a stage in the operations when it is safe to suspend them. The send operation is in many ways a voluntary operation, which then allows some other process a chance to share the cycle time of the processor. Once a process has sent a signal its operation is suspended. This kind of suspension operation is very different from that caused by the Wait operation, because the sending process is still able to continue its executions cycle. Therefore, the process does not need to wait for a signal to resume its execution. It will do so whenever it can find available processor cycles. So how is this achieved? We obviously need another queue, a ready to process queue, on which the sending process is appended.

We can now review the complete send and wait cycle:

1. The Send(S) operation that is sent from the current process must look at the S signal queue and determine if any process has previously caused a Wait(S) operation.

```
IF S queue has a waiting process THEN
   (a) Remove the first process from the S queue and resume
       this waiting process.
   (b) Place the current sending process on the ready queue.
ELSE
   Allow the current sending process to continue.
END.
```

2. The Wait(S) operation suspends the current process and inserts the process in the S queue. It then transfers to the front of the ready queue to determine if a ready process is available.

```
IF a process is available on the ready queue THEN
   Resume this ready process.
ELSE
   Deadlock.
END.
```

The deadlock situation is a fatal error. This error is caused by the programmers failure to ensure that processes cooperate at all times. It is typically caused by failing to send a Send(S) operation at the appropriate point in the program.

The implementation of Signals is given in Program 8.6. Pointer to processes are used in the queue implementation which enables us to retain the process variable for use in the process transfer operation. We will import all necessary queue operations from the Queue data abstraction given in Section 6.4.

Program 8.6 Signals

```
IMPLEMENTATION MODULE Signals;
(* This module implements the process synchronisation abstraction. *)
FROM InOut IMPORT WriteString, WriteLn;
FROM Coroutines IMPORT InitCoroutines, NewCoroutine, Transfer,
      Coroutine;
FROM SYSTEM IMPORT ADDRESS;
FROM Storage IMPORT ALLOCATE;
FROM DynamicQueue IMPORT Queue, QueueItem, NewQ, AddQ,
                              RearQ, FrontQ, IsemptyQ;
```

```
TYPE
   ProcessPointer = POINTER TO Coroutine;

   Signal = POINTER TO Processes
   Processes = RECORD
                    Process : Queue;
                END
VAR
   CurrentPointer : ProcessPointer;
   Ready : Queue;

PROCEDURE InitSignals(MemoryPoolSize : LONGINT);
BEGIN
   InitCoroutines(MemoryPoolSize);
END InitSignals;

PROCEDURE CreateSignals(VAR S : Signal);
BEGIN
   ALLOCATE(S, SIZE(Signal);
   S^.Process := NewQ();
END CreateSignals;

PROCEDURE StartProcess(P : PROC; Size : LONGINT);
VAR
   WorkSpace : ADDRESS;
   PreviousProcess : ProcessPointer;
BEGIN
   ALLOCATE(WorkSpace, Size);
   Ready := AddQ(Ready, CurrentProcess);
   PreviousProcess := CurrentProcess;
   ALLOCATE(CurrentProcess, SIZE(Coroutine));
   CreateCoroutine(P, Size, CurrentProcess^);
   Transfer(PreviousProcess^, CurrentProcess^);
END StartProcess;

PROCEDURE Send(VAR S : Signal);
VAR
   PreviousProcess : ProcessPointer;
BEGIN
   IF NOT IsEmptyQ(S^.Process) THEN
      PreviousProcess := CurrentProcess;
```

```
        CurrentProcess := FrontQ(S^.Process);
        S^.Process := RearQ(S^.Process);
        Transfer(PreviousProcess^, CurrentProcess^);
    END
END Send;

PROCEDURE Wait(VAR S: Signal);
VAR
    PreviousProcess : PreviousPointer;
BEGIN
    IF NOT IsEmptyQ(Ready) THEN
        S^.Process := AddQ(S^.Process, CurrentProcess);
        PreviousProcess := CurrentProcess;
        CurrentProcess := FrontQ(Ready);
        Ready := RearQ(Ready);
        Transfer(PreviousProcess^, CurrentProcess^);
    ELSE
        WriteString("DeadLock");
        WriteLn;
    END
END Wait;

PROCEDURE Awaited(S : Signal) : BOOLEAN;
BEGIN
    RETURN NOT IsEmptyQ(S^.Process);
END Awaited;

BEGIN
    (* Initialisation. *)
    Ready := NewQ();
    ALLOCATE(CurrentProcess, SIZE(Coroutine));
END Signals.
```

The signals abstraction gives us the high level synchronisation facilities we need to construct quite complex process models. To demonstrate the principle we will use a simple process model which consists of two processes, one of which is the main program module. The interaction of the two processes is fully synchronised by signals. Program 8.7 illustrates this principle with two interacting processes, each has a critical section enclosed within a LOOP. The main module is, of course, one of these processes. The sequence of interactions is interrupted by the eventhandler.

Program 8.7 Process synchronisation

```
MODULE ProcessSynchronisation;
FROM InOut IMPORT WriteString, WriteCard, WriteLn, WriteInt,
                  HoldScreen;
FROM Signals IMPORT Signal, InitSignals, CreateSignal,
                    StartProcess,Send, Wait;
FROM EventManager IMPORT Button;

VAR
   S : Signal;

CONST
   MemoryPoolSize = 6000;
   WorkSpace = 2000;

PROCEDURE Process2;

BEGIN
   WriteString("Process 2 has started");
   WriteLn;
   LOOP
      Wait(S); (* Guard critical section with a Wait operation. *)
      WriteString("Process 2 critical section");
      WriteLn;
      Send(S); (* Release critical section with a Send operation. *)
   END
END Process2;

BEGIN
   InitSignals(MemoryPoolSize);
   CreateSignal(S);
   WriteString("Process 1 has started");
   WriteLn;

   (* Create Process 2. *)
   StartProcess(Process2, WorkSpace);
   Send(S); (* Question - why is this Send signal required? *)
   LOOP
      Wait(S); (* Guard critical section with a Wait operation. *)
      WriteString("Process 1 critical section");
```

```
      WriteLn;
      Send(S); (* Release critical section with a Send operation. *)
   END;
   WriteString("End of Program");
   HoldScreen;
END ProcessSynchronisation.
```

The program executes as follows:

Process 1 has started
Process 2 has started
Process 2 critical section
Process 1 critical section
Process 2 critical section
Process 1 critical section
Process 2 critical section
Process 1 critical section
Process 2 critical section
....
....

A better understanding of the signaling process will be obtained if we trace the actions of this program. The current state of the ready and S queues are indicated by (ready-Queue: nil; S-Queue: nil), etc, at each stage of the program profile:

- BEGIN – Process 1 commences. (ready-Queue: nil; S-Queue: nil)
- Message – Process 1 has started.
- StartProcess – Process 1 is put on the ready-Queue. Process 2 is created and control is transferred to Process 2. (ready-Queue: Process1; S-Queue: nil)
- Message – Process 2 has started.
- Process 2 continues and next executes the Wait signal. Process 2 is suspended and placed on the S-Queue. Process 1 is taken from the ready-Queue and control is transferred to that process. (ready-Queue: nil; S-Queue: Process 2)
- Process 1 continues and executes its first Send signal. We will return to the question – *Why is this Send signal required* after we have completed this analysis? The S-Queue is examined to determine if a process is waiting. Yes, there is a waiting process, so Process 1 is suspended, it is placed on the ready-Queue and Process 2 is taken from the S-Queue. Control is passed to Process 2. (ready-Queue: Process1; S-Queue: nil)
- Process 2 continues – message Process 2 critical region.

- Process 2 next executes a Send signal. The S-Queue is examined to determine if a process is waiting. No, there is no waiting process, so continue. (ready-Queue: Process1; S-Queue: nil)

- Process 2 continues and next executes the Wait signal. Process 2 is suspended and placed on the S-Queue. Process 1 is taken from the ready-Queue and control is transferred to that process. (ready-Queue: nil; S-Queue: Process 2)

- Process 1 continues and enters its critical region for the first time. Message – Process 1 critical region.

- Process 1 next executes a Send signal. The S-Queue is examined to determine if a process is waiting. Yes, there is a waiting process, so Process 1 is suspended, it is placed on the ready-Queue and Process 2 is taken from the S-Queue. Control is passed to Process 2. (ready-Queue: Process1; S-Queue: nil)

- As the processes have their critical section enclosed within a loop, the cycle continues until broken by an *event call.*

The question posed by Program 8.7 – *Why is this Send signal required* can now be answered with ease? Without this Send signal two consecutive Wait signals would be executed. As the ready process would have been removed after the first Wait signal then there would be two waiting processes and nothing on the ready queue, resulting in deadlock.

You may have spotted that the Send operation in procedure Process 2 appears to be unnecessary. This is true when the program is executing a single process procedure on a sequential processor. However, if a concurrent processor was available or the problem had more than one process procedure then the Send operation would be essential.

A process without a critical section can easily be added to Program 8.7 as follows:

```
PROCEDURE Process3;
BEGIN
   WriteString("Process 3 has started");
   WriteLn;
   LOOP
      WriteString("Process 3 NON critical section");
      WriteLn;
      Send(S);
   END;
END Process3;
```

You may ask the question *What is the purpose of the Send signal in this process?* The signal is a voluntary operation on the part of the process, but without it the process would not relinquish control to other processes at any stage in the program execution cycle. The main program only requires minor changes to execute this extra process:

```
BEGIN
   InitSignals(MemoryPoolSize);
   CreateSignal(S);
   WriteString("Process 1 has started");
   (* Create Process 2. *)
   StartProcess(Process2, WorkSpace);
   (* Create Process 3. *)
   StartProcess(Process3, WorkSpace);
   WriteLn;

   LOOP
      Wait(S); (* Guard the critical section. *)
      WriteString("Process 1 critical section");
      WriteLn;
      Send(S); (* Release the critical section. *)
   END;

   WriteString("End of Program");
   HoldScreen;
END ProcessSynchronisation.
```

The most obvious change to the main program is the need to start Process 3. At this point a serious error would ensue if the order of the StartProcess statements were reversed. Remember that a process is suspended by a Send operation only if there is a process already waiting on the S queue. This would not be the case if Process 3 were created before Process 2. Then Process 3 would retain control for all time. Another change worth noting is that the need for the extra Send operation in the main program, to protect against deadlock, has been eliminated. The initial Send operation in Process 3, which resumes the first wait state of Process 2, has ensured that there will be a process waiting on the ready queue when the Wait operation is first executed by Process 1.

The actions of Program 8.7, with the new process added, are as follow:

```
Process 1 has started
Process 2 has started
Process 3 has started
Process 3 NON critical section
Process 2 critical section
Process 3 NON critical section
Process 2 critical section
Process 1 critical section
```

Process 3 NON critical section
Process 1 critical section
Process 1 NON critical section
Process 1 critical section
Process 2 critical section
....
....
....

This cycle of ten process interactions is then repeated. Note that the unprotected Process 3 is able to gain a greater proportion of the process time than the other processes.

8.6.2 Binary semaphore

We are now in a position to give a simple implementation of a binary semaphore in terms of signal operations. Consider Program 8.8:

Program 8.8 Binary semaphore

```
MODULE BinarySemaphore;
(* Binary Semaphore implementation. *)

FROM Signals IMPORT Signal, InitSignals, CreateSignal, Awaited,
                    Send, Wait;
VAR
   sem : CARDINAL;
   Sig : Signal;

CONST
   MemoryPoolSize = 15000;
   WorkSpace = 2000;

PROCEDURE P;

BEGIN
   IF sem > 0 THEN sem := sem - 1;
   ELSE
      Wait(Sig);
   END;
END P;
```

```
PROCEDURE V;
BEGIN
   IF Awaited(Sig) THEN Send(Sig);
   ELSE
      sem := sem +1;
   END;
END V;

BEGIN
   sem := 1; (* Initialise the semaphore. *)
END BinarySemaphore.
```

The P and V operations can now be used within processes. In the following process the semaphore operations not only guard the critical section but also synchronise the interaction of processes.

```
PROCEDURE Process1;
BEGIN
   LOOP
      P;
      WriteString("Process 1 critical section");
      WriteLn;
      V;
   END
END Process1;
```

The Synchronisation abstraction has been shown to be a powerful means by which we are able to express process interaction in a clear and efficient way. However, this abstraction does not provide any means of communicating information between the processes. In the next section we will examine methods for achieving process communication.

8.7 Process communication

Most processes need to communicate at some stage of their execution cycle, even when the processes are on the same processor. Figure 8.1 gave an example of an editor process which communicates with keyboard and screen handling processes. How we achieve these communications is of major importance, and particularly so if the processor was part of a multiprocessor system. Then the internal process communication method may have a strong influence on the available choices for external communications. Although Modula-2 does not allow us to implement our system on a multiprocessor, we should not restrict ourselves to the simplest of models which we see as adequate for a single processor. The principles we need for full concurrency can again be demonstrated using Modula-2 and quasi-concurrent methods.

8.7.1 Sharing data

The synchronisation abstraction that was described in Section 8.6 did not have any explicit mechanisms inbuilt to deal with process communication. However, this abstraction along with Program 8.7 demonstrate the use of shared variables to communicate information between processes.

The state of the Signal type was shared among the processes by ensuring that its scope extended throughout the program. The same basic idea was used in Program 8.2, where the simple buffer variable had a scope which extended throughout the program and allowed the exchange of data between coroutines. The same principle can now be used for communicating information between processes.

Let us extend the share variable method of communicating data via a simple shared buffer to a shared multiple buffer, of finite size, and use the process abstraction to solve this problem. Let the shared bounded buffer have dimension BufferSize and use the producer-consumer model to fill and empty the slots in the buffer that store the items. Program 8.9 is a simple implementation of this method. Notice that the producer process is given as a separate process procedure, but the consumer process is simply part of the MAIN process. When the producer is first started it will continue to fill the buffer slots (array elements) until the size limit of the buffer is reached; at this point the wait operation is invoked and the process is suspended. The consumer process is on the ready list and so control is passed to that process. Thereafter the processes will signal each other, enabling the processes to fill and empty the buffer slots as required, without ever trying to fill a full buffer and without ever trying to remove an item from an empty buffer.

In this example the producer process only waits on the signal full and the consumer process only waits on the signal empty. If a single signal, *S*, had been used instead of the empty / fill signals then the ability for processes to direct the signal at a particular process would be lost.

You will observe that two counting variable have been used in the program: countItem is used to keep track of the number of filled slots in the buffer at any time, and will range from 0 to BufferSize; withdrawn keeps a tally of the number of items that have been taken from buffer slots by the consumer process. The MOD BufferSize operation is necessary to keep the variable withdrawn in the range 1 to BufferSize. Using the countItem and withdrawn variables in combination allows us to cycle the deposit operation throughout the buffer slots, rather than going back to the first unfilled buffer slot each time the producer process is resumed.

Some print statements have been added to the processes so that we can observe the actions of the program:

Program 8.9 Bounded buffer

```
MODULE BoundedBuffer;
(* Bounded buffer example based on process synchronisation. *)
FROM InOut IMPORT WriteString, WriteCard, ReadCard, WriteLn,
                  HoldScreen;
FROM Signals IMPORT Signal, InitSignals, CreateSignal, StartProcess,
                    Send, Wait;

CONST
   MemoryPoolSize = 6000;
   WorkSpace = 2000;
   BufferSize = 3;

VAR
   buffer : ARRAY [1..BufferSize] OF CARDINAL;
   withdrawn : [1..BufferSize];
   countItem : [0..BufferSize];
   empty, full : Signal;

PROCEDURE Producer;
(* Template procedure for the producer process. *)

VAR
   deposit : CARDINAL;

BEGIN
   deposit := 0;
   LOOP
      IF countItem = BufferSize THEN
         Wait(full);
      END;
      (* Wait if buffer is full. *)

      deposit := deposit + 1; (* Item for buffer. *)
      buffer [(withdrawn + countItem) MOD BufferSize] := deposit;
      (* Items deposited in buffer, starting from position where the last
      item was withdrawn from the buffer by the consumer process. *)

      WriteString("Deposit in slot number ");
      WriteCard(withdrawn + countItem, 3);
      WriteLn;
```

```
      (* Increment the items in buffer count. *)
      countItem := countItem + 1;
      Send(empty);
   END;
END Producer;

BEGIN (* Main module. *)
   InitSignals(MemoryPoolSize);
   CreateSignal(full);
   CreateSignal(empty);
   countItem:=0;
   withdrawn := 1;

   (* Start producer process. *)
   StartProcess(Producer, WorkSpace);

   (* This LOOP gives the Consumer process. *)
   LOOP
      IF countItem = 0 THEN
         (* Wait if buffer empty. *)
         Wait(empty);
      END;

      WriteString("Withdrawal from slot number ");
      WriteCard(withdrawn, 3); (* Buffer slot number. *)
      WriteString("deposited item value ");
      (* Write the buffer value. *)
      WriteCard(buffer[withdrawn], 5);
      WriteLn;

      (* Decrement the items in buffer count. *)
      countItem := countItem - 1;

      (* Number of items withdrawn from buffer (range1..BufferSize).*)
      withdrawn := (withdrawn + 1) MOD BufferSize;

      Send(full);
   END;
   HoldScreen;
END BoundedBuffer.
```

The runtime actions of the program are as follows:

Deposit in slot number 1
Deposit in slot number 2
Deposit in slot number 3
Withdrawn from slot number 1 deposited item value 1
Deposit in slot number 1
Withdrawn from slot number 2 deposited item value 2
Deposit in slot number 2
Withdrawn from slot number 3 deposited item value 3
Deposit in slot number 3
Withdrawn from slot number 1 deposited item value 4
Deposit in slot number 1
Withdrawn from slot number 2 deposited item value 5
....
....

Our primary objective, to communicate data via shared variables, has been achieved. However, there are some undesirable features in our solution. Once the buffers have been initially filled, the consumer and producer processes alternate. Although this interaction need not necessarily be so in a more complex implementation, where other processes may also be sending Wait and Send signals to the Producer / Consumer processes, we should still aim to reduce the number of unnecessary signals being sent. The Send signals are sent at the end of every loop cycle; this is obviously unnecessary. A simple conditional statement to control the send operation such as:

```
IF countItem = 0 THEN Send(full) END;
```

would reduce the Send operations to a minimum. The implementation of suitable statements to remove unnecessary signal operations is left as an exercise.

8.7.2 Communications via channels

A major innovations in the 1980s was the availability of processors from which distributed memory computing systems could be built. Processes such as the Inmos transputer use simple point to point communication links to connect processors together. Although the memory in these processors is private, messages can be passed between the processors along the physical links to allow the exchange of data, or to achieve synchronisation between processors whenever this is required. The communication model that is based on this idea is known as the channel abstraction. There are two essential properties of a channel. Firstly, only two processes can be associated with a channel, the sending process and the receiving process. Note the use of the word process. The channel communication abstraction is based on the process abstraction irrespective of whether the processes reside on a single processor or on processors that are separated by a physical link. The use of the channel abstraction on a single processor is sometimes referred to as *soft channels*. Secondly, only one piece of information may be sent through the channel at any instant of time.

Processes must support a number of operations to support message passing along channels, the most important being input message and output message. Communication takes place on the channel when both the inputting and outputting processes are ready. It is therefore inevitable that some waiting is involved, as the first process to become ready must wait on the other process. An efficient implementation of channel communication would allow the descheduling of the communication process until both sending and receiving process are ready. This is, of course, only possible when the rescheduling of a different processes does not violate the correctness of the program algorithms.

As the channel abstraction does not depend on separate processors, we can use the idea for a single processor implementation in Modula-2. This again has the added advantage that the principles we are studying are extendible to a concurrent implementation.

During the execution of a set of processes it is feasible that some of these processes may require more than one channel. Therefore, a channel abstraction should be defined which includes an operation which has the ability to open several channels. The operations that are needed should first connect the input and output channels and then complete either a sending operation or a receiving operation.

A suitable definition module is given in Program 8.10.

Program 8.10 Channels

```
DEFINITION MODULE Channels;
(* Channel communication abstraction. *)
FROM SYSTEM IMPORT BYTE
TYPE Channel;

PROCEDURE OpenChannel(VAR C : Channel);
(* Opens a channel ready for connection between processes. *)
PROCEDURE ConnectInput(VAR C : Channel);
(* Attaches the opened channel to the input port. *)
PROCEDURE ConnectOutput(VAR C : Channel);
(* Attaches the opened channel to the output port. *)
PROCEDURE Input(VAR C : Channel; VAR Message ARRAY OF BYTE);
(* Input a message on the opened and connected channel. *)
PROCEDURE Output(VAR C : Channel; VAR Message ARRAY OF
BYTE);
(* Output a message on the opened and connected channel. *)
END Channels.
```

The implementation of this module is beyond the scope of this book. A good implementation can be found in Ford and Weiner, who also give an example of its use. For information on the use of channels in multiprocessor systems you should refer to a book on the programming language Occam. This language demonstrates the power of the channel abstraction and the ease with which it can be applied.

Summary

Computer models of past years were mostly based on sequential models. Computer models of the future will be based to some degree on concurrent models.

Processes are modules that execute sequentially and may interact with other processes both synchronously and asynchronously.

Coroutines are the underlying abstraction for implementing concurrency on a sequential processor. Coroutines are the basis for processes in Modula-2

When we have a number of cooperating sequential processes that share some resource, such as data, then mutual exclusion must be provided. Critical sections can be used to implement mutual exclusion in a safe and efficient manner. A Deadlock situation can occur when two or more processes are waiting for an event which can only be executed by one of the waiting processes.

Semaphores are used to solve a variety of process synchronisation problems. The signal abstraction allows process synchronisation to be achieved at the highest abstraction level.

Interprocessor communication can be achieved by sharing data or by message passing along channels.

Selected reading

Ben-Ari, M
Principles of Concurrent Programming,
Prentice-Hall,1982.
A good description of concurrency is given. The style is a little theoretical for a beginner and should be read in conjunction with of Peterson and Silberschatz.

Ford, G A and Wiener, R S
Modula-2 A Software Development Approach,
J Wiley and Sons, 1985.
This book includes a good chapter on process abstraction. It contains good implementations of Wirth's early editions of Programming in Modula-2.

Perrot, R H
Parallel Programming,
Addison-Wesley, 1987.
Parallelism and concurrency are described in an easy to follow style. There is an interesting comparison of the various language approaches to supporting parallelism.

Peterson, J and Silberschatz, A
Operating System Concepts,
Addison-Wesley, 1983.
The emphasis is on operating systems which of course depends on concurrency for its implementation. Mutual exclusion is particularly well described.

Wexler, J
Concurrent Programming in Occam 2,
Ellis Horwood, 1989.
This is of interest if you wish to study how a language can support multi-processor computing.

Wirth, N
Programming in Modula-2, Fourth Edition,
Springer-Verlag, 1988.
The fourth edition has an improved section on concurrency. This is the best reference book on the topic.

9 The hardware abstraction

9.1 The hardware abstraction

The purpose of this chapter is to introduce a simple abstract model for the hardware behind most computers and to describe the facilities that a language such as Modula-2 provides for working with this abstraction in the form of low-level programming tools. Some practical program examples for IBM-style and Macintosh machines are introduced.

The *real world* starts with data generated by some device external to the computer, and as a first step the data must be converted into a form understandable by the computer, that is the binary form of a series of zeros and ones. Conversely when the computer needs to communicate its results with the *real world*, its representation of the data must be converted from zeros and ones back into an appropriate form, often as a voltage or a current.

The devices used, for example, to measure pressures, temperatures, radiation levels etc, and then convert this form of data to voltages and currents, can be treated as abstractions provided we know how the data is constructed. The same is true in the opposite direction – out of the computer, to disk drives, the screen, another computer, etc. However it is self-evident that the data representations from and to external devices of all kinds will rarely conform to the simple data types described for Modula-2. We need to define abstractions which can map our external data onto the data types of Modula-2. Program design at this level also demands that the programmer understands the hardware itself, in particular its structure and limitations and any features which may influence the safety of a program controlling external devices – whether the controls are for a mouse or a nuclear power station! Finally we need the appropriate software tools to connect the computer program to the outside world. It is the purpose of this chapter to discuss these tools as they appear in Modula-2, and to show how they can map onto the hardware abstraction.

In contrast to most forms of worldly data, ASCII character input and output are an exception in having a pre-defined computer-friendly format, and so are understandable to most computer languages. The *character* type in some form is universal to most computer languages. But even here when we start to examine the physical means of transferring the ASCII codes, we discover that we need more than the Modula-2 data type CHAR provides.

The hardware component which sends and receives the characters, a Universal Asynchronous Receiver Transmitter (UART), needs particular binary signals from the computer to instruct it: about rates of data transmission; about the precise transmission format of the bytes of ASCII code; about the extra data bits which go to make up a transmission. We also need a particular form of control over the computer hardware itself, known as an *interrupt*, for character transmission to be efficiently and safely programmed.

9.1.2 Hardware abstractions

The interface between the computer and the outside world is only one part of the problem, another interface is needed between the programming language and the computer on which it is used. In an efficient programming language it should be possible to write the compiler for the particular computer in the language itself. Whilst there are considerable similarities between different computers from different manufacturers, the precise architecture of their hardware differs greatly.

A system which appears independent of the computer on which it is to run requires a considerable level of abstraction. An early model for this was the so called p-compiler (from UCSD Pascal). This defined an abstract model for the processor so that compilation was in terms of abstract p-codes, these in turn were interpreted according to the particular computer hardware machine codes. Whilst this system is inherently slow, it does enable programs compiled on one form of hardware to be run on a totally different form of hardware.

A simple abstract model for a computer system can be illustrated by Figure 9.1. There are four important parts to this model:

- the Central Processing Unit – CPU,
- attached memory to store data and program code,
- the connection to the outside world,
- the inter-connecting paths between the above three units.

All four can be viewed in terms of lower level abstractions of the computer system model.

Figure 9.1 An abstract model for a computer and its connections to memory and the outside world.

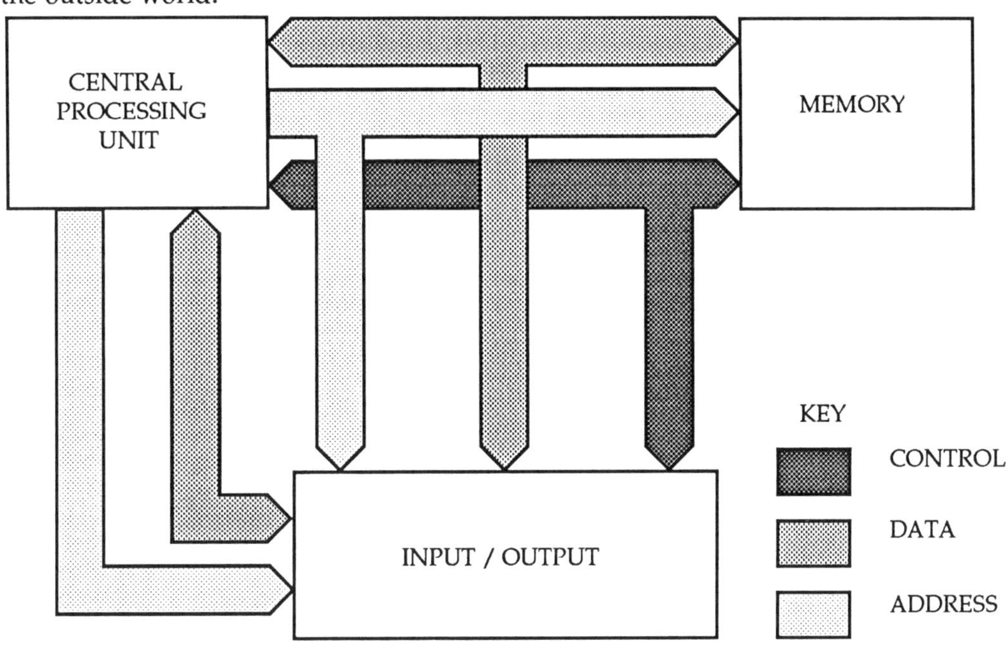

In Figure 9.1 the connections shown by the arrows represent the electrical bus connections between the three principal components of the central processing unit , the memory and the i/o. Note the alternative bus structures within the model for data and addresses.

The Central Processing Unit

The machine codes which operate a Motorola 68000 processor are meaningless to an Intel 80386 processor. An additional complication arises from the continual development of the processors themselves. The Intel processors used by the IBM-PC and its look-a-likes, starting with the 8088 in 1981, have evolved to very much more complex and powerful processor. At present there are 80486 processors in IBM-style machines, and the 80586 is on its way. A compiler written for the 8088 processor will work on the 80486 processor, but it is like putting an old model T Ford engine into a new Ford Mustang. The program language needs to be able to make use of new facilities, as well as taking into account manufacturer differences.

However, a simple abstraction for the CPU is possible since all CPUs are constructed with a very regular internal structure, including a number of code/data storage locations called *registers*. The registers are used for manipulating the data and machine code that go together to make up programs. All of the operations involved with programming are ultimately conducted *via* registers of various types.

The registers can be regarded as storage locations within the CPU itself. This abstraction is as applicable to an early (1974) processor such as the Motorola 6800 as it is to the more recent (1990) Motorola 68040.

A model for the processor registers is shown in Figure 9.2. In the model no particular function needs to be ascribed to any particular register, though some may act as accumulators (as in adding machines), some for indexing (loop counting), some for flags (binary signals), some as stack pointers, some for addresses, some for data storage, etc. An abstract model for the registers does not define their size, or number, nor does it need to.

Figure 9.2 An abstract model for the CPU registers

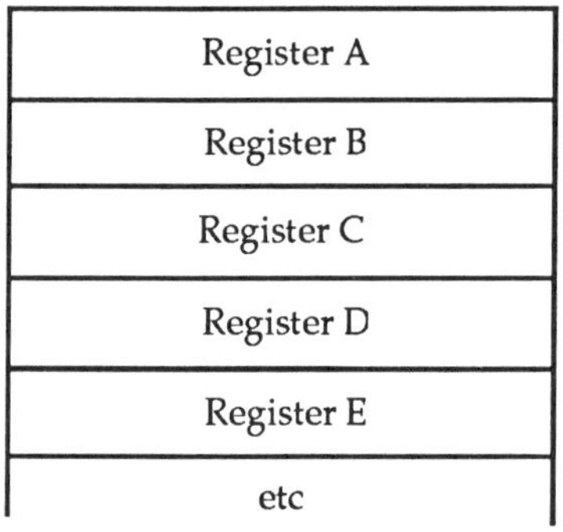

Register A
Register B
Register C
Register D
Register E
etc

The memory

The basic storage unit of all computers is the *bit* (binary digit) since this is the most convenient method to represent computer information. A decimal computer system would be possible but would require that we could reliably distinguish between ten different voltage levels! The bit is thus the basic abstraction for the machine, consequentially we need a type to represent this within the language. A binary number type is the obvious candidate, however a Boolean type could also work.

In a practical (electrical) system memory is constructed in large blocks. Within these memory blocks the common storage unit at present is the *byte* (8 bits). The byte thus forms a basic data abstraction. However a slightly larger unit may become important as processors increase in size, so that another convenient abstraction is a group of bytes, a *word*. A simple graphical model to represent this situation is shown in Figure 9.3, here the word has four bytes, applicable to 32 bit CPUs. A two byte word for 16 bit CPUs is still common.

Figure 9.3 A model for memory storage

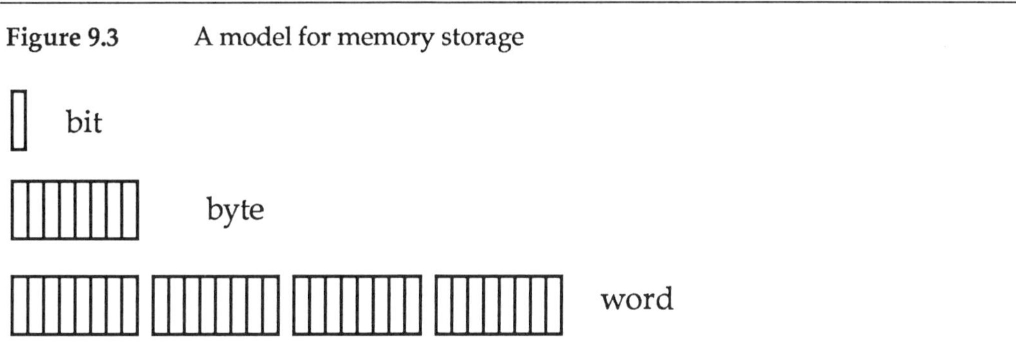

The buses

A *bus* in a computer refers to the electrical connections within the computer, and the connection to the outside world. Computer and processor manufacturers have defined many forms of bus for the various computer architectures that they develop. However, the bus represents another abstraction, within this there are sub-levels of abstraction. Thus there is an address bus, whereby the computer assigns the addresses of the memory and i/o storage, a data bus is used to transfer code and data to the memory and i/o, a control bus enables various forms of control signal to be transferred between the three principal units, and also between these units and the outside world. In the model it is important to note that the address bus is unidirectional, from the CPU to the memory and i/o, whereas the data and control buses are bidirectional. As with the registers the size of the buses have not been defined, though like memory the data and address buses are usually in units of eight.

Just as memory locations can be given specific addresses, so various forms of peripheral device can be given addresses, this provides a means whereby the computer can distinguish between these different devices. An important difference between processors appears at the address bus level. Some processors have a specific address bus to address the i/o, whereas others combine the address bus to i/o with that to memory. The former is often called *port addressed i/o*, the latter *memory mapped i/o*. If there is a separate address bus for i/o, then there is also a separate data bus.

From the point of view of the abstract programming model an important function of the control bus is to provide signal lines which can supply interrupt signals to the processor directly from the outside world (see Section 9.2.2).

9.2 Low-level facilities in Modula-2

Low-level programming refers to programs which are close to the hardware of the computer, in many situations such programming has to be done with the aid of machine code instructions written with an assembler. In 1977 when Wirth's group at

ETH in Zurich, Switzerland started to develop a computer system for a special machine called Lilith, the result was Modula-2 and they had as an aim that it:

> " was to be programmed in a single high-level language, which therefore had to satisfy requirements of high-level system design as well as those of low-level programming of parts that closely interact with the given hardware."

Modula-2 does not have any input or output instructions as a part of the language, instead i/o is made possible by the module concept, and by the provision of libraries into which input and output instructions can be confined. As was described in Chapter 7, Modula-2 has a set of tools from which all the i/o can be constructed.

9.2.1 The SYSTEM library

In order to communicate with the hardware of a particular computer, a Modula-2 compiler needs a special library module known as SYSTEM; this is intimately connected to the compiler, it does not usually appear as a library module amongst the other libraries for the particular version of Modula-2, so that there are no implementation or definition parts. However,the reference manuals for the computer will describe what SYSTEM contains. SYSTEM is usually referred to as a *pseudo-module* because of this situation, and because its contents must be known to the compiler, since they are used during the compilation of all programs through library calls to SYSTEM. The SYSTEM library facilities are used explicitly or implicitly by all of the standard library procedures supplied with a particular Modula-2 implementation.

SYSTEM can be regarded as providing part of the abstraction to represent the computer system depicted in Figure 9.1, so that it defines how a particular version of Modula-2 is to interact with a particular hardware configuration.

A minimum definition module for SYSTEM is given in Wirth's 4th Edition of Programming in Modula-2:

```
DEFINITION MODULE SYSTEM;
TYPE
   WORD; ADDRESS; PROCESS;

PROCEDURE ADR(x : AnyType): ADDRESS;
PROCEDURE TSIZE(AnyType): CARDINAL;
PROCEDURE NEWPROCESS(P : PROC; a:ADDRESS;
                         n : CARDINAL; VAR q : ADDRESS);
PROCEDURE TRANSFER(VAR from, to : ADDRESS);

(* other facilities also may be present. *)

END SYSTEM.
```

However, all practical SYSTEM libraries add many more facilities suitable for the particular computer; indeed it could be argued that these should be a necessary part of the language definition if we are to provide the abstractions described in Section 9.1. The above definition only deals with abstraction levels which relate to the computer memory, and possibly the i/o functions.

For an example of a practical SYSTEM library we take that for M2SDS (Modula-2 Software Development System) Modula-2, a version for the IBM PC machines and compatibles. M2SDS has the following export list :

```
EXPORT QUALIFIED WORD, BYTE, STRING, ADR, ADDRESS,
RegAX, RegBX, RegCX, RegDX, RegSI, RegDI, RegES, RegDS,
SIZE, TSIZE, NEWPROCESS, TRANSFER, CODE, SWI,
IOTRANSFER, SETIO;
```

This is typical of Modula-2 for Intel 80X86 based machines (where X is used to indicate the family of processors), though the identifier names and other details may vary for other Modula-2 compilers. Abstractions now appear for the processor registers, for the processor machine code, and for interrupts. Thus this is a practical system with which we can represent our full model of Figure 9.1.

The SYSTEM library for Metrowerks Modula-2 on the Apple Macintosh shows some significant differences, but again this provides a full model for Figure 9.1:

```
DEFINITION MODULE SYSTEM;
TYPE
   ADDRESS=POINTER TO BYTE;
   BYTE;
   WORD;

PROCEDURE ADR(VAR x : AnyType): ADDRESS;
PROCEDURE INLINE(x : WORD);
PROCEDURE REG(reg : INTEGER): LONGINT;
PROCEDURE SAVEREGS;
PROCEDURE SETREG(reg : INTEGER; val : T);
PROCEDURE TSIZE(AnyType): INTEGER;
PROCEDURE CAST(AnyType;x : AnyType): AnyType;
...
END SYSTEM.
```

This library also contains some procedures to manipulate INTEGER, LONGINT, REAL and LONGREAL variables. The main difference (with the standard definition from Wirth) is the omission of those types and procedures which enable programs to control multiple programming tasks, that is PROCESS, NEWPROCESS and TRANSFER, etc. Metrowerks Modula-2 moves these into another library module named Coroutines. Coroutines are described in Chapter 8.

The Apple Macintosh employs 680X0 processors, these use memory mapped i/o, so that slightly different programming facilities are needed from those with the port addressed i/o employed by IBM style machines with their Intel 80X86 processors. (Note, Metrowerks has a standard library module called System used for controlling compiled program modules, and which is nothing to do with SYSTEM).

WORD, BYTE and TSIZE

We have seen that just about the only predictable feature of much low-level computer data is that it appears as a series of 0s and 1s which are usually grouped in units of eight as bytes. Also we have seen that appropriate abstractions for the memory are bytes and words. Modula-2 compilers start by assuming that data and machine instruction codes are stored as one or more bytes. Thus an 8-bit computer would have one byte, a 16-bit computer two bytes (for example, Intel 80286 and Motorola 68000 processors), and a 32-bit computer 4 bytes as fundamental storage units (for example, Intel 80386, 80486 and Motorola 68030 processors).

The data storage unit of 1,2 or 4 bytes is called a WORD, it differs from other Modula-2 simple data types such as INTEGER or CARDINAL in that the bit pattern contained in the WORD has no specified format or meaning. It is just a collection of 8, 16, 32 or however many bits. Because of this it can only be used in assignment statements, moreover it is compatible with all other Modula-2 data types, all of which are defined to consist of one or more WORDs. At first sight this situation looks rather useless, however consider the following procedure:

```
PROCEDURE PutBinary(W : WORD);
CONST
   WordLength = 16;
VAR
   c : CARDINAL;
   b : BITSET;

BEGIN
   b := BITSET(W);
   FOR c := WordLength-1 TO 0 BY -1 DO
      IF c IN b THEN
         Write("1");
      ELSE
         Write("0");
      END;
   END;
END PutBinary;
```

This is a generic procedure which will write the binary equivalent of any type which assigns a single word to its variables – INTEGER, CARDINAL, BITSET (see below).

Our fundamental data abstraction for memory is the byte. Most computers are byte-oriented, so that WORD is a somewhat artificial unit. It is being superseded in many Modula-2 implementations by BYTE, this has the same property as WORD, namely that its individual bits have no predetermined meaning. The advantage of this type is that the type ARRAY OF BYTE is compatible with every other Modula-2 data type. Both WORD and BYTE can be used for work with the register and the memory abstractions.

The function procedure TSIZE (or SIZE) gives the number of bytes or words that a particular type or variable uses. However, notice the ambivalence over whether we are dealing with bytes or words. Most implementations work with bytes, the Wirth definition is in terms of words. Maybe in the long term, as memory becomes larger, the word will be seen to be more appropriate. TSIZE (or SIZE) are useful for determining storage requirements, particularly of RECORD types.

ADDRESS, ADR

Each WORD or BYTE of storage can be addressed at a particular memory location, this is defined by an ADDRESS, for which the definition is either:

```
TYPE
   ADDRESS = POINTER TO WORD;
```

or

```
TYPE
   ADDRESS = POINTER TO BYTE;
```

ADDRESS is thus part of the memory abstraction. Again the ambivalence arises because of the use of either WORD or BYTE. M2SDS Modula-2 has the WORD definition, MetroWerks Modula-2 the BYTE definition, but hopefully this very unsatisfactory state of affairs will be resolved by the forthcoming Modula-2 standard. The problem illustrates how difficult it is to develop abstractions for data types at the low-level end of programming.

ADDRESS, because it is defined as a POINTER, can be used as such, and is assignment compatible with POINTERs. The contents of the address can be obtained by the usual dereferencing operator.

The function procedure ADR, defined in SYSTEM, serves to determine the memory address of any variable.

Under most circumstances it is not necessary to know what the address of a particular item of data is, however with some programs, particularly those involving files or coprocesses, it is often necessary to define how much memory is to be used. The subject is generally known as *memory management*.

9.2.2 Extensions to the SYSTEM library

For all practical versions of Modula-2 it is necessary to have extended SYSTEM libraries. The extensions generally concern at least three types of operation:

- Communication with the processor registers.
- Use of short patches of machine code.
- Access to interrupts.

These follow from the discussion of the necessary abstractions for a practical computer system.

Communicating with the processor registers

The size and number of registers depend on the computer, present day typical examples such as the Intel 30386 and Motorola 68030 processors have 32 bit registers, earlier versions had 16 bit registers. Within Modula-2 an abstraction to represent the registers can simply be a set of INTEGER, CARDINAL, LONGINT or LONGCARD variables (depending on the register size) which will act as data stores, and which the compiler *knows* to associate with particular processor registers. The details must therefore be dependent on the implementation, and so are necessarily part of the SYSTEM library.

For M2SDS Modula-2 these are referred to as *pseudo-register variables*, the compiler understands that the particular variable is mapped onto the corresponding register with that name. The variables are declared as: RegAX, RegBX, RegCX, RegDX, RegSI, RegDI, RegES, RegDS, which are derived from common names for the 80X86 Intel processor registers. They are compatible with CARDINAL types. Common uses are to set up short sections of machine code, or set up an interrupt and then to read data after the interrupt. Examples are found below in the library Module Ports, in the procedures PortIn and PortOut, and also in the module PcConfiguration. It is only possible to assign data to these variables, or to read data from them, furthermore they should be written to or read from *immediately* before they are used. As the processor registers are used in the surrounding program code, their contents of course will change constantly with the operation of the program. If a data item is passed between a program and the registers then it should be kept in another variable until its immediate use, when it should be either copied into or out of the particular pseudo-register variable. The contents of the pseudo register variables are somewhat ephemeral!

There are other ways of defining processor registers, TopSpeed Modula-2 from Jensen defines a variant record structure type:

```
Registers =
   RECORD
      CASE : BOOLEAN OF
         TRUE : AX, BX, CX, DX, BP, SI, DI, DS, ES : CARDINAL;
                Flags : BITSET;
         | FALSE : AL, AH, BL, BH, CL, CH, DL, DH :SHORTCARD;
      END;
   END;
```

The advantage of this is that it keeps the registers together in one unit, and this is part of the abstraction previously described for the CPU registers. More importantly it allows the programmer to access either the full 16 bits of the register, for example, as AX, or through the FALSE part of the variant, to access the registers' top or bottom 8 bits separately, for example, as AL and AH. This can be important, for example in the procedure PortIn the processor IN instruction refers only to 8-bit data in the form that it is used. With M2SDS Modula-2 it is necessary to isolate the bottom 8 bits of the CARDINAL number of the pseudo register variable using CHR(RegAX), but with the TopSpeed data structure we could refer directly to it, for example, Register.AL .

On the Apple Macintosh, Metrowerks Modula-2 uses yet another method to access the processor registers by defining procedures to read, save and set the register contents for Motorola 68000/68020 processors, respectively:

```
PROCEDURE  SAVEREGS;
PROCEDURE SETREG(reg : INTEGER; val : T);
PROCEDURE REG(reg : INTEGER): LONGINT;
```

where reg is a constant with a value of 0-7 for the D0 to D7 data registers, or 8 to 15 for the A0 to A7 address registers. T is any simple type with a size less than or equal to four bytes, so that SETREG is generic.

Working with short embedded sections of machine code

A number of programming languages allow the programmer to include short lengths of machine code directly within the source code. This is usually called *in-line code.* One method of achieving this is to include assembler language mnemonics within the source code, in which case the compiler also acts as an assembler when it meets the assembler source code, assembling the mnemonics into machine code, and leaving the result within the compiled program. The alternative is to include pre-assembled machine code (usually) in the form of hexadecimal numbers. The codes are thus presented as data to the compiler which includes this in the instruction stream that it generates during compilation. To this end M2SDS uses a procedure called CODE, and Metrowerks uses INLINE, both of which use pre-assembled hexadecimal numbers. Thus the effect on the compiler is to interpret the data supplied as the argument to the procedure, as a list of machine codes which are inserted directly into the instruction stream of the program at the point where the CODE or INLINE call occurs. In PortIn and PortOut the hexadecimal numbers placed in this fashion (0ECH and 0EEH respectively) cause the processor to issue the machine code instructions IN or OUT. Note that the registers DX and AX are brought into use transferring the data in and out (see Section 9.3.1).

The use of in-line code is satisfactory for short sections of machine code, but needs treating with extreme caution, otherwise very unpredictable errors can be generated. As a general rule use the technique only when absolutely necessary, and if you do use it then keep the code *patches* short and comment what you do. One solution to the content of the comment statement is to give assembler mnemonics alongside of comments about what the mnemonics accomplish.

External interrupts

An interrupt enables an external signal to be recognised by the computer causing it to transfer its attention to and from another unrelated job, in the same way that we may answer a telephone call whilst interrupting a conversation to someone, then return to our conversation afterwards. Note that a telephone call is often an unexpected event, also that another more important event such as the fire alarm ringing can cause us to abandon both the conversation and the 'phone call.

If a computer is to respond to an event external to itself, then some method of signaling the processor when the event occurs must be set up. All actions external to the computer will be asynchronous, that is they will not be in time with the computer clock. Moreover, and of greater importance, the events are not predictable, so that the computer needs some method of reacting to an externally generated signal. One method to do this is by a polled loop. The computer waits in a short closed loop for a signal to arrive, when the signal appears it reacts in some way. This is usually a very unsatisfactory method for all but the simplest events since it also means that the computer is sitting doing nothing whilst it waits. All processors therefore provide one or more special (hardware) signals which can interrupt whatever the processor is doing.

Interrupt signals form part of the control bus, they are usually *active low* in that they take the form of a 5-volt line being put into a low state. When this happens the processor finishes its current machine instruction. Next, a record of the current state of the processor registers must be saved (usually explicitly by the programmer), and the interrupt is then *serviced*, that is a procedure to deal with whatever the interrupt refers to is run. When the event signaled by the interrupt is finished the processor registers are restored (by the programmer again) and the computer resumes its original task. Interrupts can also be given different levels of priority, so that an interrupt of a higher priority can itself interrupt one of lower priority.

On the 680X0 Motorola based processors interrupts are referred to as *externally generated exceptions*, or sometimes simply *exceptions*. Examples of interrupt programming are found with the M2SDS Modula-2 system, where the library procedures NEWPROCESS, TRANSFER, IOTRANSFER, SETIO form part of the SYSTEM library.

Software interrupts and exceptions

All computers need an operating system to enable the user to run the machine, very often the programmer can use the machine code programs that have been written for the operating system within the program. By using the services provided by the BIOS (Basic Input Output System) or by the DOS (Disk Operating System), or present in ROM (as with the Macintosh Toolbox), we have a readily available library of code to access a whole range of special services on the particular computer. This saves the duplication of code already present. It is possible to generate the same effect as an external interrupt signal from within the machine code controlling the processor, such an event is called a *software interrupt*. Operating system calls often take the form of these software interrupts.

On 680X0 Motorola processors the machine codes starting with the binary patterns 1010 (A hexadecimal) or 1111 (F hexadecimal) are not used by the processor, they are *unimplemented (illegal) machine instructions*. If one of these instructions appears in the compiled program code it will generate an instruction which causes the processing to jump to new code addressed by an *exception vector*. Internal exceptions coming from such illegal machine code are the Motorola equivalent of a software interrupt. Macintosh computers use this to jump to Macintosh Toolbox and Operating System routines. Proper control of a complex *windows icon mouse pointer* (WIMP) environment such as the Macintosh User Interface demands that the programmer master the use of these. In Metrowerks Modula-2 these calls are encapsulated into Manager libraries which follow the definitions described in the *Inside Macintosh* volumes.

The programming of hardware interrupts and exceptions is an advanced topic which will not be considered further here, but anyone working with low-level applications needs to be aware of these. Programming using software interrupts is much easier. For example the M2SDS SYSTEM library provides a software interrupt call, SWI, and this allows access to the IBM-PC BIOS and to the PC DOS via another library, DOSCALL. Likewise TopSpeed Modula-2 provides a DOS library. In Section 9.3.2 a module PcConfiguration, shows how a software interrupt may be used to determine. the hardware attached to a particular IBM-style PC. Similar information can be obtained about the Macintosh configuration by a call to the PROCEDURE SysEnvirons in the Utilities library module, or via the Gestalt Manager for System 7.

9.2.3 The type BITSET

The fundamental abstraction for both data and code must be the bit. Thus it is necessary to have a data type which can manipulate the individual bits of a byte or word. Whilst it is quite possible to do that *via* the CARDINAL, INTEGER or even CHAR data types, such manipulations are inherently awkward, it is much better to work in a manner which shows precisely which bit is 0 and which is 1. One solution is to allow binary numbers, however a 32 bit (or even 16 bit) binary number is rather unwieldy, difficult to read, and certainly very unmemorable. To overcome this problem Modula-2 has a standard type BITSET which is defined as:

```
TYPE
    BITSET = SET OF [0..Wordlength-1];
```

where Wordlength is just the length of the data type WORD. (Remember that this was defined as the basic storage unit for the program, and that it is normally 16 or 32 depending on the particular system.) Often :

```
BITSET = SET OF [0..15];
```

BITSET constants are represented in curly brackets so that for example

```
CONST
    Mode0AllOutputs = {7};
```

and this has a binary value (assuming a 16 bit WORD) of 0000000010000000.

BITSET refers literally to a set of bits. From the above it is seen that a binary number's bits are counted from the right, and the least significant bit, numbered 0, is on the right, so that bit 7 is the only one included in the set. This is the number appearing in the curly braces. The CARDINAL equivalent of this is 128 decimal or 80 hexadecimal. The rule for BITSET is thus that those bits which are 1 are considered to be included in the set, and appear as their bit number within the brackets of the BITSET constant or variable, those which are excluded from the set have a zero value, and do not appear in the curly braces. Because BITSET has the properties of a set, the order in which the bits are given is immaterial. The empty set is depicted as {}, and a range within a variable can be shown as {0..8} rather than {0,1,2,3,4,5,6,7,8}. The two can also be mixed, so that {0..15,30,31} is legal. Notice how much easier the latter is than the binary number 11000000000000001111111111111111.

The operators for BITSET variables are those of SETs, that is union, intersection, difference and symmetric difference. There are a number of other standard functions for sets. Thus, if two sets A and B are defined by A = {0..4} and B = {3..7}, then:

- A + B is the **union** , a logical OR of A and B, and the result is {0..7}, a set which contains the elements belonging to A, B or both sets.

- A * B is the **intersection** , a logical AND of A and B, and the result is {3,4}, those elements in both sets (see 9.3.2 below, where intersection is used to mask various bit patterns).

- A - B is the **difference**, a logical AND NOT, and the result is {0,1,2}, the elements belonging to A but not B.

- A/B is the **symmetric difference**, a logical exclusive OR, and the result is {0,1,2,5,6,7}, that is the elements of A and B which are not in both sets.

- The standard functions **INCL** and **EXCL** can be applied to the sets. INCL(B,2) returns {2,3,4,5,6,7}, EXCL(A,0) returns {1,2,3,4}. Once a BITSET variable has been initialised, then INCL and EXCL must be used for adding elements to, and removing elements from, the set.

- Whether or not a bit is present in the set can be tested with **IN**. {0} IN {0,1,2,3,4} produces TRUE.

- The standard functions **MAX, MIN, ORD, VAL, DEC** and **INC** can all be applied to BITSET variables.

You will find examples of the use of BITSET throughout the program fragments in this chapter.

9.2.4 Type transfer

Modula-2 is often described as a strongly typed language; essentially all this means is that if a variable is assigned a particular data type, then it is not permissible to assign the variable, or manipulate it, as if it were another data type. Under most circumstances we should not want to try working with CARDINAL numbers as if they were BOOLEANs, or *vice versa*. However, we may want to convert the CARDINAL variable x into its CHAR equivalent, if x represents a printable ASCII code. In this circumstance it is the programmers responsibility to ensure that x is in the range 31 to 127, that is it is actually printable. Modula-2 provides a special function to achieve this particular change of data type, so that:

```
ch := CHR(x);
```

assigns the character with ASCII code x to the CHAR variable ch. Modula-2 provides a useful range of predefined standard functions for conversions of this type; the functions do not need to be imported, they are part of the language definition:

- ORD(ch) is the converse of the CHR operation, giving the CARDINAL number for the ASCII code of ch.

- FLOAT(i) for converting INTEGER or CARDINAL numbers to the REAL number equivalent.

- TRUNC(x) for giving the INTEGER integral part of a REAL number x.

- Double length versions of FLOAT and TRUNC.

With the above functions the computer storage sizes of the types are different, CHARs occupy a byte, CARDINALs and INTEGERs two bytes, REALs four bytes. Another form of type transfer is achieved by a *type transfer function* whereby one form of type can be converted to another, or used as another type, provided that the two types *occupy the same amount of memory*, usually a word. There is an example of a type transfer in the generic procedure, PortOut in Section 9.3.2:

```
PROCEDURE PortOut(number, value : WORD);
BEGIN
   RegDX := CARDINAL(number);
   RegAX := CARDINAL(value);
   ....
   ....
END PortOut;
```

Thus number and value can have any suitable type provided they occupy a word of memory, but it is necessary for these to be interpreted in the procedure as CARDINAL data for them to be compatible with the pseudo-register variables RegDX and RegAX. Another legitimate use of a type transfer was shown in the generic procedure PutBinary, where:

```
B := BITSET(W);
```

It was necessary to cast the data passed to the procedure *via* the WORD type variable, W, into a BITSET type. By placing the identifier CARDINAL or BITSET outside a bracket like this we cause the argument within the brackets to be looked upon as a new type given by the identifier. There is no computation involved in these changes of type - merely that the compiler looks upon the argument in the brackets as another type. Other versions are possible, thus if c is a CARDINAL and i an INTEGER, the following are legal Modula-2 type transfers :

```
c := CARDINAL(i);
i := INTEGER(b);
```

It is up to the programmer to make sure that the assignment makes sense! The chances are that all of the above three examples are of dubious authenticity, conversion of INTEGER to CARDINAL etc should not be necessary. Remember that you are breaking a very fundamental rule in Modula-2 by changing the type representation of your data.

Metrowerks Modula-2 provides another function, CAST(x,T), in the SYSTEM module: a value x is interpreted as a type T. This explicit type transfer function is recommended instead of the normal version for Metrowerks programs. CAST is part of the new standard for Modula-2, but it is not yet present in all versions of compilers for the language.

9.2.5 Anchored variables

An important difference occurs between the Intel 80X86 and Motorola 680X0 processors with regard to their i/o architecture and the resulting machine code instruction sets. With Intel processors there are logically separate buses for memory and for i/o – they have *port addressed i/o,* whereas for Motorola (and DEC LSI-11), memory and input/output are on the same logical bus – they have *memory mapped i/o*. (See Section 9.1.2 on buses in the hardware abstraction description.)

Thus Intel processors use special instruction codes and have 64 kilobytes of special addresses which are only used for port addressed i/o. Hence the name of the library in Section 9.3.1, and in the example in 9.3.2 we can assign addresses to these ports :

```
CONST
    PpiaPortA  =  200H;
    PpiaPortB  =  201H;
    PpiaPortC  =  202H;
```

Thus these are the addresses used for the PortIn and PortOut procedures where we want to input or output data, in our example it is to drive a stepper motor. The specific addresses are defined *via* hardware switches on the computer interface board, here the PC-DIO48 (Bede Technologies) hardware defined below in Section 9.3.2. They represent appropriate port addresses for use with machines running MS-DOS.

For Motorola processors such as the 68020 nearly any of addresses from the 32 bit address map can be used for memory mapped i/o purposes. All that is required is that the appropriate address decoding is provided by the associated computer hardware. In practice the designers of a particular computer system define what these addresses are to be. For example on an Apple Macintosh II, which contains a 68020 processor, the addresses FFFF FFFFH to F100 0000 are set aside for the NuBus so that particular pieces of hardware may be plugged into the computer expansion slots and data transferred in and out from the devices.

In order to communicate with this kind of hardware, Modula-2 provides a method whereby a particular variable may be associated with a particular hardware memory location. These are sometimes called anchored variables. The stepping motor example of Section 9.3.2 can be modified to operate on an Apple Macintosh by substituting the variable declarations :

```
VAR
    PpiaPortA[0A00000H] =  CARDINAL;
    PpiaPortB[0A00004H] =  CARDINAL;
    PpiaPortC[0A00008H] =  CARDINAL;
    PpiaControl[0A0000CH]  =  CARDINAL;
```

Normally the addresses of variables are assigned via the compiler and linker, not by the programmer. The above facility is provided specifically to enable low-level programs which require fixed addresses to define these explicitly. For processors which use port addressing it should not be necessary to use anchored variables, since it should not be necessary to read or write directly to the memory of the computer. The module PcConfiguration in Section 9.3.3 shows the correct usage of a software interrupt.

By using the interrupt vector we can ensure that the correct data is obtained, and it is not impossible that the manufacturer may change the locations which store our information with some future software release. The vector definition will not change. If the hardware information was incorrect, and it had to be used in a program (for example to discover which form of display monitor a particular machine had) then such an error could create serious problems.

It is left to the reader to modify the Ports module to accommodate the difference between M2SDS and Metrowerks Modula-2. However, it is quite possible to leave the definition module for Ports essentially unchanged, whilst changing the implementation module to accommodate the different processor. This is of course in keeping with the fundamental ideas of Modula-2.

9.3 Modula-2 examples of low-level programs

Of necessity, the programs which follow have to use specific versions of Modula-2 for particular computers, this is the nature of low-level programming. All processors address the outside world essentially as they address their memory. Thus one group of addresses will be used for the terminal or keyboard, another for the disk drives, or for a modem or for a printer, and if you want to attach your own apparatus to the computer, the interface will have to define addresses for it.

9.3.1 Interfacing hardware

We cannot be abstract at this point – we must be specific! To demonstrate the principles behind the hardware interface it is often useful to use a *breadboard circuit*. The breadboard enables various kinds of simple hardware to be connected to the computer system when this is provided with the necessary slot interface board. The precise hardware for the motor drivers are described in *Computing in the Laboratory* by Littler and Maher.

For the IBM-style machines the example uses a PC-DIO48 digital i/o card (Bede Technologies). This provides 48 channels of digital i/o in one of the PC interface slots. The PC-DIO48 has two Intel 8255 programmable peripheral interface chips (PPIAs) on it.

For Macintosh II, with NuBus a similar board is the NB-DIO-24 digital i/o card (National Instruments). This has 24 channels of digital i/o, comprising a single PPIA. The card was used in slot A of the Macintosh NuBus interface slots. With Macintosh machines it is critical which slot is used, since these have memory mapped i/o.

9.3.2 Port input and output on MSDOS machines

A partial library module to enable input and output from the port addresses of Intel processors is given in Program 9.1:

Program 9.1

```
DEFINITION MODULE Ports;
(* This library was written for M2SDS Modula-2. *)

FROM SYSTEM IMPORT WORD;
EXPORT QUALIFIED PortIn, PortOut;

PROCEDURE PortIn(number : CARDINAL): CARDINAL;

PROCEDURE PortOut(number, value : WORD);
etc ....
END Ports.

IMPLEMENTATION MODULE Ports;
FROM SYSTEM IMPORT BYTE, WORD, RegAX, RegDX, CODE;

PROCEDURE PortIn(number : CARDINAL): CARDINAL;
   VAR
   value : CHAR;
BEGIN
   RegDX := number;
   (* Pseudo-register variable. *)
   CODE(0ECH);
   (* Machine code instruction. *)
   value := CHR(RegAX);
   RETURN ORD(value);
END PortIn;

PROCEDURE PortOut(number, value : WORD);
BEGIN
   RegDX := CARDINAL(number);
   RegAX := CARDINAL(value);
   (* Pseudo-register variables. *)
   CODE(0EEH);
   (* Machine code instruction. *)
END PortOut;
....
....
BEGIN
END Ports.
```

Program 9.1 shows that the library contains other items which we will not describe, however these are used in Program 9.2 for the stepper motor.

9.3.3 Controlling a small stepper motor with an MSDOS machine

As an example of the use of this library, the following M2SDS program fragments, which are part of a larger program, will drive a small stepper motor motor in various ways. The precise hardware for the motor need not concern us here, it is sufficient to realise that the motor has three phases which may be turned on by sending a 1 and off by sending a 0, thus three digital i/o lines are needed. The pulses to drive the motor have also to be sent at suitable time intervals, and since the motor has a finite response time very much longer than that of that of the computer it is necessary to provide pulses of tens of milliseconds duration.

The system is planned as follows :

- Many PCs provide slots or other interface board connections which enable the user to plug various forms of hardware into their machines, precisely for doing practical jobs like running motors and other equipment. Thus part of the design may involve the choice of a suitable board (see Section 9.3.1).

- Define the hardware that runs the motor. Here we use an Intel PPIA(see 9.3.1), however this is an example and in a real system we should use one of the many custom chips especially for driving motors. This would remove a lot of the work from the computer, and it would also free it for other tasks. The use of *custom* chips for driving particular forms of hardware extends the ideas about abstraction to the hardware surrounding the computer.

- Note that comments in a program should provide information about particular hardware used for running the program, cf Program 9.2.

- Pick up the various library procedures. PromptAt puts a message on the screen at a particular x-y location, QuitCheck looks momentarily whether the ESC key has been pressed for an exit to be signalled, Delay sets up software delay loops (not reliable to better than 2%, but adequate here), and ClockSpeed defines the processor clock rate.

```
FROM Ports IMPORT PromptAt, PortIn, PortOut, QuitCheck,
Delay, ClockSpeed;
```

- The screen message positions as well as the three port addresses are set up.

```
CONST
    PpiaPortA = 200H;
    PpiaPortB = 201H;
    PpiaPortC = 202H;
    PpiaControl = 203H;
    Column = 20;
```

- The PPIA chip on the DIO board needs to be configured. The 3 8-bit i/o ports can be set to work in one of three modes, 0,1,2. Here we use mode 0 for which there are in turn 16 combinations of possible input and output configurations in units of either 8 bits (ports A and B, or 4 bits (Port C). It is convenient to define a general procedure to configure the operating mode of the interface chip.

```
PROCEDURE SetConfiguration(Mode : BITSET);
(* Provides a general procedure for setting the interface
into a particular combination of inputs and outputs on a PPIA. *)
BEGIN
   PortOut(PpiaControl, Mode);
END SetConfiguration;
```

- Finally, before the procedure to drive the motor is called we need to set the correct clock speed for the particular computer that controls the motor. This is selected by means of an enumeration type, the variable for which controls a software loop provided by the Delay procedure. Thus :

```
VAR
   mcClock : ClockSpeed;
```

appears as a variable declaration, then

```
(* You need to tell the program what the machine speed is. *)
mcClock := vectra20;
(* The possible choices are : 4.77 MHz = pc477; 6.00 MHz =
at600;8.00 MHz = at800; 10.00 MHz = at1000; 20.00 Mhz =
Vectra20. *)
```

appears before the motor (or other) control program runs.

The full procedure, together with comments follows. The RunMotor procedure is part of a larger program with other examples.

Program 9.2

```
PROCEDURE RunMotor;
CONST
   Start    = 1;
   Finish   = 6;
   Row      = 1;

TYPE
   BitsOn = ARRAY [Start..Finish] OF BITSET;
   (* This type defines an array to hold the data which determines
   the motor winding(s) to be activated. *)
```

```
VAR
   setBitsOn : BitsOn;
   choice : CHAR;
   pulseDelay : CARDINAL;

   (* Provides known length pulses to drive the motor steps. *)
   leave, escapePressed : BOOLEAN;


PROCEDURE InitialiseBits();
(* The various bit patterns for activating the motor are set up. *)

BEGIN
   setBitsOn[1] := {0};
   setBitsOn[2] := {0,1};
   setBitsOn[3] := {1};
   setBitsOn[4] := {1,2};
   setBitsOn[5] := {2};
   setBitsOn[6] := {2,0};
END InitialiseBits;


PROCEDURE MotorMenu();
(* Gives a screen menu to define what the procedures do. *)

BEGIN
   Clear(); (* Screen. *)
   PromptAt(Column, Row+1, "Control of a 3-phase stepping
motor");
   PromptAt(Column, Row+2, "    ----------------------");
   PromptAt(Column, Row+4, "This will control a stepping");
   PromptAt(Column, Row+5, "motor attached to Port A bits 0,1,2");
   PromptAt(Column, Row+10, "1  -  Set motor pulse delay");
   PromptAt(Column, Row+11, "2  -  Turn motor clockwise");
   PromptAt(Column, Row+12, "3  -  Turn motor anti-clockwise");
   PromptAt(Column, Row+13, "4  -  Use half-step pulse
sequence");
   PromptAt(Column, Row+14, "5  -  Return to main program");
   PromptAt(10, Row+23, "MODULE CM1 C MUST BE ATTACHED
TO THE BREADBOARD FOR THE MOTOR TO RUN");

   (* The user is warned to have the correct hardware attached to
   the computer! *)
END MotorMenu;
```

```
PROCEDURE MenuSelection(): CHAR;
(* A menu is used to select the mode of rotation of the motor. *)
VAR
   character : CHAR;
   valid : BOOLEAN;
BEGIN
   valid := FALSE;
   REPEAT
      REPEAT
      UNTIL BusyRead();
      Read(character);
      valid := (character="1") OR (character="2") OR
             (character="3") OR (character="4") OR (character="5");
      IF valid=FALSE THEN
         Write(bs);
         Write(" ");
         Write(bel);
      END;
   UNTIL valid;
   RETURN character;
END MenuSelection;

PROCEDURE SetDelay(VAR delay : CARDINAL);
(* Control the delay between the motor winding pulses. *)
BEGIN
   PromptAt(Column, Row+20, "Give time delay in msecs >");
   WriteString("    ");
   Write(bs); Write(bs); Write(bs); Write(bs);
   ReadCard(delay);
END setDelay;

PROCEDURE TurnMotor(start : INTEGER; finish : INTEGER; step :
INTEGER);
(* A general procedure to turn the motor. *)
VAR
   element : INTEGER;
BEGIN
   LOOP
      element := start;
      REPEAT
         PortOut(PpiaPortA, setBitsOn[Element]);
         Delay(PulseDelay, mcClock);
```

```
            QuitCheck(escapePressed);
            IF escapePressed THEN
               EXIT;
            END;
            element := element+step;
         UNTIL element=finish;
      END;
   END TurnMotor;

   BEGIN (* RunMotor module. *)
      SetConfiguration({7}); (* Reset all 3 ports as outputs. *)
      leave := FALSE;
      pulseDelay := 100;
      (* Set an initial value for the delay between motor pulses. *)
      InitialiseBits();

      REPEAT
         MotorMenu();
         PromptAt(Column, Row+20, "Delay between pulses = ");
         WriteCard(PulseDelay, 5);
         WriteString(" msec");
         choice := MenuSelection();
         CASE choice OF
            | '1' : SetDelay(PulseDelay);
            | '2' : TurnMotor(1, 7, 2);   (* Clockwise. *)
            | '3' : TurnMotor(5, -1, -2); (* Anti-clockwise. *)
            | '4' : TurnMotor(1, 7, 1);   (* Half step for
                                             clockwise rotation. *)
            | '5' : Clear();   leave := TRUE; (* Quit. *)
         END;
      UNTIL Leave;
   END RunMotor;
```

The above procedure RunMotor works as follows:

- In the procedure InitialiseBits the various bit patterns for activating the motor windings are set up in an array setBitsOn. The BITSET values represent six possible ways of turning on the motor windings. By sending the array data in the sequence 1 to 6 we generate the so-called half-step movement of the motor in a forward direction. Sending data from elements 1, 3, 6 generates a single step movement, reversing the order for sending the data reverses the motor direction. It is assumed that the motor windings are to be driven by bits 0, 1, 2 of one of the PPIA ports.

- The procedure MotorMenu gives a screen menu to describe the various controls over the motor operation.

- The procedure MenuSelection is a function procedure which will respond only to the terminal input choices corresponding to the menu. A beep will sound if the wrong key is pressed.

- The procedure SetDelay is used to control the delay between pulses sent to the motor windings. No damage can be done by very short or very long pulses, strictly a check should be made that MaxCard is not exceeded.

- The procedure TurnMotor is a general (generic so far as the motor is concerned!) procedure to turn the motor. The parameters start, finish, and step define how the BITSET array variables in the array setBitsOn are to be used, hence how the motor is to turn. The combination of a LOOP..END and a REPEAT..UNTIL provides for flexibility in the control of the motor. Once started the motor turns in a particular direction until the ESC key is pressed. It is assumed that the motor is connected to port A of the PPIA.

- Finally the main program control loop sets up the PPIA interface, sets an initial pulse delay, initialises the data array setBitsOn, displays the menu and the delay time, and waits for the user to choose 1..5.

9.3.4 Software interrupts on MSDOS machines : the PC hardware configuration

Program 9.3, that follows, displays information about the hardware configuration of an IBM PC type microcomputer. Use is made of the BIOS interrupts 11H and 12H respectively. This is the preferred technique in all cases when we can use operating system vectors (software interrupts) to aid our programs. In the program the BITSET constants listed below show which bits refer to which parts of the machine. Once the coded information has been read *via* the interrupt, the BITSET constants are used to mask off all the other bits in the data with the aid of the intersection operator, and the DIV operator is used to move the bits that we need to read to the low-end of the data word. On some versions of Modula-2 this last operation can be achieved *via* a shift right operator, DIV serves just as well.

Program 9.3

```
MODULE PcConfiguration;
FROM InOut IMPORT WriteString, WriteCard, WriteLn;
FROM SYSTEM IMPORT RegAX, SWI;

CONST
   EquipmentCheck = 11H; (* Software interrupt for equipment. *)
   BaseMemoryCount = 12H; (* Software interrupt for memory size. *)
```

```
parallelMask = {14..15}; (* Bits 14,15 show the number of parallel
                             ports. *)
   serialMask = {9..11}; (* Bits 9,10,11 show number of serial ports. *)
   videoMask = {4..5}; (* Bits 4,5 indicate the video mode. *)
   coprocBit = 1;
   diskMask = {6..7};
   driveBit = 0;
   (* If bit 0 is set then the computer has at least one floppy disk drive.
   The number of disks minus one is held in bits 6,7. *)

VAR
   equipFlag : BITSET;
   memorySize : CARDINAL;
   parPorts, serPorts, video, drives : CARDINAL;

BEGIN
   SWI(EquipmentCheck);
   equipFlag := BITSET(RegAX);
   SWI(BaseMemoryCount);
   memorySize := RegAX;
   parPorts := (CARDINAL(equipFlag*parallelMask)) DIV 16384;
   serPorts := (CARDINAL(equipFlag*serialMask)) DIV 512;
   IF driveBit IN equipFlag THEN
      drives := (CARDINAL(equipFlag*diskMask)) DIV 128 + 1;
   END;
   video := (CARDINAL(equipFlag*videoMask)) DIV 16;
   WriteString("The configuration of this IBM-style PC is : -");
   WriteLn();
   WriteLn();
   WriteString("Number of parallel ports: ");
   WriteCard(parPorts, 2);
   WriteLn();
   WriteString("Number of serial ports: ");
   WriteCard(serPorts, 2);
   WriteLn();
   WriteString("Number of floppy disk drives: ");
   WriteCard(drives, 2);
   WriteLn();
   WriteString("Video mode : ");
   CASE video OF
      | 1: WriteString("40 x 25 colour");
      | 2: WriteString("80 x 25 colour");
      | 3: WriteString("80 x 25 monochrome");
```

```
    ELSE
       WriteString("Unknown video mode");
    END;
    WriteLn();
    IF coprocBit IN equipFlag THEN
       WriteString("Coprocessor chip is present");
    ELSE
       WriteString("No coprocessor chip fitted");
    END;
    WriteLn();
    WriteString("Amount of memory installed: ");
    WriteCard(memorySize, 4);
    WriteString(" Kilobytes");
    WriteLn();
END PcConfiguration.
```

The program PcConfiguration works for most PCs, but the video mode can have many more instances than in the example.

9.3.5 Machine features for a Macintosh

Discovering the machine features for the Apple Macintosh can be conducted at a much higher level of code than on MSDOS based machines. The function SysEnvirons uses the trap word A090 (hexadecimal) to help determine the software and hardware features of a given machine. (*Inside Macintosh*, Vol 5, ppV-5). The Metrowerks Modula-2 system (see p10-46 in *Metrowerks Modula-2 Reference Manual*) provides the necessary type declaration in the LUTypes library module and the procedure in the Utilities library for us to read the SysEnvRec record. The information contained in the record is self-explanatory from Program 9.4.

Program 9.4

```
MODULE MacWorld;

FROM LUTypes IMPORT SysEnvRec;
FROM MacTypes IMPORT OSErr;
FROM Utilities IMPORT SysEnvirons,SysBeep;
FROM InOut IMPORT WriteString, WriteInt, WriteHex, WriteLn,
HoldScreen;

VAR
    error: OSErr;
    theMacWorld: SysEnvRec;
    sysTop, sysBottom : INTEGER;
```

```
BEGIN
   error := SysEnvirons(1, theMacWorld);
   WriteLn;
   WriteString('I am a Macintosh ');
   CASE theMacWorld.machineType OF
      1 : WriteString('512K enhanced');
      | 2: WriteString('Plus');
      | 3: WriteString('SE');
      | 4: WriteString('II');
      | 5: WriteString('IIx');
      | 6: WriteString('IIcx');
      | 7: WriteString('SE/30');
      | 8: WriteString('Portable');
      | 9: WriteString('IIci');
      | 10: WriteString('IIfx');
      | 11: WriteString('Classic');
      | 12: WriteString('IIsi');
      | 13: WriteString('LC');
   ELSE
      WriteString('whose type number is ');
      WriteInt(theMacWorld.machineType,3);
   END;
   WriteLn;

   (* The following is necessary to sort out the syntax of the System
   version number, which is stored as, for example, $0605. *)

   WriteString('My System version is ');
   sysTop := theMacWorld.systemVersion DIV 256;
   sysBottom := theMacWorld.systemVersion MOD 256;
   WriteHex(sysTop,2); WriteString('.');
   IF sysBottom < 10 THEN
      WriteString('0');
      WriteString('.');
      WriteHex(sysBottom,1);
   ELSE
      WriteHex(sysBottom,2);
   END;
   WriteLn;
```

```
    WriteString('I have a Motorola MC680');
    CASE theMacWorld.processor OF
        1: WriteString('00 processor');
        | 2: WriteString('10 processor');
        | 3: WriteString('20 processor');
        | 4: WriteString('30 processor');
    ELSE
        WriteString('XX processor whose type number is');
        WriteInt(theMacWorld.processor,3);
    END;

    IF theMacWorld.hasFPU THEN
        WriteString(' with a MC68881 floating point processor');
        WriteLn;
    END;

    IF theMacWorld.hasColorQD THEN
        WriteString('I also have Color QuickDraw');
        WriteLn;
    END;

    WriteString('I am fitted with a ');
    CASE theMacWorld.keyBoardType OF
        0: WriteString('Macintosh plus keyboard with keypad');
        | 1: WriteString('Macintosh keyboard');
        | 2: WriteString('Macintosh keyboard with keypad');
        | 3: WriteString('Macintosh plus keyboard');
        | 4: WriteString('Apple Extended keyboard');
        | 5: WriteString('Standard Apple Desktop Bus keyboard');
    ELSE
        WriteString('Keyboard whose type number is ');
        WriteInt(theMacWorld.keyBoardType,3);
    END;

    WriteLn; WriteLn;
    WriteString("That is all I about me I'm telling!  Type any key to
continue");
    HoldScreen; (* Waits for a key press. *)
END MacWorld.
```

However, because of the large and growing family of Macintosh computers, and with the release of System 7.0 software, a powerful gestalt (configuration) manager has been introduced. If the Gestalt function is available, you should use it instead of the SysEnvirons and Environs routines. You can use the Gestalt function to determine whether all the features your application requires are present on a particular Macintosh computer (*Inside Macintosh* Vol VI, P-5).

Summary

A simple abstract model for a computer system consists of the CPU, memory, external and internal connections.

The basic storage unit of all computers is the *bit* (0 or 1). Bits are normally grouped together to form *bytes* (usually 8 bits), and bytes are grouped together to form *words* (2, 4, 8 etc bytes to a word).

External and internal connections between components of the computer are via buses. At the most basic level there is one bus for addressing the memory and i/o storage, one for transferring data, and one for sending control signals. Some systems have separate address buses (and therefore data buses) for memory and i/o.

Low-level access in programming languages must, by its nature, be hardware specific. All Modula-2 systems should have a special SYSTEM library module to provide low-level access to memory, registers etc, but the exact contents of SYSTEM will vary according to the particular implementation of Modula-2 and the computer on which it runs.

SYSTEM should provide access to the CPU registers, the ability to include embedded machine code in programs, and the ability to use interrupts. In addition, SYSTEM should also provide types such as BYTE, WORD, and ADDRESS. The built-in type BITSET is also useful in low-level programming.

An interrupt is a special signal which temporarily stops the processor at whatever it is currently doing, causing it to perform some task associated with the particular interrupt, and then resume its original task.

An interrupt allows the computer to react to external (and therefore unpredictable) events (such as the user typing a character on the keyboard), or to special internal events (such as calls to operating system routines).

Selected reading

Wirth, N
Programming in Modula-2, 4th Edition
Springer-Verlag, Berlin, 1988
See pp34, pp119, pp153. Until the Modula-2 Standard is published this provides the definitive reference for the language syntax and use.

Cooling, J
Modula-2 for Microcomputer Systems
Van Nostrand Reinhold (International), London, 1988
This is one of the few books on Modula-2 which introduces low-level programming in any detail. Its introduction to Modula-2 follows the lines of many other textbooks on the subject.

Burns, A and Wellings, A
Real-Time Systems and their Programming Languages
Addison-Wesley, 1990.
Provides a good comparative discussion of the use of Modula-2, Ada, and Occam for real-time programming. It shows how modern real time programming methods can be applied to robotics, automation and control.

M2SDS Modula-2 Software Development System Users Guide.
Interface Technologies Corporation, 1985
This is an example of one implementation of Modula-2 for IBM PC style machines. A particular interest with this version is the provision of a Modula-2 syntax editor for writing Modula-2 source code.

Metrowerks Compiler Products Modula-2 Reference Manual.
Hudson Heights, Canada, 1988-90.
This is an example of a Modula-2 implementation for Apple Macintosh machines.

Inside Macintosh, Volumes I-VI,
Addison Wesley, 1985-1991
This mammoth series (Vol VI weighs in at 3 kg!) will be needed to complement the Metrowerks Compiler for anyone involved in software design on Macintosh machines. You will also need to learn about the Macintosh Programmers Workshop (MPW). Other volumes in this series, such as Human Interface Guidelines: The Apple Desktop Interface, provides an early example of software design principles.

Littler, J and Maher, J
Computers in the Laboratory - a student guide to microprocessor interfacing.
Longman Scientific and Technical, Harlow, Essex, 1989
A beginners introduction to interfacing problems; the basic principles behind the hardware and software of computers, and interfacing components such as ADCs and DACs are described. The hardware necessary for the stepper motor example is described in detail.

Pemberton, S and Daniels, M
Pascal Implementation: The P4 Compiler,
Ellis Horwood Ltd, 1982.
A very good discussion of the construction of the p-code compiler, there are references to its background.

10 Software testing

10.1 Introduction

Specifying the problem, designing and implementing the solution are only part of the software development process. At all stages in the development of a software system we need to *test* that our solution is correct and solves the problem it is supposed to. If any part of the solution is found to be incorrect we need to modify it appropriately. The act of finding and correcting errors or *bugs* in code is called *debugging*.

Of course, it is also very important to design software that doesn't have bugs in the first place! The techniques of design and specification we have used are aimed at ensuring that our software is as correct as possible.

10.2 The need for testing

We have already seen that building software is not a linear process (although it can be represented as such). We don't start at the top with the specification, and work our way straight down to the final product. At each stage we may backtrack to try another approach or to correct a problem that has arisen. We can characterise this as a repeated series of steps:

1. Examine the problem.

2. Plan a solution.

3. Test the solution for correctness/suitability.

4. If the solution isn't good enough, go back to 1 and try again.

Many of the problems that we meet in everyday life can be solved by this approach, even though we do much of this problem solving without consciously thinking about our actions.

At the very start of the software design process we have to produce a clear and concise specification of the problem to be solved, given the customer's initial description. Even at this stage we need to check if our specification meets the customer's requirements. There is little point in going ahead with the remainder of the design and implementation, only to find that we had originally specified the wrong problem! This type of testing often appears very informal, and may include discussions with the customer of the original problem and the proposed specification.

Software prototyping may be used to test the feasibility of a design or investigate the system requirements and specification. A software prototype is a partial model of a software system, which displays some of the properties of the final system so we can evaluate the current state of the specification or design. For example, we may choose to prototype the user interface to clarify what functionality the customer wants from it.

We have already outlined how testing needs to be used in the design stage of a software solution. Modularisation and abstraction provide techniques to design a solution, but we need to ensure that the design we end up with is suitable. By suitable we mean that it must solve the specified problem, and be implementable.

In modularisation we find the abstractions which are needed to solve the problem. Some abstractions lead to auxiliary abstractions, giving a hierarchy of abstractions in the problem solution. For example, the CarPool abstraction had auxiliary abstractions Car and List. In order to see if we have modularised correctly, and chosen the correct abstractions, we need to see how the operations and types provided by the auxiliary abstractions will provide an implementation for the higher abstractions. We can determine if the abstractions are sufficient by designing each operation of the higher level abstraction in terms of the operations of its auxiliary abstractions.

In Chapter 2 we showed an example of such testing by building algorithms for some of the operations in the highest level abstraction, Requests, using the underlying data abstractions, Car and CarPool. The very fact that we could implement each operation of Requests in terms of the other abstractions shows that we probably got the modularisation right, and defined the right objects and operations.

If it had proved impossible or very difficult to implement the Requests operations in terms of our underlying abstractions we would have to think again about how the problem solution was modularised.

Once we have fully specified and designed a solution to a problem (or part of a problem) we can begin to implement our design in the target programming language. It is very easy to introduce errors at this stage, simply because there is usually no way, other than by exhaustive testing, of checking that the implementation really does meet the specification. Human nature means that errors can be introduced accidentally, and even a formal specification can be misunderstood. Ideally, we need a way of ensuring that the implementation meets the specification.

Various attempts have been made at automating the step from specification to implementation, but these generally deal only with a very restricted subset of problems, and they are not infallible. Some languages are designed to be used for both formal specification and implementation. These *executable specification languages* are still in their infancy, and tend to be restrictive in the types of problems they can easily be used to solve. Other approaches include building a special development environment for the programmer, which automatically checks to see if the programmer is keeping within the specification. Again, such systems are not good as general purpose programming tools, and often restrict the implementor to using a small subset of the implementation language.

The final goal must be to produce software which is guaranteed correct to its specification and error-free. To guarantee this we need to be able to prove that the specification is both complete and correct, and that the program meets its specification. Neither is a trivial task! Consider how we might go about proving that a program meets its specification. In order to do this we must be able to prove each part of the program, right down to proving how the individual statements of the programming language are mathematically related to each other. This is a highly time-consuming task, which cannot yet be fully automated, and is really not feasible for any but the very smallest and simplest of programs.

We say that the point of testing is to ensure that the software meets its specification, but this is not the full story. The specification may not include instructions on how the software should behave if the user uses it incorrectly, but there is very little doubt that any piece of software should behave sensibly and predictably in such circumstances. For example, if the software expects the user to give the name of a file from which information is to be read, and the file doesn't exist, the software shouldn't crash. Instead it might prompt for another file name, or report the error to the user and then exit.

Another example concerns a text editor on a well-known operating system. The editor appeared to wrap lines of text on the screen as it was typed in, so that the user didn't have to hit the return key at the end of each line to move the cursor down to the next line. Users of the editor typed in reports, letters etc without realising that the editor wasn't putting in the returns at the end of each line, so in fact each paragraph ended up as one extremely long line. The users only found out when they tried to print out their documents and the printer attempted (unsuccessfully) to print lines hundreds of characters long.

This example might just seem to be a misunderstanding of the editor by the users, but a little testing of the software with *real* users (not the people who wrote the editor) would probably have shown the way the users misused the editor, and the problem could have been corrected.

Testing a software system needs to be broken down into stages. Each part of the system should be tested and debugged in isolation from the rest of the system. This is called *unit testing.* Units are usually modules. The units can then be integrated with each other, and these larger sections tested again, until the entire system has been built-up and tested. This type of testing is sometimes called *integration testing.*

10.3 Unit testing

In unit testing we test each part or module in isolation from the other modules in the system. If we test each module we can be as certain as possible that it works correctly before integrating it into the rest of the software system.

Testing an individual module involves testing *all* the parts of the module. Usually this means testing each of the operations or procedures which the module exports for use by other modules, and testing any internal procedures which may be used by the exported procedures.

To test a procedure we need to give it some appropriate input data, and then check the resulting output. The output may not simply be a returned value; the procedure might alter one of its input variables, or produce some other side-effect, such as opening a file, or printing a message.

There are two ways of testing a module and the individual procedures it contains:

- Black box testing .
- White box testing.

10.3.1 Black box testing

In black box testing we treat the module or the procedure under test as a black box, that is we assume that we cannot see any of the implementation code. Our only knowledge of the module or procedure comes from the specification.

Modula-2 library modules consist of a specification part, the definition module, and a separate implementation part, the implementation module. For black box testing we should look only at the specification given by the definition module, and also at any user guide there may be for the module. Here is a simple scenario for black box testing:

- Using the specification of the module, build a test plan, consisting of various tests to try on the module, and the expected results for each test. The expected results are determined from reading the specification and documentation.

- Follow the test plan, checking that the results obtained are the same as the expected results. If the results differ the module is probably incorrect.

In Section 10.6 we will look at designing black box tests in more detail.

10.3.2 White box testing

For white box testing we look at the actual code implementing the module and procedures.

- Using the code, build a test plan which forces the execution to go through particular paths in the code. The test plan will consist of various tests and the expected results, as for black box testing, but these tests are derived from looking at the code itself.

- Follow the test plan, checking that the results obtained are the same as the expected results. If the results differ the module is probably incorrect.

The aim of white box testing is to check that all parts of the code work correctly in conjunction with each other. For full testing we need to test *all* paths through the code, but this is rarely possible, except for very small procedures. For example, consider the following Modula-2 procedure which takes a positive number, and prints the same number of asterisks and a message:

```
PROCEDURE Stars(c : CARDINAL);
BEGIN
   IF c > 40 THEN
      WriteString("Output will not fit on one line.");
   ELSE
      WriteString("Output will fit on one line.");
   END;
   WriteLn;
   WHILE (c> 0) AND (c <= 100) DO
      Write("*");
      c := c-1;
   END;
END Stars;
```

First, the IF statement presents two possible paths, through the first part of the IF when c is 41 or more, and through the second part when c is from 0 to 40 (remember that c is a CARDINAL), both of which then converge and go into the WHILE loop. The WHILE loop itself can be executed with values of c from 1 to 100, so there are 100 possible paths through the WHILE loop, 40 of which follow the ELSE clause and 60 of which follow the IF clause. Additionally, there is the path avoiding the WHILE loop completely, when c is 101 or more. This gives a total of 101 paths through this small procedure.

Testing each path individually is really impractical even with a procedure of this size, so instead of exhaustive white box testing we have to be satisfied with tests which follow only a subset of the possible paths through the code. In the above procedure we would supply tests which went through each part of the IF statement (for example, c=50, c=20), tests that check the lower and upper bounds of the WHILE loop (c=1 and c=100 which should go through the loop, and c=0, c=101, which should avoid the loop altogether. So we would have six or so tests rather than over a hundred! Section 10.6.1 shows how to determine what white box tests are required for a given piece of code.

10.4 Integration testing

We have seen from our examples of modularisation that the modules in a software system tend to form a hierarchy (which may have some extra interconnections). Unit testing is concerned with testing individual modules in the hierarchy, in isolation from all the other modules in the system.

During integration testing we choose parts of the hierarchy to bring together, and test that these parts work correctly with each other. Thus we start by integrating two modules, and gradually put together larger and larger parts of the hierarchy until the entire system has been integrated, and is working as a whole. As with unit testing it is usually necessary to provide test harnesses for the parts being integrated.

The overall purpose of integration testing is to pull together the various modules into a complete (preferably working) system, but to do this in a controlled manner.

10.4.1 Order of integration

There are many different strategies for determining the order in which modules are integrated. The commonest strategies are:

- Top-down, where the modules at a higher level in the hierarchy are all integrated before integrating the next level down.

- Bottom-up, which is top-down in reverse! The lowest level modules are integrated first, then the next lowest, etc.

- Sandwich integration, performing both top-down and bottom-up integration from opposite ends of the module hierarchy.

- Build integration, where we integrate modules that relate to a functional component within the system, integrating a group of modules which will span all levels in the hierarchy.

The problem with these strategies is that they impose an order of integration which may not relate to the relative importance of different parts of the software. For example, in any software system designed to be used by people who are not computer experts the user interface is probably the most important part, and it would seem worthwhile to integrate it first, so that problems can be caught as early as possible.

10.5 System testing

The idea of system testing is to ensure that a software system meets its requirements. We assume here that we are discussing a relatively large, software system, such as a database system for a hospital's records, or an airport flight scheduling system. This is where testing the various parts of the system separately, and gradually building a bigger and bigger tested unit, really pays off. Many of the errors, inconsistencies, and design problems will already have been recognized and sorted out in the earlier testing stages.

There are several, well-defined stages in system testing a commercial software system:

1. Alpha testing.
2. Beta testing.
3. Acceptance testing.

10.5.1 Alpha testing

The software is tested by the people who built it, or by other members of their company. This is sometimes called *in-house* testing, because the software company does the testing itself on its own premises, and the customers do not usually see the system at this stage.

10.5.2 Beta testing

After the alpha testing is completed the company that developed the software must find a customer who wants the product being built, and is willing to accept a free (or reduced price) copy of the software, in return for giving bug reports, on the understanding that the software is not in its final form and may contain errors. The developer can then fix the bugs as they are found. The beta test customer may get updated versions of the software with the bugs removed.

The developer must choose the customer very carefully, and make it clear that the product is not in its final form. It is also a good idea to have several beta test sites, to increase the number of people using the system, and find the bugs quicker. Of course, some software packages are custom-built for a single customer, so this customer may beta test the software.

10.5.3 Acceptance testing

The customer who wants to buy the product will be given the software to run for a short period. The customer tests the software and decides whether or not to accept it. If the customer accepts that the software is satisfactory it is purchased, otherwise the software company simply takes it away.

Often, software engineers who developed the software will work at the customer's site during acceptance testing, to help the customer with any problems and to fix any bugs that the customer finds. Extensive alpha and beta testing should reduce the likelihood of the customer finding bugs.

10.6 Designing test plans

A test plan for a module should consist of a list of tests to be run on the module, the input data, and the outputs expected. The plan can be divided into black box testing and white box testing, but some sets of test data will be performing both black and white box tests.

10.6.1 White box tests

As we have already said, the idea of white box testing is to test the various possible paths through the module. Since this is impractical in all but the shortest of modules we need some criteria for deciding which paths we test.

First, we need to ensure that every line of code in the module is tested at least once. This must include testing each branch in a selection statement, and each loop body.

Secondly, every default path in the module must be traversed at least once. A default path can occur when an IF statement has no ELSE clause, and when a loop can have zero iterations, such as a WHILE loop (but not a REPEAT loop, which is always executed at least once). For example, consider the following piece of code:

```
ReadInt(number);
IF number < 10 THEN
   WriteString("Number is less than 10.");
END;
WriteInt(number * number, 6);
WHILE number > 50 DO
   DEC(number);
END;
WriteString("Finished");
```

In this example, the IF statement has no ELSE clause. If the given number is not less than 10 (that is, if it is equal to or greater than 10), the body of the IF statement will never be entered and the next statement executed will be the WriteInt statement. The path avoiding the IF altogether is called the *default path*. Similarly, the WHILE loop can be avoided altogether, if the given number is 50 or less. The default path misses the body of the WHILE and goes straight to the WriteString statement.

The main practical problem with white box testing is determining what tests are required, so that all paths through the program are tested. As an example, lets find the white box tests needed for the AverageTemperatures program from Appendix A. Here is the program we gave:

```
MODULE AverageTemperatures;
(* Find the average of up to twenty temperatures. *)

FROM InOut IMPORT WriteString, WriteLn, ReadCard;
FROM RealInOut IMPORT ReadReal, WriteReal;

CONST
   FieldWidth = 4; (* Number display width. *)

VAR
   c : CARDINAL; (* Control variable. *)
   number : CARDINAL; (* Number of temperatures. *)
   temp : REAL; (* Temperature read in. *)
   total : REAL; (* Total of all temperatures. *)
   average : REAL; (* Average temperature. *)
   temperatures : ARRAY OF REAL; (* Temperature list. *)

BEGIN
   (* Ask user how many temperatures he will enter. *)
   WriteString("Number of temperatures to average (up to 20)? ");
   ReadCard(number);

   (* Check that it's a valid number of temperatures. *)
   IF (number > 0) AND (number <= 20) THEN

      (* Read in the temperatures. *)
      WriteString("Enter temperatures, one per line:");
      WriteLn;
      FOR c := 1 TO number
         ReadReal(temp);
         WriteLn; (* Space out input for user. *)
         temperatures := temp;
      END;

      (* Average temperatures. *)
      WriteString("Calculating average....");
      WriteLn;
      total := 0;
      FOR c := 1 TO number DO
         total := total + temperatures;
      END;
```

```
      average := total / FLOAT(number);

      (* Print out the result. *)
      WriteString("The average temperature is:  ");
      WriteReal(average, FieldWidth);
    ELSE
      (* User entered invalid number of temperatures. *)
      WriteString("Invalid number of temperatures.");
      WriteLn;
    END;
  END AverageTemperatures.
```

First we need to look for the possible paths through the program. There is only one possible path through the code until we reach the IF statement. At this point there are now two possible paths: one through the first clause of the IF statement, if number is greater than 0 and less than or equal to 20; one through the ELSE clause, if number is greater than 20. There is no default path through this IF statement because it has an ELSE clause which must be executed if the first clause fails.

Now we have to look inside the IF statement to see how many possible paths there are through each part of the IF. There are two FOR loops which will always be executed at least once, because number will always be between 1 and 20 (this is ensured by the entry condition on the IF statement). Each FOR loop will be executed *number* of times. It is rather pointless to test each possible number of iterations through the FOR loops – this would involve testing with each value of number from 1 to 20 in all possible combinations for the two loops. Instead we should choose values which test the lowest and highest number of iterations for each loop, and choose an extra value in between for a further test.

Let's see what input values are required to perform these white box tests. Consider the two possible paths through the IF statement:

- The first part of the IF clause should only be executed if number is in the range 1 to 20, so we should test the end points of this range, that is try with number=1 and number=20. We should also test that this clause is *not* entered when number is outside this range, that is try with number=0 and number=21. In addition we should try a couple of arbitrary values inside and outside this range, say number=12 and number=39.

- The second part, the ELSE clause, will therefore only be executed if number is outside the range 1 to 20 (remember that number is a CARDINAL and cannot take negative values) that is, try with number=0 and number=21. As before we also need to try a couple of arbitrary values much the same as above.

- Each FOR loop will be executed from 1 to 20 times, that is try with number=1 and number=20, also try an arbitrary value between these, say number=11.

The following table gives a summary of this information:

Code being tested	To execute code	To avoid code
IF clause	number in range 1..20	number 0 or > 20
1st FOR loop	number in range 1..20	avoid IF clause
2nd FOR loop	number in range 1..20	avoid IF clause
ELSE clause	number 0 or > 20	number in range 1..20

Now we can determine what input values we need to give to test the main paths through the code. You will see from the table below that there are two main paths to be tested, one through the first part of the IF statement and one through the ELSE part. The FOR loops are tested within the tests for the IF statement and do not require any extra tests.

Path being tested	Test
IF clause + both FOR loops	number = 1, 20, 11
ELSE clause	number = 0, 21, 39

10.6.2 Black box tests

Black box tests are needed to test if the software meets its specification. For this reason the tests are designed from looking *only* at the specification of the software.

To determine black box tests we start by reading the specification of the module, and deciding from this what input data the module requires. For each input there will be a group or class of data items which will be valid data, and, conversely, a group or class of data items which will be invalid data, and should cause an error message from the software. Once we know this we can work out some data to test each case.

For example, consider the case where a procedure is expected to read in a car registration number. Assume that from the procedure's specification we know that a car number consists of seven characters, arranged in the following way: one letter, followed by 3 digits, followed by three letters, for example, D987ESM, S584WYP, and that the letters may be upper or lower case.

Input Characteristic	Valid Class of Data	Invalid Class of Data
First character alphabetic	"a".."z" or "A".."Z"	any non-alphabetic character
Next 3 digits	"0".."9"	one non-numeric character
Next 3 alphabetic	"a".."z" or "A".."Z"	one non-alphabetic character

We have split up this input data into its various parts, and described the valid and invalid classes of data for each part. Now we need to find suitable test data to test each input characteristic.

We need to test for both the valid cases and the invalid cases.

First consider the valid input data. We need to test for both acceptance of lowercase letters and uppercase letters, possible test data might be G739HWR and g739hwr.

At first glance it might appear that we need only one test for all the invalid cases: an invalid registration number such as ?7T3PL2. However, this is not recommended. When any part of the input data is incorrect in some way we would expect an error message. If we test with data which is incorrect in more than one way, it may be hard to determine which incorrect part is causing the error report.

Even worse, what if the software was recognising errors in the first two parts of the input data, but not in the last part? A single test with all three parts incorrect will not show this up, as the software will faithfully report an error in the data. Instead, we need to test each case of invalid data separately.

Here are the tests we need to perform for the car registration number:

Characteristic under test	Test
Uppercase letters	G739HWR
Lowercase letters	g739hwr
First character non-alphabetic	%193PSU
One of next three characters non-numeric	R3T82MSE
One of next three characters non-alphabetic	H925J8U

You will often find that some of the white box tests are, in fact, also performing black box tests.

10.7 Designing test harnesses

If a software system consists of many modules, each of which may depend on each other for resources, it may be difficult to test one module without first providing the other modules it depends on. For this reason we need to build special modules round the modules we are testing, to simulate how the modules are to be used in the final system. For example, if we want to test the List data abstraction used in the Car Pool Reservation System, we need to build a program module which calls all the operations of the List abstraction, with appropriate data, and prints out the result obtained from List.

The software which is built for testing in this way is often called a *test harness*, because it is needed round the modules under test until they have been completely tested and debugged. Once this has been done the test harness can be removed.

There are several forms of test harness. The commonest are *test drivers* and *stubs*. A test driver must call all the procedures in a module, with appropriate data, and report the results. A simple test driver will have a fixed set of data, and will call the procedures in a fixed order. It is only slightly more complicated to write a simple interface to allow the user to enter appropriate data. A more complex driver will not only get some of the data from the user, but will also allow the procedures to be called in any order.

Stubs are simple, restricted implementations of modules or procedures. If a module, Mod1 say, needs resources from another module, Mod2, then it is very hard to test and debug Mod1 without first writing, testing and debugging Mod2. However, we can alleviate this problem by writing a stub for Mod2 which consists of restricted implementations of each procedure. Although restricted, each procedure should always do something which is valid, according to its specification. For example, a restricted implementation of a function to read in a character from the keyboard, might not bother to do any reading, but always return the same character. Any module using this read function to obtain a character would therefore receive a valid character from the function, although it would be restricted to always being the same character.

10.7.1 Designing test drivers

Once we have worked out the tests required for our module, we have effectively specified the test driver. It is obviously easier to build a one-off test driver just for the module under test, than to build a test driver which can be used for several modules. White box testing is usually performed first, as it is more likely to pick up simple coding errors. Black box testing is more likely to reveal errors of semantics, which make the module's actions differ from its specification.

Here is a scenario for a simple test driver:

```
Print "Test Driver for module x"
Print "Starting white box tests"

For each test
    Print "Testing x"
    Print "The input data is"
    Print the input data for this test
    Print "Running test"
    Run the test

Print "Finished white box tests"

Print "Starting black box tests"

For each test
    Print "Testing characteristic x"
    Print "The input data is"
    Print the input data for this test
    Print "Running test"
    Run the test

Print "Finished black box tests"
Print "End of testing for module x"
```

When designing a test driver consider where the data is to come from. For simple inputs it is possible to let the user interactively enter the data. For more complex inputs it may be better to store the data in a file, and have the test driver read it out of the file as necessary. Sometimes a file is essential because of the volume of test data needed, or because the module under test is expected to receive its data from a file. Another good reason for using a file to store the input data is that the tests can be repeated consistently. On balance, you will probably find that interactive data entry is best for testing programs consisting of only one or two modules, but file data entry is best once there are more modules in the program.

Similar rules apply to the test results. If the tests are few and simple, then the results could be displayed on the screen. However, if the tests are long and give lots of output, then send the results to a file. A file is an advantage because it allows you to keep a record of the previous test results, rather than having them scroll off the top of the screen and be lost.

10.7.2 Designing stubs

The idea of using stubs is to provide a framework in which to test a module, without having to implement fully all the other modules which it depends on.

We need to be careful that our stubs don't become too complicated. If we have a complicated stub which takes a long time to implement we might just as well have produced a full implementation. Additionally, the longer and more complicated the stub, the more likely it is to contain errors. Stubs need to be kept as short and simple as possible.

A stub is usually a partial implementation of a module or procedure. However, it is important that the partial implementation should follow the appropriate part of the specification correctly. Usually, a stub will only accept a subset of the inputs possible for the full specification, and may only give a subset of the possible outputs.

When you are deciding what part of the specification the stub should implement, consider making it return a *typical* value of the correct type. For example, a procedure such as CalculateCharge, from the call logger of Chapter 3, could return an average call charge. Perhaps the average might be about £5.00, so a stub for CalculateCharge could return simply return a charge of 5.0 every time it is called.

10.8 Debugging

Testing usually shows up errors (bugs) in a program. The task of correcting such errors is not always trivial, although many program writers approach it as such. Indeed, tracking down and removing errors can be the hardest and most time-consuming part of developing a piece of software. This is why we go to great lengths to avoid putting the errors there in the first place, by careful specification and testing at all stages in the design process!

However, no matter how experienced you are as a software engineer, it is extremely unlikely that you will be able to write programs that are bug free! As the software you design becomes more complex you will find more bugs creeping in to the implementations.

When you start a debugging session, decide exactly what you are aiming to achieve during the session. Write down the bugs you are trying to find, preferably with a simple input which causes them to occur. If you have any ideas on where the bugs might be, jot them down, but don't assume that they are correct!

Finding and correcting bugs should never be a haphazard business. We need to approach debugging in the same way as we devise a test plan. The stages you should go through when trying to pinpoint a bug are:

1. Find the circumstances under which the error occurs. This usually means finding various input data which causes the error to appear.

2. Try to think of a reason why the error is occurring, that is think of a possible cause for the error.

3. Try to find input data which shows this reason to be incorrect. If this happens, go back to step 2 and try to find another reason for the error occurring. If you can't show this reason to be false, you may have found what is causing the error.

4. Try to understand why you put the error into your code. Was it simply a typing error, a mistake, or a lack of understanding?

5. Decide how best to correct the error and think through the consequences of fixing it. What effect will the correction have on the rest of the program?

6. Alter your code in the way you have decided to correct the error, being careful not to introduce new errors. Then test the program again to see if the error has been removed.

10.8.1 Finding a bug!

As an example of how easy it is to introduce a bug, and how hard it can be to find even a simple bug, consider the following problem:

> Take a 2-dimensional array of real numbers, divide each element in the array by a chosen element in the array, and store the result of each division back in the original array.

We will implement a program to solve this problem which has a simple bug in it. Then we will see how the bug can be tracked down!

The initial design of a solution to this problem could be:

```
Get an array from the user
Get the index of the element to be used as the divisor
Display original array
Divide each element by the divisor
Display the array after its elements have been divided
```

For a second attempt we decide to display the array before and after its elements have been divided. Note how the following algorithm uses two nested FOR loops to go to each element in the array in turn, row by row.

```
Get size of array from user, for example, r rows and c columns.
Read in each element of the array
Get the index of the divisor, for example, row x, column y.

For each row from 1 to r do the following
   For each column from 1 to c do the following
      element at [r,c] is replaced by element/divisor
   Endfor
Endfor
Display the final version of the array
```

We'll miss out the rest of the design process and go straight from this simple algorithm to the final program in Modula-2, Program 10.1. Note that the main body of the program is very similar to the algorithm given above, but we have had to refine the reading in and writing out of the array into two procedures, ReadArray and WriteArray.

Program 10.1 A program with a bug!

```
MODULE DivideArray;

FROM InOut IMPORT WriteString, WriteLn, ReadInt, WriteInt, ReadReal,
WriteReal, ReadCard, WriteCard, HoldScreen;

TYPE
   (* A 2-dimensional 50 by 50 array of real numbers is the
   maximum size array that the program can handle. *)
   TwoDArray = ARRAY [1..50], [1..50] OF REAL;

VAR
   r, c : CARDINAL; (* Number of rows and columns in array. *)
   x, y : CARDINAL; (* Row and column index of divisor element. *)
   i, j : CARDINAL; (* General indexes for array handling. *)
   table : TwoDArray; (* The 2D array to be divided. *)

PROCEDURE ReadArray(VAR a :TwoDArray; VAR row, col : CARDINAL;
                    VAR x, y : CARDINAL);
(* Pre-condition: none.
Post-condition: variable a contains an array of row rows and col
columns, containing real numbers. Variable row contains the number of
rows in the array, variable col contains the number of columns in the
array. Variables x and y give the index of the array element which is to
be the divisor of the array. *)

BEGIN
   (* Get size of array from user. *)
   WriteString("Number of rows? ");
   ReadCard(row);
   WriteLn;
   WriteString("Number of columns? ");
   ReadCard(col);
   WriteLn;

   (* Get values for the array from the user, one row at a time. *)
   WriteString("Enter array one row at a time.");
   WriteLn;
   FOR i := 1 TO row DO
      FOR j := 1 TO col DO
         ReadReal(a[i,j]);
      END;
      WriteLn;
   END;
```

```
    (* Find the index of the divisor, by which each element is to be
    divided. *)
    WriteString("Enter position of divisor (row column) ");
    ReadCard(x);
    ReadCard(y);
END ReadArray;

PROCEDURE WriteArray(a : TwoDArray; row, col : CARDINAL);
(* Print out the contents of the array
Pre-condition: none.
Post-condition: the array is printed out row by row on the standard
output. *)

CONST
    field = 5; (* Field in which to print number. *)
    sig = 2; (* Number of significant digits. *)

VAR
    i, j : CARDINAL; (* General indexes for array handling. *)

BEGIN
    WriteLn;
    (* Print entire array. *)
    FOR i := 1 TO row DO
        (* Print a row in the array. *)
        FOR j := 1 TO col DO
            WriteReal(a[i,j], field, sig);
        END;
        WriteLn;
    END;
    WriteLn;
END WriteArray;

BEGIN
    (* Read in the array and display it. Reading in also obtains the
    size of the array (r, c) and the index of the divisor in the array
    (x,y). *)
    ReadArray(table, r, c, x, y);
    WriteArray(table, r, c);

    (* Divide each element by the divisor, and store back in array. *)
    FOR i := 1 TO r DO
        FOR j := 1 TO c DO
            table[i,j] := table[i,j] / table[x,y];
        END;
    END;

    (* Display the divided array. *)
    WriteArray(table, r, c);
    HoldScreen;
END DivideArray.
```

If we have the following starting array:

2.0	3.0	4.0
4.0	2.0	1.0
5.0	6.0	3.0

and make the divisor the element at index [3,3] (that is, the 3.0 in the bottom right of the array), the program gives the following output:

0.67	1.0	1.3
1.3	0.67	0.33
1.7	2.0	1.0

which is correct.

Now let's use the same input array, and make the divisor the element at [2,2] (that is, the element in the middle of the array). The output we obtain this time is:

1.0	1.5	2.0
2.0	1.0	1.0
5.0	6.0	3.0

which is only partly correct.

What happens if we use the element at [1,2] (that is, element in the middle of the first row)? The output is this:

0.66	1.0	4.0
4.0	2.0	1.0
5.0	6.0	3.0

The first two elements of the first row are correct, but the rest of the array is incorrect. Can you see what is happening? From the test cases we have tried we can see that every element up to and including the divisor element is divided correctly, but every element after the divisor is left unchanged. This would also account for the entire array being correct when the divisor is the bottom right element.

Now we can see what is going wrong we need to consider why it might be happening. There are two reasons why the elements after the divisor might remain unchanged in the array:

1. They are not being divided by anything at all, that is the division is not happening.

2. They are being divided by one.

If we look at the part of the code which implements the division of each element in the array:

```
FOR i := 1 TO r DO
   FOR j := 1 TO c DO
      table[i,j]:= table[i,j] / table[x,y];
   END;
END;
```

we can see that this will perform the division up to and including the element at position [r,c]. The values of r and c are supplied by ReadArray, so unless r and c are not set up correctly in ReadArray, or unless they are corrupted in some way, the above piece of code will divide every element in the table by the divisor.

The problem would therefore appear to lie elsewhere. A good technique, especially when the code is not too large, is to try to go through the motions of the code on a piece of paper. So, with the same input array as we used above, let's make the divisor the element at [1,2] which is 3.0, and write down what happens at each step in the main loop of the program.

First time round the inner loop i = 1 and j = 1, so this is the first element in the array: Element at [1,1] = 2.0, is divided by the element at [1,2] = 3.0, giving 0.66 which is stored in the array at [1,1].

Second time round the inner loop, i = 1 and j = 2, so this is the second element in the top row of the array: Element at [1,2] = 3.0, is divided by the element at [1,2] = 3.0, giving 1.0, which is stored in the array at [1,2].

Third time round the inner loop, i = 1 and j =3, so this is the third element in the top row of the array: Element at [1,3] = 4.0, is divided by the element at [1,2] = 1.0, giving 4.0, which is stored in the array at [1,3]

So, the reason for elements after the divisor appearing unchanged is now clear! When we divide the divisor by itself, we obviously get the result 1.0, which is stored back in the array. The program obtains the divisor for each division directly from the array, that is

```
table[i,j] := table[i,j] /table[x,y]
```

where table[x,y] is the divisor.

When we store the result of divisor /divisor back in the array we are changing the value of the divisor to 1.0 for all subsequent divisions. Thus, all elements after the divisor in the array are divided by 1.0, which leaves them unchanged.

The correction of this bug is quite simple, we need to keep a copy of the divisor in some appropriately named variable, and use the copy for each division, rather than getting the value from the array. We can declare a variable

```
VAR divisor : REAL;
```

and, before we enter the FOR loops, do the following assignment

```
divisor := table[x,y];
```

The line performing the division within the FOR loops then becomes

```
table[i,j] := table[i,j] / divisor;
```

It would probably be slightly neater to have the ReadArray procedure pass back the value of the divisor via a variable parameter rather than its position in the table.

10.8.2 Things to remember when debugging

Debugging is never easy, for beginners or for experienced programmers. The above example was very simple, and the error was easy to correct. In a larger piece of software errors are far harder to find, and there is the additional problem that correcting one error may reveal errors elsewhere in the code, or may introduce new errors. However, here are some useful points to remember when you are faced with the need to debug a piece of code.

- Find a simple input which causes the error to occur.
- Check that the input data you are giving is actually what is expected by the program.
- Try the simple things first. These include bugs such as:
  - Out-by-one errors in loops. Remember that a while-loop will never be entered if the entry condition fails the first time. A repeat-loop is always done at least once. A for-loop will be performed upperbound - lowerbound +1 times, because the bounds are included.
  - Uninitialised variables. Don't assume the compiler will set variables to 0 or nil values. Some do, most don't.
  - Division by zero. This will usually cause the program to crash instantly – computers cannot cope with infinity!
  - Logical conditions can get inverted. Testing for something being false, when you mean true. When you want neither a nor b to be true, testing for not(a or b), when you logically mean not(a and b).
- Decide, very carefully, what you can take for granted as being error-free. But avoid trying to pin your bugs on the compiler or the system, without checking that the fault does not lie in your code.

If an error is hard to pinpoint, it is often useful to include debugging statements in the program code. These statements can be used to print out the value of a variable (to see what happens to it during program execution), information on which procedures are being run, or which branch of an if-statement is being used, and any intermediate results which might be of use.

For example, here is the main body of the previous program, DivideArray with some debugging statements in it:

```
BEGIN
    (* Read in the array and display it.  Reading in also obtains
    the size of the array (r, c) and the index of the divisor in the
    array (x,y). *)
    ReadArray(table, r, c, x, y);
    WriteArray(table, r, c);

    (* Write out size of array and position of divisor before
    starting the divisions. *)
    WriteLn;
    WriteString("Number of rows, columns: ");
    WriteCard(r, 3); WriteString(",  "); WriteCard(c, 3);
    WriteLn;
    WriteString("Position of divisor:  ");
    WriteCard(x, 3); WriteString(",  "); WriteCard(y, 3);
    WriteLn;

    (* Divide each element by the divisor, and store back in array. *)
    FOR i := 1 TO r DO
        FOR j := 1 TO c DO
            (* Write value of divisor before starting each division. *)
            WriteString("Value of divisor:  ");
            WriteReal(table[x,y], 4, 2);
            WriteLn;
            table[i,j] := table[i,j] / table[x,y];
        END;
    END;

    (* Display the divided array. *)
    WriteArray(table, r, c);

    HoldScreen;
END DivideArray.
```

Note that we've put the statements printing out the value of the divisor inside the inner for loop, so that it is printed out before every single division performed. This is really only suitable if the input array is quite small, which we can ensure during the debugging stage.

Unfortunately, all these statements will have to be removed in the final version of the program. In a large program this can be very time consuming. When we are developing software it is often useful to be able to *turn off* the debugging statements temporarily, without removing them from the code. We can do this very easily with a Boolean variable, and some if-statements.

The idea is to ask the user, at the start of the program, whether or not debugging statements should be used. The program can read a yes or no response, and set a Boolean variable (let's call it debugging) accordingly. Each debugging statement (or group of statements) can be enclosed by an if-statement, which uses the value of debugging as the condition for running the body of the if.

We can do this in any program, procedure or implementation module (remember that the definition module does not contain any implementations, only definitions). In an implementation module we use the module body, which is often empty of any other code, to set up the value of the debugging variable. As an example of how we do this in an implementation module, this is how it can be done in ArrayUtilities:

```
BEGIN (* Main body of ArrayUtilities. *)
   WriteString("ArrayUtilities: Debugging on? (y/n)    ");
   Read(ch);
   IF (ch = "Y") OR (ch = "y") THEN
      debugging := TRUE;
   ELSE
      debugging := FALSE;
   END;
END ArrayUtilities.
```

Beware of putting in too many debugging statements; they make a program longer and harder to read. Be very careful about putting debugging statements inside a loop which may be performed a large number of times, you may end up with pages of debugging statements!

Summary

Testing ensures that a piece of software meets its specification. Testing should happen at all stages in the software lifecycle, including the specification and design stages.

Unit testing involves testing each module in isolation, before the module is integrated with the rest of the software. There are two types of unit testing which aim to test different properties of the module: black box testing and white box testing.

Black box testing - looking only at the specification of the module, derive tests and expected results, to check that the module meets its specification. Compare the expected results with the actual results. If they differ the module is not working to the specification.

White box testing - looking also at the code implementing the module, derive tests which force execution through particular paths in the code, so that all the code is covered at least once. Check that the expected results from these tests are the same as the actual results.

Integration is the act of bringing separate modules together to form the completed software system. Modules are not all integrated at once, but one module will be added at a time until all the modules are working together. Integration testing is performed at each stage of the integration process to check that the modules work correctly with each other.

System testing is performed once all the modules have been integrated into the complete system. It is usually split into three stages:

- Alpha testing – usually performed within the software company.
- Beta testing – usually performed outside the software company, but often not by the intended customer.
- Acceptance testing – performed by the customer.

Test plans for white box testing must test every line in the code at least once. For each part of the code being tested derive test data, which, when given to the module, will cause the code to be executed. Also derive test data which avoids the code.

Test plans for black box tests are derived only from the module specification, to decide the characteristics of the input data the module expects. For each input characteristic find the valid class of data and the invalid class of data, and from this derive tests for each characteristic.

Selected reading

Ould, M A, and Unwin, C (eds)
Testing in software development
British Computer Society Monographs in Informatics
Cambridge University Press, 1986
A comprehensive set of papers on software testing. A beginner may find some of it hard, but those with a little experience in writing software will gain a great deal from reading this book.

Maude, T and Willis, G
Rapid prototyping, the management of software risk
Pitman Publishing, 1991
A very readable book on the subject of rapid prototyping, and its uses in software engineering. It shows the use of rapid prototyping techniques for testing requirements specifications, initial designs, and the feasibility of very large or complex projects.

11 Algorithm complexity and efficiency

11.1 Introduction

One of the difficulties with designing an algorithm is that there is no method available that gives the *best* result. However, we have available design principles for modularisation and procedural abstraction which give the necessary methods to build programs which would be accepted, hopefully, as well designed. But are well designed programs also good programs? Unfortunately the answer is not always yes as the design principles can be applied to inappropriate ideas and algorithms which may lead to *poor* results.

In Chapter 3, we saw that a well designed recursive procedure to calculate the n'th Fibonacci number is excessively expensive to use, even when calculating small Fibonacci numbers, and useless for high Fibonacci numbers. Instead, a simple non-recursive procedure was available that is easy to apply and is inexpensive in computational cost. Unfortunately, many algorithms exhibit this behaviour of *non-linear time complexity* as the size of the program's inputs grow. If we are to attain efficient implementations of our basic program designs then it is important that we understand the behaviour of some of the standard algorithms that are available. In this way, we should be able to obtain the necessary experience to avoid methods that unnecessarily introduce nonlinear time penalties, which could otherwise occur even when the basic algorithm is well designed.

Let us examine a simple example. The set of simultaneous equations that follows consists of n equations, each of which has at most three unknown terms. In general, the i'th equation will consist of the terms x_i, x_{i-1} and x_{i+1}:

$$2x_1 + x_2 = c_1$$
$$x_1 + 2x_2 + x_3 = c_2$$
$$\cdots\cdots$$
$$\cdots\cdots$$
$$x_{n-2} + 2x_{n-1} + x_n = c_{n-1}$$
$$x_{n-1} + 2x_n = c_n$$

That is, n unknown values to be solved: $x_1, x_2, \ldots\ldots x_n$, in terms of the n known values $c_1, c_2, \ldots\ldots c_n$.

A popular method for solving systems of linear equations is known as Cramer's rule (refer to any elementary text on numerical methods). Cramer's rule is often used for pencil and paper solutions when n is small, and on a superficial examination this method may seem ideal for use on a computer. Now, part of the solution by Cramer's rule needs the evaluation of a function known as a determinant. It doesn't particularly matter if this function is unknown to you, all we need to understand is the time complexity of the evaluation of the determinant. This time complexity is easily shown to behave in proportion to n factorial. In other words, n! operations must be carried out to evaluate this function. Many scientific and engineering problems require sets of thousands or even millions of these equations to be solved, therefore if we take n = 30 the claim that this is a small set of simultaneous equations must be reasonable.

Now, 30! is $\sim 3 \times 10^{32}$ operations, a large number to say the least. But how does this relate to the time required for the calculation to be made? Let us imagine that we have access to the world's most powerful computers, then we can expect a performance of about 10^9 arithmetic operations per second. There are approximately 3×10^7 seconds in a year, so we will get 3×10^{16} operations from our supercomputer each year. So how long does it take to solve the 30 unknowns in our set of simultaneous equations?

10^{16} years!

Which is longer than the estimated life span of the universe, so what is the alternative? A little thought leads us in a new direction. Why not automate the simple substitution method we would follow if the solution was being carried out by hand. This leads to a method known as the tri-diagonal algorithm which requires approximately 10 x n operations. On the fastest computer, this would take about 10^{-7} seconds, less than the time for a wink of the eyelid. If a problem of engineering dimension was being considered then the tri-diagonal method offers a solution in reasonable time, but considering Cramer's method would be absurd.

This example more than amply illustrates the need for an understanding of the complexity of an algorithm and its alternatives before an implementation is carried out.

11.2 Complexity of algorithms

When we are measuring the amount of work that needs to be done to execute an algorithm, or to compare two algorithms which achieve the same goal, we might use the actual execution time as the metric for work. This would be wrong as many factors can affect the execution time, some of which may distort the attempt to measure the differences between algorithms. For example, the architecture of the computer, or the language used for programming, or the expertise of the programmer or even the design methodology used by the programmer may favour a particular algorithm. We need to establish a measure of the complexity of algorithms that is independent of the computer, programmer and programming language.

Start by examining what a typical algorithm consists of: a series of simple once only operations and a set of repeated operations in a bounded or conditional iteration. The once only operations usually contribute little to the total complexity of the algorithm and can be ignored, instead concentrate the analysis of complexity on the repeated operations. But even some of the repeated operations may have a low complexity and can be safely eliminated from the analysis. The expensive, that is basic operations of the algorithm must be identified and used as the basis of the complexity analysis. This means that we can analyse the complexity of an algorithm by choosing a basic operation or set of basic operations provided that the total number of operations performed by the algorithm is roughly proportional to these basic operations.

A parameter or set of parameters is needed to allow the presentation of the results of any analysis in a precise way. The amount of work needed to complete a set of operations on the standard data abstractions previously described is dependent, in some sense, on the *size* of the abstractions. Finding an item in a set or list of size 10 obviously takes more time than in one of size 3, therefore the size of the input parameters is often the parameter that is needed for presenting the analysis carried out. For example, in the factorial example, the size of the factorial, n say, is what is needed to express the complexity of the algorithm, while in the system of linear equations it is the number of equations that is important, again the value of n.

In most cases, the complexity of the algorithm can be expressed in terms of the single parameter n, that is the size of a data item or alternatively the number of data inputs:

- list – n items,
- factorial – size n,
- polynomial equations – degree n,
- one dimension array – dimension n.

But other algorithms may be more complex:

- two dimension array – dimension n x m,
- tree – spread n, depth d.

From these last two examples it can be seen that a single parameter may not be sufficient to describe the input data of the algorithm. However, most important algorithms are expressible or re-expressible in terms of the single parameter n. In the tree example, we may re-express the inputs as the number of nodes in the tree and reduce the two parameters to a single parameter. The desirability of re-expressing a set of parameters in this way has to be judged in the context of the analysis being carried out and no general rule can be applied.

When using n as a single parameter description most algorithms can be assessed as performing according to one of the following complexity classifications:

1 (Constant) This is the best behaviour that can be obtained from an algorithm. The run-time of the program is independent of the size of the input data and remains constant for all variations of the input data.

$\log_2 n$ When the complexity of the algorithm is logarithmic, we have the next best condition to constant complexity. Here, the program execution time increases with the size of n, but slower than the rate that n itself is increasing. For example, when n doubles from 64 to 128, the execution time increases by about 16%.

n Here the complexity is linear with the run-time of a program doubling when n doubles. This is the optimal performance that can be expected from a program that processes n inputs or n outputs.

$n \log_2 n$ This is a very common complexity. It arises from problems that can be divided into parts, with each separate part being processed at logarithmic speed. The whole problem is then solved as the sum of these logarithmic parts. For example, when n doubles from 64 to 128, the execution time increases by 133%, slightly worse than double.

n^2 Quadratic complexity of algorithms is used only on small problems. It arises when algorithms require the processing of all permutations of two items from n input data values. Similarly, if any three items are permuted, then the algorithm is reduced to cubic complexity, and so on.

2^n This gives exponential time complexity. The Fibonacci recursive algorithm (Chapter 3) had a property close to this. It is not good news, as even small values of n require large amounts of processing time to execute the associated programs. This is often the result of an exhaustive search method - using brute force rather than thinking through the alternative solutions to a problem to obtain a better algorithm.

n! This is awful. Factorial complexity was mentioned in the introduction. It must be avoided. This is the consequence of taking all permutations of n variables.

The relative cost of algorithms in some of the above classes can be illustrated as shown in the following table. In each column the cost of an algorithm for a particular complexity is shown *relative* to a value of the parameter n:

		Complexity		
n	$\log_2 n$	$n \log_2 n$	n^2	n!
2	1	2	4	2
4	2	8	16	24
8	3	24	64	40320
16	4	64	256	2×10^{13}
32	5	160	1024	3×10^{33}
64	6	384	4096	---
128	7	896	16384	---

In the table, we can easily see the relationship between the complexities for every doubling of the value of n. The results for the $\log_2 n$ complexity change at a rate which slows as n increases, this is very good. However, $n \log_2 n$ complexity more than doubles at each stage, and the even worse quadratic function (n^2) increases with a factor of 4 for each doubling of n. The extreme complexity given by the factorial function is unacceptable even for small increases in n.

Now, year by year computers are getting more powerful, and so the temptation is to say that complexity issues will become less important. Let us portray our analysis in a table that reflects the increased processing capability that will be obtained from the increased computer performance to be expected in the future.

Assume that the performance of a computer enables an algorithm of size n to be solved in some unit of time. As technology improves over the coming years we can expect significant increases in performance of about a million fold, even in the foreseeable future. To estimate the increased size of problem which can be solved in the same unit of time on these new computers, assume the following sizes of problem are achievable on current computers N_1, N_2, N_3, N_4 and $N_5$with algorithms of complexity

$\log_2 n$, n, n $\log_2 n$, n^2 and 2^n respectively, where $N_1 > N_2 > N_3 > N_4 > N_5$ (note, the factorial example has been replaced with one of exponential complexity). Then, the size of problem to be solved in unit time for the various algorithmic complexity for increases in future computer performance of 10, 100, 1000, and 1000000 fold are:

	Complexity				
	$\log_2 n$	n	n $\log_2 n$	n^2	2^n
Current Computers	N_1	N_2	N_3	N_4	N_5
10 times faster	$N_1 \times 30$	$N_2 \times 10$	$N_3 \times 3$	$N_4 \times 3$	$N_5 + 3$
100 times faster	$N_1 \times 600$	$N_2 \times 100$	$N_3 \times 17$	$N_4 \times 10$	$N_5 + 7$
1000 times faster	$N_1 \times 9000$	$N_2 \times 1000$	$N_3 \times 111$	$N_4 \times 31$	$N_5 + 10$
1000000 times faster	$N_1 \times 19 \times 10^6$	$N_2 \times 10^6$	$N_3 \times 5360$	$N_4 \times 1000$	$N_5 + 20$

The table shows that the benefit obtained from the extra computer performance is mostly lost if the algorithm has a high complexity. Note the exponential example where a trivial increase of +20 in size is achieved for a 1000000 fold increase in computer performance. These results indicate that a knowledge of the behaviour of the algorithm will always remain important, even if very large increases in computer performance are obtained in the future.

11.2.1 Order of an algorithm (the big-O notation)

In the last section, we gave tables of various complexity where the algorithm's performance was proportional to some factor such as n or log n. When we express the degree of complexity of an algorithm, it is normal to ignore the constants of proportionality and instead indicate the performance as an *order of magnitude* expressed, usually, in the big-O notation. Then, linear algorithms are O(n) and logarithmic algorithms are O(log n), etc.

The formal definition is as follows:

A function g(n) is said to be O(f(n)) if there exists constants K_0 and N_0 such that $g(n) < K_0 f(N_0)$ for all $n > N_0$.

This gives an upper bound on the complexity of an algorithm, that is an indication of the cost of an algorithm quite independently of input/output values or implementation details. This is sometimes called the worst case analysis as we can always expect our algorithm to perform at least as well as the order of magnitude value.

As we are ignoring the constants of proportionality, we can also ignore the base of the logarithm in the previous analysis, as $\log_k n = \log_2 n \log_k 2$. That is, the log n value in any base differs only by a constant value. Therefore, in the remainder of our analysis, we will refer to logarithmic complexity as O(log n) irrespective of the base value.

When a worst case analysis has been carried out and two algorithms are available, say O(n) and O(n log n), it would seem obvious that the algorithm with O(n) complexity should be used. But wait, is this always so? The constants K_0 and N_0 that we have chosen to ignore in the O-notation may hide important detail that show that in certain circumstances the O(n log n) algorithm is the winner. This sometimes happens, particularly for small values of n.

In general, the O-notation is a very good indication of the relative performance of algorithms and particularly so for log n algorithms. But remember, in practice, the only way you can be sure of the relative performance, for the particular circumstances in which the different algorithms will be used, is to experiment.

In many problems, the worst case analysis of an algorithm is unduly pessimistic. Usually the average case analysis is much more difficult to undertake than the worst case analysis, but if carried out it can give very useful information about the true behaviour of an algorithm. Later in this chapter we will examine the Quicksort method for placing a list of items in some desired order. A worst case analysis of this method gives $O(n^2)$ performance, but an average case analysis shows that this algorithm is likely to perform as O(n log n). In addition, the hidden constant in the average case can be shown to be very small giving an actual average performance of the Quicksort method to be 1.38 n log n, which is of course much better than the worst case analysis.

11.2.2 Simple example of complexity analysis

A simple worst and average case analysis can be carried out on a sequential search of an unordered list, that contains n entries to find the position of a particular item.

A basic set of operations must be found if a complexity analysis is to be carried out. In a search algorithm the main operation is the comparison of two list entries. The repetition of this comparison operation under the control of some loop construct is the basic set of operations needed to undertake the complexity analysis.

Worst case: The worst case is when the whole list is searched. Then the complexity is proportional to n. In the worst case, as far as the value of the complexity is concerned, it doesn't matter if the required item is in the list or not.

Average case: Suppose the item is in the list, then we could expect on average to find the item in n/2 attempts. If the item is not in the list, then again we require n attempts at finding it. If we assume that, on average, the item is in the list only half of the time then the average number of attempts needed to find the item is proportional to $\frac{1}{2}(\frac{n}{2} + n) = 3\frac{n}{4}$.

Later in this chapter, methods will be examined that would find a name in an ordered list, such as a telephone directory that contains 1,000,000 names, in about 5 search attempts, that is a method of log log n complexity.

Searching data for an item is obviously an activity that is undertaken in a wide variety of applications. Searching for an employee's record in a commercial database, and searching for the frontmost pixel in a computer graphics image are just two examples that are drawn from hundreds we could list. When searching for a data item in a random list of entries, we have to carry out a sequential search. It is far easier to devise an efficient search method if there is some order in the list. This, of course, implies that the list must first be sorted into the desired order by some routine. In the remainder of this chapter, we will examine sorting and searching algorithms and compare the computational efficiency of these algorithms.

11.3 Simple sorting methods

In this section, we will study a number of sorting algorithms. A sorting algorithm takes a number of items and rearranges them into some required order. The items could be elements of an array, or a list, or at the nodes of a graph or tree, or entries in a table, etc. To enable us to sort a number of items, we require that each item has a *key*. The key is an identifier that enables an item to be recognised in terms of the ordering required. The sorted item may contain other information beside the key; for example, a dictionary is alphabetically sorted on key words, but accompanying each key word is a set of grammatical definitions, explanations, and examples of the use of the key. In a computer graphics image, the key to a pixel would indicate distance from the observer so that the pixels can be sorted to enable hidden detail to be eliminated from the image. The information accompanying the key may, in this case, be colour and illumination intensity.

The study of sorting algorithms has two benefits. First, they are useful because of the need to sort information in many applications, and second, the algorithms are relatively easy to analyse and can give good insight to the precautions and practice that should be exercised when designing algorithms in general. From the analysis carried out, it will be seen that elementary methods of sorting n randomly arranged items are $O(n^2)$, whereas the more sophisticated methods are O(n log n) or better. However, common sense will also be an ingredient in choosing an appropriate method. For example, when small numbers of items are to be sorted it may be better to choose a simple method, but when a list is partially ordered the criteria for choosing a method may change and even reverse the preference of methods for unordered lists.

The nature of the data structure being sorted can also influence the final cost of the algorithm. To sort an array of items means that the array elements are physically moved and repositioned in another part of the array which at worst may cause all the remaining elements to be repositioned. Whereas if a linked list is being sorted only the pointer needs to be moved, a much *cheaper* operation. In most applications, the choice of data structure type is determined by criteria other than the sort requirements, but the type of data structure may influence the final choice of sorting algorithm.

11.3.1 Specification of sorting and searching algorithms

We will assume that we have specified a key type as follows:

```
TYPE    DataStructure    =    RECORD
                                  key  : KeyType;
                                  data : DataType;
                              END;
```

The data structure has been divided into two parts: the key on which we search or sort and the data part. However, for simplicity in the implementation of the sort and search algorithms we normally assume that keyType will be a simple array type.

The sorting and searching algorithms will be implemented as procedures in the appropriate section of this chapter. Here, the definition modules are given which collects the various sorting and searching methods together to give an overview of the methods available.

```
DEFINITION MODULE Sort;

(* EXPORT QUALIFIED Selectsort, Exchangesort, Insertsort,
Mergesort, Quicksort; *)

PROCEDURE Selectsort(VAR data : ARRAY OF keyType);

PROCEDURE Exchangesort(VAR data : ARRAY OF keyType);

PROCEDURE Insertsort(VAR data : ARRAY OF keyType);

PROCEDURE Quicksort(VAR data : ARRAY OF keyType; first, last :
                                              CARDINAL);
PROCEDURE Mergesort(VAR data : ARRAY OF keyType);

END Sort.
```

```
DEFINITION MODULE Search;

(* EXPORT QUALIFIED SequentialSearch, BinarySearch; *)

PROCEDURE SequentialSearch(VAR data : ARRAY OF keyType;
                                  Key : CARDINAL): CARDINAL;

PROCEDURE BinarySearch(VAR data : ARRAY OF keyType;
            key : CARDINAL): CARDINAL;

END Search.
```

Note, the open array used in each procedure has a lower index bound of zero. The upper bound of the array can be found from HIGH(data).

11.3.2 Selection sort

This is one of the simplest sort methods. The algorithm works as follows:
first find the smallest key and exchange it with the first position item; then find the second smallest key and exchange it with the second position item; continue in this way until the items are sorted.

The algorithm always *selects* the minimum value key from the items to be sorted. For each i in the set 0 to n - 1, the algorithm selects the minimum array element in data[i .. n - 1] and exchanges it with data[i].

```
PROCEDURE Selectionsort(VAR data : ARRAY OF keyType);
VAR
   i, j, n, min : CARDINAL;
   temp : keyType;

BEGIN
   n := HIGH(data); (* Find array bound. *)
   IF n > 0 THEN
      FOR i := 0 TO n - 2 DO (* This is the element to be
                                 exchanged. *)
         min := i;
         FOR j := i + 1 TO n - 1 DO
            IF data[j] < data[min] THEN (* Find the minimum. *)
               min := j
            END;
         END;
         temp := data[min]; (* Exchange data[i] with data[min]. *)
         data[min] := data[i]; (* Exchange. *)
         data[i] := temp;
      END;
   END;
END Selectionsort;
```

The method is easy to follow. In the following example start at the i'th cardinal and exchange with the minimum value:

Original keys to be sorted	63	28	75	13	8
i = 0 and j = 1 to 4.	min := 4, exchange data[0] with data[4].				
	8	28	75	13	63
i = 1 and j = 2 to 4	min := 3, exchange data[1] with data[3].				
	8	13	75	28	63
i = 2 and j = 3 to 4	min := 3, exchange data[2] with data[3].				
	8	13	28	75	63
i = 3 and j = 4 to 4	min := 4, exchange data[3] with data[4].				
	8	13	28	63	75

Sort is complete.

As in the sequential search example of section 11.2.2 a set of basic operations is required to develop the complexity analysis of the sort methods. Again the main operation is the comparison operation, used to determine the order of the items in the array. The repetition of the comparison operation is, therefore the basic operation that will be used in the complexity analysis of all the sort algorithms.

Worst case analysis

The outer loops for the algorithm ranges from 0 to n - 2, and for each of these values the inner loop ranges over a progressively smaller set of values. Taking the outer and inner loop operations together then the worst case complexity is

$$(n - 1) + (n - 2) + (n - 3) + \ldots\ldots + 1 = \frac{n}{2}(n - 1), \text{ which gives } O(n^2) \text{ complexity.}$$

At first sight this does not appear to be a good method, but let us examine the number of operations carried out during the sort. The number of comparison operations were given above, that is $\frac{n}{2}(n - 1)$. Only one exchange is made for each selection, therefore n - 1 exchanges are made in total, then:

Number of comparison operations	$= \frac{n}{2}(n - 1)$.
Number of exchange operations	$= n - 1$.

If the number of items to be sorted is low, but the items themselves contain very large data fields, then this method may be better than some of the lower order sort methods because a smaller bulk of information is moved. Remember, it is not only the number of operations that determines a method's suitability for an application, but also the cost of the operations for the particular data movements that are needed.

11.3.3 Exchange (bubble) sort

Possibly the most elementary sort method is the exchange sort, often called the bubble sort. In this method, the loop index is repeatedly passed over the items to be sorted, and when two neighbouring keys are found to be out of order then the items are exchanged. For each successive pass of the loop index the largest remaining key moves to its correct position among the items and, therefore the number of items compared may be reduced by one for each successive examination of the key. For example:

original keys to be sorted	63	28	75	13	8
i = 0 to n - 2 (that is 0 to 3)	28	63	13	8	75 (3 exchanges)
i = 0 to 2	28	13	8	63	75 (2 exchanges)
i = 0 to 1	13	8	28	63	75 (2 exchanges)
i = 0 to 0	8	13	28	63	75 (1 exchange)

This method is easily implemented:

```
PROCEDURE Exchangesort(VAR data: ARRAY OF keyType);
VAR
    i, j, n : CARDINAL;
    temp : keyType;
    notSorted : BOOLEAN;
BEGIN
    n := HIGH(data); (* Array bound. *)
    notSorted := TRUE;
    WHILE (n > 0) AND notSorted DO
        notSorted := FALSE; (* Reset stopping condition. *)
        FOR i := 0 TO n - 1 DO
            IF data[i] > data[i + 1] THEN
                notSorted := TRUE; (* Found an unsorted item. *)
                temp := data[i];
                data[i] := data[i + 1]; (* Exchange items. *)
                data[i +1] := temp;
            END;
        END;
        DEC(n);
    END;
END Exchangesort;
```

In this procedure, the BOOLEAN identifier *notSorted* ensures that only one extra pass through the items is required once the data is sorted.

Best and worst case analysis

The best performance is easy to analyse. When the original items are already sorted the algorithm will only require one traversal of the sequence of items to establish that there is no work to be done, then:

Number of comparison operations = n - 1.
Number of exchange operations = 0.

If the items are in the reverse order to the one required then the worst case sort has to be carried out. Then the inner FOR loop is executed as follows:

$$(n - 1) + (n - 2) + (n - 3) + \ldots + 1 = \frac{n}{2}(n - 1)$$

which is $O(n^2)$ complexity.

In the worst case, one exchange will occur for each comparison of the items:

Number of comparison operations $= \frac{n}{2}(n - 1)$.

Number of exchange operations $= \frac{n}{2}(n - 1)$.

The average case analysis is too difficult to carry out here, but it has been established that the complexity is about the same as the worst case:

Number of comparison operations $= \frac{1}{4}(n - 1)(n + 2)$.

Number of exchange operations $= \frac{n}{4}(n - 1)$.

As the furthest an exchanged item migrates for any comparison operation on the data is to its adjacent position, it is inevitably the slowest sorting method known. It is fast only when the data is nearly sorted. However, there are other methods, such as the insertion sort, that perform equally as well on nearly sorted data without the gross handicap suffered by the exchange sort on average data.

11.3.4 Insertion sort

An insertion sort takes an item and inserts it into its correct position in a sorted sequence of items (see the insertion operation for the list data abstraction in Chapter 6). Beginning with the (n - 2)'th item in a sequence of items that are unsorted, successively move along this sequence by comparing an item's key with those of the partially sorted items. For example:

Original keys to be sorted		63	28	75	13	8
i = n - 2	Insert data[3]	63	28	75	8	13
i = n - 3	Insert data[2]	63	28	8	13	75
i= n - 4	Insert data[1]	63	8	13	28	75
i = 0	Insert data[0]	8	13	28	63	75

The algorithm must achieve this insertion by scanning the elements in the previously sorted sequence. Each key must be compared and the item moved up one position until the appropriate point for the insertion is found. The procedure to implement this algorithm is as follows:

```
PROCEDURE Insertionsort(VAR data : ARRAY OF keyType);
VAR
   i, j, n : CARDINAL;
   temp : keyType;

BEGIN
   n := HIGH(data);
   IF n > 0 THEN
      FOR i := n - 2 TO 0 BY -1 DO
         temp := data[i];
         j := i + 1;
         WHILE (j <= n) AND (temp > data[j]) DO
            data[j - 1] := data[j]; (* Insertion. *)
            j := j + 1;
         END;
         data[j - 1] := temp;
      END;
   END;
END Insertionsort;
```

Worst case

The maximum number of comparison operations is given by the two loops FOR and WHILE, giving a total of

$$1 + 2 + \ldots\ldots + (n - 2) + (n - 1) = \frac{n}{2}(n - 1)$$

that is $O(n^2)$.

This is the behaviour we can expect when the keys are in reverse order.

Average case

The outer FOR loop always executes n - 1 times irrespective of the input data. But the inner loop execution is dependent on the key comparisons and varies between 1 and n - 1 times.

On average, only half of the sequence of items need to be probed by the WHILE loop. This gives

$\frac{n}{4}(n - 1)$ comparison operations.

When a sequence is already sorted only the position of an insertion is required. This gives linear complexity.

We can now summarise the complexity analysis for the number of operations for the three cases:

Worst :	Number of comparison operations	$\frac{n}{2}(n - 1)$.
	Number of exchange operations	$n - 1$.
Average :	Number of comparison operations	$\frac{n}{4}(n - 1)$.
	Number of exchange operations	$\frac{1}{2}(n - 1)$.
Best:	Number of comparison operations	$n - 1$.
	Number of exchange operation	1.

The insertion sort seems to be very good in two situations: when the sequence is nearly sorted and when a new insertion is required for an existing pre-sorted sequence. Even when the items are not completely sorted the insertion sort is still very good. Its complexity is better for nearly sorted files than the exchange and selection sort, and so it is a good choice whenever partially sorted sequences need to be sorted.

11.3.5 Comparative performance

We are now able to compare the three simple sorting methods, described earlier, by summarising the number of comparison and exchange operations as shown in the table:

Algorithm	Operation	Worst Case	Average Case	Pre-sorted
Selection	Comparison	$\frac{n}{2}(n - 1)$	$\frac{n}{2}(n - 1)$	$\frac{n}{2}(n - 1)$
	Exchange	$n - 1$	$n - 1$	$n - 1$
Exchange	Comparison	$\frac{n}{2}(n - 1)$	$\frac{1}{4}(n - 1)(n + 2)$	$n - 1$
	Exchange	$\frac{n}{2}(n - 1)$	$\frac{n}{4}(n - 1)$	0
Insertion	Comparison	$\frac{n}{2}(n - 1)$	$\frac{n}{4}(n - 1)$	$n - 1$
	Exchange	$(n - 1)$	$\frac{1}{2}(n - 1)$	1

Although this table gives an immediate comparison between algorithms as different as (n - 1) and $\frac{n}{2}$(n - 1), it does not indicate any difference between algorithms of identical big-O complexity. To obtain this detailed information either a very careful cost analysis of each operation must be carried out, or alternatively, experimental runs of the programs need to be carried out.

The number of data items and the size of each item can affect the outcome of these tests. Initially, we will experiment with keys that have single data items associated with each key, and with sequences of up to 2000 keys. We will first carry out the worst case experiment.

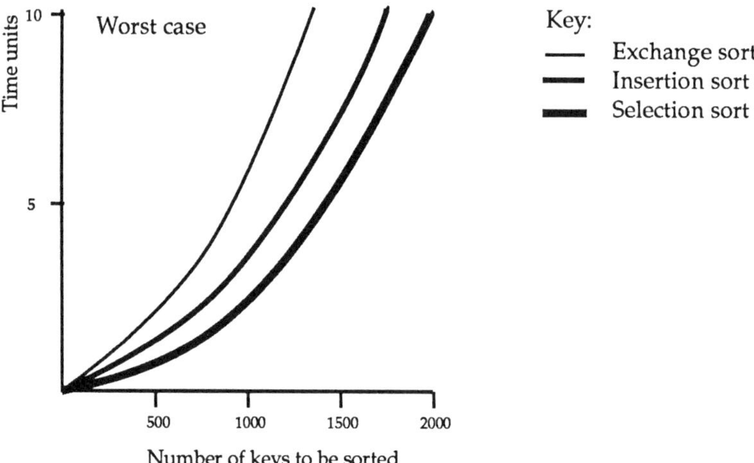

In this worst case, where the items to be sorted have their keys in the reverse order to what is needed, the selection sort is clearly the best method. The insertion sort is obviously more expensive, with the exchange sort being about twice the computational cost of the selection sort.

To make a fair comparison of these methods we also need to experiment with keys that are in random order, that is the average case, and also the most favoured case when the keys have been pre-sorted before we attempt the experiment.

Again, in both experiments, we will only use single data items with each key, and also restrict the number of keys to a maximum of 2000.

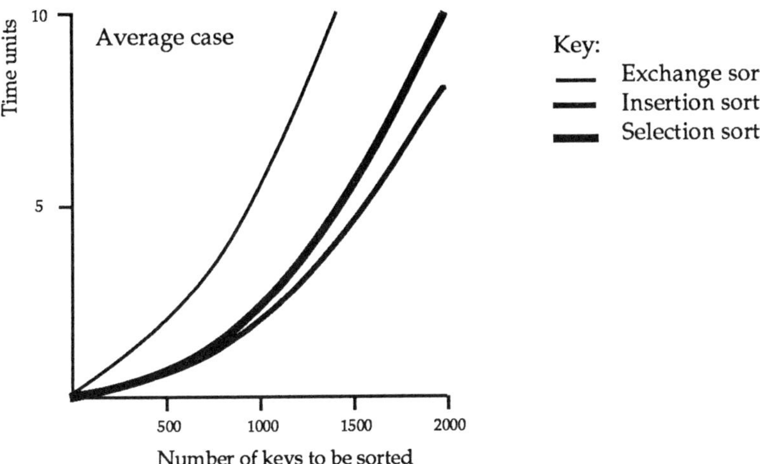

For randomly distributed keys, the insertion sort has reversed positions with the selection sort and is computationally cheaper throughout the range of keys to be sorted. The exchange sort remains in the unfavourable position of being about twice as expensive as the best method.

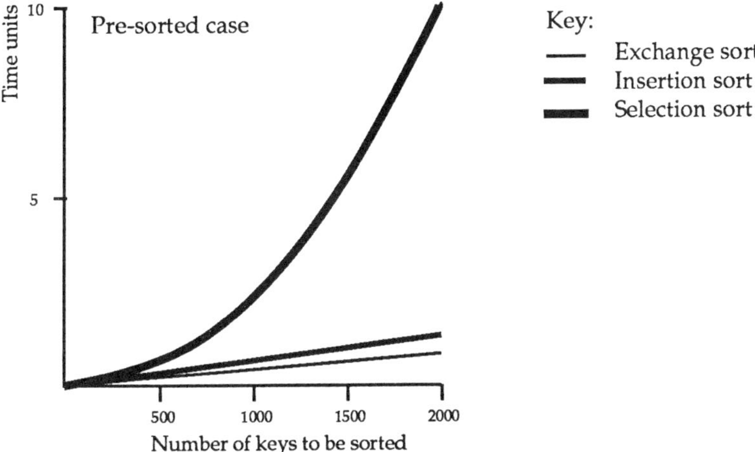

When the keys have been pre-sorted, the exchange sort is seen to be the best method for the first time. However, the insertion sort is seen to be only slightly more expensive. The selection sort shows up very badly in this situation as it takes no advantage of the ordering of the keys. It is best to forget the exchange sort as it is expensive in most cases. The only time it is the best method is for sorting pre-sorted data, which are unlikely to occur to any significant extent. The insertion sort proved to be the best method for average data, and it is also very good in the extreme cases of pre-sorted data and for worst case data.

11.3.6 Sorting large data structures

Sometimes the data associated with a single key is large and complex. In this case, we need to exercise care to ensure that these large amounts of data are not needlessly moved in the data exchange part of the sort algorithms.

When dealing with linked lists this reduces to a trivial method as all that is required is to manipulate the pointers. Taking this idea as the starting position, it is easy to develop an efficient method based on an array of pointers for any type of large data structure. To illustrate the idea, we will restrict attention entirely to sorting an array data[0 .. n - 1], but instead of exchanging the array elements we will maintain a record of the required exchanges in a pointer array - point[0 .. n - 1] so that point[0] gives the index of the smallest value of the array data[0 .. n - 1]. In this way, the number of exchanges of the full data structure can be reduced to a minimum.

In principle, any sort algorithm can be used to manipulate the pointer array. Once the pointer array has been sorted it can be used to specify the position of the full data structure, in this case the array data[0 .. n - 1]. Two alternatives are now available, first, the pointer may be used to access the required data structure without ever rearranging the data structures in the sorted order, or second, the pointer array can be used to guide the sort in the minimum number of moves.

The following procedure gives an implementation that constructs the pointer array using a modification of the insertion algorithm

```
PROCEDURE PointerArray(VAR data : ARRAY OF keyType;
            VAR point : ARRAY OF CARDINAL);
(* This procedure uses a modified insertionsort algorithm to find the
ordering of the pointer array. *)
VAR
   i, j, n, index : CARDINAL;

BEGIN
   n := HIGH(data);
   FOR i := 0 TO n - 1 DO
      point[i] := i; (* Set the initial index of the pointer array. *)
   END;
   FOR i := 1 TO n - 1 DO
      index := point[i];
      j := i;
      WHILE data[point[j - 1]] > data[index] DO
         point[j] := point[j - 1];
         j := j - 1;
      END;
      point[j] := index; (* The position of the sorted element. *)
   END;
END PointerArray;
```

At the end of this sequence of operations, the array point[0 .. n - 1] stores the indicated position of the sorted data structure (that is, array data). For example, point[2] may have the value 25, this means that the second data structure in the sorted sequence of data structures is the one in position 25 of the unsorted sequence.

Now, how do we permute the sequence if the data structures must appear in sorted order? If plenty of memory is available then the exercise is trivial. All that is required is to duplicate the data structure and then directly copy values from the duplicate to overwrite the old value in the original list. Thus, copy from position 25 in the duplicate sequence to overwrite position 2 in the original sequence, and so on.

The original assumption in this section is that we are dealing with very large data structures, in which case the large amount of spare memory required for the duplication method may not be available. In this case what is needed is a permutation algorithm that requires a minimum of extra memory and moves each data value once.

If we allocate temporary memory for a single data value it is easy to construct a permutation method as follows:

Suppose we have the cyclic set of pointer values:

```
point[0] = 3
point[3] = 27
point[27] = 22
point[22] = 0
```

Shuffle the array data value to the correct position and reset the point element to take the value of the index:

```
Set temp := data[0];
        data[0] := data[3];             point[0] := 0;
        data[3] := data[27];            point[3] := 3;
        data[27] := data[22];           point[27] := 27;
        data[22] := temp;               point[22] := 22;
```

With the aid of one temporary memory location we have completed the first cycle and inserted four data structures into their correct position; point[0], point[3], point[27] and point[22] need not be referred to again as their index and element value coincide to indicate that their data structures have already been correctly positioned. Moving to pointer point[1], etc, the algorithm may be repeated with the next cyclic set of pointer values until all elements have been permuted.

The procedure that implements this method and uses only one temporary memory location is given in the following procedure.

```
PROCEDURE Permute(VAR data : ARRAY OF keyType;
            VAR point : ARRAY OF CARDINAL);

VAR
   i, j, k, n : CARDINAL;
   temp : keyType;

BEGIN
   n := HIGH(data);
   FOR i := 0 TO n - 1 DO
      IF point[i] <> i THEN
         temp := data[i];
         j := i;
         k := n + 1;
         WHILE k <> i DO
            data[j] := data[point[j]];
            k := point[j];
            point[j] := j;
            j := k;
         END;
         data[j] := temp;
      END;
   END;
END Permute;
```

11.4 Advanced sorting methods

In this section, we will study some advanced sort algorithms that have the advantage of being *fast* in most circumstances. The idea of divide and conquer is well established in computer science. In essence, the method divides a problem into sub-problems, solves these sub-problems and finally recombines the sub-problem solutions to obtain the overall solution. A number of sorting algorithms use divide and conquer to split the original problems into smaller sort problems, but differ in the way in which the original sequence is divided and in the recombination of the sub-sorts.

11.4.1 Quicksort

This method was named Quicksort by its originator (C.A.R. Hoare) in 1962. It is regarded as the best method for general purpose sorting, but, unfortunately, its worst case performance is poor. In practice, the worst case possibility should be guarded against by taking some elementary precautions.

An array data[0 .. n - 1] is sorted by starting at an arbitrary member of the array (the pivot), data[0] say, and then moving all entries that are larger than data[0] to the right of data[0] and all entries that are smaller to the left. This new position for the pivot value is known as the partition point of the sequence of elements in the array.

For example,

Array index i:	0	1	2	3	4	5	6	7	8
Key value data[i]:	6	5	2	7	4	9	1	8	3

Take the original data[0] value as the pivot, then

i:	0	1	2	3	4	5	6	7	8
data[i]:	1	5	2	3	4	6	9	8	7

The partition point is at part = i = 5.
If we assume that a procedure is available that partitions the array in the way that we explained above and returns the value of the partition point, then we can describe the Quicksort procedure as follows:

```
PROCEDURE Quicksort(VAR data : ARRAY OF keyType;
                    first, last : CARDINAL);
VAR
   part : CARDINAL;

BEGIN
   IF first <= last THEN
   part := Partition(data, first, last);
      Quicksort(data, first, part - 1);
      Quicksort(data, part +1, last);
   END;
End Quicksort;
```

This procedure sorts the array of items by recursively calling Quicksort, with the function Partition returning the position of the pivot in the successive division of the items. The procedure partition does all the work needed in comparing and moving keys. The essential actions required from this procedure are:

(1) Return the index value *part* which identifies the final position of data[pivot] = data[part] in the sorted sequence.

(2) Re-position all the elements data[first, part - 1] which have keys less than or equal to data[part] on the left of data[part].

(3) Re-position all the elements data[part + 1, last] which have keys greater than or equal to data[part] on the right of data[part].

Next, we need to develop a strategy to achieve the partition and the ordering as required by (1), (2) and (3). Choose an arbitrary value of data[i], say data[0], and use two pointers to scan from the left (lp) and right (rp). Scan from the left until a key greater than data[0] is found; scan from the right until a key less than data[0] is found. These keys are obviously out of order and need to be exchanged:

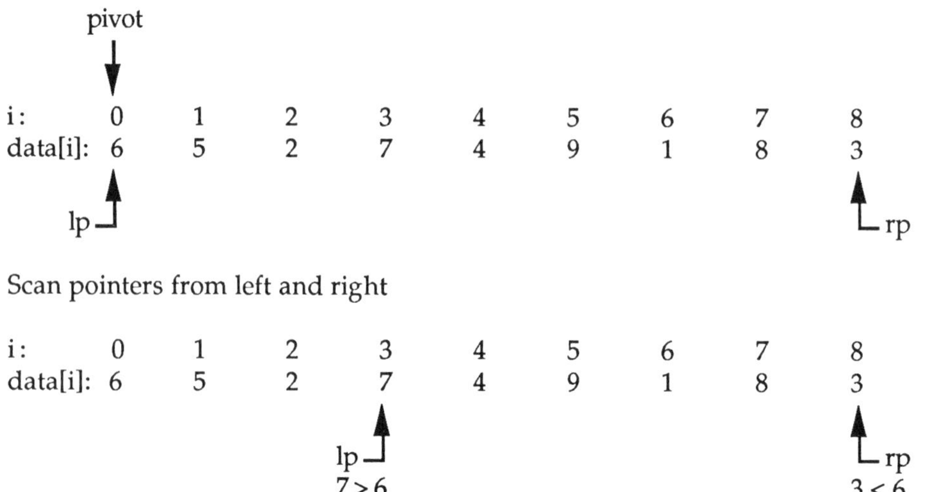

Scan pointers from left and right

Exchange data[3] and data[8] and continue scanning with pointers until all elements to the left of both pointers are less than the pivot data[0].

i:	0	1	2	3	4	5	6	7	8
data[i]:	6	5	2	3	4	9	1	8	7
						lp ↑ 9>6	rp ↑ 1<6		

Exchange data[5] and data[6]

i:	0	1	2	3	4	5	6	7	8
data[i]:	6	5	2	3	4	1	9	8	7
						rp ↑	lp ↑		

When the pointers cross, all that remains to be done is to exchange the pivot value with the key indicated by the right pointer.

i:	0	1	2	3	4	5	6	7	8
data[i]:	1	5	2	3	4	6	9	8	7

data[5] is now in its final position, that is the partition point. The two sub-sequences to the left and right of data[5] are now sorted independently by recursive calls to the Quicksort procedure.

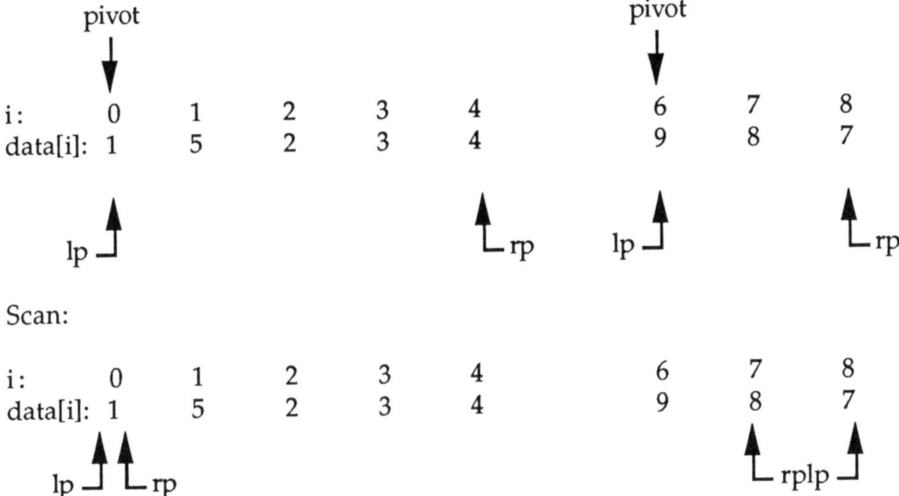

data[0] is the smallest element in sequence and remains in place. Partition is at i = 0.

Exchange data[7] and data[8] and exchange pivot with data[7].

data[0] and data[6] are now in their final positions. As there are no sub-sorts to the left of data[0] and data[6], the sort continues with the two right hand side sub-sorts.

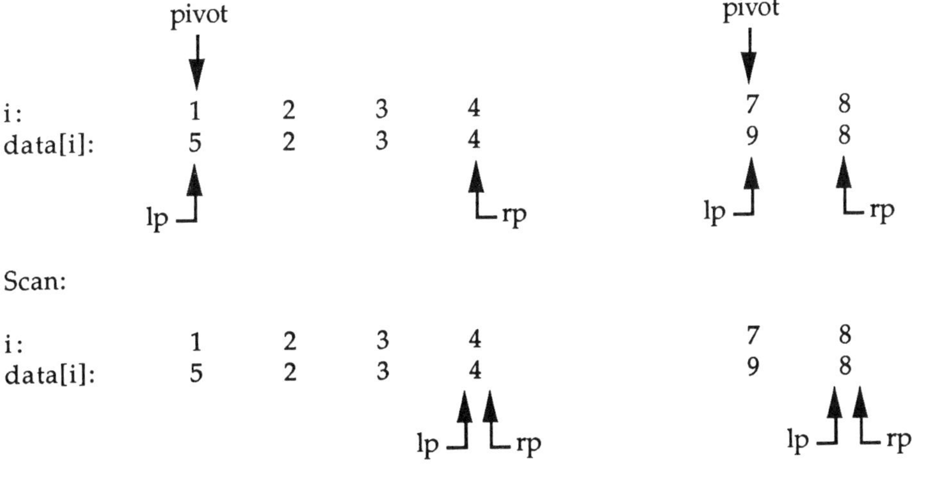

Exchange pivot with data[4], placing the pivot in its final position.

Exchange pivot with data[7], completing the sub-sort.

The original sequence has now been reduced to 3 unsorted keys:

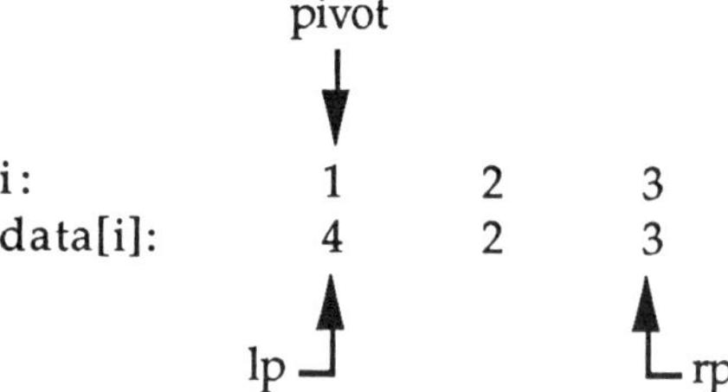

Scan:

```
i:          1    2    3
data[i]:    4    2    3
                    lp  rp
```

Exchange pivot with data[3], leaving the final keys:

```
i:          1    2
data[i]:    3    2
          lp      rp
```

which are sorted as previously. The final arrangement is, therefore:

i:	0	1	2	3	4	4	6	7	8
data[i]:	1	2	3	4	5	6	7	8	9

We can see from the small number of operations that this is an efficient method, provided that the partitioning procedure is well designed. A direct implementation of the method is as follows:

```
PROCEDURE Partition (VAR data : ARRAY OF keyType;
          first, last : CARDINAL): CARDINAL;
(* Return the partition index. *)

VAR
   leftPointer, rightPointer, part : CARDINAL;
   temp : keyType;

BEGIN
   (* Initialise pointers. *)
   leftPointer := first;
   rightPointer := last;
   WHILE leftPointer < rightPointer DO
      (* Scan from right. *)
      WHILE data[rightPointer] > data[first] DO
         DEC(rightPointer);
      END
```

```
      (* Scan from left. *);
      WHILE (leftPointer > rightPointer) AND
                              (data[leftPointer] <= data[first]) DO
         INC(leftPointer);
      END;
      (* Exchange keys at halted pointer scan position. *)
      IF leftPointer < rightPointer THEN
         temp := data[leftPointer];
         data[leftPointer] := data[rightPointer];
         data[rightPointer] := temp;
      END;
   END;
   (* Exchange pivot element with rightPointer value. *)
   part := rightPointer;
   temp := data[part];
   data[part] := data[first];
   data[first] := temp;
   RETURN part;
END Partition;
```

A few observations on the Quicksort method need to be made. First, if the pivot element is the smallest key in the sequence, then the scan must be stopped at that point. Second, when equal keys to the pivot element are present in the sequence the question arises *should one, both or neither pointer scan over them*? The best solution to this second issue has been theoretically studied and the recommendation is that both pointers stop. This feature helps to balance the partitions when many equal keys are present.

When the partition procedure successively divides the sequence of keys exactly in half we can expect the best behaviour from the Quicksort method.

To analyse the complexity of this method a theory must be established that can explain the operations carried out in a recursive program. Let C_n indicate the number of comparison operations that are made when a loop ranges over a sequence of n items. Thus, when a sequence is divided in half the number of comparison operations carried out on each sub-sequence is $C_{n/2}$.

The number of comparisons used in the Quicksort method satisfies the divide and conquer recurrence relation

$$C_n = 2\,C_{n/2} + n \quad \text{with } C_0 = 0$$

This is the classic recurrence relation that arises from a recursive program that makes a linear pass through its inputs before, during and after the input is divided into two parts. At each stage, the cost of sorting each sub-sequence is $C_{n/2}$ and n is the cost of examining each key in the full sequence.

Best case performance

Suppose that the sequence is composed of 2^k keys, that is $n = 2^k$, then for an equal partitioning at each stage, we obtain the following expression for the total number of comparisons

$$C_{2^k} = 2\,C_{2^{k-1}} + 2^k \text{ with } C_1 = 0.$$

Divide throughout by 2^k we obtain the expression

$$\frac{C_{2^k}}{2^k} = \frac{C_{2^{k-1}}}{2^{k-1}} + 1$$

therefore, by substituting this recurrence relation into the right hand side expression, $C_{2^{k-1}}$, of itself we obtain

$$\frac{C_{2^k}}{2^k} = \frac{C_{2^{k-2}}}{2^{k-2}} + 1 + 1$$

We can continue this substitution k times, therefore

$$\frac{C_{2^k}}{2^k} = 1 + 1 + 1 + \ldots\ldots + 1 = k$$

or $$C_{2^k} = C_n = k\,2^k,$$

where $2^k = n$, and $\log n = k \log_2 2 = k$.

Thus, $C_n = n \log n$.

Even though on average the partition can be expected to fall at the mid point of the sequence of keys, the solution for a random distribution of keys cannot be expected to behave quite as well as given by this result.

Average case performance

For a random distribution of keys, the partition can be expected at any position in the sequence of keys. Each key in the random sequence a[i] is likely to be the partition element with probability 1/i. After this partition the two sub-sequences are of length i - 1 and n - i.

The cost of sorting the sub-sequences is then

$$\frac{1}{n}\sum_{i=1}^{n} (C_{i-1} + C_{n-i}),$$

and the cost of comparing the pivot element with each of the other elements is n - 1, then

Total cost of comparisons C_n is

$$C_n = n - 1 + \frac{1}{n}\sum_{i=1}^{n} (C_{i-1} + C_{n-i}),$$

with $n \geq 1$ and $C_n = 1$.

To evaluate this relation, we start with the observation that C_{i-1} and C_{n-i} are symmetric, giving

$$C_n = n - 1 + \frac{2}{n}\sum_{i=1}^{n} C_{i-1}$$

and $$n\,C_n = n(n-1) + 2\sum_{i=1}^{n} C_{i-1} \qquad \text{---- (1)}$$

Rewrite (1) in terms of n - 1, we obtain

$$(n-1)\,C_{n-1} = (n-1)^2 - (n-1) + 2\sum_{i=1}^{n} C_{i-1} \qquad \text{---- (2)}$$

Subtracting (2) from (1) we obtain

$$n\,C_n - (n-1)\,C_{n-1} = n(n-1) - (n-1)(n-2) + 2\,C_{n-1}$$

Simplifying

$$n\,C_n = (n+1)\,C_{n-1} + 2n$$

and rearranging

$$\frac{C_n}{n+1} = \frac{C_{n-1}}{n} + \frac{2}{n+1}$$

$$= \frac{C_{n-2}}{n-1} + \frac{2}{n+1} + \frac{2}{n}$$

$$= \frac{C_{n-3}}{n-2} + \frac{2}{n+1} + \frac{2}{n} + \frac{2}{n-1}$$

....

....

$$\sim 2 \sum_{i=1}^{n} \frac{1}{i}$$

For large n we can treat this sum as an integral, then

$$\frac{C_n}{n+1} \sim 2 \int_{i=1}^{n} \frac{1}{i} di = 2 \log_e n$$

Converting to $\log_2$,

$$C_n \sim 1.38\, n \log n$$

This is an excellent result with the average case complexity costing only about 38% more than the best case.

Worst case performance

For each sub-sequence, of length k, the partition procedure uses k - 1 comparison operations. If the smallest element in the sequence of keys is in the first position then the partition position is also at this first element. If this occurs each time the sequence is partitioned then the total number of comparisons of keys is given by

$$\sum_{i=1}^{n} (i - 1) = \frac{n}{2}(n - 1).$$

This is as bad as the insertion sort. This worst case behaviour only happens when the sequence is already sorted in the correct order.

Improving the performance of Quicksort

Quicksort is very fast when the partition is close to or at the central position of each sub-sequence of keys. In some cases the choice of data[first] as the pivot value leads to a poor performance, such as when a sequence is nearly sorted. Among the several alternative strategies for choosing the pivot element are:

(1) using a random element,

(2) the median element of data[first], data[last] and data[midpoint].

In each case, the first element, data[first], must be exchanged with the value chosen by one of the alternative strategies. Some extra work must be done to find an alternative pivot element but this is more than offset by improving the average execution time of the method. The method is not efficient for short sequences of keys, then an alternative method should be used.

In Hoare's original paper, and in studies since, many suggestions for improving Quicksort have been made. One favoured method is to stop the recursion before the sub-sequences become small and instead use a simple sorting method, such as Insert sort, on the remaining sub-sequences. As Quicksort works best on large sequences, we then get an overall improved performance.

The recursive implementation of Quicksort will cause *first, last* and *part* to be saved on the program stack. The program stack is a piece of system software that automatically looks after all the software management that is required to oversee the actions of the recursion, however this automatic control of recursion can be computationally expensive. Then pushing and popping of the stack is an inevitable overhead of the recursion, but some of it can be avoided by directly implementing the stack in the program rather than leaving it to the compiler to handle the stack operations.

When a sequence of keys is partitioned, we create two sub-sequences. These are first checked for size and the larger is placed on the stack. The smaller sequence is then sorted without needing to be placed on the stack. By processing the smaller sequence first, the size of each successive sub-sequence will be less than half the size of the previous sub-sequence. This will require about log n entries on the stack rather than the n entries that are needed for the recursive sorting of the pre-sorted sequence. In the following non-recursive implementation, we will use the stack implementation given in Chapter 5.

```
FROM StaticStack IMPORT Stack, StackItem, Create, Push, Pop,
                        Top, IsEmpty;

PROCEDURE Quicksort (VAR data : ARRAY OF keyType;
                     first, last : StackItem);
(* Non recursive implementation. *)

VAR
   s : Stack;
   part : StackItem;
   overflow, underflow : BOOLEAN;

BEGIN
   Create(s);
   Push(s, first, overflow);
   Push(s, last, overflow);
```

```
    WHILE NOT IsEmpty(s) DO
      IF last > first THEN
        part := Partition(data, first, last);
        IF (part - first) > (last - part) THEN
          (* Test for largest sub-sequence. *)
          Push(s, first, overflow);
          Push(s, part - 1, overflow);
          first : = part + 1;
        ELSE
          Push(s, part + 1, overflow);
          Push(s, last, overflow);
          last : = part - 1;
        END;
      ELSE
        Top(s, last, underflow);
        Pop(s, last, underflow);
        Top(s, first, underflow);
        Pop(s, first, underflow);
      END;
    END;
  END Quicksort;
```

The test for the largest sub-sequence reduces the speed of the algorithm in return for a decrease in memory requirements. If speed is more important, the test can be removed, but a larger stack will be required. Note, the Boolean variables overflow and underflow should be tested and if TRUE the program should be halted.

Before we complete this section on the Quicksort method, we should ask why the divide and conquer principle has logarithmic properties. The answer is quite simple once we spot the connection with the properties of a binary tree.

In the example previously described we can display the successive stages by inserting the sorted items into the nodes of an initially empty tree. The first partition element becomes the root of the tree and successive partition elements take left or right nodes.

At each stage of the tree, a reduced amount of work needs to be done to achieve the sub-sort. The best performance is given by a balanced tree when the sub-sequences are exactly half the size of the previous sequence. Then, the work required is halved at each stage. When a pre-sorted sequence is sorted by Quicksort the tree becomes a linear sequences of nodes. This obviously gives the worst performance.

11.4.2 Merging sequences

A merging operation joins two independent sequences to form a single sequence. When merging two sequences a and b, the first entry in the resulting sequence will be the smallest entry of the two sequences. This procedure is continued until either a or b is empty, then all remaining entries can be moved to the resultant sequence.

We may wish to merge linked lists, queues or array items. This first solution uses the abstract data type DynamicQueue from Chapter 6. Assume that the keys are held in queues a and b and that the resultant queue will be held in the new queue r. Then:

```
FROM DynamicQueue IMPORT Queue, QueueItem, NewQ, AddQ,
                              RearQ, FrontQ, IsEmptyQ;

PROCEDURE Merge(a, b : Queue): Queue;
VAR
   r : Queue;
   a1, b1 : QueueItem;

BEGIN
   r: = NewQ();

   WHILE (NOT IsEmptyQ(a)) AND (NOT IsEmptyQ(b)) DO
      a1 := FrontQ(a); (* a1 is front element of a. *)
      b1:= FrontQ(b); (* b1 is front element of b. *)

      IF a1 <= b1 THEN
         r := AddQ(r, a1); (* Add a1 to rear of Queue r. *)
         a := RearQ(a); (* Remove a1 from front of a. *)
      ELSE
         r := AddQ(r, b1); (* Add b1 to rear of Queue r. *)
         b := RearQ(b); (* Remove b1 from front of a. *)
      END;
   END;

   IF NOT IsEmptyQ(a) THEN
      (* Add all remaining items in a to Q r. *)
      WHILE NOT IsEmptyQ(a) DO
         a1 := FrontQ(a);
         r := AddQ(r, a1);
         a := RearQ(a);
      END;

   ELSE
      (* Add all remaining items in b to Queue r. *)
      WHILE NOT IsEmptyQ(b) DO
         b1 := FrontQ(b);
         r := AddQ(b, b1);
         b := RearQ(b);
      END;
   END;
   RETURN r;
END Merge;
```

Instead of using queues, we will next assume the keys are held as array elements a[0 .. n - 1] and b[0 .. m - 1]

```
PROCEDURE Merge(VAR a, b, r : ARRAY OF keyType);

VAR
    i, j, k, n, m : CARDINAL;
    temp : keyType;

BEGIN
    n := HIGH(a);
    m := HIGH(b);
    i := 0;
    j := 0;
    k := 0;
    WHILE (i <= n - 1) AND (j <= m - 1) DO
        IF a[i] < b[j] THEN (* Add a. *)
            r[k] := a[i];
            INC(i);
        ELSE
              r[k] := b[j]; (* Add b. *)
              INC(j);
        END;
        INC(k);
    END;
    IF i > n - 1 THEN
        WHILE j <= m - 1 DO
            r[k] := b[j];
            INC(j);
            INC(k);
        END;
    ELSE
        WHILE i <= n - 1 DO
            r[k] := a[i];
            INC(k);
            INC(i);
        END;
    END;
END Merge;
```

The analysis of this procedure is quite easy. After comparison a key is moved to array r and never again referred to. Thus the two lists are merged after at most n + m - 1 comparisons.

In this implementation, we have assumed that there is sufficient memory available for the resultant array r. Space can be conserved by dynamically overlapping the arrays a and b and re-using the space vacated by moved keys. Some spare capacity in the array is necessary to implement this last method.

11.4.3 Mergesort

Another example of divide and conquer is given by the Mergesort algorithm. Once we have an efficient merge procedure this method is very easy to implement. This is one of the most efficient methods of sorting, easy to understand and simple to implement. Mergesort divides the sequence of keys into two equal halves and recursively sorts the halves separately. The sorted halves are then merged by a suitable modification to the above procedure to merge adjacent sub-sequences of the same original sequence. The new merge procedure has the heading:

```
PROCEDURE Merge(VAR data : ARRAY OF keyType;
          first, mid, last : CARDINAL);
```

Then we can implement the Mergesort procedure as

```
PROCEDURE Mergesort(VAR data : ARRAY OF keyType;
              first, last, CARDINAL);
VAR
   mid : CARDINAL;

BEGIN
   IF first < last THEN
      mid := (first + last) DIV 2;
      Mergesort(data, first, mid);
      Mergesort(data, mid + 1, last);
      Merge(data, first, mid, last);
   END;
END Mergesort;
```

Performance of Mergesort

The work done in Mergesort is identical to that of the best Quicksort, that is n log n comparison. When n is not a power of 2, the successive subdivision will not always break into two equal parts and the complexity will be slightly worse. However, the Mergesort algorithm is recognised as about optimal for an algorithm that is based on simple comparisons of keys. It does suffer from the need for a duplicate array to implement the merge procedure. This is one of the main reasons that Quicksort is still regarded as the best choice of algorithm for general sorting.

11.5 Searching methods

Searching and retrieving items of information from an ordered list is one of the fundamental operations in computer science. As in sorting, a key is used to mark the entry point to a record of information.

Typical applications are searching a bank account, or a reservation system for a specific key, or in an artificial intelligence application where sets of keys are being matched in some way. Search operations are often combined with other operations such as insert or delete a record, or merge two sets of records at some key.

In each of the following examples, we will assume that the sequence of keys has been pre-sorted. As in the sort sections of this chapter, the records will be represented by simple data structures, but the procedures can be adapted to search more complex data structures with little effort.

11.5.1 Sequential search

This first method makes no use of the fact that the sequence is in order. The idea is to sequentially search the sequence until the key is found. Why are we considering a method which appears to be trivially simple? Because it is sufficient to illustrate the search principle and also it is an adequate method for small sequences of keys. We start by initialising the search index to 0 and then look for the key in array data.

```
PROCEDURE SequentialSearch(VAR data : ARRAY OF keyType;
                                key : keyType): CARDINAL;

VAR
   i, n : CARDINAL;
   notFound : BOOLEAN;

BEGIN
   n := HIGH(data);
   i := 0;
   notFound := TRUE;
   data[n] := key; (* Sentinel. *)
   WHILE (i <= n) OR notFound DO
      IF data[i] = key THEN
         notFound := FALSE;
      ELSE
         INC(i);
      END;
   END;
   RETURN i;
END SequentialSearch;
```

In this procedure, the sentinel ensures that the algorithm succeeds when the key is not found. The array data must have spare capacity at i = n for the method to work, and a test against the sentinel value must be made to detect that the key was not found.

If the keys are duplicated many times, this method would only find one of them. However, the algorithm can be easily adapted to find other records with the same key. Let the entry index point to the procedure be *enter*, then

```
PROCEDURE SequentialSearch (VAR data : ARRAY OF keyType;
                        key: keyType; enter : CARDINAL): CARDINAL;

VAR
   i, n : CARDINAL;
   notFound : BOOLEAN;

BEGIN
   n := HIGH(data);
   data[n] := key;
   notFound := TRUE;
   WHILE (enter <= n) OR notFound DO
      INC(enter);
      IF data[enter] = key THEN
         notFound := FALSE;
      END;
   END;
   RETURN enter;
END SequentialSearch;
```

By starting with the index enter = -1 and repeatedly executing

enter := SequentialSearch (data, key, enter);

we can obtain the complete set of records associated with the value key.

The first of these search procedures was used in Chapter 5 in the implementation of the IsIn procedure, used to sequentially search a list.

The computational complexity of this search is the easiest to establish. If we ignore the ordering of the sequence then we can always expect n comparison operations for an unsuccessful search and on average n/2 comparison operations for a successful search.

When the order of a list is taken into account we obtain an improvement in the performance of the unsuccessful search, because the search can be terminated if the key is exceeded. The complexity property of this unsuccessful search is now identical to the successful search, that is it is as likely to terminate after the first element as at the last element, giving an average n/2 complexity.

Perhaps, we should comment on what is meant by ordering a list before we move to the next section. Generally, we mean that it is ordered in the sense of the sorted items that we discussed earlier in this chapter. However, this is not the only ordering that is important in computer science. The frequency that an item is accessed is an alternative criteria for ordering, where items are ordered according to this frequency distribution with the most frequently accessed item being first on the list, etc.

11.5.2 Binary search

The O(n) complexity of the SequentialSearch method is not difficult to improve. We know from our study of divide and conquer methods, such as Quicksort and Mergesort, that considerable advantage can be obtained from successively dividing a problem in half.

The obvious method is similar to the way we manually search a telephone directory. When searching for the name *Smith*, we would not start from the front and search linearly, instead we would probably open the directory roughly in the middle. Having opened a page to a name beginning with, say, *K* we would know that Smith is in the second half of the directory. So, dividing the remainder of the directory in half, we open to a name beginning with, say, *U*. The next division is going to be between the first and second attempt. Continuing in this way, we soon find the required entry. As humans, we usually do a little better than a simple division. Using our experience, we usually bias the division in one direction. For the moment, let us assume that we always divide the directory in equal halves. Then the surprising result we obtain is that a directory containing 30 million entries can have a single entry found by a search involving about 25 comparison operations.

A numerical example will illustrate this very simply. Find the key = 8 in the following ordered list:

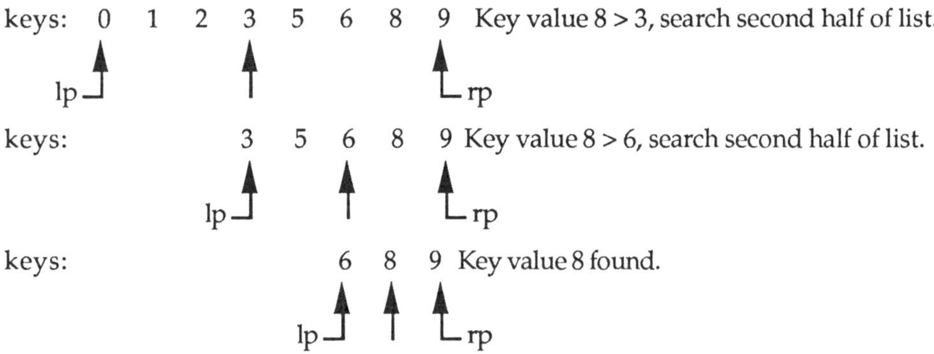

Key value 8 found in three comparison operations. Now increase the number of elements to sixteen and repeat the search to find the key = 23:

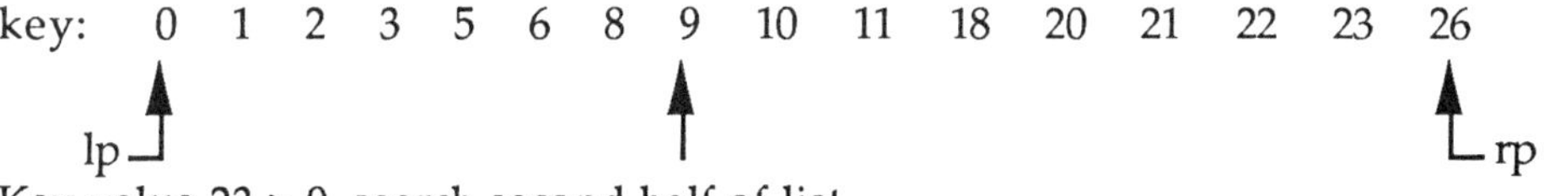

Key value 23 > 9, search second half of list.

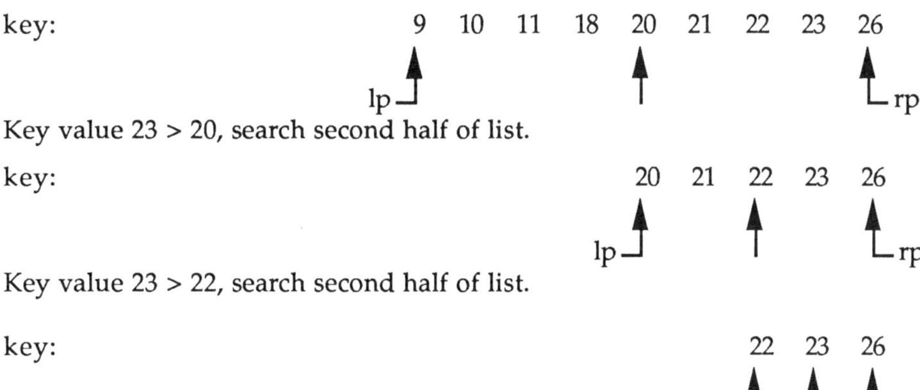

Key value 23 > 20, search second half of list.

Key value 23 > 22, search second half of list.

Key value 23 found in four operations.

So we can double the size of the list for the cost of only one extra comparison operation. This is the classic result from an optimum divide and conquer method, that is O(log n).

To find a key by this method only three possibilities are open:

1. key < middle position key: key is in first half of list

2. key > middle position key: key is in last half of list

3. key = middle position key: key is found

This set of conditions can be implemented by using pointers to the start and end of the list or sub-list and then by applying the sub-division method repeatedly until the key is found, or a failure reported:

```
PROCEDURE BinarySearch(VAR data : ARRAY OF keyType;
            key : CARDINAL): CARDINAL;
VAR
   leftPointer, rightPointer, mid, n : CARDINAL;
   notFound : BOOLEAN;

BEGIN
   n := HIGH(data);
   leftPointer := 0;
   rightPointer := n - 1;
   notFound := TRUE;
   WHILE notFound OR (leftPointer < rightPointer) DO
      mid := (leftPointer + rightPointer) DIV 2;
      IF key = data[mid] THEN
         notFound := FALSE;
      ELSIF key < data[mid] THEN
         rightPointer := mid - 1;
```

```
          ELSE
             leftPointer := mid + 1;
          END;
       END;
       IF notFound THEN
          RETURN n; (* Sentinel value. *)
       ELSE
          RETURN mid;
       END;
    END BinarySearch;
```

The return of the sentinel, n, indicates an unsuccessful search. This extra element must be allowed and tested for in this implementation.

Complexity analysis

This is a divide and conquer method with the search space being exactly halved at each step. A program that halves its inputs at each step always satisfies the recurrence relation

$$C_n = C_{n/2} + 1, \quad \text{with } C_1 = 0.$$

We will again assume that n is a power of two, that is $n = 2^k$, which gives

$$C_{2^k} = C_{2^{k-1}} + 1$$

Substituting this relation into the right hand side

$$C_{2^k} = C_{2^{k-2}} + 1 + 1$$

....

....

$$= C_{2^0} + k - 1$$

$$= k$$

As $n = 2^k, C_n = \log n$

Although this solution has assumed that n is a power of 2, in practice it has been found that the number of comparison operations required for a general value of n is still ~ log n.

Multiple keys will not be found by the implemented procedure, but only a small modification is needed if multiple keys are required. Once a key has been found, then a simple sequential search in both directions from the initial key is all that is required to find multiple keys.

Binary search only works for ordered sequences, therefore the insertion operation for a new key has a high penalty as it requires the complete sequence to remain in order. For an array of items this will require on average the movement of n/2 elements.

Decision tree

A decision tree can be used to illustrate a binary search for a given key. A decision tree for an input of n elements in a sequence a is constructed as follows:

1. n nodes are labelled from 0 to n - 1.
2. The root of the tree is labelled with the midpoint index of the original sequence.
3. Subsequent nodes are labelled according to the mid point positions of the sub-sequences to the left and right of the parent node.

A decision tree for 16 elements is therefore:

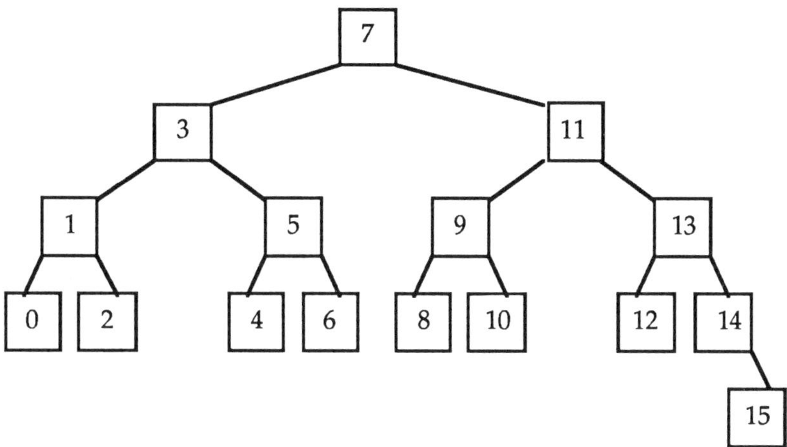

We have been able to construct this tree without any knowledge of the key values, the structure was determined entirely from knowing the number of elements in the sequence. This means, of course, that the search structure is predetermined.

11.5.3 Interpolated binary search

In the introduction to the binary search method we described how to bias the search when looking for a name in a telephone directory. This concept can be formalised and used in conjunction with the binary search technique.

The midpoint assignment, mid: = (leftPointer + rightPointer) DIV 2, should be replaced by an expression that reflects the expected position of the key. First, re-express the above assignment as follows:

$$\text{part} := \text{leftPointer} + \frac{1}{2}\,(\text{rightPointer} - \text{leftPointer}).$$

We now replace the factor 1/2 by a factor that biases the partitioning of the sequence. With a well chosen bias factor it should be possible to estimate a partition point which is much closer to the required key. The principle underlying the new expression

part : = leftPointer + bias (rightPointer - leftPointer)

is linear interpolation. If it is assumed that the directory has nearly evenly distributed names, it works as follows

The first partition gave a key name beginning with M when the mid point assignment is used. The principle of linear interpolation can be illustrated as below:

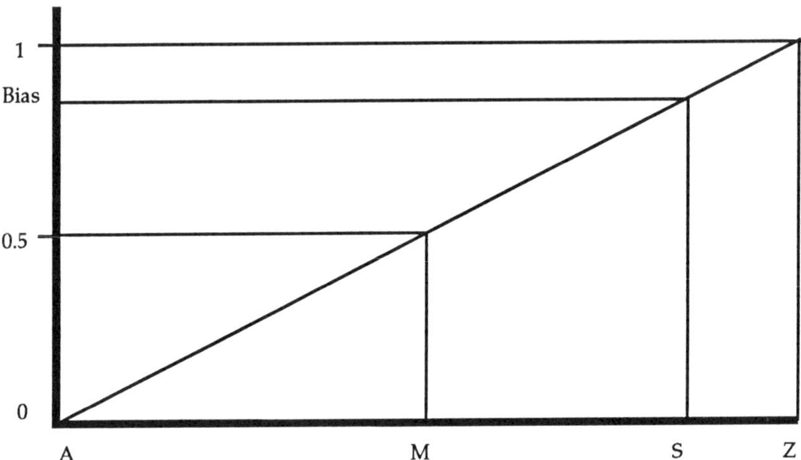

S is the 19'th letter in the alphabet, so if we use a bias factor of 19/26, the estimate would be close to the required key, even on the first attempt. Assume this division gives a key value beginning with T. As T is larger then S in the ordered list, the interpolation must now be on the interval [A, T]. A bias factor of 19/20 will give a partition point very close to the required key. To implement the method, the interpolation expression must be supplemented by a mechanism for estimating the bias factor. This mechanism has to be designed for the application in hand as no general method can be given. The idea relies on the keys being evenly distributed, otherwise the method can fail to improve the convergence rate of the normal binary search method. Uneven distribution is a feature of directories and Smith would not normally be found at the partition point 19/26 along the sequence of names. However, even here we can outperform the normal binary search.

Complexity estimate

The full analysis of this method is difficult, but the result is worth reporting because of its remarkable properties. For evenly distributed keys, interpolated binary search is O(log log n). This means that an item held within a sequence of 10^{10} items can be found in 5 comparison operations. Even though this is a remarkable result for large n, it may still be better when searching short sequences to use the normal binary search method rather than pay the overhead of calculating the bias factor.

11.5.4 Binary search tree

The full description of the binary search tree was given in Section 5.7.1. Here, we will restrict attention to the complexity of the search and insertion operation.

Complexity analysis

The average complexity of the binary search tree for both insertion and search is given by the average distance between the root of the tree and the node with the required key.

Given n nodes in the binary tree, we first need to sum the total node operations in the tree. Assuming that each node contributes one comparison operation and that the root node contains the i'th largest key, then the i - 1 and n - 1 sub-trees contribute C_{n-1} comparison operations, where

$$C_{n-1} = \frac{1}{n} \sum_{i=1}^{n} (C_{i-1} + C_{n-i})$$

In addition, the root node contributes one comparison operation to each of the n - 1 sub-nodes, therefore the total number of comparison operations is given by:

$$C_n = n - 1 + \frac{1}{n} \sum_{i=1}^{n} (C_{i-1} + C_{n-i})$$

This is the number of comparison operations to find each of the n nodes, therefore to find the average comparison operations per node this equation must be divided by n

$$\frac{C_n}{n} = \frac{n-1}{n} + \frac{1}{n^2} \sum_{i=1}^{n} (C_{i-1} + C_{n-i})$$

If the Quicksort complexity given in Section 11.4.1 is divided by n then an identical expression to the above is obtained. Using the solution to the Quicksort recurrence relation, the average number of comparison operations needed for a single search operation is:

$$C_n = \log n$$

It can be shown that an unsuccessful search has approximately the same complexity.

The solution to the above recurrence relation uses the assumption that there is symmetry between C_{i-1} and C_{n-i}. This implies that the tree is balanced, which in turn implies that the keys are randomly distributed over the sequence. If the keys are not randomly distributed, as in a sorted sequence, then the tree will not be balanced. In the worst case, the search reduces to a linear method with complexity n.

11.5.5 The complexity of sorting and searching algorithms

From the discussion in this chapter, we have seen that complexity can be regarded in a number of ways. The most obvious, and given the most attention, is the work complexity. Some algorithms, such as the exchange sort, proved to be so grossly inefficient that further consideration would be regarded as foolish. However, the work required to achieve a result, such as a sort or search, is not the only complexity consideration. In addition, we should always consider memory complexity and intellectual complexity.

As memory has become cheaper in relative terms, this consideration may be thought to be less important than perhaps a few years ago. But this is not necessarily so. The advantage of very fast computers has made possible the solution of problems that were previously considered to be too time consuming. The hallmark of this class of problems is that they are invariably large in memory requirements. Therefore, any algorithm that requires extra memory, such as the Mergesort algorithm, may be unacceptable.

The intellectual complexity may be regarded by some as unimportant, because with sufficient effort most of us can solve difficult problems. But there is a cost to pay, our time is expensive, usually more so than computer time, and the return for our effort may not be adequate compensation for the higher cost. Also, intellectually difficult algorithms are more bug prone than simple algorithms. Development time is likely to be larger and testing must be more exhaustive.

A recursive implementation is usually simple to write and understand, but this is often an area where extra work for an alternative solution does pay rewards. A non recursive implementation of a program always outperforms a recursive implementation. Removing errors from a recursive solution is invariably more difficult than removing errors from a non recursive solution and so the extra effort needed to write the non recursive solution can often be repayed in the time saved in debugging activities.

Summary

The time needed to compute solutions to different algorithms of a given problem can vary from seconds to billions of years. Therefore, the complexity of an algorithm should be established before it is implemented. The poor choice of an algorithm will not necessarily be adequately compensated for by increasing the power of computers. Exponential and factorially complex algorithms will always remain prohibitively expensive to compute and are unacceptable for all problems. The variety of sorting and searching algorithms make them ideal for comparing the complexity of different computing strategies.

Simple sorting methods, such as insert sort and select sort, can be effective in most circumstances, however the exchange sort has a very high complexity and should,therefore be avoided. Divide and conquer methods can be applied with good effect. The complexity analysis of the quick sort and merge sort methods show very good properties. Although the merge sort is faster it requires considerably more memory, therefore the quicksort method is usually favoured.

As recursion can be expensive to execute it may be beneficial to implement recursive sorting methods, such as the quick sort method, directly by explicitly employing a stack.

Sequential searches are of O(n) complexity. If the data is unordered then this method must be employed. However, for ordered data the principle of divide and conquer may be used as a binary search or extrapolated search to considerably accelerate the search. Therefore, it is possible to search an ordered list with O(n log log n) complexity.

Selected reading

Aho, A.V., Hopcroft, J.E. and Ullman, J.D.
The design and analysis of computer algorithms
Addison-Wesley, 1974.
This one of the original and still the best book on the design and analysis of algorithms. The complexity issues are given clear and precise descriptions. It is not a book for the beginner but the more advanced student will derive great benefit from this text.

Harel, D.
Algorithmics – The spirit of computing
Addison-Wesley, 1987.
The efficiency, inefficiency and even intractability of algorithms is given a thorough but enjoyable analysis. The style is light but the content is accurate. This book should be in the personal library of every computer scientist.

Kingston, J.H.
Algorithm and data structures
Addison-Wesley, 1990.
This is an advanced treatment of the complexity and correctness of algorithms. The mathematics is fairly rigourous but is not difficult for senior students. The examples on searching and sorting are written in Modula-2 with very good commentary on the advantages of each method.

Knuth, D.E.
The art of computer programming Vol 3 Sorting and searching
Addison-Wesley, 1973.
This is an advanced book and must be regarded as the standard work on sorting and searching for the professional programmer.

Sedgewick, R.
Algorithms in C
Addison-Wesley, 1990.
Although the programming language used is C, the reader will find a wealth of useful information in this book. The examples on searching and sorting are particularly well described. Many methods not covered here, such as heap and radix sort, are given detailed attention.

A Using Modula-2

A.1 Overview of Modula-2

The programming language we use for the examples throughout the book is Modula-2. Modula-2 was designed by Niklaus Wirth, well known as the designer of many programming languages, in particular Pascal, one of Modula-2's predecessors. The first Modula-2 compiler was released in 1981 and since then the language has gradually worked its way through the computing community, becoming particularly popular for large-scale software development and teaching.

Modula-2 has features which allow us to use the important software engineering principles of abstraction, data hiding (which is central to data abstraction and object-oriented design), problem decomposition and modularisation. Also important for teaching, Modula-2 has a very simple syntax, and is a small language, even though the concepts it implements are central to advanced software engineering.

We will work through the basic features of Modula-2 in this appendix, using simple programs to illustrate each new idea. The more complex features which allow abstraction, data hiding and modularisation are dealt with in detail in the main body of the book. The treatment of Modula-2 here is particularly suitable for those who have little or no experience of programming. It is suggested that beginners read this appendix immediately after Chapter 2.

We will assume that you have a computer, a Modula-2 compiler and you know how to type in, compile and run a program. The examples in the rest of the book are implemented in Metrowerks Modula-2 PSE, on an Apple Macintosh. However, in this appendix we have tried to keep things as general as possible, so for those of you using Metrowerks Modula-2 you will have to make a couple of small additions to the programs shown here before you can see their output. After the first example program we will show you what to add.

We start straight away with the problem of displaying a simple message on the terminal screen – displaying messages or results in some way or another is very important, since there is little point in writing a program to calculate the answer to life, if there is no way of finding out the result!

```
MODULE FirstLook;
(* Display an important message on the terminal. *)

FROM InOut IMPORT WriteString, WriteLn;

BEGIN
   WriteLn;
   WriteString("Hello Modula-2 World!");
   WriteLn;
END FirstLook.
```

This program (when compiled, linked and run) gives the following output:

```
Hello Modula-2 World!
```

It should run without alteration on nearly all Modula-2 implementations, but for those of you using Metrowerks Modula-2 on an Apple Macintosh, here is what the program should look like

```
MODULE FirstLook;
(* Display an important message on the terminal. *)
FROM InOut IMPORT WriteString, WriteLn, HoldScreen;
BEGIN
   WriteLn;
   WriteString("Hello Modula-2 World!");
   WriteLn;
   HoldScreen;
END FirstLook.
```

The difference is that we have added an operation called HoldScreen as the last operation in the program and note that it also appears on the third line of the program. HoldScreen keeps open the output window used by the program to display its results on the screen. If you tried the first version using Metrowerks on an Apple Macintosh you will know why this is needed (because the window is closed so fast that no one has time to read what's in it). HoldScreen needs to be the last operation in your program (if it is supposed to display information on the computer screen). You must also remember to import it from the InOut library (this is what the reference to HoldScreen on line 3 is doing).

For those of you using other compilers please ignore all this and carry on!

Now we know what the program does, let's look inside to see how the internal workings display a message. Each line in the program has a particular meaning and use, so we will examine each in turn.

The program commences with the line

```
MODULE FirstLook;
```

which states the name of our program or *module* – FirstLook. In Modula-2 all programs consist of one or more modules; this program is quite simple and so has only one module.

Next we have a piece of text enclosed by (* and *). This is a comment: comments are used to describe what a program does, or how it does it, to a human reader. They are ignored by the compiler, and play no part in the program itself – they are simply a means of conveying information to the reader. The use of comments is obligatory to all rational programmers. Just bear in mind that any reader of your program is unlikely to be psychic and may not be able to work out what your program is meant to do solely from the code. Additionally, as you write programs to solve more complex problems, you will find that you need the comments as much as anyone else, to remind you how your own code works. Modula-2 allows comments to be placed in just about any position inside a program, and to extend over multiple lines. Some examples of commented code are given below.

```
WriteString(" the total is "); (* Print message. *)
(* Calculate the new value for total. *)
total := total + 1;
```

We are also allowed to *nest* comments inside each other. This can be useful if we want to place comment brackets around a section of code to prevent it being executed. For example,

```
number := 5;
(* By-pass reading in of number
WriteString("enter a number : ");
ReadInt(number); (* Get number from user. *)  *)
square := number * number;
```

In this program fragment, the WriteString and ReadInt statements are commented out and will not be executed when the program is run.

Now we come to a feature of Modula-2 which is very important for software engineering – the *import* statement. The line

```
FROM InOut IMPORT WriteString, WriteLn;
```

is an example of an import statement. Modula-2 is a language which is designed to allow existing problem solutions to aid in the solving of new problems. It does this with *library modules.* Library modules can be thought of as a lending library, from which a program can *borrow* ready-made problem solutions by using import statements. These solutions are really sets of Modula-2 instructions, which perform a specific task or tasks: in computer science they are more usually called procedures or functions.

A typical Modula-2 program will contain several import statements. The import statement in FirstLook is a request to borrow the procedures WriteString and WriteLn from the standard library InOut. The import statement must come near the top of the program text, so that the required procedures are imported before any attempt is made to use them. Every implementation of Modula-2 provides a set of standard library modules, which contain procedures for solving some very common problems, such as getting data into a program, printing out results and performing mathematical calculations. In addition, the programmer can create his or her own libraries of procedures, which can be reused in many different programs.

We have now reached the line consisting only of the word BEGIN. Although this seems a small and inconsequential statement it is in fact rather important, since it marks the start of the main workings of the program module – the part which does the job of printing out the message using the imported procedures. This part of the program is called the *module body,* and it is terminated by the END statement at the bottom of the program. Inside the BEGIN and END statements is another list of statements, which are executed sequentially when the program is run.

The first statement inside the module body, WriteLn, is a use of the procedure imported from library module InOut. WriteLn sends a newline command to the terminal screen, causing the cursor to move down from its current position to the beginning of the next line.

The next statement uses procedure WriteString (also imported from InOut). WriteString displays a string of characters on the terminal screen, where the string is indicated by enclosing the characters to be displayed in either double or single quotes. Further examples of valid WriteString statements are:

```
WriteString("  Hello  ");
WriteString("54000 black space ships.");
WriteString("   ");
WriteString('Answer "Yes" or "No" ');
```

The module body of FirstLook uses only WriteLn and WriteString to produce the output shown earlier.

Examining program FirstLook, you should see that all the statements except BEGIN,

END, the last WriteLn and the comment, are terminated by a semicolon. This is not done simply to increase the amount of typing needed to write a program, but because semicolons are required by Modula-2 to separate one statement or language block from another. The semicolons are therefore used as *statement separators*.

It is difficult at first to understand when a semicolon is needed, but the general rule is that a semicolon is not needed before the first statement in a sequence or after the last statement in a sequence. Thus the word BEGIN and the last WriteLn do not have semicolons after them. The rules of Modula-2 do allow an extra semicolon to be inserted after the last statement of a sequence; this has the effect of inserting an extra, empty statement.

Having statement separators allows us to place several statements on one line, such as:

```
WriteLn; WriteString("Hello");
WriteLn; WriteString("Modula-2 World");
```

However, this is not generally considered to be good programming style. In fact, rather than putting several statements on one line, you should consider leaving blanks lines at strategic positions in your programs, to make them easier to read and understand.

You may still be wondering why the END and the comment do not have semicolons at the end of them. The comment has its own delimiters, (* and *); once the compiler recognises the first (* it ignores everything until it sees the corresponding *). The END statement is the last statement of the module body, and also the last statement in the entire module. The syntax of Modula-2 dictates that it must have the name of the module after it, and it must be terminated by a full stop. This full stop indicates the end of the entire module.

Before we go any further into the details of Modula-2 let's take a quick look at how program FirstLook is laid out on the page. Note the way some lines are indented, and some blank lines have been left in the text of the program. The indentation is to highlight the structure of the program and make it easier to read. If we write FirstLook without any indentation:

```
MODULE FirstLook;
(* Display an important message on the terminal. *)
FROM InOut IMPORT WriteString, WriteLn;
BEGIN
WriteLn;
WriteString("Hello Modula-2 World!");
WriteLn;
END FirstLook.
```

it isn't so easy to understand. You should always indent your programs to display their structure, and leave blank lines where necessary to divide up the program into logical parts. Try to use the styles of indentation and layout that we have used throughout this chapter; indentation styles tend to vary very little between programmers (except in the size of the indent), and you will see very similar styles in other books on Modula-2 (and, indeed, most other programming languages).

A.2 Reserved words and syntax

We haven't yet explained why some of the words in FirstLook are in upper case, or why they are arranged in a certain way in the program. All the uppercase words are *reserved words* which have special meanings to Modula-2.

Reserved word	Description
MODULE	Indicates the start of a program module.
BEGIN	Indicates the start of the module body.
END	Indicates the end of the entire module.
FROM, IMPORT	Used to borrow procedures from a library module.

The reserved words of Modula-2 are always written in uppercase. Unlike English, Modula-2 is case-sensitive, so words like

BEGIN, begin, Begin

are taken as different words in Modula-2, although they all have the same meaning in English.

Just as English has rules of syntax which tell us how to construct correct sentences, so each programming language has its own syntax, which governs how we construct statements and programs. If we don't use the syntax correctly our statements and programs will not make any sense to the compiler, and will not therefore be executable.

The syntax of Modula-2 insists on a certain ordering of parts inside a module or program. Thus, a program always commences with a MODULE statement, this is followed by any IMPORTs required, then any declarations (which we will meet later in this appendix), the BEGIN statement, the module body, and finally the END statement.

A.3 Data handling

Most programs need data, which is manipulated by the statements in the module body to produce results of one form or another. This data comes in many forms, from weather pictures transmitted as a sequence of digits by an orbiting satellite, to a piece of text typed in by a user. Modula-2 insists that we *declare* any data before we use it. Declaring data means that we state, usually at the top of a module, all the data items we are going to use in the module body. Each data item is declared by giving it a unique name (unique to the module) by which it can be referred to in the program and stating what sort of data item it is. For example, if it is an array of real numbers or a character or a record etc.

A.3.1 Constants

Let's consider how we might write a program which calculates the number of working hours in a typical week, and prints out the result. We will assume that a working day runs from 9am to 5pm, so that the number of working hours in a day is eight. Here is one way of using declared data in such a program:

```
MODULE WorkingHours;
(* Calculate and display the number of working hours in a week. *)

FROM InOut IMPORT WriteString, WriteLn, WriteInt;
CONST
   WorkingDays = 5; (* Working days in week. *)
   DailyWorkHours = 8; (* Working hours in day. *)
   WeeklyWorkHours = WorkingDays * DailyWorkHours;
                    (* Number of working hours per week. *)

BEGIN
   WriteString("Number of working hours in a week is: ");
   WriteInt(WeeklyWorkHours, 3);
   WriteLn;
END WorkingHours.
```

This program illustrates the simplest form of data in Modula-2, constants. Constants are data items which have a fixed value, for example, the integer 42 is a constant. WorkingHours declares three constants, using the reserved word CONST, in the declaration section of the program. Each data item is given a name and this name is then used to refer to the data item throughout the module body and in other declarations. The program uses constants and procedures imported from InOut to print out the number of working hours in a week. Procedure WriteInt displays an integer number on the terminal: it must be given the integer number to display (WeeklyWorkHours in this example) and the minimum field width (number of spaces) in which to print this number (three spaces in this case).

We could have produced the same result as the above program without using declared constants:

```
MODULE WorkingHours2;
(* Calculate and display the number of working hours in a week. *)

FROM InOut IMPORT WriteString, WriteLn, WriteInt;

BEGIN
   WriteString("Number of working hours in a week is: ");
   WriteInt(40, 3);
   WriteLn;
END WorkingHours2.
```

Comparing this to the earlier version you should agree that the first program is far easier to understand. WriteInt(40, 3) could mean anything, but WriteInt(WeeklyWorkHours, 3) is much clearer. It would be even better to have declared the field width as a constant too, perhaps called FieldWidth, so that the WriteInt statement would look like this:

```
WriteInt(WeeklyWorkHours, FieldWidth);
```

This is also a good reason for choosing meaningful names for programs, procedures and data items.

The three constants used in WorkingHours are quite straightforward: WorkingDays and DailyWorkHours are given the values 5 and 8 respectively; WeekyWorkHours is a constant expression, since it contains only constants, and will have the value 40. Here are some further examples of valid Modula-2 constants and constant expressions:

```
pi = 3.1416;
FirstLetter = "A";
Greeting = "Good Morning";
TwoPi = 2.0 * pi;
```

A.3.2 Variables

Declaring constants in our programs is useful, but doesn't allow us to use data items whose values can change. For example, if we wish to write a program to read in a character from the terminal keyboard, we need to declare a data item in which to store the character. We need a data item whose value is allowed to change because we cannot know in advance which character the user of the program will type at the terminal, so we cannot set up the data item to be a constant.

Data items whose values are allowed to change are called variables; they are declared using the Modula-2 reserved word VAR. Here is an example of how we might use a variable in a program which reads a single character from the terminal keyboard and prints it out again:

```
MODULE ReadACharacter;
(* Read character from the keyboard, and write out again. *)

FROM InOut IMPORT Read, Write, WriteString, WriteLn;

VAR
   ch : CHAR;

BEGIN
   WriteString("Type a character and press return..  ");
   Read(ch);
   WriteLn;
   WriteString("You typed the character ..  ");
   Write(ch);
   WriteLn;
END ReadACharacter.
```

This program contains a declaration of one variable data item called ch. The value of ch becomes the character typed on the keyboard, which is read in by the procedure Read (Read reads a single character; Write displays a single character). The CHAR after ch declares what class of data objects ch belongs to – the class of a data object is more usually called its *type*. Type CHAR means that ch is a character (rather than an integer or a real number etc.) and can therefore take the value of any valid character, such as "!" or "g". Most implementations of Modula-2 use a set of characters called the ASCII character set. They are defined in Appendix B. The ASCII character set includes all the characters you would expect (upper and lowercase letters, digits, punctuation), and a few unusual ones.

The type of a data item is essential because it tells us two very important things about the item:

- The range of values which the data item can assume. For example, if we are using the ASCII character set there are 128 possible characters for a data item of type CHAR.

- The operations which can be performed on or with the data item. For example, addition and subtraction are valid operations for integer numbers, but not for characters.

Modula-2 provides us with some ready-made classes or types for our data items which already have their range of values and operations defined. These ready-made types are as follows:

Type name	Meaning
CHAR	Characters, for example, a, !, F.
INTEGER	Integer numbers, for example, 0, 56, 23100, -4567
CARDINAL	Positive integers, for example, 0, 432, 3, 34500
REAL	Real numbers, for example, 2.13, 0.0, -32.009, 2.3E2.

A.3.3 Identifiers

The names which we use when declaring constants and variables, such as ch and WorkingDays, are called *identifiers*. We also use identifiers for the names of procedures and modules, such as InOut, FirstLook and WriteLn. Modula-2 places certain restrictions on the characters we can use in identifiers, and the way in which those characters are arranged. Here are some valid identifiers:

```
ReadACharacter
Write
count20
newword
STOP2
dailyPayRate
```

The following identifiers are illegal for the reasons given:

BEGIN	This is a Modula-2 reserved word and reserved words cannot be used as identifiers.
day temp	Spaces are not allowed in identifiers.
night-temp	Illegal character "-".
20stop	An identifier is not allowed to start with a digit.

The valid characters for identifiers are: alphabetic, "a"– "z" and "A"– "Z", and numeric, "0"– "9" (although a numeric character cannot be the first character in an identifier). Most Modula-2 implementations do not place any restrictions on the length of identifiers, but you should be sensible about how long (or how short) you make them.

As Modula-2 is a case-sensitive language it is customary for programmers to take advantage of this by using both uppercase and lowercase characters in identifiers, to make their programs more readable. Here are some of the most commonly used ways of writing different kinds of identifiers:

- Library names, procedure and function names usually start with a capital letter, and every new word within the identifier starts with a capital letter. For example,

  ```
  InOut
  WriteString
  ```

- Variables can either be entirely in lowercase or can start with a lowercase letter and have each word within the identifier starting with a capital letter. For example,

  ```
  newword
  dailyPayRate
  ```

  We use the latter method for variables in all our program examples.

- Constants are often entirely in uppercase, or can be defined in the same way as library and procedure names. For example,

  ```
  MAXSIZE
  FieldWidth
  ```

  We have chosen to use the latter method in our program examples.

A.3.4 Expressions and assignments

So far we have only described how to declare constant values and expressions, read a data value into a variable and write things out. This doesn't allow us to do more complex operations or calculations with data. Consider the task of creating a short program to read in a number from the user and print out its square and its cube.

The algorithm for this problem is given below:

```
Ask user to enter a number
Read in the number
Square the number
Print out the square
Cube the number
Print out the cube
```

Here is the Modula-2 solution:

```
MODULE SquareAndCube;
(* This program reads in an integer number typed by the user, and
prints out the square and cube of the number. *)

FROM InOut IMPORT WriteString, WriteLn, WriteInt, ReadInt;
CONST
   FieldWidth = 6; (* Width of number display. *)
VAR
   number, square, cube : INTEGER;

BEGIN
   (* Get the number from the user. *)
   WriteString("Enter a number: ");
   ReadInt(number);
   WriteLn;

   (* Calculate the square and cube. *)
   square := number * number;
   cube := square * number;

   (* Display the results. *)
   WriteString("The square is:  ");
   WriteInt(square, FieldWidth);
   WriteLn;
   WriteString("The cube is: ");
   WriteInt(cube, FieldWidth);
   WriteLn;
END SquareAndCube.
```

The following two lines,

```
square := number * number;
cube := square * number;
```

are examples of assignment statements. The right hand sides of these assignment statements are expressions. Note that the calculation of the cube uses the previously calculated square, which saves a multiplication. The := can be read as *becomes* or *takes the value of*, thus square takes the value of number*number, and cube takes the value of square*number. Other examples of valid assignments and expressions are:

```
circumference := 2.0 * pi * radius;
answer := 6 * 7;
total := 0;
total := total + 1;
```

The final one of these calculates total+1, and assigns this value back to total itself, thus increasing the value of total by 1.

Modula-2 places certain restrictions on expressions and assignments, concerning the types of the variables and constants used. In general you are not allowed to mix variables or constants of different types in an assignment or an expression. For example, if we declare the following variables:

```
VAR
    i : INTEGER;
    c : CARDINAL;
    ch : CHAR;
```

the following assignments are illegal:

```
i := ch;
c := 1.05 * 2;
r := i + c;
```

There are some exceptions to this rule, and some ways of circumventing it, which are discussed later.

A.4 Simple data types

We have already said that Modula-2 provides several ready-made data types, so we will now look at them in more detail.

A.4.1 Type INTEGER

Modula-2's type INTEGER consists of integer numbers which may be positive, negative or zero. It does not include numbers with decimal points. The range of integers that can be used is restricted by the particular computer on which you are running Modula-2. A 16-bit computer will typically provide a range of -32768 to +32767.

We can do all the expected operations on data items of type INTEGER:

+	addition
-	subtraction and negation
*	multiplication
DIV	integer division
MOD	modulus/remainder

The operations +, - and * are straightforward, they act on integers to produce integer results, but why do we have DIV instead of the more obvious / operator? DIV is integer division and it always gives an integer result. The statement

```
x := y DIV z;
```

assigns to x the truncated result of dividing y by z. The need for a division operator which produces an integer result is clearer when we remember that mixing different types in expressions and assignments is not generally acceptable. Consider the result of 5/2, which is 2.5. This is a real number and cannot be assigned to a variable of type INTEGER (we will meet type REAL later). However 5 DIV 2 produces an integer result, 2, which can be assigned to a variable of type INTEGER. It should also be remembered that division by zero is undefined on a computer (because computers have considerable trouble with the concept of infinity) and any attempt to do this will cause a program to fail as soon as the computer tries to execute the division.

The other strange operation for type INTEGER is called MOD, which is short for modulus.

```
x := y MOD z;
```

This gives the (integer) remainder of y divided by z. Here are some examples of DIV and MOD,

```
4 DIV 2 = 2
10 DIV 3 = 3
10 MOD 3 = 1
4 MOD 2 = 0
2 MOD 5 = 2
```

Let's consider a small problem where we might need to use integer data. Let us take the problem of calculating a person's annual income tax bill. First we must define the problem more clearly.

We want to calculate a tax payer's yearly tax bill, given his yearly income and the number of children he has. Assume that one third of the income (less any allowances) must be paid as tax. There is a personal allowance of £6000, and an allowance of £1000 per child. An initial algorithm for solving this problem will be:

```
Get annual income from user
Get number of children from user
Calculate total amount of allowances
Calculate total amount of taxable income
Calculate tax payable
Display tax payable
```

Get annual income and *Get number of children* are quite straightforward, consisting simply of displaying appropriate messages and reading in numbers. The three calculations are also simple:

Calculate total amount of allowances:
total allowances = (£1000 * number of children) + £6000

Calculate total amount of taxable income:
taxable income = income - total allowances

Calculate tax payable:
tax payable = 1/3 * taxable income

We can put all this together in a Modula-2 program:

```
MODULE Taxes;
(* Program to calculate amount of tax payable per year by a tax payer,
given his yearly income and the number of children he has.  The
program calculates the tax payable to be one third of the annual
income after any allowances have been deducted.  There is a
personal allowance of £6000 and an allowance of £1000 per child. *)

FROM InOut IMPORT WriteString, WriteLn, WriteInt, ReadInt;

CONST
   ChildAllowance = 1000; (* Allowance per child. *)
   PersonalAllowance = 6000;
   FieldWidth = 6; (* Number display width. *)

VAR
   income : INTEGER; (* Total yearly income. *)
   numberOfChildren : INTEGER;
   totalAllowances : INTEGER; (* Personal + children. *)
   taxableIncome : INTEGER; (* Income - allowances. *)
   taxPayable : INTEGER; (* Total tax payable. *)

BEGIN
   (* Get income and number of children from user. *)
   WriteString("Enter total yearly income (For example, 12500): ");
   ReadInt(income);
   WriteLn;
   WriteString("Enter number of children:  ");
   ReadInt(numberOfChildren);
   WriteLn;

   (* Calculate total allowances. *)
   totalAllowances := (numberOfChildren *
            ChildAllowance) + PersonalAllowance;
```

```
    (* Calculate taxable income. *)
    taxableIncome := income - totalAllowances;

    (* Calculate tax payable. *)
    taxPayable := taxableIncome DIV 3;

    (* Tell user tax payable. *);
    WriteLn;
    WriteString("Tax payable is:  ");
    WriteInt(taxPayable, FieldWidth);
END Taxes.
```

Note the use of DIV to obtain an integer result, and how the algorithm description provides some of the comments for the final implementation in Modula-2.

A.4.2 Type CARDINAL

Modula-2's type CARDINAL is similar to INTEGER in that it also refers to the counting numbers, that is positive whole numbers and zero. On a 16-bit computer a typical range for CARDINAL is 0 to +65535. Since CARDINAL only covers positive integers, it has a larger positive range than that of type INTEGER. The operations of type INTEGER are also valid for CARDINAL.

We will consider a small problem in which we can use CARDINAL numbers – reading in a positive number, and displaying its value in octal (base 8) and hexadecimal (base 16). The initial algorithm for this problem is very simple:

```
Get number from user
Display value of number in octal
Display value of number in hexadecimal
```

You are probably thinking that converting a number from decimal into octal and hexadecimal is not quite such a small problem as we have suggested. If we really did have to write conversion procedures then it wouldn't be so small, but the problem stated that the number should be displayed in octal and hexadecimal – it didn't mention anything about converting the number. Still, you may be saying, this is the same problem – just displaying a decimal number in octal and hexadecimal means converting it. Luckily we can cheat! In the Modula-2 tradition of borrowing ready-made problem solutions from libraries, we can borrow the procedures WriteOct and WriteHex from library module InOut. WriteOct, when given a decimal number, displays it on the terminal in octal, and WriteHex (not surprisingly) will display it in hexadecimal. So our problem is practically solved:

```
MODULE OctHex;
(* Read a positive integer from the terminal, and display
it again in octal (base 8) and hexadecimal (base 16). *)

FROM InOut IMPORT WriteString, WriteLn, WriteOct, WriteHex,
ReadCard;

CONST
   FieldWidth = 6; (* Number display width. *)
VAR
   number : CARDINAL;

BEGIN
   (* Ask user to enter a number. *)
   WriteString("This program displays a given decimal number in
octal and in hexadecimal.");
   WriteLn;
   WriteString("Enter a (positive) integer: ");
   ReadCard(number);
   WriteLn;

   (* Display in octal. *)
   WriteString("The number in octal is: ");
   WriteOct(number, FieldWidth);
   WriteLn;

   (* Display in hexadecimal. *)
   WriteString("The number in hexadecimal is: ");
   WriteHex(number, FieldWidth);
   WriteLn;
END OctHex.
```

A.4.3 Type REAL

Many applications require real numbers, and Modula-2 provides type REAL for such situations. Some examples of valid REAL numbers in Modula-2 are:

0.0032
-5.6
8.
897.0

Note that there must always be at least one digit before the decimal point, but there don't have to be any digits after the decimal point.

Modula-2 also allows us to represent real numbers using exponential notation. This can be very useful for representing very large or very small numbers. Here are some examples of exponential notation:

32.124E2	which is	3212.4
1E10	which is	10000000000.0
12.2E1	which is	122.0
2.3E-6	which is	0.0000023

Most of the operations available for REAL are the same as those for INTEGER and CARDINAL, except for the division operator which returns a real result:

+ addition

- subtraction and negation

* multiplication

/ real division, this gives a REAL result.

Modula-2 also provides several libraries of extra operations for real numbers: in some Modula-2 implementations InOut contains input and output facilities for reading in and displaying real numbers, but in others you may find real number input and output in a separate library called RealInOut. There is also usually a library called MathLib0, which contains mathematical functions such as sin, cos etc.

We need to use real numbers in many mathematical problems, for example, consider writing a program which will calculate the circumference and area of a circle when given its radius. The algorithm for this problem is quite simple:

```
Get the radius from the user
Calculate the circumference
Print out the result
Calculate the area
Print out the result
```

In Modula-2:

```
MODULE Circles;
(* Given the radius of a circle, calculate its circumference & area. *)
FROM InOut IMPORT WriteString, WriteLn, ReadReal, WriteReal;
CONST
   FieldWidth = 6; (* Number display width. *)
   SigDigits = 4; (* Number of significant digits to display. *)
   Pi = 3.1416; (* Or more accurately, Pi := 4.0 * ArcTan(1.0); *)
```

```
VAR
   radius, circumference, area : REAL;

BEGIN
   (* Ask user to enter radius. *)
   WriteString("Enter radius of circle: ");
   ReadReal(radius);
   WriteLn;
   (* Calculate and display circumference. *)
   circumference := 2.0 * Pi * radius;
   WriteString("The circumference is:  ");
   (* Some versions of WriteReal require an extra parameter,
   indicating the number of significant digits to display. *)
   WriteReal(circumference, FieldWidth, SigDigits);
   WriteLn;
   (* Calculate and display area. *)
   area := Pi * radius * radius;
   WriteString("The area is:  ");
   WriteReal(area, FieldWidth, SigDigits);
   WriteLn;
END Circles.
```

Precision

We have to be very careful when using numbers (particularly real numbers, very large numbers, and very small numbers) on a computer, because their precision depends on the number of significant digits to which the computer can store them. When using a 32-bit word, seven significant digits is normal. This means that two numbers which differ in only the eighth significant digit will be indistinguishable to the computer. For example,

2000000.0 + 0.00000001

will give the result

2000000.0

You should never expect calculations done on a computer to be exact – and in complex calculations expect errors that are caused by rounding errors, which are accumulating at every stage of the calculation. When accuracy is needed you may have to increase the word length for the arithmetic to 64-bits, that is *LONG* words. In addition, always carefully consider the order in which calculations are made. Errors can be cancelled out or compounded by choosing the appropriate order of operations.

A.4.4 Type CHAR

Modula-2's type CHAR allows our programs to use character data. Characters are not stored as such inside the computer: instead each character is assigned a number, called its ordinal value, which is used to represent it inside the computer. Each character has a different ordinal value. Most implementations of Modula-2 use a standard set of ordinal values called the ASCII set. Many different programming languages and computers represent characters using the ASCII representation. Appendix B contains the ASCII representations of the 128 characters of type CHAR, giving their ordinal values in decimal, octal (base 8) and hexadecimal (base 16).

If you look at the ASCII table you will see that the different characters are grouped together in sensible blocks, so that all the digits are together, as are the lowercase alphabet and the uppercase alphabet. Because of this, Modula-2 allows us to use the relational operators to do direct comparisons between the characters within each grouping, thus

"A" < "B" < "C" < .... < "Z"
"a" < "b" < "c" < .... < "z"
"0" < "1" < "2" < .... < "9".

It is sometimes useful to know the *ordinal* value of a character, so Modula-2 provides an operation, ORD, for doing this.

ORD("x") = 120
ORD("A") = 65

The ordinal values range from 0 to 127, one for each of the 128 characters, and ORD returns the values as CARDINAL numbers. But remember, not all of these characters are printable, especially those with the lower ordinal values. We can also go in the opposite direction, starting with an ordinal value and obtaining the corresponding character, using an operation called CHR. For example,

CHR(120) = "x"
CHR(65) = "A".

CHR and ORD are mutually inverse, so

CHR(ORD(120)) = "x",
ORD(CHR("x")) = 120.

We can use ordinal values to write a program which reads a lowercase letter, and writes it out again in uppercase. How can we do this? If we look at the ASCII table, we can see that for each letter the ordinal value of the lowercase letter is 32 higher than that of the corresponding uppercase letter. For example, "A" has ordinal value 65, and "a" has ordinal value 92. Thus the assignment

```
upperCh := CHR( ORD(lowerCh) - 32 );
```

where upperCh and lowerCh are of type CHAR, and lowerCh is a lowercase letter, will assign the corresponding uppercase letter to upperCh. Here is the algorithm:

```
Read a character
Convert to uppercase character
Display uppercase character
```

The complete program is very short:

```
MODULE ToUpper;
(* Read in a lower case letter and print it out again in uppercase.*)

FROM InOut IMPORT WriteString, WriteLn, Write, Read;

VAR
   lowerCh, upperCh : CHAR;

BEGIN
   (* Read in character. *)
   WriteString("Enter a lowercase letter:  ");
   Read(lowerCh);
   WriteLn;
   (* Find corresponding uppercase character. *)
   upperCh := CHR( ORD(lowerCh) - 32 );
   (* Write out resulting character. *)
   WriteString("The character in uppercase is: ");
   Write(upperCh);
   WriteLn;
END ToUpper.
```

You will probably have noticed that this program can't cope with invalid input. What happens if the user enters a space or a question mark instead of a lowercase letter? (Hint: look at the ASCII table in Appendix B.)

A.5 Sequence control

Our Modula-2 programs have so far only used direct sequencing, where statements are executed in the order in which they appear. In the earlier section on algorithm design we discussed some other methods of sequence control:

Conditional branching	if x then do y otherwise do z
Bounded iteration	do y exactly n times
Unbounded iteration	1. while x do y 2. do y until x.

Modula-2 provides constructs which match these forms of sequence control. We will look at how these constructs are implemented in Modula-2 in the following sections.

A.6 Conditional branching

This is done with the IF statement, which is of the form

```
IF condition 1 THEN statement sequence 1
ELSIF condition 2 THEN statement sequence 2
ELSIF condition 3 THEN statement sequence 3
- - - -
ELSIF condition n - 1 THEN statement sequence n - 1
ELSE statement sequence n
END;
```

Where a statement sequence is evaluated only if its associated Boolean expression condition is TRUE, otherwise the statement sequence following ELSE is executed.

A.6.1 Boolean expressions and type BOOLEAN

The conditions we use in IF statements are called *Boolean expressions* – the value of a Boolean expression is either true or false, there are no other possibilities. The Boolean value of an expression is its *truth value* – whether it is true or whether it is false. For example,

3 > 2	has Boolean value	true
1 = 1	has Boolean value	true
10 > 12	has Boolean value	false
7 <= 3	has Boolean value	false.

The operators used here are called relational operators, some of which we met briefly in the section on type CHAR. Here is a full list:

Symbol	Meaning
<	less than
>	greater than
<=	less than or equal to
>=	greater than or equal to
=	equals
# or <>	not equal to.

The result of a relational operator is always a Boolean value. Modula-2 allows the use of Boolean values by providing type BOOLEAN which has two possible values,

TRUE and FALSE. A variable of type BOOLEAN can therefore only be TRUE or FALSE. There are also three operators for BOOLEAN: AND, OR and NOT, which can be used on BOOLEAN variables and expressions. We can define these operations with a truth table:

x	y	NOT x	x AND y	x OR y
TRUE	TRUE	FALSE	TRUE	TRUE
TRUE	FALSE	FALSE	FALSE	TRUE
FALSE	TRUE	TRUE	FALSE	TRUE
FALSE	FALSE	TRUE	FALSE	FALSE

Here are some examples of BOOLEAN expressions and operators in use:

```
ReadCard(x);
ReadCard(y);
IF x >= y THEN
   max := x;
ELSE
   max := y;
END;

noBugs := TRUE;
programWorks := FALSE;
IF programWorks AND noBugs THEN
   programmerHappy := TRUE;
ELSE
   programmerHappy := FALSE;
END;

summer := (temperature >= 75) AND sunny;
IF summer THEN
   WriteString("Time for a holiday!");
END;
```

In the above code fragments noBugs, programWorks, programmerHappy and summer are all BOOLEAN variables. A common mistake made when using BOOLEAN variables is to assume that a statement such as:

```
WriteString(programmerHappy);
```

will print out either TRUE or FALSE, depending on the Boolean value of the given variable, in this case programmerHappy. This does **not** work – TRUE and FALSE are simply names for some internal representation of type BOOLEAN. WriteString expects to be given a string of characters between quotes, such as "hello !", which it will write out on the terminal, or a variable of type ARRAY OF CHAR, which we will meet later. The variable programmerHappy is neither a string of characters between quote marks nor of type ARRAY OF CHAR (in fact it is of type BOOLEAN), so WriteString cannot print it. If you want to print out the Boolean value of an expression or variable you must write the code to do so yourself, for example:

```
IF programmerHappy THEN
   WriteString("TRUE");
ELSE
   WriteString("FALSE");
END;
```

You must remember that the string of characters represented by "TRUE" is not the same as the Boolean value TRUE. Try experimenting to see what error messages your compiler gives when you give WriteString something unexpected to display.

A.6.2 An alternative to IF – the CASE statement

The CASE statement is another form of conditional branch, which is generally thought to be more elegant than the IF statement in some situations. Here is an example of a CASE statement:

```
CASE programmerHappy OF
   FALSE : WriteString("FALSE");
  | TRUE : WriteString("TRUE")
END;
```

This has exactly the same effect as the previous IF statement. A CASE statement can also have a trailing ELSE, which acts exactly like the ELSE of an IF statement, being a catch-all for cases which don't meet any of the given conditions:

```
CASE day OF
     1 :  WriteString("Monday")
   | 2 :  WriteString("Tuesday")
   | 3 :  WriteString("Wednesday")
   | 4 :  WriteString("Thursday")
   | 5 :  WriteString("Friday")
   | 6 :  WriteString("Saturday");
          WriteLn;
          WriteString("Don't get up today!")
   | 7 :  WriteString("Sunday");
          WriteLn;
          WriteString("Mow the lawn.");
ELSE
      WriteString("Invalid day number.");
END;
```

The ELSE statement will be entered if day is not 1, 2, 3, 4, 5, 6, or 7.

The general form of a CASE statement is given below:

```
CASE expression OF
        case-label-1 : statement-sequence-1;
   |    case-label-2 : statement-sequence-2;
   |    case-label-3 : statement-sequence-3;
ELSE
   statement-sequence;
END;
```

The vertical bar separates each choice in the CASE, and is needed because the statement sequence associated with each choice can be one statement or many statements.

The case labels must be constants, so the following CASE statement is illegal:

```
CASE price OF
      <= 20 : canBuy := TRUE;
   |  > 20 : canBuy := FALSE;
END;
```

If more than one label applies to a particular case, then the labels can be separated by commas, that is

```
CASE character OF
        "Y", "y" : WriteString("Yes");
   |    "N", "n" : WriteString("No");
ELSE
   WriteString("Invalid character");
END;
```

The main difference between the CASE and the IF concerns the ELSE clause. In an IF statement, if the ELSE clause is missing and all the choices in the IF fail, control simply falls through to the statement which comes after the end of the IF statement. However, in a CASE statement without an ELSE clause, if all the choices in the CASE fail when the code is run, the program itself will fail immediately.

A.7 Unbounded iteration

Modula-2 provides constructs which mirror both *while x do y* and *do y until x*. These are called WHILE loops and REPEAT loops respectively.

A.7.1 The WHILE loop

Consider the problem of reading in a string of characters one at a time, until some *end of text* character is read. We have already seen an algorithm for this problem:

```
Read a character
While character isn't "." do
   Process character
   Read next character
Endwhile
```

We can now write this in Modula-2, using a WHILE loop:

```
Read(ch);
WHILE ch <> "." DO
   (* Here we would process ch in some way. *)
   Read(ch);
END;
```

The END statement corresponds to the Endwhile statement in our algorithm. The Modula-2 WHILE tests the condition at the top of the loop, before the statements in the body of the loop are executed. In our example, if the first character typed is "." the test ch <> "." will fail on the first attempt and the body of the loop will never be executed, causing control to move to the statement following the end of the loop. Here is a complete program which counts the occurrences of a given letter in a string of characters typed in at the terminal. The user must enter both the letter to be counted and the text. The algorithm will be as follows:

```
Read letter to count
Set count to zero
Read text, adding one to count each time letter occurs
Display count
```

This can be refined further to produce a more detailed algorithm:

```
Ask user what letter to count
Ask user to enter text, terminated by a full stop
Set letterCount to zero
Read a character
While character isn't "." do
   If character = letter then
      Add one to letterCount
   Endif
   Read next character
Endwhile
Display letterCount
```

Writing this in Modula-2 we obtain the following program:

```
MODULE  LetterCounter;
(* Count the occurrences of a given letter (entered by the user) in a
string of characters, which is typed in at the terminal by the user.
The character string must be terminated by a full stop.  A letter must
be an alphabetic character "a".."z" or "A".."Z". *)

FROM InOut IMPORT WriteString, WriteLn, WriteCard, Read;

CONST
   FullStop = "."; (* Terminates input string. *)
   FieldWidth = 3; (* Number display width. *)

VAR
   letter : CHAR; (* Letter to be counted. *)
   ch : CHAR; (* Character read in. *)
   letterCount : CARDINAL; (* Occurrences of letter. *)

BEGIN
   (* Ask user to enter letter to be counted. *)
   WriteLn;
   WriteString("Enter letter to be counted ");
   WriteString ('"a".."z "or "A".."Z"): ');
   Read(letter);
   WriteLn;
   IF ((letter >= "a") AND (letter <= "z")) OR
      ((letter >= "A") AND (letter <= "Z")) THEN
      (* We have a valid letter. *)
      letterCount := 0;

      (* Ask user to enter text. *)
      WriteString("Enter text, ending with a full stop.");
      WriteLn;

      (* Read in characters and count occurrences. *)
      Read(ch);
      WHILE ch <> FullStop DO
         IF ch = letter THEN
            (* Add one to letterCount. *)
            letterCount := letterCount + 1;
         END;
         (* Read next character. *)
         Read(ch);
      END;
```

```
        (* Display total occurrences of letter. *)
        WriteLn;
        WriteString("The number of occurrences is: ");
        WriteCard(letterCount, FieldWidth);
        WriteLn;
    ELSE (* Not a valid character. *)
        (* Display an error message and finish. *)
        WriteLn;
        WriteString("Not a valid character.");
        WriteLn;
    END; (* IF *)
END LetterCounter.
```

Note that we have added some error checking to make sure that the user only enters a valid character to be counted. This is done by an IF statement which controls entry to the main body of the program, so that the text is only requested and read if the user has given a valid character to count, that is. a letter. If the character given is invalid the ELSE clause will be entered, and an error message is printed out.

A.7.2 The REPEAT loop

This type of loop is most useful when some task has to be performed at least once. If we return to one of our earlier programs, SquareAndCube, which read in an integer and printed out its square and its cube, we can modify this program so that it can be used for more than one number in each execution. To do this we will alter the algorithm first. The initial algorithm for the program was:

```
Ask user to enter a number
Read in the number
Square the number
Print out the square
Cube the number
Print out the cube
```

Now we want an iterative construct which can go around this whole algorithm, so that the user is asked repeatedly to enter a number. This also suggests that we need to consider how the user is to stop the program, so that it doesn't keep asking for numbers until the next power cut. One way would be to ask the user each time round the iteration if another number is to be entered, and stop the iteration if the response is no. If we use a do-loop for the iteration we need a condition to test at the end of the loop.

```
Do the following
    Ask user to enter a number
    Read in the number
    Square the number
    Print out the square
```

```
      Cube the number
      Print out the cube
      Ask if user wants to enter another number
      Read in the response typed
   Until the response is negative
```

Remember, the body of a do-loop is executed at least once, because the test for stopping the iteration is at the bottom of the loop. This is the opposite situation to a while loop, where the test is at the top, so that the body of the loop need not be executed at all.

This algorithm can now be written in Modula-2, using the equivalent of do y until x – the REPEAT loop, which is of the form:

```
REPEAT
   (* Statements go here. *)
UNTIL condition;
```

where condition is a Boolean variable or expression.

Here is the program, incorporating such a loop:

```
MODULE SquareCube2;
(* Reads positive integers from the terminal and displays their
squares and cubes. *)

FROM InOut IMPORT WriteString, WriteLn, WriteInt, ReadInt, Read;

VAR
   number, square, cube : INTEGER;
   response, eol : CHAR;

BEGIN
   number := 0;
   REPEAT
      (* Get the number from the user. *)
      WriteString("Enter a number: ");
      ReadInt(number); Read(eol);

      (* Calculate the square and cube. *)
      square := number * number;
      cube := square * number;
      (* Display the results. *)
      WriteString("The square is:  ");
```

```
        WriteInt(square, FieldWidth);
        WriteLn;
        WriteString("The cube is:  ");
        WriteInt(cube, FieldWidth);
        WriteLn;

        (* Find out if user wants to stop. *)
        WriteString("Enter another number? (y/n): ");
        Read(response); Read(eol);
    UNTIL (response = "n") OR (response = "N");
END SquareCube2.
```

If you examine the code closely you will see that the iteration (and the program) will finish when the user types "n", and continue if any other character (not just a "y") is typed. The answer "n" causes BOOLEAN variable stop to be set to TRUE, so the condition on the UNTIL is now true, stopping the iteration and exiting the REPEAT loop.

There is also something in the code which you may find surprising. After the ReadInt(number) and Read(response) statements we have a Read(eol) statement, where eol is declared as a CHAR variable. You are probably wondering why we need to read another character after both ReadInt(number) and Read(response). When you type in the number and the response you also press the return (or enter) key to indicate that you have finished typing. The Read(eol) statement reads the return (also called the end-of-line character or eol) that you type, and puts it into the variable eol. We don't do anything with this variable, but if we don't read the return character the next Read statement will find it waiting to be read in. Try removing these two Reads and see what happens to the program.

Some implementations of ReadInt and Read will read and throw away the return that you type and in such cases the two extra Read statements will have to be removed for the program to work correctly.

A.7.3 The LOOP

There is yet another loop in Modula-2 which can provide unbounded iteration – this is called the LOOP statement. A LOOP statement looks like this:

```
LOOP
    statement-sequence
    IF condition THEN
        EXIT;
    END;
    statement-sequence
END;
```

When the condition to the IF statement is true, the EXIT statement will be executed, which causes control to leave the LOOP and move to the next statement after the end of the LOOP. The LOOP construct is useful in situations where you want to exit from the middle of a loop rather than from the top or the bottom. Alternatively, it can be used to produce an infinite loop by leaving out the EXIT statement. Of course, one usually wants to avoid programs with infinite loops which never terminate, but some programming situations, such as multi-programming, do need non-exiting loops. In most cases LOOPs are better written using WHILE or REPEAT loops. Here is an example where use of LOOP is quite valid:

```
LOOP
   WriteString("Enter number to square: ");
   ReadInt(number);   Read(eol);
   WriteLn;
   IF number = 0 THEN
      EXIT;
   END;
   (* Process number. *)
   number := number * number;
   WriteString("The square is:  ");
   WriteInt(number, 6);
   WriteLn;
END;
```

A.8 Bounded iteration

This type of iteration takes the form *do x exactly y times*. It is particularly useful when an algorithm needs to do a task or tasks a fixed number of times. You will also find bounded iteration is useful when using arrays (another means of storing data, which will be discussed later).

A.8.1 The FOR loop

We will use bounded iteration to display a message on the terminal a fixed number of times. The Modula-2 form of bounded iteration is called the FOR loop. FOR loops often appear at first glance to be rather confusing constructs. Here is a FOR loop which will display the message "hello" five times:

```
FOR count := 1 TO 5 DO
   WriteString("hello");
   WriteLn;
END;
```

The confusing part is at the top of the loop, where we have

```
FOR count := 1 TO 5 DO
```

You may well be wondering what count is for. Count will have been declared as a variable of type INTEGER or CARDINAL, and it is called the *control variable* of the FOR loop. Each time round the loop count will be automatically incremented by 1. The body of the loop is executed for each value of count, from 1 up to and including 5. Note that the control variable doesn't have to be called count, it can be called anything you like, so long as it is declared as a variable of type INTEGER or CARDINAL.

The general form of a FOR loop is slightly more complicated:

```
FOR controlVariable := expression1 TO expression2
            BY constantExpression DO
     statement sequence
END;
```

Expression1 is the starting value for controlVariable, and expression2 is the limit. ConstantExpression is the increment or decrement, to be applied to controlVariable each time round the loop; if constantExpression is positive it is an increment, if negative it is a decrement. If BY constantExpression is missing then an increment of 1 is assumed. Note that the control variable must be either INTEGER or CARDINAL, **not** REAL. The control variable is incremented (or decremented) each time round the loop until its value passes that of the limit (expression-2).

The control variable can be referred to inside the FOR loop, for example:

```
FOR c := 2 TO 10 BY 2 DO
   WriteCard(c,2);
   WriteLn
END;
```

will print out:

```
   2     4     6     8     10
```

But once the FOR loop has been exited and control has transferred to the next statement in the program, the value of the control variable becomes undefined, and no attempt should be made to use it without assigning a new value to it. Thus, if we did a WriteCard(c,2) after the above FOR loop we might expect the value 10 to be printed out again (and in some implementations it will be!), but Modula-2 rules state that there is no guarantee of this being the case. It is therefore extremely bad programming practice to try to use the control variable's value after the end of the FOR loop unless you assign a new value to it first.

A.9 User-defined scalar data types

The data types we have looked at so far are all completely provided by Modula-2. For example, type CARDINAL comes complete with the range of values allowed for examples of the type (which will vary between different computers), and the set of operations allowed on the type. As we have seen from Chapter 1, such simple data types are not sufficient for solving many problems. Modula-2 provides a way for users to define their own types, and to build *structured data types* which allow more than one item to be stored in a single variable of such a type. Structured data types are extremely important for implementing data abstractions.

The data types we have seen so far are all *scalar data types*. The values of a scalar type are indivisible or atomic objects, that is they cannot be split up into smaller objects. The values of a structured type are not atomic objects, instead each value can be split into several other objects. Put another way, a value of a structured type is a compound or aggregate of several other values. A queue at a bus stop can be thought of as a single object, but it can also be broken down into smaller objects – the people which make up the queue.

There are two scalar types we have not looked at so far, because they are user-defined types, and not provided in a fully defined state by Modula-2 – enumeration types and subranges.

A.9.1 Enumeration types

These are a form of do-it-yourself type, which the user can define. For most types there is an implicit range of values which a variable of the type can assume, but in an enumeration the possible values are explicitly stated or *enumerated* by the programmer. The values of an enumeration type, called *identifiers*, are actually names which are chosen by the programmer. Here are some examples of enumeration types:

```
TYPE
    Colours = (blue, red, green);
    Days = (Monday, Tuesday, Wednesday, Thursday,
        Friday, Saturday, Sunday);
```

In effect, we are defining constants, because each identifier in the enumerated type is a constant of the data type. A particular identifier can only appear in one enumeration type in a program, so

```
TYPE
    PrimaryColours = (blue, red, green);
    Colours = (blue, red, green, yellow, cyan, orange);
```

will not be allowed.

The items of an enumerated type appear in a well-defined order – the order in which they are declared in the enumeration. This order defines the results of the relational operators on items in an enumeration type. Each item in an enumeration has a value associated with its position in the enumeration, called its *ordinal value*. This is similar in concept to the ordinal values of the characters in the ASCII character set.

The first item in an enumeration always has ordinal value zero. Given the following enumeration type,

```
TYPE
   Car = (Peugeot, Renault, Ferrari, Ford, Rover);
```

the ordinal values of the items are:

Peugeot	0
Renault	1
Ferrari	2
Ford	3
Rover	4

The ordinal values are worked out for you by Modula-2, and you can refer to them by using the ORD and VAL operations.

What operations can we perform on an enumeration type? All the relational operators such as >, <=, # etc. are valid for enumerations, and additionally,

ORD	Ordinal value
VAL	Inverse of ORD
INC	Increment
DEC	Decrement

Given the following declarations,

```
TYPE
   CarParts = (Chassis, Engine, Gears, Wheels, Lights);

VAR
   part : CarParts;
   number : CARDINAL;
```

we can do the following assignments:

```
part := Engine;            (* Part gets value Engine. *)
number := ORD(part);       (* Number gets value 1. *)
part := VAL(CarParts, 3);  (* Part gets value Wheels. *)
part := DEC(part);         (* Part gets value Gears. *)
```

However, these assignments are invalid:

```
part := Exhaust;           (* Exhaust isn't in CarParts. *)
part := VAL(CarParts, 12); (* No item in CarParts with this
                              ordinal value. *)
```

Enumeration types can be used to add clarity to a program. For example, the months of the year are widely used in many business and accounting packages, and whilst they can be referred to by number (from 1 to 12 say), it is clearer to declare a suitable enumeration which names the months.

A.9.2 Subranges

Sometimes we might want to restrict the range of a scalar data type, for example,

```
TYPE
    Sixties = [1960..1969];
    Capitals = ["A".."Z"];
    Range = [-1..5];
```

A subrange type is declared by giving it a name (which should not clash with any existing type names), and declaring the range in square brackets, as shown above. The first value is the *lower bound* of the range (the lowest value a variable of this type can assume) and this is separated by two full stops from the *upper bound* (the highest allowable value for a variable of this type).

Given the above type declarations, if we have a variable of type Sixties it is only allowed to take values from 1960 to 1969 (inclusive). If we try to assign a value outside this range, for example, 1990 or -231, the program will immediately abort with an appropriate error message, such as *subrange out of bounds*. Similarly, we cannot assign a lower case letter to a variable of type Capitals, nor can we assign the numbers 34 or -3 to a variable of type Range. A variable of a subrange type can only assume one value from the subrange at any one time.

Every subrange will be a contiguous subset of a scalar data type (such as CARDINAL, INTEGER or CHAR), but not type REAL. By *contiguous* we mean that the values must occur next to each other, with no gaps between them. Luckily, the Modula-2 way of declaring a subrange makes it difficult to declare a non-contiguous subrange!

The scalar type of which the subrange is a subset is called the *base type* of the subrange. The compiler works out the base type at compilation time, by looking at the values of the lower and upper bounds. For example, the base type for Sixties is type CARDINAL, the base type for Capitals is type CHAR, and that for Range is INTEGER. Mixing types in a subrange is illegal, and if you think about it, doesn't make sense anyway. The following subranges are illegal:

```
LetterNumber = ["a"..10];
Backwards = [12..0];
Reals = [3.0..6.0];
```

The first of these is illegal because it mixes two types (and is therefore meaningless); the second is illegal because it is in the wrong order, it should be [0..12]; the third is illegal because it uses real numbers.

We can, if required, declare a variable to be a subrange without using a type declaration to name the subrange, so we could have:

```
VAR
    capitalLetters : ["A".."Z"];
    sixties : [1960..1969];
```

but in general it is better to declare an appropriate type, especially if you have several variables declared with the same subrange.

You need to be careful not to over-use subranges in your programs. Although they can prevent variables going out of range, the way in which they do so is not very elegant – if a subrange variable goes outside the appropriate range your program will abort immediately. This is not a good way of coping with an error, so be sure to include code in your program which checks to see if a value is invalid before it is assigned to a subrange, and takes appropriate action if it is. For example, if we have the variables,

```
    hippyYear : Sixties;
    year : CARDINAL;
```

we might have the following check:

```
WriteString("Which year in the sixties?  ");
ReadCard(year);
WriteLn;
WHILE (year < 1960) OR (year > 1969) DO
    WriteString("Invalid year, try again:  ");
    ReadCard(year);
    WriteLn;
END;
hippyYear := year;
```

In the above code fragment we use an ordinary CARDINAL variable to read in the value of the year entered by the user, instead of using hippyYear. This prevents the program aborting if the user types a year outside the given range. A WHILE loop is used to force the user to enter a valid year. Only when the loop is finished do we assign the year read in to hippyYear.

A.10 Structured data types

We have so far shown how to declare single data items of a particular type, but many situations need to use groups of data items. For example, if we want to read in a word typed at the terminal, we would really like to be able to store the characters as one data item, rather than putting each character into a separate variable. If we have to store the characters of a word in separate variables the problems are two-fold. Firstly we need as many variables as there are characters in the word, so this might mean anything from one to twenty variables (or more), and secondly we must declare all twenty variables, even though most of the time we will only be using five or ten, because we don't know beforehand how large each word will be.

Similarly, if we need to read in a list of daytime temperatures and perform several operations on this list, we would like to have a way of storing these temperatures all together, so that we can refer to them collectively by one name, and still access each one individually when needed.

A.10.1 The SET type

The simplest form of structured data type is the SET data type. In Modula-2, sets are a limited implementation of mathematical sets; that is unordered collections of objects chosen from some universal set.

Sets can cause problems because they may be confused with enumerations or subranges. In fact, sets can be built out of enumerations and subranges. For example, given the following enumeration, representing possible faults in a car:

```
TYPE
    Faults = (BatteryFlat, AlternatorDead, NoLight, NotSparking);
```

then we can declare a set type to hold the set of faults which might belong to one particular car:

```
TYPE
    FaultSet : SET OF Faults;
```

In this case our universal set is the enumeration Faults, and the set we build can contain zero or more objects from this universal set. If we have a variable carFaults, which is of type FaultSet, we can initialise it to be the empty set (the set with no elements) by the following assignment:

```
carFaults := FaultSet{};
```

This is a rather strange assignment statement, so what does it all mean? First of all, we use curly brackets { } to indicate a particular set in Modula-2. In Modula-2, every set type we declare has a *base type*. The base type of a set is the type of the universal set from which our elements are being drawn. We already know that in the above example the universal set is the enumeration of possible car faults, so the base type of the set FaultSet is Faults.

```
TYPE
    BinaryDigits = SET OF [0..1];
    OctalDigits = SET OF [0..7];
```

In these examples we have declared our sets to use subranges of type CARDINAL as their universal sets. This means that the base types of BinaryDigits and OctalDigits are the same – type CARDINAL. If we have a set {1}, is it of type BinaryDigits or is it of type OctalDigits? To prevent such ambiguity in our programs, Modula-2 insists that we always indicate what type a set belongs to. So, for example, given the variables,

```
VAR
    binary : BinaryDigits;
    octal : OctalDigits;
```

the following assignments are possible:

```
    binary := BinaryDigits{1};
    octal := OctalDigits{1, 3, 5, 7};
```

We indicate the type of a set by preceding the set in curly brackets by the name of the type to which it belongs.

Most of the time, we don't want to state the values in a set; instead we want to be able just to add and remove values, and to see if a particular value is actually in the set. The set of car faults is one example where we would want to make the fault set for a particular car initially empty, and then add faults into the set as they are spotted. Once we have built a suitable fault set for the car, we might pass it onto another part of the program, which uses the set to produce a fault report.

To do this, Modula-2 provides operations for adding items to a set and removing items from a set. To add an object into a set we use the INCL operation (short for *include*), and to remove an object from a set we use the EXCL operation (short for *exclude*).

Let's see an example of a set in use. We will design a small program which uses FaultSet and Faults to build a set of faults for a car, entered by the user. Here is the initial algorithm:

```
Initialise the fault set to empty
Tell the user the names and numbers of the faults
Repeat the following
    Ask the user to enter a fault number
    Read fault number
    If fault number is valid then
        Add corresponding fault to fault set
    Otherwise
        Tell user that fault number is invalid
    EndIf
    Ask if user wants to enter another fault number
    Read response
Until the response is no
```

In Modula-2 we will have the following code:

```
MODULE FaultyCars;
(* Build a set of faults for a particular car. *)

FROM InOut IMPORT WriteString, WriteLn, ReadInt, Read;
TYPE
   Faults = (BatteryFlat, AlternatorDead, NoLights,
   NotSparking);
   FaultSet = SET OF Faults;

VAR
   response, eol : CHAR; (* User response. *)
   number, i : INTEGER; (* Fault number from user, loop index. *)
   fault : Faults; (* Fault corresponding to fault number. *)
   carFaults : FaultSet; (* Faults for one car. *)

BEGIN
   (* Tell user the possible faults for a car. *)
   WriteString("Possible faults are:  ");
   WriteString("0: Battery Flat, 1: Alternator Dead");
   WriteLn;
   WriteString("2 : No Lights, 3 : Not Sparking");
   WriteLn;

   (* Initialise variables. *)
   response := "y";
   carFaults := FaultSet{};

   REPEAT
      (* Get fault number from user. *)
      WriteString("Enter fault number: ");
      ReadInt(number); Read(eol);
      WriteLn;
      (* Check fault number. *)
      IF (number >= 0) AND (number <= 3) THEN
         (* Number is valid, add fault to set. *)
         fault := VAL(Faults, number);
         INCL(carFaults, fault);
      ELSE
         (* Number is invalid. *)
         WriteString("Invalid fault number.");
         WriteLn;
      END;
      (* Ask user if there are any more faults. *)
      WriteString("More faults to enter? (y/n): ");
```

```
        Read(response);  Read(eol);
    UNTIL response = "n";
    (* Now print out the set of car faults. *)
    WriteLn;
    WriteString("The set of faults for the car is:  ");
    WriteLn;
    FOR i := 0 TO 3 DO
        (* For each fault in Faults, see if it is in carFaults, and if
        so print it out. *)
        fault := VAL(Faults, i);
        IF fault IN carFaults THEN
            CASE fault OF
                BatteryFlat:
                    WriteString("Battery Flat");
                    WriteLn;
              | AlternatorDead :
                    WriteString("Alternator Dead");
                    WriteLn;
              | NoLights :
                    WriteString("No Lights");
                    WriteLn;
              | NotSparking :
                    WriteString("Not Sparking");
                    WriteLn;
            ELSE
                WriteString("Invalid fault");
            END;
        END;
    END;
END FaultyCars.
```

This program will build a set of car faults from the information given by the user. We have also added a piece at the end which will print out the contents of the fault set built up by the user of the program. The algorithm for this part is:

```
For each fault in Faults do the following
    if the fault is in carFaults then
        print out the appropriate fault description
    endif
endfor
```

A FOR loop is used to allow us to see if each fault in Faults is present in carFaults. A CASE statement is used to print the appropriate fault description for each fault that is in carFaults.

A.10.2 The ARRAY type

An array is a list of data items:

7.0, 2.5, 12.31, 6.3, 0.05

All the data items in an array must have the same type, so they must be all REAL or all CHAR etc. We need to be able to refer to each item in an array individually – this is done by *indexing* the array with a suitable range of numbers:

1	2	3	4	5	Index
7.0	2.5	12.31	6.3	0.05	Array

The data item at index 1 is 7.0, the data item at index 4 is 6.3, and so on.

Here is a declaration of an array variable in Modula-2, which could be used for storing a list of temperatures:

```
VAR
    temperatures : ARRAY [1..20] OF REAL;
```

The [1..20] is the index range of the array; temperatures is indexed from 1 through to 20, and so can store 20 real numbers. The first location in the array has index 1, the second location has index 2, and so on. We could have declared the index to start from 0 and go up to 19,

```
temperatures : ARRAY [0..19] OF REAL;
```

which would still give us space to store 20 temperatures, but would make the index of the first location 0, that of the second location 1 and so on.

The general form of an array variable declaration is:

```
name : ARRAY [lowerBound..upperBound] OF dataType;
```

Note that the lowerBound and upperBound, which constitute the array index, must be whole numbers (either integers or cardinals). DataType is the type of items which can be stored in the array. An array can only store items of one type, the type defined in the variable declaration.

It is possible to have negative bounds for the index, but gaps in the range are not allowed:

```
anArray : ARRAY [-5..5] OF CHAR;
```

This is a valid example of an array with one negative bound (note that it has eleven storage locations). The index of the array is also called a *subrange*. The type of this subrange is assumed to be CARDINAL, unless it contains a negative value, when it is assumed to be INTEGER, which is the case with anArray above. UpperBound mustalso be greater than lowerBound, so, for example, we cannot index an array from 100 down to 1.

Two and multi-dimensional arrays are declared in a similar way:

```
name : ARRAY [l1..u1], [l2..u2], .... [ln..uN] OF Datatype;
```

where the l1and u1, etc., are the lower and upper bounds of the successive dimensions of a N dimensional array (note, the maximum value of N depends on the compiler implementation. For example:

```
board : ARRAY [1..8], [1..8] OF BlackOrWhite;
```

gives an 8 x 8 two dimensional array of black or white values which could be used to represent a chess board.

UWe will be using the first version of the temperatures declaration for our examples. How can we assign a value to an array location? This can be done with an assignment statement:

```
temperatures[1] := 65.3;
temperatures[2] := 62.7;
```

and so on. The square brackets indicate the index (that is, the location) at which the value should be stored. We can also use a variable (of the correct type) to refer to a location in the array:

```
VAR
   position : CARDINAL;
   ....
BEGIN
   ....
   position := 5;
   temperatures[position] := 75.0;
   ....
END;
```

This assigns the value 75.0 to location 5 in the array. Note that if an index is given that is not in the defined range (1 through to 20 inclusive, in this case), the program will fail when it is run, as soon as an attempt is made to refer to an invalid array location.

We can now use an array in a program which reads in up to twenty temperatures and prints out their average. We need to consider how the user can indicate that he has entered all the temperatures he wants averaged – we could ask the user to enter the number of temperatures he is going to give, before he starts typing them in, which would allow us to use a FOR loop.

```
Ask user how many temperatures he wants to enter
Store in number
Set index to 1

(* Read in the temperatures. *)
Do the following number times
   Read in a temperature
      Store in array at position index
   Add 1 to index
Enddo

Set total to 0
Set index to 1

(* Total the temperatures. *)
Do the following number times
   Get value stored in array at position index and add to total
   Add 1 to index
Enddo
Calculate average
Print out average
```

In Modula-2 we get the following program:

```
MODULE AverageTemperatures;
(* Find the average of up to twenty temperatures. *)

FROM InOut IMPORT WriteString, WriteLn, ReadCard,ReadReal,
WriteReal;

CONST
   FieldWidth = 4; (* Number display width. *)
   SigDigits = 4; (* Number of significant digits to display. *)

VAR
   c : CARDINAL; (* Control variable. *)
   number : CARDINAL; (* Number of temperatures. *)
   temp : REAL; (* Temperature read in. *)
   total : REAL; (* Total of all temperatures. *)
   average : REAL; (* Average temperature. *)
   temperatures : ARRAY [1..50] OF REAL; (* Temperature list. *)

BEGIN
   (* Ask user how many temperatures he will enter. *)
   WriteString("How many temperatures to average (up to 50)? ");
   ReadCard(number);
   (* Check that it's a valid number of temperatures. *)
```

```
IF number <= 20 THEN
   (* Read in the temperatures. *)
   WriteString("Enter temperatures, one per line:");
   WriteLn;
   FOR c := 1 TO number DO
      ReadReal(temp);
      WriteLn; (* Space out input for user. *)
      temperatures[c] := temp;
   END;

   (* Average temperatures. *)
   WriteString("Calculating average....");
   WriteLn;
   total := 0.0;
   FOR c := 1 TO number DO
      total := total + temperatures[c];
   END;
   average := total / FLOAT(number);

   (* Print out the result. *)
   WriteString("The average temperature is: ");
   WriteReal(average, FieldWidth, SigDigits);
ELSE
   (* User entered invalid number of temperatures. *)
   WriteString("Invalid number of temperatures.");
   WriteLn;
END;
END AverageTemperatures.
```

There are several points to note in this program. Firstly, in transferring from the algorithm to Modula-2 we find that a separate variable for the index is not needed – we can use the control variable c to index the array of temperatures. Working through arrays is a common use of FOR loops, and is one of the reasons why FOR loops have explicit control variables (so that the control variable can be used for the array index). Secondly, in our earlier discussion about arithmetic, we said that it was generally invalid to use variables of different types in assignments and expressions. Here, however we have used number (which is a CARDINAL) in the calculation of average (which is a REAL), by using a *type conversion* function, that is

```
average := total + FLOAT(number);
```

FLOAT is used to convert number from CARDINAL to REAL. There is another type conversion function, TRUNC, which takes a REAL number and converts it into a CARDINAL, by throwing away the part after the decimal point (note that TRUNC does **not** round the number).

A.10.3 Character arrays

Arrays of characters are very widely used, so we will take a more detailed look at them. We will return to the problem of reading in a word and storing it as a single data item – this is an obvious case for using an array of characters. A possible definition for a word is:

```
VAR
   word : ARRAY [0..24] OF CHAR;
```

which allows us words of up to 25 characters.

Before we go any further, it is worth mentioning that Modula-2 regards strings as arrays of characters, where the lower bound of the array index is zero, and the upper bound is n-1 for a string of n characters. The following code fragments will produce exactly the same output:

```
WriteString("Hello");

CONST
   Greeting = "Hello";
   ....
   WriteString(Greeting);

VAR
   greeting : ARRAY [0..4] OF CHAR;
   ....
   greeting := "Hello";
   WriteString(greeting);
```

The length of a string of characters is the same as or less than the size of the array. Since a string may be shorter than the array in which it is stored we need some means of indicating where in the array the string ends. To do this we store a special character in the unused part of the array. This character is called *null,* and its special attribute is that it is not printable or displayable in any way whatsoever. Since we can't display the null character we can only refer to it by its ordinal value in the ASCII table, 0. Thus CHR(0) is the null character.

Let's look at what happens to array variable greeting when different length strings are assigned to it.

greeting := "Hello";

H	e	l	l	o

greeting := "Hi"

H	i	CHR(0)	CHR(0)	CHR(0)

greeting := "Salutations";

S	a	l	u	t

greeting := "";

CHR(0)	CHR(0)	CHR(0)	CHR(0)	CHR(0)

This last example is called a null string, which is indicated by the two quote marks without any gap between them. It is a completely empty string, and will have no effect on the output when displayed using WriteString.

A.10.4 Array type declarations

Instead of just using arrays directly in variable declarations (as shown in the previous examples), we can declare new array types, in the TYPE declaration section of our programs. This is similar to the way in which we declared enumerations and subranges. The following type declaration, declares a new, user-defined type, TemperatureList, which is an array type:

```
TYPE
    TemperatureList = ARRAY [1..20] OF REAL;
```

Now we can declare a variable of this new type,

```
VAR
    temperatures : TemperatureList;
```

This type declaration can help to clarify a program if a meaningful name is chosen for the type, and can also help to prevent mistakes when writing the program. For example if we have the following variable declarations, where temperatures is for storing temperature values, and prices is for storing prices,

```
VAR
    temperatures : ARRAY [1..20] OF REAL;
    prices : ARRAY [1..20] OF REAL;
```

then the following assignments will be allowed by Modula-2, because prices and temperatures are of the same type:

```
temperatures[4] := prices[3];
prices[1] := temperatures[1] + 5.0;
```

Syntactically these are quite correct, but semantically there is no justification for assigning a price into an array of temperatures, or for adding five to a temperature and assigning it into an array of prices. By using suitable type declarations, we can prevent such problems.

```
TYPE
    TemperatureList = ARRAY [1..20] OF REAL;
    PriceList = ARRAY [1..20] OF REAL;

VAR
    temperatures : TemperatureList;
    prices : PriceList;
```

Now the assignments are invalid and will produce errors at compilation time, because temperatures and prices are now of different types.

Let's try and design a program which draws a simple bar chart of some given input data. The user must first state how many bars there are to be in the chart, and then enter the size of each bar. The program should then display the bar chart sideways (because this makes it much easier than displaying a vertical bar chart) with the size printed at the end of each bar. So, a typical input might look like this:

```
5
12
23
9
3
10
```

and the corresponding output should look like this:

```
*****5
************12
***********************23
*********9
***3
**********10
```

We need to use several of the concepts we have met in this chapter, such as arrays, FOR loops and IF statements. First we need to design the algorithm:

```
Get number of bars from user - store in barCount
Do the following barCount times
    Read a bar size.
    Store in bar chart array
Enddo
```

```
(* Print out bar chart. *)
Do the following barCount times
    Get a bar size from bar chart array
    Do the following bar size times
            Print a "*"
    Enddo
    Print bar size
    Move to next line
Enddo
```

Now here it is in Modula-2:

```
MODULE DrawBarChart;
(* Displays a horizontal bar chart, given the number of bars to display
and the size of each bar (as positive integers). *)

FROM InOut IMPORT WriteString, WriteLn, ReadCard, WriteCard,
Write;

CONST
    FieldWidth = 3; (* Number of spaces to print out a number. *)
    MaxChart = 24; (* Max number of bars allowed in chart. *)

TYPE
    BarChart = ARRAY [1..20] OF CARDINAL;

VAR
    barCount : CARDINAL; (* Number of bars. *)
    barSize : CARDINAL; (* Size of current bar. *)
    chart : BarChart; (* The bar chart array. *)
    c, d : CARDINAL; (* Loop indexes. *)

BEGIN
    (* Get number of bars from user. *)
    WriteString("Enter number of bars (up to 20): ");
    ReadCard(barCount);
    WriteLn;

    (* Read in bar sizes. *)
    FOR c := 1 TO barCount DO
        WriteString("Enter bar size: ");
        ReadCard(barSize);
        WriteLn;
        chart[c] := barSize;
    END;

    (* Print out bar chart. *)
```

```
    FOR c := 1 TO barCount DO
       barSize := chart[c];
       FOR d := 1 TO barSize DO
          Write("*")
       END;
       WriteCard(barSize, FieldWidth);
       WriteLn;
    END;
 END DrawBarChart.
```

To print out the bar chart we have used one FOR loop to print each bar in turn that is

```
FOR c := 1 TO barCount DO
   (* Print bar c. *)
END;
```

We have used another FOR loop to print the asterisks for each individual bar that is

```
FOR d := 1 TO barSize DO
   Write("*");
END;
```

Using one loop or one sequence control structure within another is often called *nesting*. Since all control structures just contain statement sequences we can have a WHILE loop inside an IF statement or a REPEAT loop inside a CASE statement. If you look back at some of the programs demonstrating sequence control you will see some more examples of nesting.

A.10.5 Records

Arrays provide us with a means of grouping data items of the same type. However, consider the situation where we want to store all the details about each employee in a small computer company. The information to be stored for each employee consists of:

Name	–	String
Position	–	String
Salary	–	Real number
Payroll reference	–	Positive integer.

We can declare these data items as separate variables:

```
VAR
   name : ARRAY [1..20] OF CHAR;
   position : ARRAY [1..20] OF CHAR;
   salary : REAL;
   payrollRef : CARDINAL;
```

but it would be preferable to place them all together under one name, as we did with the array of temperatures. Unfortunately, we cannot use an array because of the restriction that all data items in an array must be of the same type. However, Modula-2 provides us with another do-it-yourself data type called the RECORD.

In Chapter 2, we used records in the car pool reservation system, where the details of each car in the car pool were stored as records containing several pieces of information about the car. Similarly, a Modula-2 RECORD consists of a group of named slots, each of which can hold a data item. When a RECORD is declared we also declare the name and type of each slot.

```
TYPE
   EmployeeRecord =
      RECORD
         name : ARRAY [1..20] OF CHAR;
         position : ARRAY [1..20] OF CHAR;
         salary : REAL;
         payrollRef : CARDINAL;
      END;

VAR
   employee1, employee2 : EmployeeRecord;
```

Now we have declared a RECORD, we need a means of accessing each slot. In the car pool example of Chapter 2, we defined our own operations for accessing each slot in a record, but, luckily Modula-2 provides the operations for us, although the syntax looks slightly strange at first:

```
variableName.slotName
```

For example,

```
employee1.salary
```

refers to slot salary in record variable employee1, and

```
employee2.salary
```

refers to slot salary in record variable employee2.

We can use the assignment statement to put a value into a record field, or use a field in an expression (provided it is of the correct type). For example:

```
bonus := 500.0;
employee1.salary := employee1.salary + bonus;
WriteString(employee1.name);
WriteLn;
WriteReal(employee1.salary, 8);
```

where the record type and its variables are as defined above, and bonus is of type REAL.

A.10.6 The WITH statement

As you can see from the previous example, using records often leads to very long identifiers in our code. Not only can this prolong typing in a program, but, more importantly, such code can often be hard to read. There is a special construct provided by Modula-2, to shorten the identifier names we have to use when referencing record variables; this is the WITH statement. Here is the above code fragment inside a suitable WITH statement:

```
WITH employee1 DO
   bonus := 500.0
   salary := salary + bonus;
   WriteString(name);
   WriteLn;
   WriteReal(salary, 8, 8);
END;
```

The general form of a WITH statement is:

```
WITH recordVariable DO
   statement sequence
END;
```

where recordVariable is the name of a record variable, for example, employee1 or employee2.

What happens if one of the fields in the record variable has the same name and type as another variable in the program? For example:

```
VAR
   salary : REAL;
   bonus : REAL;
   employee : EmployeeRecord;
   ....
   salary := 20000.0;
   WITH employee DO
      salary := 12500.0;
      bonus := 500.0
      salary := salary + bonus;
      WriteString(name);
      WriteLn;
      WriteReal(salary, 6, 6};
   END;
```

In the above program fragment we have declared salary as a REAL variable, in the declaration section of the program, but it is also one of the field names of the record variable employee. Outside the WITH statement we are referring to the global salary (the one declared at the top of the program). So which salary is being referred to inside the WITH statement? Inside a WITH statement the record field names take preference over any global variables of the same names, so inside we are referring to employee.salary.

Selected reading

Problem-solving and structured programming in Modula-2
Koffman, B.
Addison-Wesley, 1988
This is a beginner's introduction to programming in Modula-2. The language is introduced as a means of implementing problem solutions, and there are good examples on how to analyse problems. A very comprehensive introduction to programming.

Modula-2, a seafarer's guide and shipyard manual
Joyce, E.
Addison-Wesley, 1985
One of the best beginner's introductions to Modula-2, but may unfortunately be out of print and hard to find. If you like a light hearted approach, this is the book for you. It is a very clear, simple, but comprehensive introduction to Modula-2.

Modula-2, a software development approach
Ford, G and Wiener, R.
J. Wiley and Sons, 1985
Once you have mastered the basic syntax of Modula-2, and you can write simple programs, this book provides an excellent introduction to the more complex features of the language, such as library modules, data abstractions, data hiding etc. It does assume that you already have some programming experience.

Programming in Modula-2, 4th Edition
Wirth, N.
Springer-Verlag, 1990
This is the seminal tome on Modula-2. It is very definitely a language reference manual, and is not really suitable for beginners. However, no booklist on Modula-2 would be complete without it!

B The ASCII character set

Ordinal number			Character
Decimal	Octal	Hexadecimal	
0	000	00	nul
1	001	01	soh
2	002	02	stx
3	003	03	etx
4	004	04	eot
5	005	05	enq
6	006	06	ack
7	007	07	bel
8	010	08	bs
9	011	09	ht
10	012	0A	lf
11	013	0B	vt
12	014	0C	ff
13	015	0D	cr
14	016	0E	so
15	017	0F	si
16	020	10	dle
17	021	11	dc1
18	022	12	dc2
19	023	13	dc3
20	024	14	dc4
21	025	15	nak
22	026	16	syn
23	027	17	etb
24	030	18	can
25	031	19	em
26	032	1A	sub

27	033	1B	esc
28	034	1C	fs
29	035	1D	gs
30	036	1E	rs
31	037	1F	us
32	040	20	space
33	041	21	!
34	042	22	"
35	043	23	#
36	044	24	$
37	045	25	%
38	046	26	&
39	047	27	'
40	050	28	(
41	051	29	)
42	052	2A	*
43	053	2B	+
44	054	2C	,
45	055	2D	-
46	056	2E	.
47	057	2F	/
48	060	30	0
49	061	31	1
50	062	32	2
51	063	33	3
52	064	34	4
53	065	35	5
54	066	36	6
55	067	37	7
56	070	38	8
57	071	39	9
58	072	3A	:
59	073	3B	;
60	074	3C	<
61	075	3D	=
62	076	3E	>
63	077	3F	?
64	100	40	@
65	101	41	A

66	102	42	B
67	103	43	C
68	104	44	D
69	105	45	E
70	106	46	F
71	107	47	G
72	110	48	H
73	111	49	I
74	112	4A	J
75	113	4B	K
76	114	4C	L
77	115	4D	M
78	116	4E	N
79	117	4F	O
80	120	50	P
81	121	51	Q
82	122	52	R
83	123	53	S
84	124	54	T
85	125	55	U
86	126	56	V
87	127	57	W
88	130	58	X
89	131	59	Y
90	132	5A	Z
91	133	5B	[
92	134	5C	\
93	135	5D	]
94	136	5E	^
95	137	5F	_
96	140	60	`
97	141	61	a
98	142	62	b
99	143	63	c
100	144	64	d
101	145	65	e
102	146	66	f
103	147	67	g
104	150	68	h

105	151	69	i
106	152	6A	j
107	153	6B	k
108	154	6C	l
109	155	6D	m
110	156	6E	n
111	157	6F	o
112	160	70	p
113	161	71	q
114	162	72	r
115	163	73	s
116	164	74	t
117	165	75	u
118	166	76	v
119	167	77	w
120	170	78	x
121	171	79	y
122	172	7A	z
123	173	7B	{
124	174	7C	|
125	175	7D	}
126	176	7E	~
127	177	7F	del

C Built-in functions and standard library procedures

C1 Symbols and reserved words

Symbols		Reserved words (in uppercase)		
+ plus	= equal	AND	FOR	QUALIFIED
- minus	# not equal	ARRAY	FROM	RECORD
* multiplication	< less than	BEGIN	IF	REPEAT
/ real division	> greater	BY	IMPLEMENTATION	RETURN
:= becomes	<> not equal	CASE	IMPORT	SET
& and	<= less/equal	CONST	IN	THEN
. stop	>= greater/equal	DEFINITION	LOOP	TO
, comma	.. range indicator	DIV	MOD	TYPE
; separator	: type indicator	DO	MODULE	UNTIL
(open bracket	) close bracket	ELSE	NOT	VAR
[array subscripts	] array subscripts	ELSIF	OF	WHILE
{ open set	} close set	END	OR	WITH
↑ dereference	| or (case)	EXIT	POINTER	
(* open comment	*) close comment	EXPORT	PROCEDURE	
~ not				

C2 Built-in data types (typical range)

Type	Range	Storage
INTEGER	All integers between -32768 and 32767.	16 bits (2 bytes)
CARDINAL	All the counting numbers between 0 and 65535.	16 bits (2 bytes)
BOOLEAN	Either TRUE or FALSE.	8 bits (1 bytes)
REAL	The finite set of real numbers between -3.38E38 and 3.38E38 that can be represented by the mantissa.	32 bits (4 bytes)
CHAR	The ASCII characters.	8 bits (1 byte)
ADDRESS	Compatible with type LONGCARD and with all POINTER types.	32 bits (4 bytes)
BYTE	Smallest addressable unit. Compatible with all types of two bytes length.	8 bits (1 byte)
WORD	Two consecutive bytes beginning at an even address.	16 bits (2 bytes)
BITSET	The set of integer values from 0 to 15.	16 bits (2 bytes)
LONGINT	All the integers between -2147483648 and 2147483647.	32 bits (4 bytes)
LONGCARD	All the counting numbers between 0 and 4294967295.	32 bits (4 bytes)
LONGREAL	The finite set of real numbers between -1.79D308 and 1.79D308 that can be represented by the mantissa.	64 bits (8 bytes)

C3 Type conversion

Function	Description	Argument type	Result type
BITSET(c)	Converts CARDINAL to BITSET	CARDINAL	BITSET
CARDINAL(i)	Converts INTEGER to CARDINAL.	INTEGER	CARDINAL
CAST(x,T)	Value x is converted to type T	any	T
INTEGER(c)	Converts CARDINAL to INTEGER	CARDINAL	INTEGER
FLOAT(i)	Converts INTEGER or CARDINAL to the REAL equivalent.	INTEGER or CARDINAL	REAL
FLOATD(li)	Converts LONGINT or LONGCARD to the LONGREAL equivalent.	LONGINT or LONGCARD	LONGREAL
TRUNC(r)	Truncates a REAL to a CARDINAL.	REAL	CARDINAL
TRUNCD(lr)	Truncates a LONGREAL to a LONGCARD.	LONGREAL	LONGCARD

C4 Memory function procedures

Function	Description	Argument type	Result type
ADR(x)	Returns the address of variable x.	any	ADDRESS
SIZE(T)	Returns the number of bytes needed to store the type.	T	CARDINAL
TSIZE(T)	Returns the number of bytes needed to store the type. Must be used if T is a variant record type.	T	INTEGER

C5 Standard function procedures

Function	Description	Argument type	Result type
ABS(x)	Absolute value of x.	REAL, INTEGER, CARDINAL	REAL, INTEGER, CARDINAL
HIGH(A)	UPPER BOUND of ARRAY A (indexed from 0).	an open ARRAY	CARDINAL
MAX(T)	Maximum value of type T.	any type T	T
MIN(T)	Minimum value of type T.	any type T	T
ODD(x)	TRUE if x is odd, FALSE otherwise.	CARDINAL or INTEGER	BOOLEAN

C6 Character function procedures

Function	Description	Argument type	Result type
CAP(ch)	Gives the uppercase equivalent of character ch.	CHAR	CHAR
CHR(c)	Gives the ASCII character whose ordinal number is c.	CARDINAL	CHAR
ORD(x)	Ordinal value of x.	INTEGER, CARDINAL, CHAR or enumeration type	CARDINAL
VAL(T,o)	Inverse of ORD.	T is the type, and o its ordinal value	T

C7 Standard procedures

Procedure	Description
DEC(x)	Decrement x, x:=x-1, where x is an INTEGER, CARDINAL, CHAR or enumeration type.
DEC(x,n)	Decrement x by n, x:=x-n, where x and n are the same type from INTEGER, CARDINAL, CHAR or enumeration type.
EXCL(S,e)	Removes element e from set S.
HALT	Terminates program.
INC(x)	Increment x, x:=x+1, where x is an INTEGER, CARDINAL, CHAR or enumeration type.
INC(x,n)	Increment x by n, x:=x+n, where x and n are the same type from INTEGER, CARDINAL, CHAR or enumeration type.
INCL(S,e)	Adds element e to set S.

C8 Operator precedence

Precedence	Operators of same precedence are executed from left to right							
First (highest)	NOT	~						
Second	*	/	DIV	MOD	AND	&		
Third	+	-	OR					
Fourth	=	#	< >	<	<=	>	>=	IN

C9 MathLib0 function procedures

Function	Description	Argument type	Result type
ArcTan(r)	Inverse Tan function.	REAL (radians)	REAL
Cos(r)	Cosine function.	REAL (radians)	REAL
Entier(r)	Truncates a real number to its integer part.	REAL	INTEGER
Exp(r)	Exponential function.	REAL	REAL
Ln(r)	Natural logarithm of r.	REAL	REAL
Real(i)	Converts integer i to real equivalent.	INTEGER	REAL
Sin(r)	Sine function.	REAL (radians)	REAL
Sqrt(r)	Square root function.	REAL (positive values only)	REAL
LONG functions	All maths functions are available in LONGREAL versions.		

D Exercises

1 Building software

1.1 Undertake a full life cycle analysis for organising and managing a three day pop festival. Start by drawing up a requirements specification of the festival which includes the number of artists and the size of the audience. The concert is to be an annual event, and alternates the venue between the UK and the USA. The analysis must provide for the split venue.

1.2 The C programming language is frequently referred to as the Industry Standard. Is this statement true? You will need to research what languages are used throughout industry and not restrict yourself to the languages used by systems programmers.

1.3 Fortran has been the most used programming language for engineering and scientific computing since the 1950s. Is this situation likely to continue? Investigate the trends in language usage by interviewing practicing engineers and scientists.

1.4 Which high level languages are most appropriate for developing operating systems on personal computers, minicomputers, networked workstations and mainframe computers. If you conclude that different languages are appropriate for each class of computer then how can you reconcile these differences to enable communications to be made between these classes of computer.

1.5 Give a detailed review of why Modula-2 is a better language for a beginner to use to learn programming skills rather than using Basic, Fortran, Pascal or C.

1.6 Take the points listed in the software life cycle and expand each point into a full discussion of its role and importance in the development of quality software.

1.7 Identify the requirements of a simple airline reservation system that is able to find all the flights available to a particular destination on a certain date and allow the travel agent to make a reservation according to the preferences of the passenger. The specification must allow for a passenger to be wait list on the preferred flight.

1.8 Work out the requirements of a computer aided software system to help a non specialist determine the requirements of a project. The computer aided system must ensure that contradictory requirements are eliminated.

1.9 In a large software project, it is desirable that some of the development is carried out in parallel. By referring to the software life cycle, discuss which aspects of this cycle (or sub cycles) can be undertaken in parallel and which should be constrained to be developed sequentially.

1.10 In the past, software maintenance has consumed a large proportion of software costs. Why has this been so, and how can we hope to minimise the cost of future changes in implementations of software products?

2 Modularisation and data abstraction

2.1 Given the following problem description, find the data abstractions needed to implement a solution to this problem. State informally (in English, no need for axioms) the various objects and their associated operations.

An air cargo company requires software to simulate its service between four remote islands. The service consists of a single cargo plane which can hold up to ten full crates. Passengers wishing to travel between the islands may also use the plane, but four passengers take up the space needed for one crate. The plane will not fly between islands unless it is fully loaded with crates and/or passengers. On each island the freight is loaded on a first come, first served basis. Passengers queue separately to the freight, but freight has priority over passengers, so if there are ten crates and four people to fly, the people will have to wait for the next flight.

2.2 A dequeue is a special kind of queue where items can be added to and removed from either end of the queue (that is, a *double-ended queue*). Alter the formal specification of the Queue abstraction into the Dequeue abstraction. Several extra operations will be required.

2.3 Find the object(s) and operations required to specify a Clock data abstraction.

Clock must hold both the date and the time of day. Hint: to find the operations needed, consider the operations allowed on a digital watch.

2.4 Conventional music notation is shown on a five line stave. The pitch of a note is determined by its vertical position on the stave, where the higher the note is up the stave, the higher its pitch. A symbol called the clef indicates the pitch of each line in the stave. Each pitch of note on the treble clef stave has a name, these are shown below:

c d e f g a b c d e f g a b c

Notes are played from left to right along the stave. Each note must be held for a certain length of time. Vertical bar lines are used to divide up the stave into smaller time units. Assume that there are four equal length notes to each bar, for example:

Specify the data abstraction(s) needed to represent music on the treble clef stave. Give the operations informally only (you don't need to write axioms). If you have some knowledge of music you may wish to include time signatures, key signatures and different length of note.

2.5 Find and formally specify (as far as possible) the data abstractions required for the airline reservation system of Exercise 1.8.

3 Procedural abstraction

3.1 Design and implement (in a program module) a procedural abstraction which gives the ability to define a small text window anywhere on the computer screen, and display any (short) message in it. The position of the text window and the message should be passed as parameters to the procedure. This procedural abstraction can be very useful for displaying information (such as hints, error messages etc.) to the user of a program.

3.2 Simulations, such as the air cargo service in Exercise 2.1, often deal with situations that depend on events which occur in some random or semi-random way. For example, the arrival of freight and passengers for the plane will be at random intervals, and the time at which the plane leaves will depend on these intervals (because the plane will not leave until it is full).

Given a random number generation function called Random (check to see if your Modula-2 implementation provides something similar), design and implement a procedure which generates a random number between two integer values x and y. Use this procedure to generate a series of time intervals between 1 and 30 minutes (using whole minutes only), representing the arrival of items in the freight and passenger queues for the cargo plane.

Hint: given a random number r (assuming r is an integer), generated by Random, the following statement will give each integer value between x and y-1 an approximately equal number of times:

```
result := (y - x) * r + a
```

3.3 Use an n x n array to represent a maze that has been mapped to a n x n grid. Use this array to define a path through the maze, and by randomly filling (or otherwise) complete the definition of the maze. Once the maze has been defined rediscover the path through the maze by using a 'turn left first' strategy at the junctions. On failure, backtrack to the previous junction and try the next right path, again using a 'turn left first' strategy at further junctions, with backtracking on failed paths. Record the successful path. On the screen show the initial maze, the complete search for path (including backtracking), and the successful direct walk through the maze.

You should use a recursive algorithm to implement the search strategy.

4 Modules for abstraction

4.1 Implement the Clock data abstraction in a library module, so that any other module can implement and use Clock. Extend the abstraction to implement an alarm operation which tells the user when a particular time is reached. A record data structure will be useful when you are deciding how to represent the date and time.

4.2 The procedural abstraction of Exercise 3.1, for displaying a message in a text window, could be useful in many situations. So that it is more easily re-usable put this procedure into a new TextUtilities library module.

4.3 Design and implement as a function (in the TextUtilities library module) a procedural abstraction which takes a text string (comprising some question), displays that text in a text window on the screen, and reads in a yes/no response typed in at the keyboard. Allow the answer to be given as a single character, "y" or "Y" for a positive response, and "n" or "N" for a negative response. The function must only accept a valid response, and must not return until the user has given a valid response.

4.4 Alter the elevator simulation to accept multiple floor requests. Include in the simulation a random generation of requests. Assume that the elevator takes 20 seconds to travel between adjacent floors and 60 seconds to load and unload at each floor.

5 Standard data abstractions

5.1 Find suitable data representations for the air cargo service abstractions of Exercise 2.1. Give Modula-2 type declarations for these data representations and show why you believe them to be suitable.

5.2 Implement, in a library module, the Dequeue data abstraction which you specified in Exercise 2.2.

5.3 There is one more kind of queue abstraction which is common in computing, this is the *priority queue.* In a priority queue items are not ordered by time of arrival, but by some priority criterion. Each item inserted into a priority queue has some priority associated with it. This could be represented as a number from 1 to 10 say, with 1 being the highest priority, and 10 being the lowest priority. When an item is inserted into a priority queue it is inserted after all items of the same priority, and before all items of lower priority.

Formally specify the Priority Queue data abstraction, and implement it in a library module. You should see a similarity between the Ordered List of Chapter 5 and the Priority Queue.

5.4 Find suitable data representations for the Music abstraction(s) of Exercise 2.4. Give Modula-2 type declarations for these data representations.

Using these data representations and the operations you defined in 2.4, implement the abstraction(s), in a library module, so that a user can type in music for the treble clef stave by giving the names of the notes as lower case letters a to g. If you have included sharps and flats, and different note lengths you will need to specify and implement a syntax for the user to enter this information about an individual note.

Design and implement a program which uses the Music abstraction(s) to read in simple pieces of music and display the music graphically on the treble clef stave. You can choose to show the music on the stave as it is entered, or to wait until the user has finished and display it all at once.

As an extra problem, you might like to allow the user to edit the music in some way, after it has been entered and displayed.

6 Implementing dynamic data structures

6.1 Using the formal specification of the Set data abstraction shown in Chapter

2, implement dynamic, generic sets. Your Set implementation should be able to cope with sets of integers, sets of records, sets of list etc.

6.2 Simulate the movement of trucks in a shunting yard consisting of three sidings. Trains arrive in the shunting yard one at a time, each containing a mixture of trucks for various destinations. The trucks are labelled 1, 2 or 3 (for destinations 1, 2 and 3 respectively). The shunter must split up the original train into new trains, each consisting of trucks for one destination only, with each new train on a different siding . Thus a train brought into the yard for shunting may provide up to three new trains, each residing in a separate siding.

The input data for the simulation should consist of a list of truck numbers, 1, 2 and 3, which constitute the original train, in the order in which they appear in this train. The output produced should be a display of the movements of the trucks as they are shunted into their new trains. NOTE: the shunting engine only has sufficient power to move one truck at a time.

Find the data abstractions required for this simulation and design and implement a system which satisfies the above informal specification.

6.3 The Binary Tree data abstraction is, as shown in Chapters 5 and 6, a non-linear data abstraction, where each item in a binary tree has one parent and up to two descendants. Other forms of Tree abstraction allow items to have more than two descendants, but an item will still have only one parent.

A more general non-linear data abstraction is the Graph. Each item in a graph may have zero or more parents (called *predecessors*) and zero or more descendants (called *successors*). Two items or nodes in a graph can be joined by a line or *arc*. Nodes which are joined by an arc are adjacent and can be represented by a tuple (x, y), where x and y are the nodes. A graph may be connected or disconnected, that is:

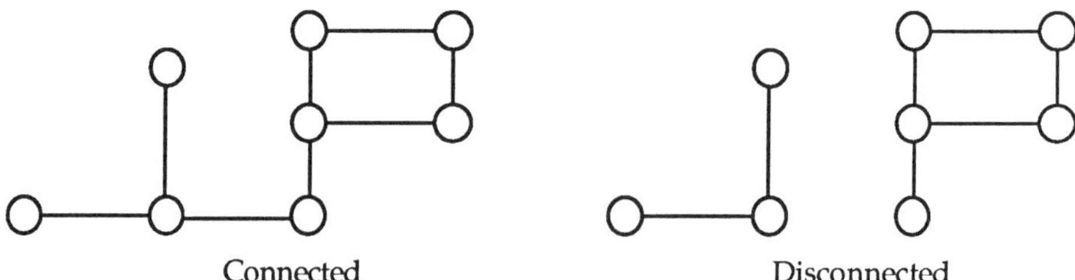

A path is a sequence of nodes $n_1, n_2, ..., n_m$), where for i = 1 to m, each pair of nodes (n_i, n_{i+1}) is adjacent.

Try to formally specify the Graph data abstraction, and implement it as a dynamic, generic data structure. Then return to the maze problem of Exercise 3.3 and re-implement it, using a graph to represent the maze. (Note: this is a hard exercise!)

7 Input/Output abstractions

7.1 Alter the music implementation of Exercise 5.4 to allow the user to store music in files, and display the contents of such files. Retrieved music should be displayed graphically as before.

7.2 Design and implement a program which reads words from a text file, and builds a binary tree of all the different words in the text. The tree should only contain one occurrence of each word. As its output the program should display (i) an alphabetical list of words in the text, showing the number of times each word occurred in the text, and (ii) a list showing the words ranked by frequency of occurrence in the text, with the most frequent word at the top of the list.

7.3 The BDVLC problem of Chapter 2 requires a file (or group of files) in which to store the driver records and their associated information. The number of individual driver records will be in the millions and so sequential access to such a file would be impossibly slow. If we allow a random access file, how could this file be structured to allow fast access to individual driver records? Consider the possibility of using some form of index into the file.

8 Process abstraction

8.1 A database may be accessed either for reading or writing by a number of users. A writer must have exclusive access to the database, but many writers may have simultaneous access. Devise a solution to this problem using

(i) monitors

(ii) conditional critical regions

8.2 In the implementation of the signal module in Chapter 8 a signal can be lost if a process sends a signal before another process has executed a wait operation. Change the implementation so that a premature send operation is remembered and executed after the wait operation has been received.

8.3 In the eight queens problem the eight queens are placed on a chessboard in such a way that none can attack another. Queens are allowed to attack each other only if they are in the same row, column or diagonal. Write a parallel program that uses a coroutine to generate the 92 solutions to this problem and a further coroutine to check the correctness of the result.

8.4 Implement the elevator example from Chapter 4 and Exercise 4.4 using coroutines. Initiate a new coroutine at the first occurrence of a particular floor request. An existing coroutine should be suspended in favour of a coroutine that holds a request for an earlier earlier floor. Priority must always be given to an existing direction of travel. Use the random interval generator of Exercise 3.2 to simulate floor requests.

8.5 Use coroutines to implement the car wash simulation of chapter 2.

8.6 Use coroutines to design a simulator for training air traffic control officers. The coroutines will need to represent a number of incoming and outgoing aircraft, each with the attributes of speed, elevation and direction.

9 The hardware abstraction

9.1 In driving a stepper motor, the purpose is to demonstrate the use of the bit handling facilities in Modula-2. Write a program to turn the motor. Place an adjustable delay of 1-200 milliseconds between each bit charge. Design the program to allow control of the motor by different sequences of bits, so that it is possible to turn the motor the desired number of steps either forwards or backwards.

9.2 Write a random number generator coroutine that uses the system clock to seed the number generator.

10 Software testing

10.1 Your TextUtilities library module from Exercises 4.2 and 4.3, contains two relatively small procedures. As far as you can, perform black and white box testing on these procedures.

10.2 Design a test plan for black box testing of the Clock data abstraction of Exercise 4.1. Build a test harness to perform this testing. Input for the tests and output from the tests should be stored in text files.

10.3 How would you approach testing the random event generator of Exercise 3.2

11 Algorithm complexity and efficiency

11.1 If one algorithm executes as n log n and another as $O(n^2)$, what can you infer about the relative performance of these algorithms.

11.2 The towers of Hanoi problem is as follows. Three pegs are labelled a, b and c. On peg a is placed a set of n disks, each with a centre hole to allow the disks to be threaded onto the pegs. The disks increase in size with the largest at the base of the peg. The objective is to move the pile of disks one at a time onto another peg without ever placing a larger disk over a smaller disk. Design a recursive algorithm to solve this problem. Analyse the algorithm and find its complexity.

11.3 List the advantages and disadvantages of the sorting methods described in this chapter.

11.4 Analyse the complexity of your implementation of the shunting yard problem given in Exercise 6.2. How could you improve the efficiency of your implementation?

11.5 Experiment with varying sets of sort keys, n, for the binary search algorithm implemented recursively and non recursively. Plot (Time for recursion)/(Time for non recursion) against n and analyse the result.

11.6 Modify the exchange sort to avoid unnecessary comparisons between keys by keeping a record of where the last interchange occurred in each traversal of the FOR loop.

11.7 If a queue was used instead of a stack to implement the non-recursive QuickSort, what effect would you expect this change to have on complexity issues and memory requirements? Find a case where the runtime stack that implements the recursive version of QuickSort grows to O(n), where n is the number of key items. Modify the QuickSort method to choose the pivot element at random. What is the complexity of this method?

11.8 Implement the interpolated binary search method for a telephone directory. Analyse the complexity of your interpolation formula and estimate its cost advantage, or otherwise, in comparison to a normal binary search. Assume that the directory contains 30 million entries.

11.9 Implement a non-recursive binary tree search that prints the keys values in order.

A Using Modula-2

A.1 Alter Module FirstLook to display your own name on the screen. (Simple output, compiling and running.)

A.2 Alter the program of A.1 to read in a positive integer, i and print out your name i times. Try having it print your name on a new line each time, and then try just leaving a few spaces between each print out. (For loops, variables, simple input and output.)

A.3 Write a program which reads in a length given in feet and inches, and displays it in metres and centimetres. Note: 1 metre is approximately 39.371 inches. (Constants, variables, simple calculations, reals.)

A.4 Write a program, which calculates the number of bits of storage available on a 1.44 megabyte floppy disk. Note: 1 byte = 8 bits, 1 megabyte = 1024 * 1024 bytes. (Constants, reals, mixed type calculations.)

A.5 Write a program which, given a height above ground (in metres) calculates the length of time taken (in seconds) for an object dropped from this height to hit the ground. The distance, d, travelled in t seconds is given by the formula:

$$d = 1/2\,Gt^2$$

G is the gravitational constant, and can be taken as 9.80665. (Simple arithmetic, mixed type calculations, reals.)

A.6 Write a program which finds the roots of a quadratic equation $ax^2 + bx + c = d$, where a, b, c and d are entered by the user. Consider carefully how you would calculate the values of x. (Simple arithmetic, mixed type calculations, reals.)

A.7 Write a program which calculates the factorial of an integer n (given by the user), where n! = n * (n-1) * (n-2) *.......* 2 * 1. When you have met recursion in Chapter 5, re-implement this program using recursion. Compare the speeds of the two versions of your factorial program. (For loops.)

A.8 Write a program which reads text (typed in by the user) one character at a time until a full stop is read, then outputs the total number of characters typed in, and the number of occurrences of each vowel (a, e, i, o, u) in the text. (Loops, conditional branching.)

A.9 WriteHex and WriteOct will only display octal and hexadecimal conversions of cardinal numbers on the screen. Write a program which actually converts a cardinal number given by the user, to both an octal and a hexadecimal number. The program should then display all three versions of the number. Your program must not use WriteHex or WriteOct, but must store the octal and hexadecimal versions of the given number in two appropriate variable. (Loops, arrays.)

A.10 Write a program which reads in today's date as three cardinal numbers, for example, 25 12 92. The program should then display the given date in full, for example: 25th December 1992. (Conditional branching, case statements.)

A.11 Design a RECORD type which could be used to store the title, author, publisher, publication date and number of pages for a particular book. Design an ARRAY type which can be used to store ten of these records. Write a program which gets the user to enter the required information for several books, and then prints out a list of the books, showing author, title and number of pages for each book entered, in descending size order (based on the number of pages). (Records, arrays.)

A.12 If your Modula-2 implementation provides a simple graphics library (Metrowerks does) design a name logo for yourself, and use the routines from the graphics library to implement it. Your logo should include your surname somewhere in it. If you wish, leave this exercise until you have read about procedures and functions in Chapter 5, so that you can use them in your program. (Using libraries, loops, branching, procedures.)

Index